Digital Image Processing

A Practical Introduction Using Java

To Judi, Matthew and Louise

Digital Image Processing

A Practical Introduction Using Java

Nick Efford

School of Computer Studies
University of Leeds

An imprint of **Pearson Education**

Harlow, England · London · New York · Reading, Massachusetts · San Francisco · Toronto · Don Mills, Ontario · Sydney
Tokyo · Singapore · Hong Kong · Seoul · Taipei · Cape Town · Madrid · Mexico City · Amsterdam · Munich · Paris · Milan

Pearson Education Limited
Edinburgh Gate
Harlow
Essex
CM20 2JE
England
and Associated Companies throughout the world

Visit us on the World Wide Web at:
www.pearsoned-ema.com.

First published 2000

© Pearson Education Limited 2000

The programs in this book have been included for their instructional value. They have been tested with care but are not guaranteed for any particular purpose. The publisher does not offer any warranties or representations nor does it accept any liabilities with respect to the programs.

ISBN 0-201-59623-7

British Library Cataloguing-in-Publication Data
A catalogue record for this book can be obtained from the British Library.

Library of Congress Cataloging-in-Publication Data
Efford, Nick.
   Digital image processing: a practical introduction using Java / Nick Efford.
     p. cm.
   Includes bibliographical references and index.
   ISBN 0-201-59623-7 (alk. paper)
   1. Image processing–Digital techniques. I. Title.

TA1637.E35 2000
621.36'7'0285–dc21   99-087172

10 9 8 7 6 5 4 3 2 1
05 04 03 02 01 00

Typeset by 56
Printed and bound in the United States of America

Contents

List of Figures

List of Tables

List of Algorithms

List of Program Listings

Preface

Digital image processing is not a new phenomenon; techniques for the manipulation, correction and enhancement of digital images have been in practical use for over thirty years—an early application being the removal of defects from images obtained by NASA's unmanned lunar probes—and the underlying theoretical ideas have been around for a lot longer. We don't have to look very far these days to see an example of image processing at work. It has insinuated itself into many different areas of human endeavour, ranging from small-scale activities such as desktop publishing and healthcare, through to activity on the largest scales imaginable: the search for natural resources on Earth, or the study of other planets, stars and galaxies in our universe.

But there is a revolution happening right now in the field of digital imaging. No longer is this subject the sole province of the trained professional. Digital imaging is becoming part of everyday life. We can see evidence of this in the constant exposure we have to computer generated imagery and special effects through film and television; in the ever widening range of digital still and video cameras on sale to the general public at rapidly falling prices; and in the increasing numbers of new PCs that are sold already bundled with scanners or digital cameras, photo-quality printers and image manipulation software—allowing computer users the freedom to experiment with techniques that, only a decade ago, were confined to the laboratories of engineers and computer scientists. The days of photographic film as the standard medium for routine imaging tasks are, it seems, numbered—as are the days when only the specialist had the tools and skills necessary to do anything other than merely take a photograph.

Becoming digital may have been inevitable, but a major accelerating factor in this change has surely been the internet or, more specifically, The World-Wide Web. The Web provides the medium through which millions of images are moved daily between computers at all points of the globe. The phenomenal growth of the Web has undoubtedly helped to make digital imaging more important than ever before, but digital imaging techniques have also helped to speed the growth of the Web; downloading of image-laden web pages across communications links of modest bandwidth is feasible only because many of those images have been compressed to small sizes using techniques from the realm of image processing. (These techniques are discussed further in Chapter 12.) This symbiotic relationship between the internet and imaging is certain to continue.

Of course, the internet has been the breeding ground for many exciting new technologies in recent years, one of the most notable being Java. Java has established itself as a major new programming language, one that seems particularly well-suited to the development of software in today's network-centric environments. But if the internet and imaging are linked, and Java is a key technology of the internet, it follows that there is a link between Java and digital imaging—a link that is a major motivating factor for this book.

A great many books on image processing have appeared in recent years, so why add to the collection? What does this book, in particular, have to offer? Many existing texts give the subject a strong electrical engineering or physics perspective, or present a rigorous treatment of the subject that can be comprehended fully only if the reader possesses advanced mathematical skills. Others adopt a less theory-bound, more practical approach, but lack the examples or the software tools that would allow readers to develop their own image processing applications. Where software tools are provided, they are often inflexible and platform-specific.

This book provides a practical introduction to image processing, avoiding unnecessary mathematical detail and focusing more on the computational aspects of the subject. It is aimed at a broad audience, but is likely to appeal most strongly to the computer enthusiast with some programming experience, or to those on an undergraduate computing course. I have tried to balance the conceptual with the practical; my intent is that the book should both explain the concepts *and* provide the computer-literate reader with the means of experimenting with those concepts, in order to achieve a deeper understanding of this complex and fascinating subject. The vehicle for this experimentation is Java. On the CD-ROM accompanying this book, you will find Java classes that you can use to develop your own, highly sophisticated image processing software. You will also find numerous ready-to-run tools, with which you can perform image processing experiments whether or not you have experience of programming in Java. Note that the book generally gives more emphasis to the explanation of concepts than to the description of programming techniques—so much of the text should be easily digestible by those lacking the skills or inclination to indulge in programming.

The book is divided into twelve chapters. Most of these conclude with recommendations for further reading, along with a few exercises. A significant proportion of these exercises are programming projects using the tools provided on the CD-ROM. The first few chapters deal with the acquisition, digitisation and basic manipulation of images, and address the question of how images may be represented in Java programs. After this, one chapter deals with techniques for the enhancement of brightness, contrast and colour in images. A major part of the book is devoted to so-called 'neighbourhood operations', which may be used to blur or sharpen images, remove noise and detect edges. This is followed by another major chapter on what is probably the most difficult subject, conceptually, in the entire book: the processing of images in the frequency domain.

Geometric operations on images, ranging from simple scaling and rotation up to complex, piecewise warping operations, are covered. Another chapter gives a brief introduction to the vast topic of image segmentation, the process by which meaningful features are extracted from images. The penultimate chapter of the book examines morphological image processing techniques, and the book concludes with a review of the various data compression algorithms that have been applied to images. A glossary of image processing terms is also provided.

I hope that you enjoy reading the book and using the software that comes with it. It is my belief that, as we begin a new millennium and digital image processing expands into the frontiers opened up by the internet, there is a need for presentations of the subject based on tools designed for these new frontiers. I hope that this book helps in some small way to address that need.

Acknowledgements

I would like to thank my colleagues Roger Boyle and David Hogg, of the School of Computer Studies at the University of Leeds, for their continuing support. I am very grateful to Keith Mansfield of Pearson Education for taking on board this project, and for his words of advice and encouragement. Finally, I can't thank my wife Judi enough for her patience and understanding in the face of many late nights and weekends spent at the keyboard.

Nick Efford
September 1999

CHAPTER 1

Introduction

1.1   What are images?

In the broadest possible sense, images are *pictures*: a way of recording and presenting information visually. Pictures are important to us because they can be an extraordinarily effective medium for the storage and communication of information. Consider the familiar example of the photograph (Figure 1.1). We use photography in everyday life to create a permanent record of our visual experiences, and to help us share those experiences with others. In showing someone a photograph, we avoid the need for a lengthy, tedious and, in all likelihood, ambiguous verbal description of what was seen. This emphasises the point that humans are primarily *visual* creatures. We rely on our eyes for most of the information we receive concerning our surroundings, and our brains are particularly adept at visual data processing. There is thus a scientific basis for the well-known saying that 'a picture is worth a thousand words'.

Figure 1.1   Example of a photograph, rich in information.

Photography is the imaging technique with which we are most familiar, simply because the information it records is similar to that which we receive using our eyes. Both human vision and photography require a light source to illuminate a scene. The light interacts with the objects in the scene and some of it reaches the observer, whereupon it is detected by the eyes or by a camera. Information about the objects in the scene is recorded as variations in the intensity and colour of the detected light. A key point is that, although a scene is (typically) three-dimensional, the image of that scene is always two-dimensional.

There are other forms of energy, besides light, that can be used to create images. Light is merely the visible portion of the **electromagnetic (EM) spectrum** (Figure 1.2), which includes such things as x-rays and microwaves. EM radiation is produced by the oscillation of electrically charged material, and has wave-like properties. It travels rapidly, at approximately 300,000 kilometres per second, allowing near-instantaneous imaging of events as they occur. Another useful property of EM radiation, for imaging purposes, is its tendency to travel in straight lines. This means that many of the geometric characteristics of objects in a scene are preserved in images of that scene. EM radiation can interact with matter in different ways, depending on its wavelength. Images acquired at different wavelengths may have very different properties, and we may need to be aware of these differences when seeking appropriate image processing techniques.

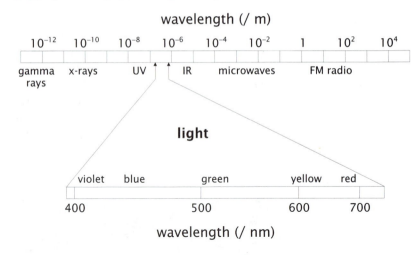

Figure 1.2   The spectrum of electromagnetic radiation.

The visible portion of the spectrum occurs between wavelengths of approximately 400 and 700 nanometres (nm)[1]. Within this region, wavelength is perceived as *colour*; light at 550 nm appears green, whereas light at 700 nm is seen as red. At shorter wavelengths, EM radiation carries larger energies. In the x-ray region of the spectrum (at a wavelength, λ, of around 10^{-10} m), it carries sufficient energy to penetrate a significant volume of material. X-ray images therefore reveal the internal structure of objects that are opaque to light—the human body being a prime example (Figure 1.3).

---

[1]   1 nanometre = 10^{-9} metres

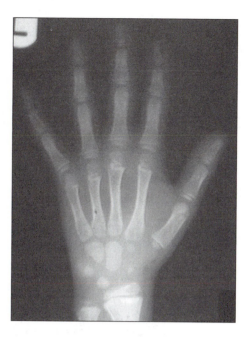

Figure 1.3 X-ray image of a child's hand.

At still shorter wavelengths, EM radiation manifests itself as gamma rays, which are a common product of radioactive decay. Gamma rays are highly penetrating and, like x-rays, have medical applications. Whereas x-rays provide information on anatomy and internal structure, gamma ray imaging provides information on *function* [50]. Typically, the patient ingests a substance that is 'tagged' with a radioactive tracer. This tracer is taken up in varying amounts by different tissues in the body, according to their level of activity. A device known as a gamma camera collects gamma ray photons emitted by body tissues and forms an image from them. Vigorous, diseased tissue such as a tumour will often appear as a bright region in images of this kind.

EM radiation with wavelengths longer than that of light also has its uses. Copious quantities of infrared (IR) radiation are emitted from warm objects, so IR imaging can be used to locate people or moving vehicles even in conditions of total darkness. 'Synthetic aperture radar' (SAR) imaging techniques use an artificially generated source of microwaves ($\lambda = 1$–100 cm) to probe a scene. Radar is unaffected by cloud cover, and it has provided us with detailed images of the surface of Venus—a planet hidden from view at shorter wavelengths. Radar images can be difficult to interpret, owing to geometric distortions inherent in the imaging process, and to the presence of a significant noise component termed 'speckle'.

We need not restrict ourselves to images based on the interactions of EM radiation with matter. In fact, any quantity that varies in two dimensions can be used to create an image. Consider, for example, Figure 1.4, showing the continent of Antarctica. This might look like a photograph obtained from space, but it is actually a rendering of a *digital elevation model* (DEM) for the continent. Brightness in this image represents height. The process of acquiring the data needed to form the image differs radically from the processes involved in, say, photography; however, this does not prevent us from manipulating the image in just the same way as a photograph.

Figure 1.4   Digital elevation model of Antarctica, rendered as an image.

1.2   What is image processing?

Image processing is a general term for the wide range of techniques that exist for manipulating and modifying images in various ways. Photographers and physicists can perform certain image processing operations using chemicals or optical equipment; in this book, however, we concern ourselves solely with *digital* image processing, i.e., that which is performed on digital images using computers. We will consider not only how digital images may be manipulated and enhanced, but also how they may be acquired, stored and represented in computer memory.

Digital imaging actually predates modern computer technology; newspaper pictures were digitised for transatlantic transmission via submarine cable in the early 1920s [20]. However, true digital image processing (DIP) was not possible until the advent of large-scale digital computing hardware. The early motivation for the development of DIP techniques came from the space programme; in 1964, NASA's Jet Propulsion Laboratory used computers to correct distortions in images of the lunar surface obtained by the Ranger 7 probe. Now, more than three decades later, DIP finds applications in areas as diverse as medicine, military reconnaisance and desktop publishing.

1.2.1 Example: contrast enhancement

Manipulation of brightness, contrast and colour in images is very common. Often, there is a need to increase the contrast in an image, to make certain features clearly visible for the purposes of human interpretation. In Figure 1.5(a), for example, we see an image of a car in which very little detail is visible. It is a simple matter to increase both brightness and contrast in this image, making it easier to identify the vehicle and read its number plate (Figure 1.5(b)). We can envisage various scenarios—criminal investigations, for example—in which this might be important. Chapter 6 discusses this class of techniques in detail.

(a)   (b)

Figure 1.5 Example of contrast enhancement. (a) Image of a car with an unreadable number plate. (b) Result of contrast stretching.

1.2.2 Example: removal of motion blur

Many image processing operations are meant to remove or suppress the defects present in images. Some defects manifest themselves as a blurring of the image. For example, imagine a military scenario in which an enemy aircraft must be identified from an image, but the speed of this aircraft is such that the image suffers from motion blur (Figure 1.6(a)).

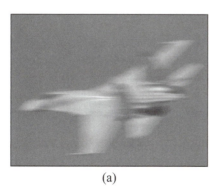
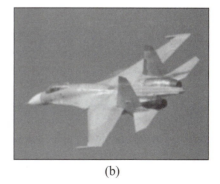

(a)   (b)

Figure 1.6 (a) Image of a jet degraded by motion blur. (b) Undegraded image.

Provided that we have accurate knowledge of how the aircraft was moving at the time of image acquisition, a technique known as deconvolution can be applied to remove the motion blur and hence assist identification (Figure 1.6(b)). This technique is discussed in Chapter 8.

1.2.3   Example: image warping

Image warping and morphing techniques are frequently used to produce special effects in advertisements, music videos and movies. Figure 1.7 shows how the image of a face can be distorted in an unnatural way. A more serious application for warping is the correction of various geometric distortions that result from the image acquisition process. Warping may also be used to *register* two or more images of the same scene, acquired at different times or with different instruments. Techniques for manipulating image geometry are discussed in Chapter 9.

(a)   (b)

Figure 1.7   Example of image warping. (a) Input image. (b) Output image.

1.3   Exercises

1. What problems might we experience when creating images of the human body using x-rays?

2. The digital elevation model depicted in Figure 1.4 is a two-dimensional array of height measurements rendered as an image. Can you think of any other examples of images that have been synthesised from data in this manner?

3. If you own a photograph album, look through it and identify any photographs that you consider to be flawed or disappointing in some way. For each photograph, try to decide whether anything could be done to correct its defects using image processing. (You might like to repeat this exercise once you have read more of the book and have a better idea of what is possible.)

4. Anyone who has used a bitmap editing package such as Adobe Photoshop® or Corel PhotoPAINT® has done some image processing, perhaps without even realising it. If you have access to such a package, experiment with its facilities and then make a list of the different types of operation that can be performed. (By the end of this book, you will understand how many of these operations work.)

CHAPTER 2

Imaging

Imaging is the process of acquiring images. In this chapter, we consider how images are obtained using an electronic camera and compare this mode of imaging with the way in which our eyes acquire images. We also consider briefly some examples of three-dimensional imaging technology.

2.1   Introduction

Imaging is shorthand for image acquisition, the process of sensing our surroundings and then representing the measurements that are made in the form of an image. The sensing phase distinguishes image acquisition from *image creation*; the latter can be accomplished using an existing set of data, and does not require a sensor. (An example of this is the digital elevation model depicted in Figure 1.4.)

2.1.1   Passive and active imaging

We can classify imaging as either *passive* or *active*. Passive imaging employs energy sources that are already present in the scene, whereas active imaging involves the use of artificial energy sources to probe our surroundings. Passive imaging is subject to the limitations of existing energy sources; the Sun, for example, is a convenient source of illumination, but only during daylight hours. Active imaging is not restricted in this way, but it is invariably a more complicated and expensive procedure, since we must supply and control a source of radiation in addition to an imaging instrument.

Active imaging predominates in the medical field, where precise control over radiation sources is essential in order to facilitate an accurate diagnosis and safeguard the patient's health. Active imaging is also becoming an important tool in remote sensing. Earth-orbiting satellites that carry sensors tuned to the visible region of the EM spectrum are unable to acquire useful images for areas of the surface that are in darkness, or that suffer from excessive cloud cover. Satellites equipped with synthetic aperture radar, on the other hand, can acquire data continuously, regardless of the time of day or the weather conditions.

2.1.2 Energy sources

We have seen, in Chapter 1, that all regions of the EM spectrum are suited to imaging. Nevertheless, there are good reasons to prefer light for imaging, except where the application demands otherwise:

- Light is familar, and is inherently safe.
- Light can be generated reliably and cheaply.
- Light is easy to control and process with optical hardware.
- Light can be detected easily.

The last point is important. Sensors for the visible and near-IR regions of the spectrum can be manufactured cheaply from silicon—which exhibits a useful response to radiation at these wavelengths. Also, the use of silicon allows a sensor to be integrated with its associated signal processing electronics, further reducing manufacturing costs.

For the reasons given above, we shall concentrate on imaging equipment that uses light. We shall examine in detail how images are acquired by an electronic camera and compare its performance with that of our own imaging 'hardware': our eyes.

2.2 The electronic camera

2.2.1 Camera optics

A camera uses a lens to focus part of the visual environment onto a sensor. The most important characteristics of a lens are its magnifying power and its light gathering capacity. The former can be specified by a *magnification factor*,

$$m = \frac{\text{image size}}{\text{object size}}.$$

By similar triangles, we can also say that

$$\frac{v}{u} = \frac{\text{image size}}{\text{object size}},$$

where u is the distance from an object to the lens and v is the distance from the lens to the image plane (see Figure 2.1). Hence

$$m = \frac{v}{u}. \tag{2.1}$$

It is usual to express the magnifying power of a lens in terms of its **focal length**, f, the distance from the lens to the point at which parallel incident rays converge (Figure 2.1). Focal length is given by the lens equation,

$$\frac{1}{f} = \frac{1}{u} + \frac{1}{v}. \tag{2.2}$$

The units for f are usually millimetres.

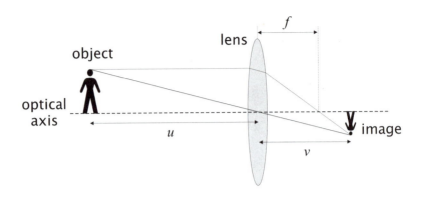

Figure 2.1 Image formation using a lens.

We can combine Equations 2.1 and 2.2 and rearrange to give an expression for f in terms of u and m:

$$f = \frac{um}{m+1}. \tag{2.3}$$

This is useful, since it allows us to select an appropriate lens for any desired magnification and object distance. Consider, for example, a scenario in which we need to form an image of a 10-cm-wide object, 50 cm away, on a sensor measuring 10 mm across. The magnification factor we require is

$$m = \frac{\text{image size}}{\text{object size}} = \frac{10}{100} = 0.1.$$

Hence the focal length should be

$$f = \frac{um}{m+1} = \frac{500 \times 0.1}{1.1} \simeq 45.5,$$

i.e., we need a lens with a focal length of approximately 45 mm.

The light gathering capacity of a camera lens is determined by its **aperture**. This can be no larger than the diameter of the lens itself, and it is usually made smaller than this by means of a diaphragm—a circular hole of adjustable size, incorporated into the lens. It is normal to express the aperture of a lens as an 'f number'—a dimensionless value obtained when focal length is divided by aperture diameter. Most lenses offer a sequence of fixed apertures (e.g., f2.8, f4, f5.6, f8, f11) that progressively halve the total amount of light reaching the sensor.

All lenses suffer from defects or *aberrations*, which can affect image quality. **Spherical aberration** arises when central and off-centre light rays are brought to a focus at different distances from the lens, resulting in blurred images. **Coma** occurs for obliquely-incident light when the off-centre rays come to a focus to one side of the central ray position, producing comet-shaped images of point objects. The surface of best focus for a lens is domed rather than planar, with the result that focus varies across an image acquired using a flat sensor. **Field curvature** measures the severity of this effect. Geometric distortion may also be a problem, particularly for lenses with small focal lengths. The tendency for straight lines to be bowed inwards, towards the centre of image, is termed **pincushion distortion**; the tendency for straight lines to be bowed outwards is termed **barrel distortion**.

The lens of a camera typically consists of several separate lens elements, designed so that, in combination, they partially compensate for the aforementioned aberrations. The effects of aberrations can also be reduced by making the lens aperture as small as possible. This confers additional benefits: depth of field (the range of distances at which an object will be in focus) is increased; also, small apertures restrict the passage of light to the central part of the lens, which has the highest resolving power. However, small apertures also cut down the amount of light falling on the sensor, thereby reducing the sensitivity of the instrument and, consequently, the quality of the image.

2.2.2 CCD sensors

The charge-coupled device, or **CCD**, is a sensor based on modern semiconductor technology. CCDs have become the sensor of choice in imaging applications because they do not suffer from geometric distortion and have a linear response to indicident light—unlike the vacuum tube technology that preceded them.

A CCD comprises an array of discrete imaging elements, or **photosites**, manufactured in silicon. The physical area of the array is small, typically less than 1 cm^2. When light falls on a CCD, each photosite accumulates an amount of electric charge proportional to the illumination time and the intensity of incident illumination. A photosite has a finite capacity of about 10^6 charge carriers, which places an upper limit on the brightness of objects to be imaged. A saturated photosite can overflow, corrupting its neighbours and causing blooming.

All CCDs produce thermally-generated charge, indistinguishable from charge produced by illumination. Hence, even in darkness, there will be some output from a CCD. This output is often called the **dark current**. In specialist applications such as astronomy, where light levels are extremely low and exposures are long, the dark current is a potentially significant source of noise. In such applications, CCDs are cooled to reduce dark current effects.

Figure 2.2 shows the architecture of a simple 'full-frame' CCD. In order to retrieve image data, the accumulated charge must be shifted from the photosites in the imaging area into an output register, and thence to an amplifier that (typically) outputs a serial video signal. The charge shifting process is shown schematically in Figure 2.3. Sets of electrodes associated with the photosites are energised in sequence to transfer packets of charge toward the output. A 'transfer clock' generates a waveform for this purpose. The process is highly efficient; there is virtually no loss of charge, even for packets of charge shifted from the furthest parts of the array. A defective photosite or electrode can prevent the advance of charge down a column, giving rise to a black line in the image.

In the simple architecture of Figure 2.2, a mechanical shutter is required to keep light away from the photosites during readout, lest there be smearing. Hence, this type of CCD is best suited to still image capture. Applications such as broadcast video use a 'frame transfer' architecture instead, in which the entire contents of the imaging area are shifted rapidly into a storage buffer that can be accessed whilst the imaging area is integrating the next frame.

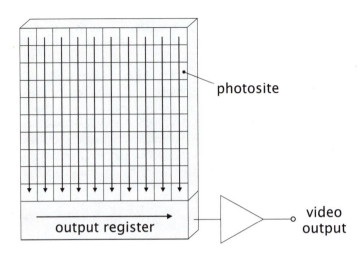

Figure 2.2 Architecture of a CCD.

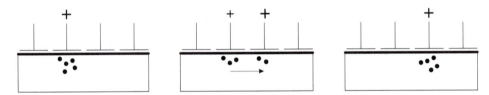

Figure 2.3 Charge coupling in a CCD.

2.3 The human eye

2.3.1 Structure

The human eye (Figure 2.4) is almost spherical in shape, with a diameter of approximately 20 mm. At the front of the eye is the *cornea*, a tough, transparent tissue that provides protection and carries out initial focusing and concentration of incoming light. Behind the cornea is the *iris*, a diaphragm that can expand or contract to control the amount of light entering the main body of the eye. (Its central hole, the *pupil*, varies in diameter from 2 mm to about 8 mm.) Final focusing of the incoming light rays is perform by the *lens*, a transparent structure assembled from layers of fibrous cells. The lens absorbs about 8% of light in the visible region of the spectrum, absorption being highest at shorter wavelengths. Excessive amounts of IR or UV radiation can cause damage to lens proteins.

The lens is suspended within the eye by means of the *ciliary fibres*, which are attached to *ciliary muscles*. An important difference between the lens of the eye and the lenses of artificial imaging instruments is that the former is flexible; it can change its shape by means of the ciliary muscles in order to adjust focus. The lens flattens to focus on distant objects and becomes thicker in order to focus on nearby objects.

When the eye is properly focused, a sharp image of the outside world forms on the

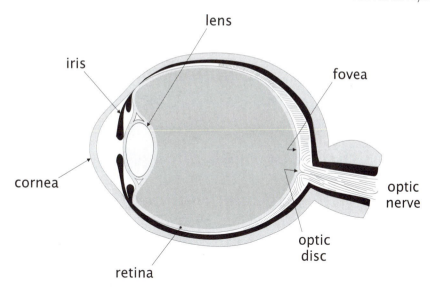

Figure 2.4 Structure of the human eye.

retina. This is a thin, photoreceptive layer covering about 200° of the eye's inner surface. The function of the retina is analogous to that of a CCD. However, the retina contains two different types of cell that act as photosites: **rods** and **cones**. There are about 120×10^6 rods and 8×10^6 cones in the human eye, distributed across the retina as shown in Figure 2.5. Note that, unlike a typical CCD, the photoreceptors are distributed non-uniformly. The cones are concentrated in a small region, approximately 1.5 mm in diameter, located where the optical axis intersects the retina. This region, the **fovea**, contains about 300,000 cones. By comparison, a medium-resolution CCD will have a similar number of photosites contained within an area of about 7 mm × 7 mm. The superb eyesight of birds of prey is partially explained by the fact that, compared with humans, they have four times as many photoreceptors packed into the fovea.

The distribution of photoreceptors is radially symmetric about the fovea, with the exception of a region about 20° from the optical axis. This region, the *optic disc*, contains no photoreceptors and corresponds to a perceptual *blind spot*. It is the point where connections from the photoreceptors are gathered into the *optic nerve*, which conveys visual information to the brain in the form of electrical impulses. Note that, although there are nearly 130 million photoreceptors in the retina, the optic nerve contains only a million fibres; evidently, a substantial amount of data integration and processing takes place within the retina itself. In this respect, the eye differs from a CCD-based camera, which typically relays all its data to an external computer for processing.

The optic disc and the blind spot are consequences of the fact that the retina is 'inside-out'; that is, the photoreceptors are not the innermost layer of cells, and, furthermore, they point *away* from the light. This curious arrangement is common to all vertebrates, for whom the retina has evolved as an outgrowth of the brain. Throughout the retina, the neurons that gather information from photoreceptors lie directly above those photoreceptors and

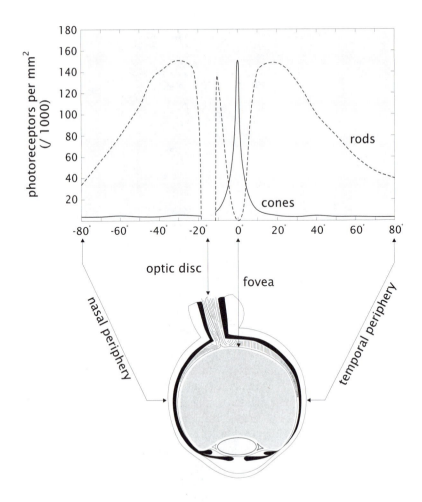

Figure 2.5 Distribution of rods and cones across the human retina.

represent an obstacle to the passage of incoming light. The exception is the fovea, where the retina is thinner because much of the overlying structure has been peeled away. This thinness is crucial for sharp vision.

Cones come in three varieties. Very roughly, we can think of the three types as being sensitive to red, green and blue light, respectively. Note that a cone merely signals that light has arrived: colour perception is possible because the signals from many cones, of all three types, are combined. This is done at a very early stage of processing. Each cone is connected to its own nerve end; thus, it is cones which give us the ability to resolve fine detail. Rods are not colour sensitive, and several are connected to a single nerve end. Moreover, they are found only outside the fovea, where they are far more numerous than cones. Consequently, rods serve to give us a lower-resolution picture of the entire field of view.

Cones require plenty of light to operate; they are responsible for **photopic** ('bright-light') vision. Rods are sensitive to low levels of illumination, and give rise to **scotopic** ('dim-light') vision. Creatures with a preponderance of rods in their retinae, such as the owl, therefore tend to be active at night, whereas those with a preponderance of cones, such as the squirrel, tend to be active only during daylight hours.

2.3.2 Properties of the human visual system

The human visual system is capable of adapting to an enormous range of light levels—far greater than that of any electronic imaging system. The upper and lower limits on intensity (the glare limit and the scotopic threshold, respectively) differ by a factor of 10^{10}. Of course, our visual system cannot cope with such a huge intensity range simultaneously. It accomplishes the task by means of changes in the overall sensitivity of the eye, a phenomenon termed **brightness adaption**. The total range of intensity levels that can be discriminated simultaneously is small compared with the total adaption range. A typical person can perceive a few dozen different intensity changes at a single point in an image. However, as the eye roams around the image, the average background level changes, allowing a different set of intensity changes to be detected.

There is a complex relationship between perceived brightness and light intensity. The former is, in fact, a logarithmic function of the latter. This can be seen in Figure 2.6, which shows a staircase of intensities ranging from black to white. A fixed intensity increment was used to generate this image, but to our visual system this increment appears to vary, being larger for the high intensity steps at the right of the image than for the low intensity steps at the left.

Figure 2.6 A staircase of increasing intensity.

Figure 2.6 illustrates another interesting phenomenon. Although each vertical band is uniform, we perceive it to be slightly brighter or darker near its edges than at its centre. This is known as **Mach banding**. The phenomenon is a direct consequence of the way in which the visual system amalgamates input from neighbouring photoreceptors[1] so as to sharpen

---

[1] We will see how the effect can be replicated with image processing when we consider the Laplacian operator in Chapter 7.

everything we see and increase visual acuity.

When light arrives at a photoreceptor, it triggers chemical processes that, ultimately, result in the transmission of an electrical signal along a nerve fibre. These chemical processes last for several milliseconds, so the output from a photoreceptor is a time-averaged response. Electronic cameras can respond much more rapidly. As a consequence of the temporal smoothing performed by the retina, there is a 'critical flicker frequency', below which we perceive the individual flashes of a blinking light, and above which the flashes fuse into a single, continuous image. Early motion pictures suffered from a visible flicker because their frame rates were not high enough for the eye to integrate the individual frames.

2.4   Three-dimensional imaging

A camera creates images that are projections of some limited part of our three-dimensional world onto a two-dimensional plane. If we can somehow invert this projective transformation, we can recover information about the three-dimensional world from images. Unfortunately, a single image does not contain sufficient information to invert the projection. There is ambiguity because a given feature in the image could correspond to a large distant object or a small nearby object. This ambiguity can be resolved using multiple views of the scene.

2.4.1   Stereoscopy

Our two eyes give us binocular vision. A point in the scene that we are viewing projects onto one point on the retina of the left eye and a different point on the retina of the right eye. The points are different because our eyes are separated by a few centimetres. The separation of the points is termed the **disparity**. There is an inverse relationship between disparity and depth in the scene; disparity will be relatively large for points in the scene that are near to us and relatively small for points that are far away.

Following this principle, stereoscopic imaging uses a pair of images of the same scene obtained from cameras located at slightly different positions. Standard formulae exist to calculate depth from disparity, given adequate knowledge of imaging geometry (i.e., camera separation and focal length). However, a major problem is the detection of corresponding points in the left and right images, a process known as stereo matching.

2.4.2   Computed tomography

A range of techniques exist for imaging three-dimensional structure inside solid objects such as the human body. They require a source of EM radiation that penetrates the object; light is not suitable because solid objects tend to be opaque to radiation at visible wavelengths. X-rays are normally transmitted through the object. Sometimes, a radiation source is placed inside the object and the emitted radiation is detected. In medical imaging applications, this is done by having the patient ingest a substance that has been 'tagged' with a radioisotope. Gamma rays emitted by the radioactive decay of this radioisotope pass through the body to a detector.

X-ray computed tomography (x-ray CT) is performed using a CT scanner. Figure 2.7 shows two possible configurations of this instrument. The CT scanner builds up a three-dimensional image of an object as a sequence of parallel, two-dimensional slices, each separated by some small fixed distance. Each slice is computed from multiple, one-dimensional 'views'. A single view records the intensities of x-rays transmitted through the object in a particular plane and from a particular direction. The x-ray source and (in some scanners) the detector array rotate to obtain different views, all in the same plane but with different orientations. A complete set of views will cover 180° in steps of a few degrees.

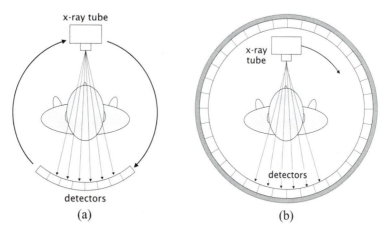

Figure 2.7 CT scanner configurations. (a) Rotating detectors. (b) Stationary detectors.

Reconstruction of a two-dimensional image from these one-dimensional views is carried out by a technique known as filtered backprojection. In effect, this technique expands or projects each one-dimensional view back along the beam axis into the image plane. Summing these backprojected images over all views yields an image showing a cross-section through the object. There is an inverse relationship between the sum computed at any point in this image and the opacity of the object at that point; small values occur at points where the object is relatively opaque to x-rays and large values occur at points where it is relatively transparent.

We can illustrate how backprojection works with a simple example. Let us suppose that the circle in Figure 2.8 represents a cross-section through a cylindrical object of some kind. The projection of this shape in any direction has the form plotted in Figure 2.9(a). Backprojecting this view into two dimensions yields images such that in Figure 2.9(b). Now let us imagine that we have a set of these views, obtained from different directions. Backprojecting and summing these views produces images like those of Figure 2.10. We can see that, as the number of views being summed increases, the reconstructed image more closely resembles the original cross-section[2].

---

[2] This is a fairly crude example. The reconstructed image will always be a little blurred compared with the cross-section, however many views are summed. Filtered backprojection solves this problem by incorporating a filtering operation that sharpens the image. Chapters 7 and 8 explain how operations of this kind can be performed.

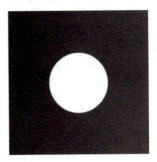

Figure 2.8 A shape to be reconstructed by backprojection.

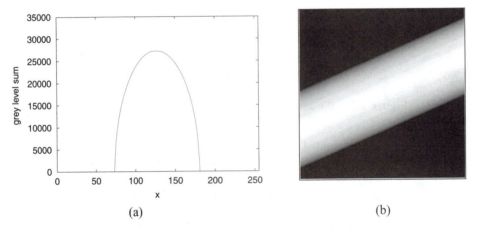

(a)   (b)

Figure 2.9 (a) Projection of the shape in Figure 2.8. (b) Backprojection of (a).

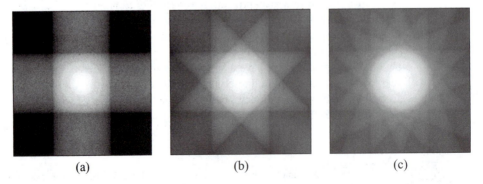

(a)   (b)   (c)

Figure 2.10 Reconstruction by backprojection. (a) Sum of two backprojected views. (b) Sum of four backprojected views. (c) Sum of eight backprojected views.

2.5 Further reading

Awcock and Thomas [4] describe camera optics and sensor technology in some detail. Further information on CCDs and other types of sensor can also be found in Castleman's book [9]. A highly technical, in-depth description of CCD technology is presented by Janesick et al. [26]. The standard formats for the signals output by video cameras are explained in detail by Baxes [5].

Volume I of Glassner's *Principles of Digital Image Synthesis* [17] gives much more detail on the human visual system. It covers topics such as depth and colour perception that we have barely touched on here.

Stereoscopic imaging is discussed in a great many articles and books, especially those that focus on computer vision rather than the lower-level topic of image processing [9, 20, 25, 42, 45, 46].

Baxes [5] gives a basic introduction to computed tomography. A slightly more thorough treatment is presented by Castleman [9]. Webb [50] discusses in considerable detail all aspects of tomographic medical imaging using x-rays and gamma rays. Webb also presents extensive discussion of magnetic resonance imaging (MRI), a powerful technique in which 3D images of the body are formed by detecting radio waves emitted from the nuclei of hydrogen atoms resonating in a magnetic field. The complexity of MRI is such that further discussion lies beyond the scope of this book. Issues relating to the visualisation of 3D image data from MRI or computed tomography are discussed by Lichtenbelt et al. [28].

2.6 Exercises

1. A camera with a lens of focal length 35 mm acquires images of an object measuring roughly 50 cm across its largest dimension. Assuming that the object fills the 10 mm × 10 mm array of the camera's CCD, how far away is the object?

2. How might the sensor found in a flatbed scanner differ from the CCD found in a camera? What are the problems that can arise when scanning a document, and how might these problems manifest themselves in the scanned image?

3. Suppose that we have a CCD with a defective photosite, resulting in a black line of missing data in the image. Suggest an operation that might correct this defect in the image. (You might wish to revisit this problem after reading the next chapter.)

4. Write Java programs to compute projections of an image and then reconstruct that image from projections.

CHAPTER 3

Digital images

In this chapter, we consider the process of creating a digital image from data acquired by a camera or some other kind of imaging instrument. We also consider how such images are represented within the memory of a computer in order that image processing operations can be carried out on them.

3.1   Introduction

As we have seen in Chapter 2, the optics of an imaging system will focus a continuous, two-dimensional pattern of varying light intensity and colour onto a sensor. The pattern is defined in a coordinate system whose origin is conventionally defined as the upper-left corner of the image (Figure 3.1). We can describe the pattern by a function, $f(x, y)$. For monochrome images, the value of the function at any pair of coordinates, x and y, is the intensity of the light detected at that point. In the case of colour images, $f(x, y)$ is a vector-valued function. Section 3.4 gives further details of how colour can be represented by a vector.

The function $f(x, y)$ must be translated into a discrete array of numerical data if it is to undergo computer processing. This *digital* representation is only an approximation of the original image, but that is the price we must pay for the convenience of being able to manipulate the image using a computer. Translation of $f(x, y)$ into an appropriate numerical form is accomplished by the processes of **sampling** and **quantisation**. For standard video signals, both processes are usually carried out by a single piece of hardware, known as an **analogue to digital converter** (ADC).

(0,0)

Figure 3.1 Coordinate system for an image.

3.2   Sampling

Sampling is the process of measuring the value of the image function $f(x, y)$ at discrete intervals in space. Each sample corresponds to a small, square area of the image, known as a **pixel**. A digital image is a two-dimensional array of these pixels. Pixels are indexed by x and y coordinates, with x and y taking integer values.

A CCD sensor consists of a discrete array of photosites, so it has, in effect, already sampled the radiation pattern that falls on it. However, in conventional video cameras these samples are converted into an analogue video signal for compatibility with the majority of video equipment in use today.

A single frame from a standard video signal is already discrete in the y dimension, consisting of either 525 or 625 lines of data. Sampling the signal therefore involves measuring its amplitude at regular time intervals during the segments of the signal that correspond to each line. This makes the image discrete spatially in the x dimension.

Video standards enforce a particular **sampling rate** for a video signal. An RS-170 video signal, for instance, has 485 active lines and each frame must have an aspect ratio of 4:3, so there must be $485 \times (4/3) = 646$ samples per line. In practice, a few lines and samples are trimmed from the signal to give an array of pixels with dimensions 640×480. To produce such an image, a temporal sampling rate of around 12 MHz is required.

With a digital 'still picture' camera, things are somewhat simpler, as there is no need to convert samples from the CCD into an analogue form and then resample. Neither is there a requirement to conform to broadcast video standards. Such cameras typically produce images with dimensions of 1024×768, 1280×1024, etc. These dimensions are chosen to suit display standards originating from the computer industry (e.g., SVGA). Much higher resolutions than those of broadcast video are possible, and a 4:3 aspect ratio is not enforced (although this is often preferred).

Other types of imaging equipment operate under different constraints. In medicine, for example, radioisotope imaging devices produce images that are, of necessity, sampled very coarsely. This is because images are formed from gamma ray photons emitted by radioactive material inside the patient. For safety reasons, the quantity of this material is small, hence there are relatively few photons emitted. It is therefore necessary to integrate photon counts over a relatively large area in order to obtain statistically meaningful results [50]. An area the size of the chest, for example, might be represented by a 64×64-pixel array.

3.2.1 Spatial resolution

The spatial resolution of an image is the physical size of a pixel in that image; i.e., the area in the scene that is represented by a single pixel in the image. For a given field of view, dense sampling will produce a high resolution image in which there are many pixels, each of which represents the contribution of a very small part of the scene; coarse sampling, on the other hand, will produce a low resolution image in which there are few pixels, each representing the contribution of a relatively large part of the scene to the image.

Spatial resolution dictates the amount of useful information that can be extracted from an image. Figure 3.2 illustrates this point emphatically with an image that is displayed at three different resolutions. You may conduct your own experiments on the effects of varying

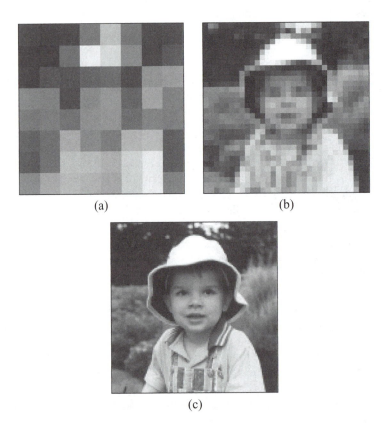

(a) (b)

(c)

Figure 3.2 Effect of resolution on image interpretation. (a) 8×8 image of a scene. (b) 32×32 image. (c) 256×256 image.

spatial resolution by running the `ResolutionSimulator` application, as described in the Exercises section at the end of this chapter.

In deciding whether a digital image has been sampled appropriately, we must consider the rapidity with which the value of $f(x, y)$ changes as we move across the image. This rate of change is measured by **spatial frequency**. Gradual changes in $f(x, y)$ are characterised by low spatial frequencies and can be represented adequately in a coarsely-sampled image; rapid changes are characterised by high spatial frequencies and can be represented accurately only in a densely-sampled image. Wherever possible, the sampling that we choose for an image should satisfy the **Nyquist criterion**. Essentially, this states that the sampling frequency should be at least double the highest spatial frequency found in the image. If we sample an image coarsely, such that the Nyquist criterion is not met, then the image may suffer from the effects of **aliasing**.

Figure 3.3 illustrates how aliasing can occur when sampling a quantity that varies in one dimension. (You can imagine this as a variation in intensity along an arbitrary line in a 2D image.) In aliasing, a signal of a certain frequency that has been undersampled can appear

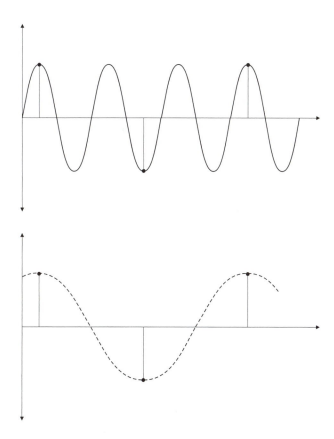

Figure 3.3 Aliasing in one dimension. Top: an undersampled waveform. Bottom: aliased reconstruction of waveform from samples.

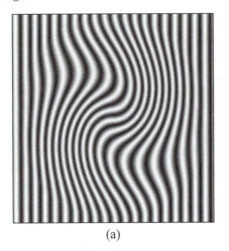 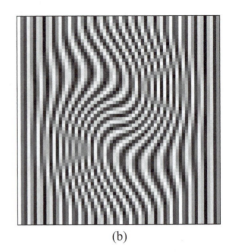

(a) (b)

Figure 3.4 Aliasing artefacts in digital images. (a) Image without aliasing. (b) Coarsely-sampled version, showing aliasing artefacts.

to be of a lower frequency upon reconstruction. This has the effect of distorting the signal, introducing frequency components that are unrepresentative of the original data. Figure 3.4 shows the visible effect of aliasing in an image containing strong periodic variations in intensity.

We will not, in general, have advance knowledge of the highest spatial frequency present in an image. Consequently, the sampling process is normally preceded by **anti-aliasing**. This is a filtering operation designed to remove frequencies that exceed half the sampling rate achieved by the ADC hardware, thereby guaranteeing that the Nyquist criterion is met.

3.2.2 Sampling pattern

When sampling an image, we need to consider not only the sampling rate, but also the physical arrangement of the samples. A rectangular pattern, in which pixels are aligned horizontally and vertically into rows and columns, is by far the most common. Unfortunately, a rectangular sampling pattern leads to ambiguities in pixel connectivity. Figure 3.5(a) suggests that the chain of shaded pixels labelled A–D separates two regions of unshaded pixels, but this is not so; if we allow B and C to be connected diagonally, then it follows that E and F are also connected—in which case, the chain is not continuous and the two groups of unshaded pixels form a single region.

A second problem with rectangular patterns is an inconsistency in distance measurement. Suppose that each pixel in Figure 3.5(a) represents a region of the scene that is 1 mm wide and 1 mm high. The distance between pixels C and D is thus 1 mm; however, the distance between pixels B and C is not 1 mm but $\sqrt{2}$ mm, by simple trigonometry. Hence, the actual distance travelled when we move by a fixed number of pixels in the image depends on the direction in which we move.

These problems would be solved by a hexagonal sampling pattern (Figure 3.5b). Here, diagonal neighbours are properly connected, and the distance travelled in an image does

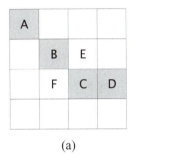

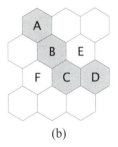

(a)　　　　　　　　(b)

Figure 3.5 Connectivity of different sampling patterns. (a) Rectangular pattern. (b) Hexagonal pattern.

not depend on direction. Despite these advantages, a hexagonal pattern is seldom used. It cannot portray accurately the large number of horizontal and vertical features found in many images, and, in any case, sensors and display hardware generally do not support hexagonal sampling.

The rectangular and hexagonal patterns described above are uniform, with the result that one part of an image is as important as any other part. This is useful in images intended for eventual human interpretation, for which prediction of where viewers will direct their attention is impossible. In other situations, where attention can be predicted or controlled, a non-uniform sampling scheme may be profitable. In particular, a **log-polar** sampling pattern has some interesting and useful properties. Figure 3.6 shows an array of pixels that conforms to this pattern. The pixels of this array are sectors with a fixed angular size and a radial size that increases logarithmically with increasing distance from the centre. This gives high resolution near the centre of the array and low resolution in the periphery. Such an arrangement satisfies the conflicting requirements of good resolution and wide field of view. However, a camera using a sensor with this sampling pattern must always point towards the most interesting or important part of the scene, to ensure that it lies in the

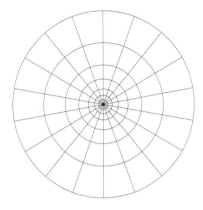

Figure 3.6 A log-polar array of pixels.

centre of the array and is therefore imaged at the highest possible resolution. This is known as an *attentive vision* strategy.

Note that the photoreceptor distribution in the human retina broadly resembles that of a log-polar array. The part of the image that forms on the fovea is densely sampled by the tightly packed, well connected cones in that part of the retina; the remainder of the image is coarsely sampled by a more sparse population of rods. The human visual system supports attentive vision by means of eye, head and even body movements, thereby ensuring that the features of interest are always imaged using the fovea.

A pixel coordinate in a log-polar array is specified by a radial index, r, and a sector index, θ. If we plot these indices in Cartesian space, it becomes clear that changes in scale cause translations along the r axis, whereas rotation causes a cyclic shift along the θ axis. This

(a) (b)

(c) (d)

Figure 3.7 Benefits of log-polar sampling. (a) Original image. (b) Log-polar resampled version of (a). (c) Rotated image. (d) Log-polar resampled version of (c). This is equivalent to (b) after circular shifting, such that pixels moving beyond the right side border of the image reappear on its left side.

greatly simplifies scale- and rotation-invariant object recognition and matching tasks. This idea is illustrated in Figure 3.7.

You can experiment further with log-polar sampling by running the `LogPolar` application, as detailed in the Exercises for this chapter.

3.3 Quantisation

It is usual to digitise the values of the image function, $f(x, y)$, in addition to its spatial coordinates. This process of quantisation involves replacing a continuously varying $f(x, y)$ with a discrete set of **quantisation levels**. The accuracy with which variations in $f(x, y)$ are represented is determined by the number of quantisation levels that we use; the more levels we use, the better the approximation.

Conventionally, a set of n quantisation levels comprises the integers $0, 1, 2, \ldots, n - 1$. 0 and $n - 1$ are usually displayed or printed as black and white, respectively, with intermediate levels rendered in various shades of grey. Quantisation levels are therefore commonly referred to as **grey levels**. The collective term for all the grey levels, ranging from black to white, is a **greyscale**.

For convenient and efficient processing by a computer, the number of grey levels, n, is usually an integral power of two. We may write

$$n = 2^b, \tag{3.1}$$

where b is the number of bits used for quantisation. b is typically 8, giving us images with 256 possible grey levels ranging from 0 (black) to 255 (white). Some ADCs are not capable of quantising to 8 bits, producing 6-bit or 7-bit images instead (although these may subsequently be represented in memory using 8 bits per pixel). The specialised equipment used in medicine and astronomy may produce images quantised using 10 or even 12 bits.

Figure 3.8 shows how the number of quantisation levels affects image quality. The differences between 8-bit and 6-bit images are almost imperceptible. Coarser quantisation creates a 'false contouring' effect in an image, although this will not necessarily hamper interpretation.

You can investigate the effect of varying the number of quantisation levels on image interpretation using the `QuantisationSimulator` program, as decribed in the Exercises.

3.4 Colour

3.4.1 The RGB model

Much of our technology for creating and displaying colour is based on the empirical observation that a wide variety of colours can be obtained by mixing red, green and blue light in different proportions. For this reason, red (R), green (G) and blue (B) are described as the *primary colours* of the additive colour system. Not all colours can be obtained in this way, but the technique is a powerful one, nonetheless. It would seem to suggest that a colour image can be formed by making three measurements of scene brightness at each pixel, using the red, green and blue components of the detected light. We can do this by

(a)   (b)

(c)

Figure 3.8   Effect of quantisation on image interpretation. (a) 4 levels. (b) 16 levels. (c) 256 levels.

using a colour camera, in which the sensor is able to measure radiation at red, green and blue wavelengths for all points in the image, or by using a monochrome camera in conjunction with three special filters that block all but a narrow band of wavelengths centred on red, green and blue, respectively.

In a colour image conforming to the RGB model, the value of $f(x, y)$ is a vector with three components, corresponding to R, G and B. In a normalised model, these components each vary between 0.0 and 1.0. R, G and B can be regarded as orthogonal axes defining a three-dimensional colour space. Every possible value of $f(x, y)$ is a point in this 'colour cube'. The primary colours red, green and blue are at the corners $(1, 0, 0)$, $(0, 1, 0)$ and $(0, 0, 1)$; the colours cyan, magenta and yellow are at the opposite corners; black is at the origin; white is at the corner furthest from the origin (Figure 3.9). Points on a straight line joining the origin to the most distant corner represent various shades of grey.

Since each of the three components—red, green and blue—is normally quantised using 8 bits, an image made up of these components is commonly described as a **24-bit colour**

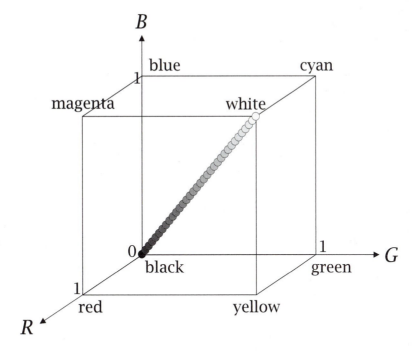

Figure 3.9 The RGB colour cube.

image. Because each primary colour is represented to a precision of 1 part in 256, we can specify an arbitrary colour to a precision of about 1 part in 16 million[1]; that is, around 16 million colours are available in a 24-bit image.

Despite its importance in image acquisition and display, the RGB model is of limited use when processing colour images, because it is not a *perceptual* model. In perceptual terms, colour and intensity are distinct from one another, but the R, G and B components each contain both colour and intensity information. Models which decouple these two different types of information tend to be more useful for image processing.

3.4.2   Other colour models

The **CMY model** has as its primaries cyan (C), magenta (M) and yellow (Y). These are the primary colours of the subtractive system that describes how colour is produced from pigments. A CMY colour is derived from an RGB colour as follows:

$$\begin{bmatrix} C \\ M \\ Y \end{bmatrix} = \begin{bmatrix} 1 \\ 1 \\ 1 \end{bmatrix} - \begin{bmatrix} R \\ G \\ B \end{bmatrix}. \tag{3.2}$$

---

[1] This is because $256^3 = 16{,}777{,}216$.

We can, in theory, produce almost any colour on paper by mixing cyan, magenta and yellow inks. In practice, this process cannot produce a satisfactory black, so a fourth component labelled K and representing black pigment is added, resulting in the **CMYK model**. This is the model that is used when generating hardcopy versions of digital images using colour printers (see Section 5.4.2).

The **HSI model** is more suitable than the RGB model for many image processing tasks. Its three components are hue (H), saturation (S) and intensity (I). H and S specify colour. H specifies the dominant pure colour perceived by an observer (e.g., red, yellow, blue) and S measures the degree to which that pure colour has been 'diluted' by white light. Because colour and intensity are independent, we can manipulate one without affecting the other.

HSI colour space is described by a cylindrical coordinate system and is commonly represented as a 'double cone' (Figure 3.10). A colour is a single point inside or on the surface of the double cone. The height of the point corresponds to intensity. If we imagine that the point lies in a horizontal plane, we can define a vector in this plane from the axis of the cones to the point. Saturation is then the length of this vector and hue is its orientation, expressed as an angle in degrees.

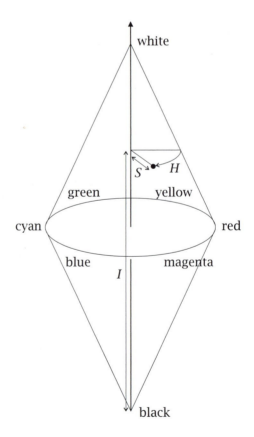

Figure 3.10 The HSI colour space.

A rather complicated geometric transformation maps a colour from RGB space to HSI space or vice versa. Gonzalez and Woods [20] give a detailed derivation of the conversion formulae. Implementations of these formulae in C are given by Pitas [37] and by Crane [11]. Rather than creating equivalent Java implementations, we can take advantage of conversion code built into Java's Color class. The HSICalc application on the CD uses this code to convert an RGB colour into an HSI colour. The RGB colour is specified on the command line as a triplet of 8-bit integers; the HSI colour is written to standard output as three numbers in the range 0.0–1.0. Source code for this program is shown in Listing 3.1.

LISTING 3.1 A program to convert RGB colours into values of hue, saturation and intensity. A conversion method from Java's **Color** class is used.

```java
import java.awt.Color;
import java.text.DecimalFormat;

public class HSICalc {

  public static void main(String[] argv) {

    if (argv.length > 2) {

      int[] rgb = new int[3];
      for (int i = 0; i < 3; ++i)
        rgb[i] = Integer.parseInt(argv[i]);

      float[] values = Color.RGBtoHSB(rgb[0], rgb[1], rgb[2], null);
      String[] labels = { "H=", "S=", "I=" };
      DecimalFormat floatValue = new DecimalFormat("0.000");
      for (int i = 0; i < 3; ++i)
        System.out.println(labels[i] + floatValue.format(values[i]));

    }
    else {
      System.err.println("usage: java HSICalc r g b");
      System.exit(1);
    }

  }

}
```

3.5 Image representation

So how do we go about representing a digital image in a Java program? The Java 2 platform provides a convenient representation for images that makes the implementation of image processing software relatively straightforward; nevertheless, it is highly instructive to consider first how we might create our own representation in Java, before examining in Chapter 4 the solution provided as a standard part of the Java API. We assume here that the reader is familiar with Java and with the basic concepts of object-oriented programming; if a refresher course is required, the books by Niemeyer and Peck [35], Winder and Roberts [51], Eckel [13] and Horstmann [23] are highly recommended.

3.5.1 8-bit greyscale images

Usually, a single, quantised value is associated with each pixel of an image. It is normal to use eight bits for quantisation, in which case the value at each pixel can be stored using one byte of memory. The Java language has a `byte` data type, so a simple way of representing such an image in a Java program would be as a two-dimensional array of bytes:

```
byte[][] image = new byte[512][512];
```

This code creates storage for an 8-bit, 512 × 512 image. Clearly, it would not be possible to represent a larger image using this array. Also, a considerable amount of storage space would be wasted if the images being processed were much smaller than the array. A better solution is to determine the precise storage requirements at run time:

```
int width, height;
...
// determine appropriate
// values for width and height
...
byte[][] image = new byte[height][width];
```

It is interesting to compare this Java code with the equivalent code written in another language, such as C++:

```
int width, height;
...
unsigned char** image = new unsigned char*[height];
for (int i = 0; i < height; ++i)
  image[i] = new unsigned char[width];
```

Arrays in C++ lack the necessary flexibility, since their dimensions are fixed at compile time. Hence we use a *pointer* instead[2]. Significantly, the code required to create a pointer and allocate two-dimensional storage to it is rather more complex than the equivalent Java code.

C++ does not have a byte data type, but `unsigned char` can be used instead because a character in C++ occupies one byte. Values of this type are interpreted as integers in the

---

[2] To be more precise, we are using a pointer to a pointer.

range 0–255 in arithmetic expressions, whereas Java's `byte` type is treated somewhat less conveniently as a value in the range −128 to 127.

An image class

In the previous examples, three variables are used to define an image: two integers that specify its dimensions and a 2D array of bytes that holds the image data. It can be tiresome to juggle all of these variables, particularly in programs that create numerous images. A better approach is to define an **image class** that encapsulates these three attributes. An instance of this class—an **image object**—therefore contains not only the pixel data but also variables that store the dimensions of the image.

An image class should support the notion of *information hiding*. The image dimensions and pixel data should be made private to the image object and access to these variables should be possible only by invoking the public methods that form the **interface** to the class. These methods should be implemented in such a way that clients of the class are denied the opportunity of putting an image object into an invalid state, e.g., by setting image width to zero.

Separating interface from implementation in this manner encourages the programmer using the class to think in terms of the behaviour of an image object, or the services it provides to client programs, rather than the details of exactly how the pixel data are stored. It has the further advantage that the implementation is free to change (e.g., become more efficient) without affecting clients of the class, provided that the interface remains the same. For example, we might choose to replace the two-dimensional array of bytes used for pixel data storage by a one-dimensional array. There are a number of reasons for doing this, not least the fact that it simplifies the task of reading image data from or writing image data to a file. (Section 3.7 gives further reasons.)

These considerations lead to a design like that outlined in Figure 3.11. This has `private` instance variables to store image width and height, together with `public` methods `getWidth` and `getHeight` that simply return the current values of these variables to the client[3]. There is also a `private` array of bytes, which holds the image data, plus methods `getPixel` and `setPixel` to retrieve and modify pixel values. Note that `getPixel` returns an `int` value, although pixel values are represented internally as bytes. Values of type `byte` in Java are taken to lie in the range −128 to 127, whereas we require an integer in the range 0–255. The client need never be aware of this implementation detail because the `getPixel` method performs the conversion. The constructor of the class, which is responsible for creating `ByteImage` objects, takes parameters w and h, representing the desired width and height of the image.

In a client program, an image is created like so:

```
ByteImage image = new ByteImage(100, 100);
```

A method should, in general, check its parameters, to ensure that an object is not put into an invalid state by a client. In some cases, we can rely on the inherent

---

[3] We follow Sun's JavaBeans convention here. Thus, methods that inspect the state of an object have names prefixed with 'get', whereas methods that modify its state in some fashion have names prefixed with 'set'.

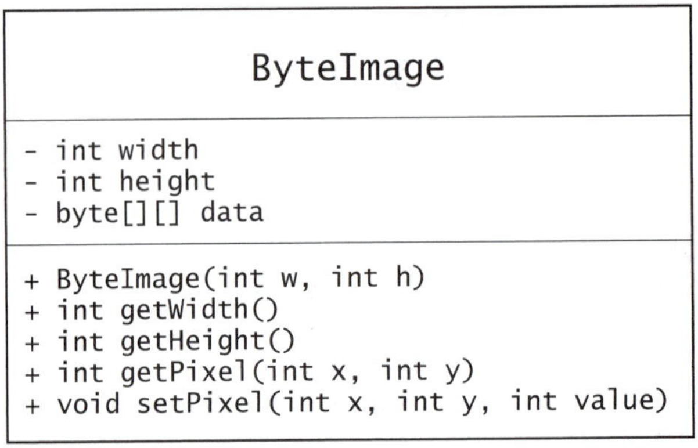

```
                    ByteImage

  - int width
  - int height
  - byte[][] data

  + ByteImage(int w, int h)
  + int getWidth()
  + int getHeight()
  + int getPixel(int x, int y)
  + void setPixel(int x, int y, int value)
```

Figure 3.11 A simple class to represent 8-bit greyscale images. This diagram uses a variation of the standard UML notation. The class is represented as a rectangle divided into three compartments. The top compartment names the class, the middle compartment lists its instance variables and the bottom compartment lists its methods. A − prefix indicates that a variable or method is private; a + prefix indicates that it is public.

robustness of Java and its tendency to throw **exceptions** when runtime error conditions occur. For example, when allocating storage for an array of pixels with new, a NegativeArraySizeException will be thrown if either dimension has a negative value[4]. Similarly, an ArrayIndexOutOfBoundsException will occur if the array subscripts used to access a pixel are out of range. Thus there is no particular need for getPixel or setPixel to check that the values of x and y are in the ranges 0 to width−1 and 0 to height−1, respectively. However, we can implement different behaviour if we wish. For instance, setPixel could check that x and y are within the permitted ranges and simply do nothing if this is not the case, rather than throwing an exception.

The new pixel value passed to setPixel must be checked explicitly. In this case, we have three options:

1. Ignore the value if it is not in the range 0–255.
2. Enforce a 0–255 range by treating negative values as 0 and values greater than 255 as 255.
3. Throw an exception if the value is out of range.

To implement option 3, we must define our own exception class that extends Exception, and modify the definition of setPixel to indicate that the method throws an instance of this new exception class.

The ByteImage class depicted in Figure 3.11 uses a two-dimensional array for the storage of pixel values. This means that a pixel at coordinates (x, y) has its value stored in the array element data[y][x][5]. We are free to change this and use a *one-dimensional* array

---

[4] Although no exception is thrown, unfortunately, if either dimension has a value of zero.
[5] We are assuming a 'row-major' ordering of values here; the opposite arrangement would also work, in which case a pixel at (x, y) would have its value stored in data[x][y].

of bytes if we wish. For instance, we could define the array as follows:

```
private byte[] data;
```

The implementations of the constructor, getPixel and setPixel would then have to change. A pixel at coordinates (x, y) would now correspond to the array element data[y*width+x]. In effect, y*width represents an offset which identifies the start of each row of pixels in the 1D array. For added efficiency, these offsets could be precalculated and stored in another array. This would avoid the need for a multiplication every time a pixel was accessed.

Provided that the *interface* of the ByteImage class—as defined by the parameters, return types and behaviour of its methods—remains the same, client code will be unaffected by this change of implementation.

One reason for making this change is that operations such as copying an image in memory, reading it from a stream or writing it to a stream become much easier. Copying of image data, for instance, can be accomplished with a single call to the System.arraycopy method if the data are in a 1D array. Similarly, output of image data to a stream can be implemented with a method as simple as this[6]:

```
public void write(OutputStream out) throws IOException {
    out.write(data);
}
```

3.5.2 Other data types

Some sources of images, particularly those in the medical field, routinely produce data which cannot be represented as 8-bit integers. The pixel values in images from x-ray CT scanners in hospitals, for instance, are often represented using 16-bit signed integers, which may range in value from $-32,768$ to $32,767$ [50]. Because two bytes are used for each pixel, these images require twice the storage space of 8-bit images. In Java, 16-bit integers are represented by variables of type short. If 16 bits are not sufficient, we can use the wider int type, which has 32 bits and can represent values between approximately -2×10^9 and 2×10^9. An image containing an int array will occupy four times as much space in memory as an image of the same dimensions in which pixel values are represented with bytes.

The byte, short and int types allow us to represent a moderate range of values exactly, and are sufficient for most imaging applications. On occasion, it may be beneficial to use floating-point numbers—which can represent an enormous range of values with a limited, albeit useful, precision. Java's float data type supports values as large as 3.4×10^{38} or as small as 1.4×10^{-45}, and a still wider range is possible using double.

Floating-point images are sometimes useful as a means of storing the intermediate results of some image processing operation, particularly if it is important that the fractional part of a calculation is preserved. Floating-point images may also be used in scientific imaging applications, where the exact values measured by an instrument are important and loss of precision due to excessive quantisation is undesirable.

---

[6] We ignore here the need to store image dimensions along with the data. This is considered further in a later section.

LISTING 3.2 Program to print limits for the primitive types. The limits are defined as static constants in the standard Java 'wrapper' classes `Byte`, `Short`, `Integer`, `Float` and `Double`.

```
1   public class Limits {
2     public static void main(String[] argv) {
3       java.io.PrintStream s = System.out;
4       s.println("Min byte value   = " + Byte.MIN_VALUE);
5       s.println("Max byte value   = " + Byte.MAX_VALUE);
6       s.println("Min short value  = " + Short.MIN_VALUE);
7       s.println("Max short value  = " + Short.MAX_VALUE);
8       s.println("Min int value    = " + Integer.MIN_VALUE);
9       s.println("Max int value    = " + Integer.MAX_VALUE);
10      s.println("Min float value  = " + Float.MIN_VALUE);
11      s.println("Max float value  = " + Float.MAX_VALUE);
12      s.println("Min double value = " + Double.MIN_VALUE);
13      s.println("Max double value = " + Double.MAX_VALUE);
14    }
15  }
```

The simple program in Listing 3.2 prints the range of values that can be represented with each of Java's primitive types. (This program can be found in the `Apps` directory on the CD.)

3.5.3 Representation of colour

A colour image is usually represented using the RGB model (see Section 3.4.1). 24-bit quantisation is typical, with 8 bits used for each component. For the purpose of representation in a computer program, such an image can be regarded as a set of three distinct 'planes' of data, one for each component. A design based on this notion is shown in Figure 3.12.

Alternatively, we can imagine that the image consists of a single array of data, each element of the array being a triplet of R, G and B values. Another class is needed to represent the RGB triplet. We can devise our own or use Java's `Color` class from the `java.awt` package. A design which uses this class is shown in Figure 3.13.

Which approach is best? In the design of Figure 3.12, it is much easier to manipulate the red, green and blue components independently as separate images, but retrieving the colour of a single pixel requires three array access operations. In the design of Figure 3.13, pixel colour can be retrieved by indexing an array once only, but separate manipulation of the different colour components is more difficult to accomplish.

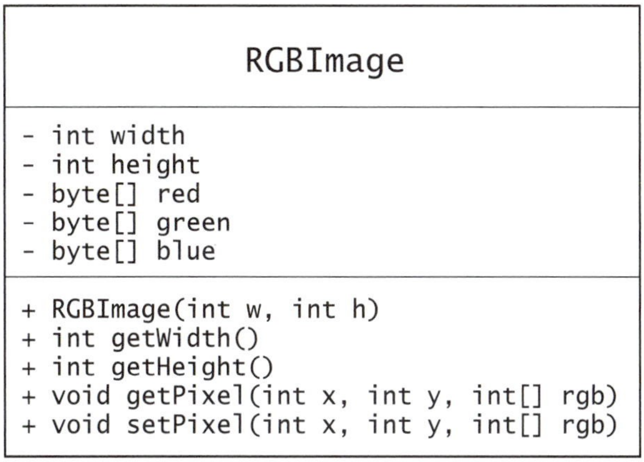

RGBImage
- int width
- int height
- byte[] red
- byte[] green
- byte[] blue
+ RGBImage(int w, int h)
+ int getWidth()
+ int getHeight()
+ void getPixel(int x, int y, int[] rgb)
+ void setPixel(int x, int y, int[] rgb)

Figure 3.12 A class for RGB images in which the red, green and blue components are stored in separate arrays.

RGBImage
- int width
- int height
+ RGBImage(int w, int h)
+ int getWidth()
+ int getHeight()
+ Color getPixel(int x, int y)
+ void setPixel(int x, int y, Color c)
1
1..*
Color

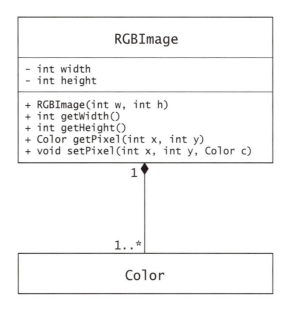

Figure 3.13 A class for RGB images that uses an array of `Color` objects.

3.6 Volumetric data

Although images are two-dimensional, there are instances where *three-dimensional* data are acquired. In x-ray CT imaging, for example (Section 2.4), a 'stack' of images representing parallel slices through the body are obtained. Other techniques which provide 3D data include nuclear magnetic resonance imaging and confocal microscopy. In each case, the images are slices through a third, spatial dimension. Video data can likewise be regarded as three-dimensional, although the third dimension is, in this case, time.

Here, we use the term **volume** to describe a 3D dataset. We will further assume that the third dimension is spatial. Each element of a sampled volume is termed a **voxel** (by analogy with pixel). The structure of a volumetric dataset is shown in Figure 3.14.

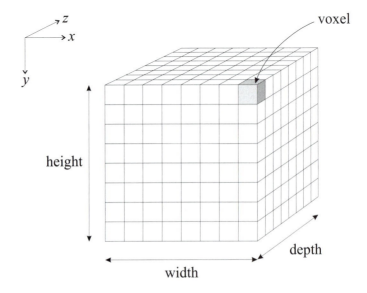

Figure 3.14 A volumetric dataset can be viewed as a 3D array of voxels.

Our previous definition of an image class can be extended in a straightforward manner to accommodate a third spatial dimension, giving us the design in Figure 3.15. A 3D array of bytes is used here, but we could equally use any of the other primitive numeric data types provided by Java. We could also use a 1D array for storage, as explained earlier—in which case each voxel is addressed as

```
data[sliceSize*z + width*y + x]
```

where `sliceSize = width*height`. Again, we can use the approach of storing precomputed offsets for each slice and each row within a slice in order to minimise the number of multiplications that must be done to access a voxel.

```
┌─────────────────────────────────────────────────────────┐
│                     ByteVolume                          │
├─────────────────────────────────────────────────────────┤
│  - int width                                            │
│  - int height                                           │
│  - int depth                                            │
│  - byte[][][] data                                      │
├─────────────────────────────────────────────────────────┤
│  + ByteVolume(int w, int h, int d)                      │
│  + int getWidth()                                       │
│  + int getHeight()                                      │
│  + int getDepth()                                       │
│  + int getVoxel(int x, int y, int z)                    │
│  + void setVoxel(int x, int y, int z, int value)        │
└─────────────────────────────────────────────────────────┘
```

Figure 3.15 Structure of a simple volume class.

3.7   Object-oriented programming with images and volumes

Although we tend to regard images and volumes as distinctly different entities, at some fundamental level they are both represented using an array of data. There are certain operations for which the organisation of data in this array is irrelevant. Consider, for example, the task of calculating the mean of all the samples in the dataset. For an image, this involves iterating over all pixels, summing the values, and then dividing by the number of pixels; for a volume, we must iterate over all voxels, sum the values and then divide by the number of voxels. If we have implemented our image and volume classes using 2D and 3D arrays, respectively, then the iteration process differs, so different pieces of code are required for what are, essentially, identical tasks. However, if we have implemented storage for both images and volumes using a 1D array, then *identical* pieces of code perform the calculation.

Obviously, it is wasteful to have identical pieces of code in two separate classes. Instead, we can share this code between our image and volume classes by means of **inheritance**. For example, we can define a base class containing the array of data and then derive image and volume classes from it. The base class represents an abstract view of the data as a mere sequence of samples, and the derived classes impose a particular spatial interpretation on the dataset. The base class can have methods which do not depend on the interpretation of values in the array—such as a method to compute mean sample value. This method is inherited by, and is therefore available to, both the image class and the volume class. The relationship between the three classes is depicted in Figure 3.16.

Now let us consider the issue of other data types. The design in Figure 3.16 supports only 8-bit data, but we have seen that it is sometimes necessary to use wider integer types or floating point types to represent pixel and voxel values. In C++, this need could be accommodated easily by using **templates** for the array, image and volume classes of Figure 3.16. Unfortunately, Java lacks this feature, so it is necessary to create separate classes for each data type. Figure 3.17 shows how these classes can be implemented using inheritance. (We show only classes used for image representation here, although the discussion below applies equally to volumetric data.)

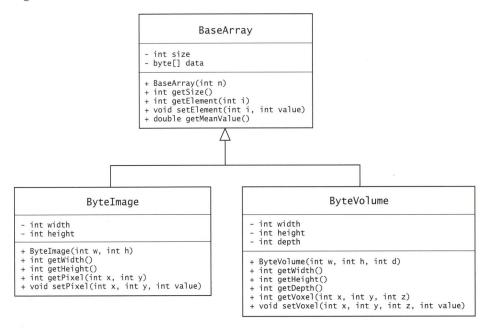

Figure 3.16 Inheritance hierarchy for simple 8-bit image and volume classes. BaseArray is responsible for image storage and for providing sequential access to data; ByteImage imposes a 2D interpretation on the data sequence and provides appropriate methods to access pixels by 2D indexing; ByteVolume imposes a 3D interpretation on the data and provides methods to access voxels via 3D indexing.

The main change from the design of Figure 3.16 is that the class BaseArray and the image class derived from it are now **abstract classes**. It is not possible to create instances of BaseArray or ByteImage in a program; however, a program may create instances of a concrete (i.e., non-abstract) class derived from ByteImage and subsequently manipulate that object using references to a BaseArray or a ByteImage. We would work with ByteImage if we required our code to function with any image, regardless of pixel data type; we would work with BaseArray if our code had to work with both images and volumes.

The BaseArray class of Figure 3.17 contains no data. It stores the size of (i.e., number of samples in) the dataset, and contains abstract methods getElement() and setElement() to retrieve and modify an array element. The implementations of these methods appear in the derived class that actually contains the pixel/voxel data. The methods use double values, allowing for the possibility that the pixel/voxel data type could be anything from byte up to double. The getMeanValue() method, implemented here because calculation of the mean sample value does not require knowledge of the spatial organisation of the data, uses the getElement() method to obtain sample values, which are summed in order to compute a mean value.

The ByteImage class represents a lower level of abstraction, imposing a 2D interpretation on the data. Concrete methods exist to inspect image width and height, and there are abstract

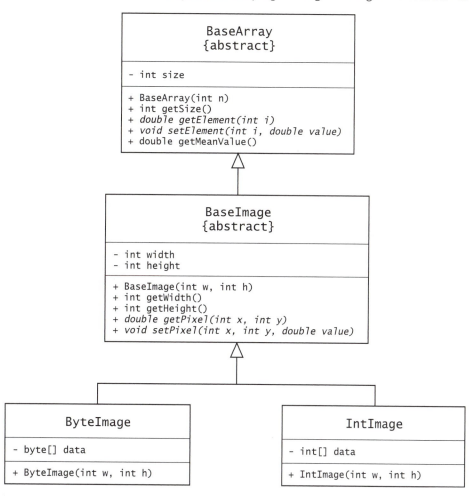

Figure 3.17 An inheritance hierarchy for images with different pixel data types. Italics signify an abstract method, for which an implementation must be provided by a derived class.

methods `getPixel()` and `setPixel()` which retrieve or modify the value of a pixel that is indexed by its *x* and *y* coordinates.

Concrete image classes are derived from `BaseImage`. For each pixel data type, we have a separate class. Figure 3.17 shows only the `ByteImage` and `IntImage` types, suitable for representing 8-bit and 32-bit integer-valued images. These concrete classes contain the arrays that store pixel data. They also contain implementations of the abstract data access methods declared in `BaseArray` and `BaseImage`. Note that these methods have to return or accept `double` values, despite the fact that the concrete classes shown in the diagram store `byte` and `int` data. The implementations of `getElement()`, `setElement()`, `getPixel()` and `setPixel()` can use casts to convert between `double` and `byte` or `double` and `int`.

LISTING 3.3 Example of polymorphism.

```
1   public class Mean {
2
3     public static void print1(ByteImage image) {
4       System.out.println("mean value is " + image.getMeanValue());
5     }
6
7     public static void print2(BaseImage image) {
8       System.out.println("mean value is " + image.getMeanValue());
9     }
10
11    public static void print3(BaseArray array) {
12      System.out.println("mean value is " + array.getMeanValue());
13    }
14
15  }
```

Although this approach may seem rather complex, its advantages soon become apparent when we consider a simple example. The class Mean in Listing 3.3 contains three static methods, each of which can be used to compute the mean of an image and print the resulting value on the console. The method print1() can be invoked only on ByteImage objects. The method print2() takes a BaseImage parameter, so it can be invoked on objects of type ByteImage, IntImage, FloatImage, etc. The method print3() takes a BaseArray parameter, making it completely general. We can pass *any* image object to it, or, indeed, any volume object; methods print1() and print2() are therefore superfluous.

Note that print3() will function correctly even with instances of image or volume classes that *haven't yet been implemented*—provided that such classes are derived from BaseImage or the equivalent BaseVolume class and that they implement the getElement() method declared as abstract in BaseArray. It is not necessary for the Mean class to be recompiled. This is an example of **polymorphism** at work. The concept of polymorphism is central to object-oriented programming, and it is exploited frequently in the Java API.

3.8   Further reading

Our discussion of sampling and quantisation is fairly qualitative. Sampling is dealt with much more rigorously by Castleman [9], who devotes an entire chapter to the subject. Useful discussion may also be found in the books by Gonzalez and Woods [20], Gomes and Velho [19], and Glassner [17].

A fairly simplistic view of colour is presented here; a far more thorough treatment is given in books by Gomes and Velho [19] and by Glassner [17]. One important colour model that we have not mentioned is the YC_bC_r model. This is an internationally-recognised standard for digital video, and is the colour model used by the JPEG and MPEG image and video compression techniques discussed in Chapter 12. In this model, Y, known as the luminance component, contains all of the intensity information. Colour is represented by the two colour difference components, C_b and C_r. Since intensity is more significant, perceptually, than colour, C_b and C_r can be quantised using fewer bits than Y.

There are many ways of representing images in computer memory. Lyon [29] presents some Java image classes rather different from those described in this chapter. Other texts [25, 37, 48, for example] generally give examples written in C, but it can be instructive to compare these with Java implementations.

This chapter illustrates how basic object-oriented concepts are useful in developing software to support image processing. Deeper insights into object-oriented techniques using Java can be gained from the books by Eckel [13] and Horstmann [23].

The class diagrams in this chapter follow Unified Modelling Language (UML) conventions. UML is emerging as the industry-standard notation for describing object-oriented designs. An accessible introduction to UML and software engineering in general is given by Pooley and Stevens [38]. The book by Alhir [1] is more of a reference manual.

3.9   Exercises

1. Using the `ResolutionSimulator` application on the CD, investigate the relationship between spatial resolution and our ability to recognise image content. Faces are a particularly good choice of image for this type of experiment. Use an image of a well-known person and start with the lowest resolution, increasing resolution until you can recognise the person. (The fact that you already know the identity of the person may influence the results; to avoid any bias, try the experiment on some friends who have not seen the image at full resolution.)

2. An outdoor scene contains a fence consisting of fence posts 6 cm across, spaced 6 cm apart. A camera observing the scene captures a 30 m length of this fence within its field of view. Output from the camera is sampled to give 256×256 images. What kinds of artefacts might we see in these images? Perform some calculations to support your argument and to determine the conditions under which these artefacts will not be present.

3. Run the `LogPolar` application on the CD and verify that a scale change merely translates an image along the r axis.

4. Using the `QuantisationSimulator` application on the CD, investigate the relationship between image content and the number of bits required to quantise an image adequately.

5. Implement the `ByteImage` class of Figure 3.11 and write a suitable driver program to test that `ByteImage` objects behave correctly.

6. Why does `ByteImage` not provide methods `setWidth` and `setHeight` ?

7. Improve `ByteImage` by defining additional instance variables and methods that would be useful in a simple image class.

8. Compare the image classes described in this chapter with data structures for image representation in other programming languages, such as C [25, 37, 48]. What are the advantages of using Java instead of these other languages? What benefits does the object-oriented approach convey? In what ways are these other implementations superior to the Java implementation presented here?

CHAPTER 4

Images in Java

This chapter describes how images are represented in Java programs. We examine the classes that have been available to represent and manipulate images since version 1.0 of the language and compare them with the newer and more powerful classes introduced into the language via the Java2D API. These classes are used extensively in the Java programs presented in subsequent chapters. We also consider briefly the Java Advanced Imaging API, an optional extension to the language that supports more advanced modes of operation.

4.1 Images in Java 1.0/1.1

Older versions of Java (1.0 and 1.1) supported image manipulation via the Image class[1] and a small number of related classes. The Image class is part of the java.awt package, and its helpers are part of java.awt.image. Although the Image class remains useful, it suffers from some limitations that hinder the implementation of conventional image processing programs.

4.1.1 Loading images

The limitations of Image first become apparent when we attempt to load image data into a program. This is accomplished by the getImage() method, which is directly available to Java applets. The method takes a URL specifying the location of the image as its parameter. Applications can obtain a java.awt.Toolkit object and call its getImage() method:

```
Image image = Toolkit.getDefaultToolkit().getImage(file);
```

---
[1] Note that Image is an abstract class; when you manipulate an Image object, you are actually working with an instance of a platform-specific subclass.

45

Toolkit has a version of getImage() that loads an image from a local file, as shown above, and another version that loads an image from a URL.

On all platforms, getImage() can be guaranteed to understand the file formats used for GIF and JPEG images. A number of Java implementations also provide support for the XBM image format that is used on X Windows platforms. It is possible (although not trivial) to create and install a 'content handler' class for some other image format [35], thereby allowing getImage() to handle that new format; alternatively, we can create a class that handles image loading itself, rather than relying on getImage(). One way of doing this is to implement the ImageProducer interface described in Section 4.1.2.

The use of URLs by getImage() reflects Java's 'network-centric' perspective. Java programs, be they applets or applications, are able to load image data from remote sites on the internet. But what happens if there is a slow connection to a remote site? Java solves this problem by loading images *asynchronously*, in a separate thread. This leaves the applet or application free to perform other tasks—such as creating and displaying a graphical user interface or handling user interaction of some kind—whilst waiting for delivery of image data to be completed.

A call to getImage() returns immediately; it sets up image loading but does not load any image data itself. Image retrieval is initiated when we call a method that requires image data. For applets or graphical applications, this is usually the drawImage() method, used to display the image on a component of some kind. The prepareImage() method can also be used trigger image data retrieval. Both of these methods take as one of their parameters an object implementing the ImageObserver interface. An ImageObserver object provides a method called imageUpdate() that will be called from the thread carrying out image loading whenever new information about the image becomes available. The Component class of Java's Abstract Windowing Toolkit (AWT)—from which all GUI components are derived—implements the ImageObserver interface, so objects such as Applet, Button, Canvas, etc, can monitor image loading and act appropriately when an image has been fully loaded.

Although clearly advantageous in some respects, asynchronous image loading makes the implementation of a straightforward, console-based (i.e., non-graphical) image processing program more complicated than usual. This is because we must somehow guarantee that image loading has completed before attempting to process the image. We could do this by implementing ImageObserver and supplying an imageUpdate() method that initiates processing once loading has completed; however, a more convenient approach may be to use a MediaTracker. This class forces image loading to begin and provides methods to check the status of an image or simply wait until loading of that image has finished.

Listing 4.1 shows how MediaTracker can be used to fake synchronous image loading in a console-based application. The class listed here implements a method called readImage() that returns a fully-loaded Image object (assuming that there were no problems with accessing or reading from the image file). Line 6 sets up loading of data from the specified file into image. Line 7 creates the MediaTracker that will monitor loading of the image data. Note that a MediaTracker must be constructed with a Component as a parameter. In applets or GUI-based applications, this presents no problems, since there is always a Component of some kind available. In a console-based application, there is no Component available, but we must still create one for the MediaTracker to use. Of course, Component itself cannot be instantiated, being an abstract class. We could simply create an instance of Canvas,

---

> **LISTING 4.1** Synchronous loading of image data into an **Image** object.

```java
import java.awt.*;

public class ImageTest {

  public static Image readImage(String file) {
    Image image = Toolkit.getDefaultToolkit().getImage(file);
    MediaTracker tracker = new MediaTracker(new Component() {});
    tracker.addImage(image, 0);
    try { tracker.waitForID(0); }
     catch (InterruptedException e) {}
    return image;
  }

  public static void main(String[] argv) {
    if (argv.length > 0) {
      Image image = readImage(argv[0]);
      // do something with image...
    }
  }

}
```

Button or any other AWT component and pass this to `MediaTracker`'s constructor, but a neater and more satisfactory approach is to create an instance of an anonymous inner subclass of Component[2]. This is done with

```java
new Component() {}
```

which is shorthand for

```java
class TemporaryComponent extends Component {}
new TemporaryComponent();
```

Line 8 of Listing 4.1 registers `image` with `tracker` and initiates loading. The second parameter of the call to `addImage()` is a numerical identifier for the image. Lines 9 and 10 block until the image with the specified identifier has loaded or an `InterruptedException` is thrown. At line 11, the image should, barring any errors, have been loaded completely, so a reference to it can be safely returned to the caller of `readImage()`.

4.1.2 Producers and consumers

Image handling in Java 1.0/1.1 is driven by the availability of image data. This is sometimes described as the 'push model' of image processing. Java supports this model by

---

[2] If you are unfamiliar with the concept of inner classes, Eckel [13] provides a thorough explanation.

means of the producer-consumer paradigm (Figure 4.1). Classes that handle images can operate as producers or consumers of image data, implementing the `ImageProducer` or `ImageConsumer` interfaces as appropriate. An image producer can generate pixel values itself or acquire pixels from some external source (e.g., from a file with a format that is not supported by `getImage()`). Its job is to forward the pixel data to one or more consumers. The consumers register their interest in an image with the producer and, as image data become available, the producer calls methods of those consumers to transfer the data to them. Image consumers work behind the scenes to facilitate the display of images on AWT components such as `Canvas`. Other examples of image consumers are considered in Section 4.1.3.

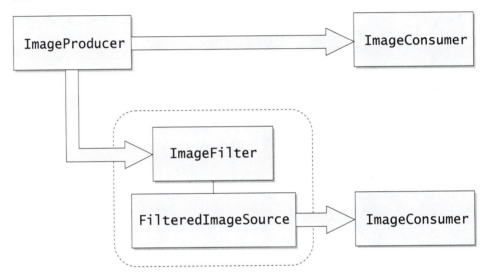

Figure 4.1 Java's producer-consumer model for image handling.

At its simplest, the producer-consumer paradigm has a single producer feeding pixels to a single consumer. The former will typically obtain pixel data from an input stream or from memory and the latter will normally display those pixels on an AWT component of some kind. We can think of pixel data flowing along a pipeline from producer to consumer. To process the image, we can interrupt this pipeline, inserting an operation that modifies pixel values in some way. To fit in with the producer-consumer paradigm, this operation must consist of an image consumer to acquire the pixel data and an image producer to pass the processed data on to the original consumer. Java provides the `ImageFilter` and `FilteredImageSource` classes to fulfil these roles (see Section 4.1.3).

An example of an image producer is `MemoryImageSource`. This class produces pixels from data in a user-specified array. That array could be filled with data generated by a program, or it could contain data read from a file that has a format unsupported by Java[3]. Arrays of type `byte` or `int` can be used. The abstract class `ColorModel` specifies

---

[3] Actually, in the latter case, a better approach is to implement a special image producer to handle other formats.

how values in the array are to be interpreted. We must create an instance of a concrete subclass of ColorModel and pass it to the MemoryImageSource constructor along with the array of pixel data. The AWT provides two concrete subclasses: IndexColorModel and DirectColorModel. The former can be used to specify a greyscale and the latter is used to specify RGB colour.

For example, let us suppose that we wish to create a greyscale image 320 pixels wide and 200 pixels high from an array of bytes called data. The first step is to create the appropriate IndexColorModel, using

```
byte[] grey = new byte[256];
for (int i = 0; i < 256; ++i)
  grey[i] = (byte) i;
ColorModel greyModel =
  new IndexColorModel(8, 256, grey, grey, grey);
```

IndexColorModel expects three arrays, specifying the values of red, green and blue associated with each index. By definition, the values of red, green and blue are equal for all indices in greyscale images, so only one array needs to be created.

The next step is to create a MemoryImageSource object to act as producer of pixel data. The Image object can then be created from this producer by means of the createImage() method:

```
ImageProducer producer =
  new MemoryImageSource(320, 200, greyModel, data, 0, 320);
Image image = Toolkit.getDefaultToolkit().createImage(producer);
```

This example assumes a non-graphical application. If the code was featuring in an applet, the createImage() method of that applet could be used instead of using a Toolkit. The array data is a one-dimensional array of type byte. A left-to-right, top-to-bottom ordering of pixel values is assumed. The last two parameters passed to the MemoryImageSource constructor require some explanation. The first is the index of the first image pixel in the array. This is usually 0; it might be a value other than 0 if a single array is used to hold pixel data for more than one image. The second and final parameter is the amount of space in the array that is devoted to a single row of image pixels. This is usually the same as the width of the image, although it can be larger (in which case the extra bytes are skipped when moving from one row to the next).

Now let us suppose that the image is an RGB colour image. This is slightly simpler to deal with. Although we could create an instance of DirectColorModel to specify that pixel values are RGB colours, this is not strictly necessary, as the default ColorModel for images is an RGB model. Hence, we can create the Image object as follows:

```
ImageProducer producer =
  new MemoryImageSource(320, 200, data, 0, 320);
Image image = Toolkit.getDefaultToolkit().createImage(producer);
```

If a MemoryImageSource is used as the producer, the ability to display or manipulate portions of the image as data become available is lost [55].

The main difference between this code and the previous example for a greyscale image, aside from the absence of an explicit `ColorModel`, is the fact that `data` is now a one-dimensional array of `int`. One integer from this array is associated with each pixel. This integer is 32 bits wide, so it has the capacity to hold the 8-bit red, green and blue components of a pixel's value. The remaining 8 bits are used for the alpha component, which represents pixel transparency. The ordering of red, green, blue and alpha is shown in Figure 4.2.

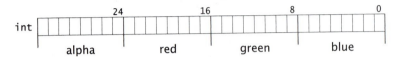

Figure 4.2 Red, green, blue and alpha values packed into a single integer.

4.1.3 Acquiring and processing pixel data

The `PixelGrabber` class

Having created an `Image` object, how do we access its pixels? The `ByteImage` class described in Chapter 3 had methods `getPixel()` and `setPixel()` for this purpose, but `Image` has nothing resembling these. This is a frustrating but necessary restriction, given that images are loaded asynchronously and there are no guarantees that an `Image` object has any data associated with it.

Of course, if the producer of pixels for this image is a `MemoryImageSource` and we have retained a reference to the array containing the pixel data, then we can inspect or modify a pixel's value simply by accessing the appropriate element of the array. But what if the image was created by a call to `getImage()`? In that case, the only way of accessing pixels is to follow the producer-consumer paradigm and use an image consumer. Fortunately, we don't have to implement this ourselves, as Java has a class called `PixelGrabber` to perform this task. `PixelGrabber` can acquire pixel data synchronously or asynchronously. It can store pixel values in a user-specified array or create a suitable array itself. For details of all the various ways in which a `PixelGrabber` can be used, see the *Java AWT Reference* [55] or a similar text; here, we give just one example to illustrate how a `PixelGrabber` might be used in a console-based application.

Listing 4.2 shows a Java application that uses `getImage()` to read an image and `PixelGrabber` to retrieve its pixel values. Line 9 creates the `PixelGrabber` object. The parameter passed to the constructor are: the `Image` object from which data are required; the x and y coordinates of the upper-left corner of the block of pixels to be grabbed; the width and height of the block to be grabbed; and a Boolean flag to indicate whether the `PixelGrabber` should force the use of an RGB colour model for the grabbed data. In this case, we are grabbing the entire image, so 0 is used for the x and y coordinates. Width and height are not yet known because image data are loaded asynchronously, but we are allowed to specify -1 for both dimensions, signifying that the width and height of the image should be used, once they have been determined. The final parameter is `false`, indicating that we will let the `PixelGrabber` decide how to interpret the grabbed data. In line 10, a call to the `grabPixels()` method acquires the data. This method blocks until the

LISTING 4.2 Example of how `PixelGrabber` may be used to acquire pixel data from an **Image** object.

```java
import java.awt.*;
import java.awt.image.PixelGrabber;

public class ImageTest {

  public static void processImage(String infile, String outfile) {
    Image image = Toolkit.getDefaultToolkit().getImage(infile);
    try {
      PixelGrabber grabber = new PixelGrabber(image, 0, 0, -1, -1, false);
      if (grabber.grabPixels()) {
        int width = grabber.getWidth();
        int height = grabber.getHeight();
        if (bytesAvailable(grabber)) {
         byte[] data = (byte[]) grabber.getPixels();
         // process greyscale image...
        }
        else {
          int[] data = (int[]) grabber.getPixels();
          // process colour image...
        }
      }
    }
    catch (InterruptedException e) {
      e.printStackTrace();
    }
  }

  public static final boolean bytesAvailable(PixelGrabber pg) {
    return pg.getPixels() instanceof byte[];
  }

  public static void main(String[] argv) {
    if (argv.length > 1) {
      processImage(argv[0], argv[1]);
      System.exit(0);
    }
    else {
      System.err.println("usage: java ImageTest <infile> <outfile>");
      System.exit(1);
    }
  }

}
```

data have been acquired, returning true if acquisition was successful and false otherwise. An InterruptedException can also be thrown if another thread interrupts acquisition.

In this example, the PixelGrabber itself is responsible for allocating storage space for the pixel data. To obtain a handle on this storage we must call the PixelGrabber's getPixels() method. The returned array will be of type byte[] if the image has an IndexColorModel (which could mean that it is a greyscale image). The array will be of type int[] if the image has a DirectColorModel (indicating that it is an RGB colour image). Actually, getPixels() returns an Object, but we can use Java's instanceof operator to check whether this is, in fact, an array of bytes (line 27). If so, we can cast it to byte[] and assign the result to a byte[] variable (line 14); otherwise, we must cast the returned object to int[] and assign it to an int[] variable (line 18). In the former case, pixel grey levels are simply the values stored in the array; in the latter case, the red, green and blue components of a pixel's value are packed into a single integer and must be retrieved using bitmasks. We can do this ourselves, using

```
int red = data[i] & 0xff0000;
int green = data[i] & 0xff00;
int blue = data[i] & 0xff;
```

but this assumes that these bitmasks describe how red, green and blue values have been packed into integers. In practice, this is highly likely to be the case, but it might not be true—so a better approach may be to ask the PixelGrabber for the ColorModel of the image and use methods of the ColorModel to unpack red, green and blue values:

```
ColorModel model = grabber.getColorModel();
int red = model.getRed(data[i]);
int green = model.getGreen(data[i]);
int blue = model.getBlue(data[i]);
```

The ImageFilter class

We now know enough to carry out image processing operations on Image objects in Java 1.0/1.1; we can load the image via getImage(), get the pixel data with PixelGrabber, modify the array of pixels as required and convert them back into an Image using MemoryImageSource. A more elegant variation of this approach is to use the ImageFilter and FilteredImageSource classes in the java.awt.image package. An ImageFilter object specifies what happens to pixel values. To process an image with this ImageFilter, we must create an instance of FilteredImageSource, passing the image's producer and the ImageFilter in as parameters. The FilteredImageSource acts as the producer for the processed pixels and can be used to create a new Image object:

```
Toolkit toolkit = Toolkit.getDefaultToolkit();
Image image = toolkit.getImage(filename);
ImageFilter filter = new ImageFilter();
FilteredImageSource newSource =
 new FilteredImageSource(image.getSource(), filter);
Image newImage = toolkit.createImage(newSource);
```

This example uses `ImageFilter`, which simply forwards image data without modifying pixel values in any way. To do anything useful, we must use one of the subclasses of `ImageFilter` supplied with Java or implement our own subclass. Table 4.1 lists the filter classes provided with Java version 1.1 onwards and Figure 4.3 shows the relationships between these classes. Further information on using these classes can be found in many Java books [35, 55, for example], so we shall not discuss them further here.

Table 4.1 `ImageFilter` classes provided for image processing in Java 1.1.

Class	Description
`ImageFilter`	'Null' filter; has no effect on images.
`RGBImageFilter`	Abstract base class for filter classes that modify pixel values.
`CropImageFilter`	Crops the image to the specified rectangular region.
`ReplicateScaleFilter`	Scales an image by duplicating or removing rows and columns of pixels.
`AreaAveragingScaleFilter`	Scales an image with anti-aliasing.

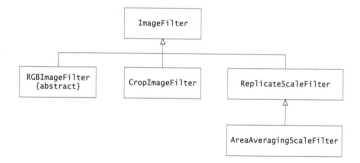

Figure 4.3 Relationship between the various `ImageFilter` classes available in the `java.awt.image` package.

4.2   The Java2D API

The producer-consumer approach is conceptually sound but rather clumsy for straightforward image processing applications in which we can guarantee the availability of image data—when the image is loaded from a local disk, for example. In these cases, an image class similar to the `ByteImage` class described in Chapter 3 is more suitable. This deficiency has been addressed with the introduction of the Java2D Application Programming Interface (API) into Java. With the release of Java 2, Java2D has become one of the standard APIs provided with the language.

The Java2D API consists of a number of classes, distributed amongst the old packages `java.awt` and `java.awt.image` and six new packages: `java.awt.color`, `java.awt.font`, `java.awt.geom`, `java.awt.print`, `java.awt.image.renderable` and `com.`

`sun.image.codec.jpeg`. The classes enhance significantly Java's 2D graphics capabilities relative to what was possible in earlier versions of the language. Many of the new classes support operations that are of limited relevance to images and image processing. We ignore those classes here and concentrate on the classes used for image representation: `BufferedImage`, `ColorModel`, `Raster`, `SampleModel`, `DataBuffer` and their subclasses. The reader interested in the broader capabilities of Java2D should consult Knudsen's *Java 2D Graphics* [27] for more information.

Note that the new features of Java2D augment, rather than replace, the image handling classes of Java 1.0/1.1. (This is one reason why we dwelled so long on these classes in Section 4.1.)

4.2.1 The `BufferedImage` class

The `BufferedImage` class is provided specifically to support what Sun describe as 'immediate mode', i.e., a mode of operation in which pixel values are known to be in memory, allowing operations to be performed immediately without the need to wait for the delivery of image data. With this mode of operation, it is possible for an image class to have methods that access individual pixel values, making the implementation of image processing software a lot more straightforward. Note that `BufferedImage` is a subclass of `Image`; we are therefore free to substitute `BufferedImage` for `Image` wherever the latter is used.

A `BufferedImage` object has the structure shown in Figure 4.4. It consists of a `ColorModel` and a `Raster`. The `Raster` holds the image data. Every pixel in the `Raster` has one or more *samples* associated with it. The `ColorModel` specifies how these samples are interpreted. The number of colour components specified by the `ColorModel` must match the number of samples per pixel provided by the `Raster`. There are three concrete subclasses of `ColorModel` that specify different interpretations of pixel data.

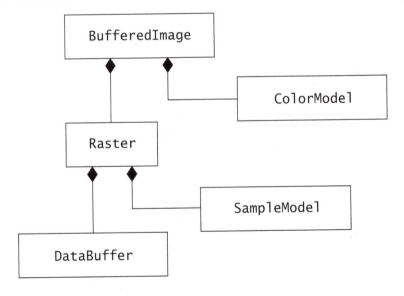

Figure 4.4 Composition of a `BufferedImage` object.

Table 4.2 Selected types of `BufferedImage`.

Constant	Description
TYPE_BYTE_BINARY	1-bit sample for each pixel; 8 samples packed into a byte.
TYPE_BYTE_GRAY	8-bit sample for each pixel, stored in a byte.
TYPE_USHORT_GRAY	16-bit sample for each pixel, stored in a `short`.
TYPE_3BYTE_BGR	8-bit blue, green and red samples, each stored in one byte.
TYPE_INT_RGB	8-bit red, green and blue samples, packed into an `int`.

`DirectColorModel` and `IndexColorModel` were available in Java 1.0/1.1 and have already been discussed (Section 4.1.2). Java2D introduces a third subclass of `ColorModel`, called `ComponentColorModel`. This supports representations in which a pixel's samples correspond directly to the components of the colour model.

The `Raster` of a `BufferedImage` can be further decomposed into a `DataBuffer` and a `SampleModel`. The `DataBuffer` is simply a wrapper for the array or arrays used to store pixel data. The `SampleModel` specifies how the array elements managed by the `DataBuffer` are translated into the samples of a particular pixel.

The constructor of `BufferedImage` takes image dimensions and image type as its parameters. Image type is specified by an integer constant defined in the `BufferedImage` class. There are thirteen different standard types, representing different combinations of `ColorModel` and `SampleModel`. Table 4.2 lists a selection of these standard types. (The others are described in detail by Knudsen [27].) The most useful types for our purposes are `TYPE_BYTE_GRAY` and `TYPE_3BYTE_BGR`, representing greyscale and colour images, respectively. Both of these types use a `ComponentColorModel`, there being one component in the case of greyscale images and three in the case of colour images. `TYPE_BYTE_BINARY` is also useful for binary images (see Chapters 5, 10 and 11), which consist only of black and white. Samples for this image type can have the values 0 or 1. A single bit is used to represent each sample.

The dimensions and type of an existing `BufferedImage` object can be queried using the methods `getWidth()`, `getHeight()` and `getType()`. Its `ColorModel` can be retrieved with `getColorModel()`. Pixel values can be inspected or modified by means of the methods `getRGB()` and `setRGB()`. These methods are overloaded so that they can be used to manipulate single pixels or rectangular blocks of pixels (Table 4.3). Note that `getRGB()` and `setRGB()` represent each pixel's value as an integer, into which alpha, red, green and blue components are packed as illustrated in Figure 4.2. Packing is done re-

Table 4.3 Methods `getRGB()` and `setRGB()` provided by the `BufferedImage` class.

```
int getRGB(int x, int y)
int[] getRGB(int x, int y, int w, int h, int[] data, int offset, int
 scansize)
void setRGB(int x, int y, int value)
void setRGB(int x, int y, int w, int h, int[] data, int offset, int
 scansize)
```

gardless of the underlying representation used for pixel values. This is inefficient when the image has a ComponentColorModel. Suppose, for example, that we have an image of type TYPE_3BYTE_BGR, which stores red, green and blue in separate array elements. The getRGB() method gives us these three components packed into an integer. To process a pixel, we must extract red, green and blue values from this integer. When we have finished, we must pack the processed values into another integer and pass this integer to setRGB(), which promptly extracts red, green and blue values and stores them in the appropriate elements of the array(s) used for data storage.

Confusion and inefficiency can also arise when using getRGB() and setRGB() on greyscale images. For example, suppose that we have an image of type TYPE_BYTE_GRAY, and that a particular pixel in that image has a grey level of 50. The value returned by getRGB() for that pixel is −13487566! The explanation for this seemingly bizarre result becomes clear if we look at the binary representation of this number and compare it with Figure 4.2:

11111111	00110010	00110010	00110010
$\alpha = 255$	$R = 50$	$G = 50$	$B = 50$

A value of −13487566 corresponds to an alpha of 255 (signifying an opaque pixel) and red, green and blue values of 50—which was the grey level stored in the image. This makes sense because, when the red, green and blue components of a colour are equal in magnitude, that colour is seen as a shade of grey. Nevertheless, it is still frustrating that an unnecessary conversion of a grey level into a colour has been done.

Now suppose that we wish to modify the grey level of that pixel, changing it to 100. To do this with setRGB(), we must assume that red, green and blue are all equal to 100 and pack these identical values into an integer, as indicated in Figure 4.2. This can be done by judicious use of the left shift and logical OR operators, but it would clearly be a lot easier if we could manipulate pixel grey level directly.

Because of these problems, it is generally more convenient to manipulate pixel values at a lower level, using methods of the underlying Raster object.

4.2.2   Raster and WritableRaster

Java2D's Raster class contains methods that manipulate the samples of a pixel directly, without the potentially wasteful interpretation imposed by a ColorModel. Note that Raster is a read-only class; its methods can be used to inspect pixel values but not to modify them. A subclass of Raster, called WritableRaster, adds methods that change a pixel's value.

The pixel access methods of Raster and WritableRaster fall into two broad classes: pixel methods and sample methods. The basic pixel methods are getPixel() and setPixel(). These operate on arrays of int, float or double representing the set of samples associated with a single pixel. Also available are methods getPixels() and setPixels(), which operate on a rectangular block of pixels specified by upper-left corner coordinates, width and height. The basic sample methods are getSample() and setSample(). These operate on a specified sample from a single pixel. Also available are getSamples() and setSamples(), which operate on a particular sample of each pixel in a rectangular block specified by upper-left corner coordinates, width and height. The methods are summarised in Tables 4.4 and 4.5.

Table 4.4 Methods provided by the `Raster` class to inspect pixel values.

```
int[] getPixel(int x, int y, int[] data)
float[] getPixel(int x, int y, float[] data)
double[] getPixel(int x, int y, double[] data)
int[] getPixels(int x, int y, int w, int h, int[] data)
float[] getPixels(int x, int y, int w, int h, float[] data)
double[] getPixels(int x, int y, int w, int h, double[] data)
int getSample(int x, int y, int band)
float getSampleFloat(int x, int y, int band)
double getSampleDouble(int x, int y, int band)
int[] getSamples(int x, int y, int w, int h, int band, int[] data)
float[] getSamples(int x, int y, int w, int h, int band, float[] data)
double[] getSamples(int x, int y, int w, int h, int band, double[] data)
```

Table 4.5 Methods provided by `WritableRaster` to modify pixel values.

```
void setPixel(int x, int y, int[] data)
void setPixel(int x, int y, float[] data)
void setPixel(int x, int y, double[] data)
void setPixels(int x, int y, int w, int h, int[] data)
void setPixels(int x, int y, int w, int h, float[] data)
void setPixels(int x, int y, int w, int h, double[] data)
void setSample(int x, int y, int band, int value)
void setSample(int x, int y, int band, float value)
void setSample(int x, int y, int band, double value)
void setSamples(int x, int y, int w, int h, int band, int[] data)
void setSamples(int x, int y, int w, int h, int band, float[] data)
void setSamples(int x, int y, int w, int h, int band, double[] data)
```

The parameter band used by the sample-based methods is always 0 for greyscale images; for RGB colour images, it can be 0, 1 or 2, corresponding to the red, green and blue bands (or channels or components) of the image.

Note that the `getPixel()`, `getPixels()` and `getSamples()` methods have two modes of operation. We can supply these methods with an existing array of `int`, `float` or `double`, ignoring the return value of the method; or we can pass in `null` as the array parameter, in which case the method allocates storage and returns a reference to the array.

Let us look at a simple example to illustrate how these methods are used in practice. Suppose that we have a greyscale `BufferedImage` called `image` and we wish to divide all its grey levels by two. This can be done with the following code:

```
WritableRaster raster = image.getRaster();
int value;
```

```
for (int y = 0; y < image.getHeight(); ++y)
  for (int x = 0; x < image.getWidth(); ++x) {
    value = raster.getSample(x, y, 0) / 2;
    raster.setSample(x, y, 0, value);
  }
```

The first line obtains a `WritableRaster` for the image. We then iterate over each pixel of the image, retrieving its grey level with one method call, dividing it by two and then writing the scaled value back into the image with another method call.

4.2.3   The `DataBuffer` classes

Working with `BufferedImage` objects at the `Raster` level is sufficient for most tasks, but on occasion it may be more convenient or more efficient to descend to the `DataBuffer` level. For example, let us suppose that we wish to write the pixel data of a greyscale image to a file in binary form. We could do this on a pixel-by-pixel basis, using `getSample()`. A more direct approach is illustrated by the following code:

```
OutputStream output =
  new BufferedOutputStream(new FileOutputStream(file));
DataBufferByte db =
  (DataBufferByte) image.getRaster().getDataBuffer();
output.write(db.getData());
```

`DataBufferByte` is the concrete subclass of `DataBuffer` used to manage storage for image types such as `TYPE_BYTE_GRAY` and `TYPE_3BYTE_BGR`. (Other subclasses are `DataBufferShort`, `DataBufferUShort` and `DataBufferInt`.) The `getData()` method call returns a byte array that can be passed directly to the `write()` method of the output stream.

4.2.4   `RasterOp`, `BufferedImageOp` and `BufferedImageFilter`

Java2D supports the processing of `BufferedImage` objects through the `RasterOp` and `BufferedImageOp` interfaces. Classes that implement these interfaces can perform operations in which a single output image is generated from a single input image. We shall defer any further discussion of these interfaces until Chapter 6; in that chapter and in subsequent chapters you will see many examples of classes that implement `BufferedImageOp` to carry out various different image processing operations.

The `BufferedImageFilter` class acts as a bridge between the 'old' approach to image processing in Java, involving the use of `ImageFilter` classes, and the new approach, in which `BufferedImage` objects are processed with a `BufferedImageOp`. Essentially, a `BufferedImageFilter` converts a `BufferedImageOp` into an `ImageFilter` that processes `BufferedImage` objects according to the producer-consumer paradigm.

4.2.5   Reading a `BufferedImage`

The package `com.sun.image.codec.jpeg` contains classes to support the reading of images from, and writing of images to, datastreams that have been compressed using the

JPEG compression technique (see Chapter 12). The main workhorse is JPEGCodec, a factory class with static methods that manufacture instances of JPEGImageDecoder (for reading images) and JPEGImageEncoder (for writing them). For example, to load an image from the file in.jpg, we do the following:

```
FileInputStream fileStream = new FileInputStream("in.jpg");
JPEGImageDecoder input = JPEGCodec.createJPEGDecoder(fileStream);
BufferedImage image = input.decodeAsBufferedImage();
```

Writing the image out to a new JPEG file is equally straightforward:

```
FileOutputStream fileStream = new FileOutputStream("out.jpg");
JPEGImageEncoder output = JPEGCodec.createJPEGEncoder(fileStream);
output.encode(image);
```

4.3   Java Advanced Imaging

The Java Advanced Imaging API, abbreviated here to JAI, is a relatively recent development. At the time of writing, it was still in beta testing and was somewhat buggy. JAI is an extension to Java and is not part of the standard Java 2 platform. It builds on the image processing capabilities introduced through the Java2D API, adding support for float and double pixel data types, *tiled images* and operations that have more than one input image. (Tiled images facilitate more efficient partial processing of an image, particularly as image dimensions become large.)

An arbitrary image processing task is performed in JAI by linking together various operators in a *processing graph*. This graph is rather like a map that specifies the paths along which image data can flow from one operator to another. The graph is evaluated in one of three different ways in order to produce one or more output images. In the *rendered execution model*, the source of image data associated with an operator is fixed at the moment that the operator object is created. This means that a processing graph always generates the same results, regardless of whether the input images have changed. In the *renderable execution model*, the graph is not evaluated at the time that it is created; instead, processing is deferred until a request for rendering is made. The request propagates backwards and causes image data to be pulled through the graph—hence the term 'pull model' sometimes used to describe this type of processing. In this model, any changes that occur to the input images before the request for rendering will be reflected in the output. The third execution model is the *remote execution model*. This allows an image processing task to be distributed across a number of networked machines.

JAI promises to be a significant enhancement of Java's image processing capabilities. However, we do not consider it further in this book; instead, we concentrate on developing image processing tools using the standard APIs of the Java 2 platform. The main advantage of this approach is that the programs described here will work on any system running Java 2; JAI, on the other hand, is not part of the standard distribution and is not guaranteed to be available on all systems that support Java. In any case, our aim here is to explore the fundamental operations of image processing and see how they can be implemented using Java. The comparatively straightforward model for image processing provided by classes such as BufferedImage and BufferedImageOp means that programming issues do not obscure our educational objectives. The greater sophistication of JAI means that programming issues tend to dominate when using this API, at the expense of those educational objectives. We also note here that JAI comes complete with many standard image processing operations built in. There is little practical benefit to 'reinventing the wheel' in JAI. By using only the standard Java classes, however, we can be sure that there is both educational and practical value in the programming that we do.

4.4   Further reading

For more detail on image handling in Java 1.0/1.1, see *Exploring Java* by Niemeyer and Peck [35] or *Java AWT Reference* by Zukowski [55]. The definitive guide to the Java2D API is Knudsen's *Java 2D Graphics* [27]. A very good text on all aspects of Java programming is Eckel's *Thinking in Java* [13].

Sun's Java website holds information on the Java2D and Java Advanced Imaging APIs. The former is at http://java.sun.com/products/java-media/2D/index.html and the latter is at http://java.sun.com/products/java-media/jai/.

4.5   Exercises

1. Examine the Java program below. Explain why it prints −1 twice on the console when it is executed with a GIF or JPEG image specified as a command line argument, and outline a simple modification that will enable the program to perform in the expected manner.

```
import java.awt.*;

public class ImageTest1 {
  public static void main(String[] argv) {
    if (argv.length > 0) {
      Image img = Toolkit.getDefaultToolkit().getImage(argv[0]);
      System.out.println(img.getWidth(null));
      System.out.println(img.getHeight(null));
    }
  }
}
```

2. Write an application or applet that

   (a) Reads a GIF or JPEG image into an Image object
   (b) Uses PixelGrabber to extract a square region of pixels from the centre of the image, the dimensions of this region being half those of the image
   (c) Uses MemoryImageSource to create a new Image from the extracted data
   (d) Displays the new image

Write the equivalent program using `CropImageFilter` and compare the performance of the two programs.

3. The `BufferedImage` class can represent images having different pixel data types. Chapter 3 described an alternative approach in which a different class is used for each data type, the common attributes and behaviour being inherited from an abstract base class. Compare and contrast these two approaches. (If you know C++, you might like to also consider how features such as templates provide yet another way of representing images that have different pixel data types.)

4. Write a program that reads JPEG-compressed greyscale image data into a `BufferedImage` and then iterates over all pixels in the image to determine the minimum, maximum and mean grey levels, writing this information to `System.out`.

5. Write a program that reads a colour image from a JPEG file into a `BufferedImage` object and then counts the number of pixels with a colour similar to some reference colour. This reference colour should be specified as red, green and blue values on the command line. 'Similar' in this case means that the distance between a colour and the reference colour in RGB space is less than 10. What happens when you attempt to run the program on a greyscale image?

Basic image manipulation

This chapter discusses key issues relating to the storage, display and printing of digital images and gives practical examples in Java where appropriate. It also considers basic pixel manipulation tasks such as expanding or shrinking an image and extracting regions of interest. The chapter concludes with a brief examination of simple algebraic operations on images.

5.1 Storage

5.1.1 Storage media

Storage for digital images may be categorised as *short-term*, *online* or *archival*.

Short-term storage is memory-based, employing either the general-purpose RAM of the host computer or the dedicated memory of a 'framestore'. The latter is a piece of specialised hardware that provides storage space for one or more images and facilitates rapid access by the host computer. Framestores may provide hardware support for fast 'zoom and roam' operations (analogous to examining a picture by moving a magnifying glass over it). Memory-based storage is fast, but it is normally *volatile*, meaning that image data are no longer available once the supply of power to the hardware has been interrupted. Memory is also the most expensive form of storage.

Online storage is non-volatile and allows relatively rapid access to image data. It is typically provided by the host computer's own hard disk. Disk-based storage is slower but substantially cheaper than memory-based storage.

Archival storage is used for the long-term archiving of image data. It typically employs removable media, and access to data is slow compared with fixed-disk or memory-based storage. A key advantage, however, is that data can be exchanged easily. The standard

3.5-inch, high-density diskettes used with personal computers have a limited capacity, sufficient for five 512×512, 8-bit greyscale images, or a single 512×512, 24-bit colour image (assuming no data compression). Magnetic tape can have a storage capacity several thousand times greater than that of the lowly 3.5-inch diskette. Recordable CD technology is becoming commonplace. CDs can store approximately 650 Mbyte and they are considerably more robust than magnetic tape; their shelf life estimated to be in excess of thirty years, compared with approximately seven years for tape.

5.1.2   File formats

When placing images into online or archival storage, it is important to select an appropriate **file format**. This will determine not only how the image data are stored, but also what additional information is stored with the pixel values. Many file formats adhere to the simple model shown in Figure 5.1, in which an image file consists of a header segment and a data segment. The header will contain, at the very least, the width and the height of the image—since it is impossible to display or process any image without knowledge of its dimensions. The headers of most file formats begin with a **signature** or 'magic number'—a short sequence of bytes designed to identify the file as an image with that specific format.

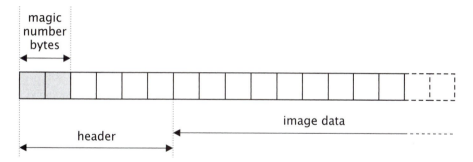

Figure 5.1   Basic structure of an image file.

File formats can be grouped roughly into three categories. **Device-specialised formats** have been tailored for use with specific pieces of computer hardware. The structure of the image file may be chosen to facilitate rapid display on a particular type of workstation, for example. The disadvantages of device-specialised formats include their lack of portability, their inefficiency when used with other hardware, and the tendency of the format to change when hardware is updated.

Software-specialised formats are those designed by a software vendor to be used with a particular program or class of programs. Examples include the PCX and Windows bitmap (BMP) formats commonly found on PCs, or the MacPaint format used on Apple Macintosh computers. The advantages and disadvantages are similar to those for device-specialised formats.

Interchange formats are designed to facilitate the exchange of image data between users, via removable storage media or computer networks. It is essential that they are usable with the widest possible range of hardware and software. Image compression (see Chapter 12) is often a standard feature of interchange formats, since it reduces storage requirements and transmission times. Examples of common interchange formats are

- GIF (Graphic Interchange Format)
- PNG (Portable Network Graphics)
- JFIF (JPEG File Interchange Format)
- TIFF (Tagged Image File Format)
- PGM (Portable Grey Map)
- FITS (Flexible Image Transport System)

GIF and JFIF[1] are the *lingua franca* for images on the World-Wide Web. PNG is a replacement for GIF which was developed when legal problems arose with GIF. Both PNG and PGM are described in more detail later.

Interchange formats often support the storage of arbitrary, user-defined information with the image data. This allows processing of images in a variety of situations. In astronomy, for example, it is important that we know the exact circumstances of data acquisition when carrying out image analysis. The FITS format used for astronomical images guarantees this by allowing a large amount of relevant information to be placed in the header.

Simple file formats have headers of fixed size. The various pieces of information needed to process an image are located at fixed offsets from the start of the file. For example, if the magic number occupies four bytes, then bytes 5–8 and 9–12 might be used to store image width and height, respectively. *Tagged* formats do not require that information is stored at fixed locations in an image file; instead, they make use of special strings or codes to identify particular items of data. Examples of tagged formats are FITS, which uses ASCII strings as tags; PNG, which uses four-byte sequences of uppercase or lowercase characters; and TIFF, which uses numeric codes.

5.1.3 The PBM, PGM and PPM formats

Let us examine a simple image format in more detail. The PGM format mentioned earlier is a popular format for greyscale images on Unix systems. It is one of a small family of closely-related formats; the others, PBM ('portable bitmap') and PPM ('portable pixmap'), are used to represent binary images and RGB colour images, respectively.

These formats are distinguished by the two-character signatures shown in Table 5.1. There are two signatures per format because there are two different methods of data storage possible with each format: ASCII storage, in which pixel values are stored in ASCII decimal form; and 'raw' or binary storage, in which pixel values are stored as bytes.

The header of a PBM, PGM or PPM file begins with the appropriate signature, followed by one or more whitespace characters. (A single newline is typically used.) One or more comment lines, each beginning with the # character, may follow if desired. Typically, these will give some indication of the origin of the image or the subject matter that it depicts.

Next in the header are the width and height of the image as ASCII decimal values, separated by whitespace. PBM files have no further header information, but PGM and

---

[1] This is known colloquially as 'JPEG format'. However, the JPEG compression algorithms are actually independent of any file format; indeed, JPEG compression is supported by the TIFF file format.

Table 5.1 Signatures of the various PBM, PGM and PPM image formats.

Signature	Image type	Storage type
P1	binary	ASCII
P2	greyscale	ASCII
P3	RGB	ASCII
P4	binary	raw bytes
P5	greyscale	raw bytes
P6	RGB	raw bytes

PPM files contain a third integer value, again in ASCII decimal form, representing the maximum allowable pixel value. This can be less than 255, to signal that fewer than 8 bits are required for image representation. For ASCII-based PGM or PPM files, it can be greater than 255, indicating that the image is quantised using more than 8 bits[2].

In the ASCII formats, the header is separated from the image data by whitespace. In an ASCII PBM file, pixel values are represented by the characters '1' and '0', interpreted as black and white, respectively. In an ASCII PGM file, grey levels are stored as ASCII decimal values, separated by whitespace. In an ASCII PPM file, the colour of each pixel is stored as a triplet of ASCII decimal values (in the order red, green, blue), each separated from each other and from the surrounding pixel colours by whitespace. In any of the ASCII formats, no line should exceed 70 characters in length.

In the raw formats, the header is separated from the image data by a single character of whitespace. (By convention, a newline is used.) In raw PGM files, each pixel value is stored as a single byte. In raw PPM files, each pixel's colour is stored as a triplet of bytes (in the order red, green, blue). In a raw PBM file, each pixel value occupies just one bit of storage. This is achieved by packing eight pixel values into each byte of data. If necessary, each row of the image is padded out such that its width is a multiple of eight. This ensures that a single row is represented by a whole number of bytes.

Figure 5.2 shows a very simple 7×7 greyscale image and its representation as ASCII and raw PGM files. The main advantage of the ASCII format is that pixel values can be examined or modified very easily using a standard text editor. (Of course, this is likely to be practical only for relatively small images.) Files in the raw format cannot, in general, be viewed or edited in the same way, since they usually contain many unprintable characters[3]. (The example in Figure 5.2 is an exception.)

The advantage of the raw format is that it is much more compact; in a raw PGM file, pixel values are coded using only a single character, but in an ASCII PGM file, as many as four characters may be required for each pixel value—with the result that ASCII files consume up to four times as much space as raw files.

---

[2] Although this is perfectly legal, most public domain software supporting these formats assumes that PGM and PPM files store 8-bit and 24-bit images, respectively.

[3] Pixel values in the range 32–126 are represented by printable ASCII characters.

```
P2
# a simple PGM image
7 7 255
 120 120 120 120 120 120 120
 120 120 120  33 120 120 120
 120 120 120  33 120 120 120
 120  33  33  33  33  33 120
 120 120 120  33 120 120 120
 120 120 120  33 120 120 120
 120 120 120 120 120 120 120
```

```
P5
# a simple PGM image
7 7 255
xxxxxxxxxx!xxxxxx!xxxx!!!!!xxxx!xxxxxx!xxxxxxxxxx
```

Figure 5.2 A simple image and representations of it as ASCII and raw PGM files. In general, the contents of a raw PGM cannot be listed in this way due to the presence of unprintable characters.

5.1.4   The portable network graphics (PNG) format

The PNG image format is one of the newer formats. Its development was motivated by legal problems relating to the patented compression algorithm used in GIF images. However, the format has evolved into something considerably more sophisticated than a simple replacement for GIF. The latest version of the PNG specification and other relevant information can be obtained via FTP from `ftp://ftp.uu.net/graphics/png/`; there is also a web site for PNG at `http://www.cdrom.com/pub/png/`.

The PNG format supports: greyscale images with up to 16 bits per pixel; indexed colour images with a 256-colour palette; and RGB colour images with up to 16 bits per component, or 48 bits per pixel. For images with fewer than 8 bits per pixel, multiple values can be packed into a single byte to reduce file size. The data stream is always compressed using a variant of the LZ77 algorithm described in Chapter 12. This compression algorithm is *lossless*, i.e., the original data stream can be restored without any loss of information. (In contrast, JPEG compression is lossy—so an image is changed slightly by a cycle of compression and decompression.)

For display purposes, PNG allows 'gamma correction' information to be stored with an image. This allows display software to compensate for the nonlinear characteristics of a display device and makes it possible to display the image so that it looks the same on different devices.

PNG also supports the notion of transparency. In an indexed colour image, we can specify that a particular entry in the palette is a 'transparent colour'. The display software may choose to ignore pixels with this colour, making whatever is behind the image visible at those locations. More generally, PNG supports the use of an 'alpha channel', which specifies transparency on a pixel-by-pixel basis. An alpha value of 0 signifies that a pixel is fully transparent, and therefore invisible when displayed; an alpha of 255 (for 8-bit images) signifies that the pixel is fully opaque, such that it hides whatever is behind it when displayed; intermediate values indicate some degree of blending of pixel grey level or colour with that of the background.

File structure

A PNG file consists of an eight-byte signature, followed by a series of **chunks**. Each chunk consists of: a 32-bit integer giving the number of bytes in the chunk's data field; a four-byte code to indicate chunk type, consisting of uppercase and lowercase letters; zero or more data bytes; and a 32-bit cyclic redundancy check (CRC) for the chunk, which a PNG decoder can use to test whether the chunk data are valid. Table 5.2 gives some examples of chunk types.

Every PNG file must contain a chunk of type IHDR, representing the image header. The header specifies, amongst other things, the dimensions, colour type and bit depth of the image. Colour type indicates whether the image is a greyscale or colour image and whether colour is represented by RGB values at every pixel or by an index into a colour palette. It also indicates whether alpha values are stored with each pixel. Bit depth is the number of bits used to represent each component of a pixel's value. Bit depths of 1, 2, 4, 8 or 16 are possible, although not all depths are permitted for all colour types.

Every PNG file must contain one or more IDAT chunks which hold the image data. If

Table 5.2 Various chunk types in the PNG file format. A lowercase first letter for a chunk type indicates that the chunk is not critical to proper interpretation of a PNG file. A lowercase last letter indicates that it is safe to simply copy the chunk from an input file to an output file as it will not become invalid if we change the image data in any way.

Chunk type	Usage
IHDR	image header
IDAT	image data
IEND	end of image file
PLTE	colour palette
gAMA	gamma correction
pHYs	pixel's physical dimensions
tEXt	textual comment
tIME	time of last modification

there is more than one IDAT chunk, they must appear consecutively, with no intervening chunks. The data within an IDAT chunk are compressed.

Finally, every PNG file must end with an IEND chunk, which marks explicitly the end of the datastream.

5.2 Reading and writing images in Java

We saw in Chapter 4 that GIF and JPEG images are supported implicitly in Java. Loading of a GIF or JPEG image into an `Image` object can be initiated with a call to the `getImage()` or `createImage()` methods of the `Applet` and `Toolkit` classes. For general image processing, this mechanism has a number of limitations:

- It is read-only; there is no support for *writing* images in these formats.
- It cannot be extended easily to support other formats.
- It loads images asynchronously, so special measures may need to be taken to delay processing until loading has completed.

With Java 2, explicit handling of JPEG image files is supported via the classes of the `com.sun.image.codec.jpeg` package. These classes make it possible to load image data synchronously into `BufferedImage` objects, which is much more convenient for general image processing. It is also possible to write image data to a JPEG file.

One problem with this is that JPEG compression is lossy (see Chapter 12). This means that every cycle of reading and writing an image degrades it a little more. A JPEG file is perhaps best used as the *final* destination for an image—a way of archiving it in the most compact manner possible, once we are sure we have applied all the necessary processing to it. We therefore need additional support for image formats that do not degrade the image in any way.

5.2.1   PBM, PGM and PPM images

Zukowski [55] presents a class PPMDecoder that can read colour images in the PPM format. The ASCII and raw binary variants of the format are both supported. The class follows the producer-consumer paradigm of Java 1.0/1.1 and implements the ImageProducer interface. Instances of the class generate data for Image objects.

Jef Poskanzer, designer of the PBM, PGM and PPM formats, has written a more general PPMDecoder class that can handle all three formats, along with a PPMEncoder class that writes data in the raw PPM formats. The decoder and encoder implement the ImageProducer and ImageConsumer interfaces, respectively. Again, instances of these classes are intended for use with Image objects. The source code for these classes is available from http://www.acme.com/java/.

In this section, we describe the key features of our own decoder and encoder classes for PBM, PGM and PPM images. These classes support the ASCII variants of the three formats and not the binary variants; we assume that other, more appropriate formats will be used if more compact storage is desired.

A decoder

The design of the decoder is depicted in Figure 5.3. The class, named PPMDecoder, implements an interface called ImageDecoder. The reason for this will be explained shortly. The practical consequence of this is that the class must implement a method called decodeAsBufferedImage() which does the job of reading image data and returning it in the form of a BufferedImage object.

As Figure 5.3 indicates, a PPMDecoder object has an instance of java.io.Reader called reader and an instance of java.io.StreamTokenizer called parser (plus a number of simple integer instance variables). Readers are used in Java programs for character-based input—which is precisely what we require here, given that the decoder is intended to handle the ASCII versions of the PBM, PGM and PPM formats. In the PPMDecoder class, reader acts simply as a source of data for parser. It is parser that does the hard work of breaking up the data stream into *tokens* which must then be interpreted as elements of the header, pixel values, etc.

The default constructor for a PPMDecoder creates a decoder object that takes data from standard input (System.in). The other constructors create decoders that take data from an arbitrary InputStream or a named file. The default constructor and file-based constructor are actually defined in terms of the stream-based constructor. Its implementation is shown in Listing 5.1. The stream passed to the constructor is first transformed into a Reader by wrapping it in an InputStreamReader, and the resulting object is then buffered using BufferedReader to improve efficiency. We then create parser and configure it to treat all lines beginning with # as comments and ignore them. Finally, the private method readHeader() is called to parse the header information.

Information obtained from the header is stored in the instance variables type, width, height and maxValue. 'Get' methods are defined for these variables so that clients of a PPMDecoder object can inspect their values. The getType() method returns an integer code indicating whether the input stream has data in PBM, PGM or PPM format. The predicates isBinary(), isGrey() and isRGB() fulfil a similar role.

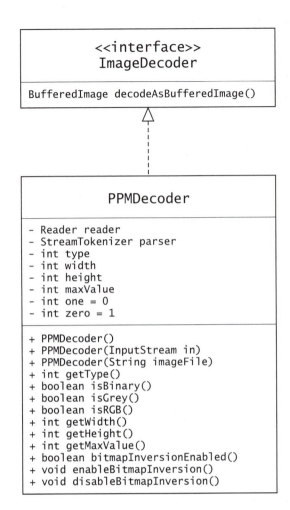

Figure 5.3 UML diagram showing the design of the PPMDecoder class.

LISTING 5.1 One of the constructors for a PPMDecoder.

```
public PPMDecoder(InputStream in)
  throws IOException, PPMDecoderException {
    reader = new BufferedReader(new InputStreamReader(in));
    parser = new StreamTokenizer(reader);
    parser.commentChar('#');
    readHeader();
}
```

The remaining methods and instance variables of Figure 5.3 deal with the special case of PBM files. The specification of the PBM format states that, contrary to what one might expect, PBM files are encoded such that a value of 1 represents black and a value of 0 represents white[4]. By default, a PPMDecoder conforms to the specification and inverts PBM data on input so that a '1' from the file is stored as 0 and a '0' from the file is stored as 1. This 'bitmap inversion' can be disabled or enabled, as required.

Image data are not read from the stream until the method decodeAsBufferedImage() is called. This delegates the task to one of the private methods parsePBM(), parsePGM() or parsePPM(). The code for parsePGM() is shown in Listing 5.2. This method creates an 8-bit or 16-bit greyscale image, as appropriate, and gets a WritableRaster object with which it can address the pixels of that image (lines 10 and 11). Nested for loops iterate

LISTING 5.2 Method that reads PGM data into a greyscale image.

```
1   private BufferedImage parsePGM() throws IOException,
2     PPMDecoderException {
3
4     int imgType;
5     if (maxValue > 255)
6       imgType = BufferedImage.TYPE_USHORT_GRAY;
7     else
8       imgType = BufferedImage.TYPE_BYTE_GRAY;
9
10    BufferedImage img = new BufferedImage(width, height, imgType);
11    WritableRaster raster = img.getRaster();
12
13    for (int y = 0; y < height; ++y)
14      for (int x = 0; x < width; ++x) {
15        parser.nextToken();
16        if (parser.ttype == StreamTokenizer.TT_EOF)
17          throw new EOFException("image appears to be truncated");
18        if (parser.ttype != StreamTokenizer.TT_NUMBER)
19          throw new PPMDecoderException(
20            "non-numeric value for pixel at ("+ x + "," + y + ")");
21        raster.setSample(x, y, 0, (int) parser.nval);
22      }
23
24    return img;
25
26  }
```

---

[4] This makes sense if we think of PBM images as being printed, rather than displayed on screen.

over all pixel coordinates. For every pixel, `parser` skips whitespace where necessary and obtains a new token (line 15), which should be numeric since no other characters are allowed in the data segment of a PBM, PGM or PPM file. This value is then written to the raster at the current coordinates (line 21).

The following fragment of Java code shows how one might read an image from a PGM file named on the command line of the application.

```
PPMDecoder pgm = new PPMDecoder(argv[0]);
BufferedImage image = pgm.decodeAsBufferedImage();
```

An encoder

The design of the encoder is depicted in Figure 5.4. The PPMEncoder class implements the ImageEncoder interface, meaning that it must provide a method encode() which takes the image to be encoded as a parameter. A PPMEncoder uses `writer`, an instance of `java.io.PrintWriter`, to output image data in ASCII form. Constructors for the class mirror those of the decoder; the default constructor creates a PPMEncoder that writes to standard output (`System.out`) and the other two constructors create encoders that write to an arbitrary output stream and to a named file. Code for the latter is shown in Listing 5.3.

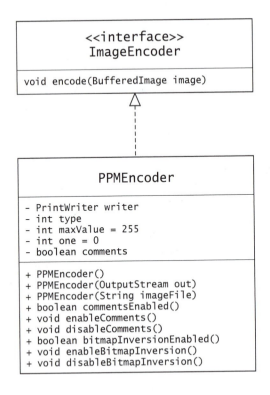

Figure 5.4 UML diagram showing the design of the PPMEncoder class.

LISTING 5.3 One of the constructors for a `PPMEncoder`.

```
public PPMEncoder(String filename) throws IOException {
  writer = new PrintWriter(
          new BufferedWriter(
            new FileWriter(filename)));
}
```

As in `PPMDecoder`, there are methods to control the inversion of binary images when writing to PBM files. The predicate `commentsEnabled()` indicates whether a comment line will be added to a PBM, PGM or PPM file. The methods `enableComments()` and `disableComments()` turn this behaviour on and off, respectively. The comment line, if added, simply records the time and date of file creation.

The task of actually encoding the image in PBM, PGM or PPM format is carried out by the `encode()` method. When passed an image, this method checks its type and hence determines the most appropriate format for the image. It writes a header and then calls one of the private methods `writePBM()`, `writePGM()` or `writePPM()` to write the image data.

5.2.2 Creating your own format: an example

The ASCII versions of the PBM, PGM and PPM formats are easy to read and write, but are not particularly compact. The raw versions of these formats are more compact, but they mix ASCII and binary data in the same file, which is not particularly elegant. For this reason, we present our own simple, pure binary format in this section. We shall call this the 'SIF format', SIF being an acronym for *Simple Image File*. The SIF format supports 8-bit greyscale and 24-bit RGB colour images, which may or may not be compressed using a lossless technique. (We support data compression in SIF images because implementing it in Java is very straightforward, thanks to the classes supplied in the standard `java.util.zip` package.) In colour images, a pixel's colour components are stored in BGR order rather than RGB order, since this makes it possible to write the image more efficiently in some situations.

A SIF image has a twelve-byte header. The first four bytes are the signature. This is followed by a pair of 32-bit integers representing the width and height of the image, respectively. All remaining bytes in the file are compressed or uncompressed image data. The signature is used to indicate image type and compression status, as indicated in Table 5.3.

Table 5.3 Image types supported by the SIF format.

Signature	Image type
GIMG	8-bit greyscale, uncompressed
gIMG	8-bit greyscale, compressed
CIMG	24-bit RGB colour, uncompressed
cIMG	24-bit RGB colour, compressed

We can design SIFEncoder and SIFDecoder classes similar to those created for PBM, PGM and PPM files. The design of SIFEncoder is shown in Figure 5.5. SIFEncoder objects are constructed and used in exactly the same way as PPMEncoder objects. Internally, a SIFEncoder uses a DataOutputStream for output. This is the most appropriate stream class to use when writing binary data. The only other instance variable is a Boolean flag to indicate whether image data should be compressed when written. Methods are provided to check this flag and to set or reset it.

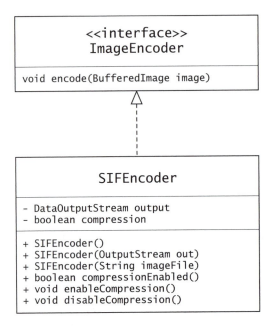

Figure 5.5 UML diagram showing the design of the SIFEncoder class.

The implementation of SIFEncoder's encode() method is shown in Listing 5.4. There are two distinct cases to deal with when writing image data. The first (lines 10–20) is when the image passed to encode() stores its pixel values as single bytes (representing grey level) or groups of three bytes (representing the blue, green and red colour components). In this special case, the way that data are stored in memory by a BufferedImage object matches the way that we wish to store the data in the file. We can therefore access the image's data buffer directly (lines 10 and 11) in order to write the data in a more efficient manner. If compression is not required, a single call to the output stream's write method will deliver the data buffer's entire contents to the stream (line 18); if compression is required, we must create an instance of DeflaterOutputStream from the normal output stream and write the data buffer contents to it.

Of course, the image may store data in such a way that we cannot merely dump the contents of its data buffer to the output stream. An example is a colour image that packs red, green and blue values into a single integer (i.e., an image of type BufferedImage.TYPE_INT_RGB). Such cases are dealt with by lines 27–42 of encoder(). We start by creating a Raster

LISTING 5.4 Java method to encode an image in the SIF format.

```
1    public void encode(BufferedImage img) throws IOException, SIFEncoderException {
2
3      writeHeader(img);
4
5      if (img.getType() == BufferedImage.TYPE_BYTE_GRAY
6       || img.getType() == BufferedImage.TYPE_3BYTE_BGR) {
7
8        // Access the data buffer directly
9
10       DataBufferByte db = (DataBufferByte) img.getRaster().getDataBuffer();
11       byte[] data = db.getData();
12       if (compression) {
13         DeflaterOutputStream deflater = new DeflaterOutputStream(output);
14         deflater.write(data, 0, data.length);
15         deflater.finish();
16       }
17       else {
18         output.write(data);
19         output.flush();
20       }
21
22     }
23     else {
24
25       // Write the image pixel-by-pixel
26
27       Raster raster = img.getRaster();
28       if (compression) {
29         DeflaterOutputStream deflater = new DeflaterOutputStream(output);
30         for (int y = 0; y < img.getHeight(); ++y)
31           for (int x = 0; x < img.getWidth(); ++x)
32             for (int i = 2; i >= 0; --i)
33               deflater.write(raster.getSample(x, y, i));
34         deflater.finish();
35       }
36       else {
37         for (int y = 0; y < img.getHeight(); ++y)
38           for (int x = 0; x < img.getWidth(); ++x)
39             for (int i = 2; i >= 0; --i)
40               output.write(raster.getSample(x, y, i));
41         output.flush();
42       }
43
44     }
45   }
```

object with which we can address individual pixels. Then, for each pixel, we retrieve samples in reverse order (blue, then green, then red) and write directly to the output stream (line 40) or, if compression is required, to an instance of `DeflaterOutputStream` that we have wrapped around the original output stream (line 33).

5.2.3 PNG images

The SIF format is simple and convenient, but it is not very flexible. Also, it is a 'personal' image format; existing tools cannot read or write the format, so SIF images cannot be exchanged easily with others. It is therefore useful to support a recognised interchange format for compressed images, and PNG is an ideal candidate.

Writing a PNG decoder and encoder from scratch would be a challenging task, given the sophistication of the format. So, rather than do this, we will use an existing implementation from Visualtek (http://www.visualtek.com/PNG/). This package provides classes called PNGDataDecoder and PNGDataEncoder which are suitable for our purposes. However, they are not used in quite the same way as the encoder and decoder classes that we have already developed for PBM, PGM, PPM and SIF images. We can hide this fact from users and present them with a consistent set of encoder and decoder classes by creating two 'wrapper' classes, PNGDecoder and PNGEncoder.

Figure 5.6 shows the design of the PNGDecoder class. As far as clients of PNGDecoder are concerned, PNGDecoder objects behave in much the same way as PPMDecoder or SIFDecoder objects. They can be constructed from input streams or named files, they can be queried for information on image dimensions and they can be tested to see whether the

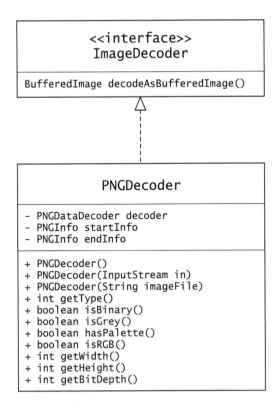

Figure 5.6 UML diagram showing the design of the PNGDecoder class.

image is a greyscale image or a colour image. Internally, a `PNGDecoder` is composed of an instance of `PNGDataDecoder`, called `decoder`, and two instances of `PNGInfo`, called `startInfo` and `endInfo`. All of the decoding is done by `decoder`. The two objects `startInfo` and `endInfo` store critical information that may appear in chunks before and after the image data. The 'get' methods of `PNGDecoder` retrieve their information from `startInfo`.

5.2.4   Putting it all together

So far, we have developed three encoder classes and three decoder classes to deal with five different image formats. The decoders all behave in the same way: they can be constructed to read from standard input, an arbitrary input stream or a named file; and they can be made to read image data into a `BufferedImage` by calling the `decodeAsBufferedImage()` method. Likewise, the encoders all behave in the same way; they can be constructed to write to standard output, an arbitrary output stream or a named file; and they can be made to write image data by calling the `encode()` method with a `BufferedImage` as a parameter.

The only visible difference between these classes and the JPEG encoder and decoder in Java's `com.sun.image.codec.jpeg` package is in the way that we create a new decoder or encoder. We can conceal this difference if we hide the standard JPEG decoder and decoder inside wrapper classes, as we did for the PNG format. Figure 5.7 shows the structure of these wrapper classes.

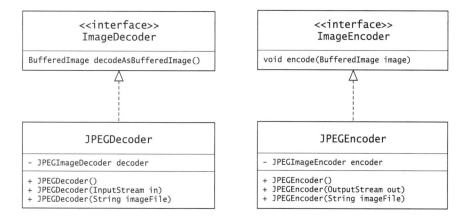

Figure 5.7 UML diagrams showing the design of the `JPEGDecoder` and `JPEGEncoder` wrapper classes.

So we now have a consistent set of classes for reading and writing images in the PBM, PGM, PPM, SIF, PNG and JPEG formats. Every decoder class reads image data using the method `decodeAsBufferedImage()`, so we can define an **interface** that specifies this method and have each class implement the interface. Similarly, every encoder class writes image data using the method `encode()`, so we can define an interface that specifies this method and have each class implement it. The two interfaces are called `ImageDecoder` and `ImageEncoder`.

This seems like an unnecessary complication, but in fact it allows us to write polymorphic code. An example of this appears in Listing 5.5. This shows a class `ImageFile` containing two static methods. The first of these, `createImageEncoder()`, takes a filename as a parameter, examines the suffix of the filename and returns a new encoder object appropriate to that filename. The other method, `createImageDecoder()` does the same but returns the most appropriate decoder object.

LISTING 5.5 A class with factory methods that create encoder and decoder objects appropriate to particular filenames.

```
1    public class ImageFile {
2
3      public static ImageEncoder createImageEncoder(String file)
4        throws IOException, ImageEncoderException {
5        if (file.endsWith(".pbm") || file.endsWith(".pgm") || file.endsWith(".ppm"))
6          return new PPMEncoder(file);
7        else if (file.endsWith(".sif"))
8          return new SIFEncoder(file);
9        else if (file.endsWith(".png"))
10         return new PNGEncoder(file);
11       else if (file.endsWith(".jpg") || file.endsWith(".jpeg"))
12         return new JPEGEncoder(file);
13       else
14         throw new ImageEncoderException("cannot determine file format");
15     }
16
17     public static ImageDecoder createImageDecoder(String file)
18       throws IOException, ImageDecoderException {
19       if (file.endsWith(".pbm") || file.endsWith(".pgm") || file.endsWith(".ppm"))
20         return new PPMDecoder(file);
21       else if (file.endsWith(".sif"))
22         return new SIFDecoder(file);
23       else if (file.endsWith(".png"))
24         return new PNGDecoder(file);
25       else if (file.endsWith(".jpg") || file.endsWith(".jpeg"))
26         return new JPEGDecoder(file);
27       else
28         throw new ImageDecoderException("cannot determine file format");
29     }
30
31   }
```

For example, if we pass the filename `test.png` to `createImageEncoder()` then a `PNGEncoder` that writes to a file of that name is created and returned. If, however, the filename `test.sif` is passed to the method then it creates and returns a `SIFEncoder`. This works because the method returns an object of type `ImageEncoder` and, since each of our encoder classes implements the `ImageEncoder` interface, instances of each class can be regarded as `ImageEncoder` objects.

This concept is used frequently in the Java API. Methods like `createImageEncoder()`

are described as **factory methods** because their job is to create objects of an appropriate type. Since client code manipulates these objects via an interface that is common to all of them, it need never know the actual type of object that has been created. A practical example of this is shown in Listing 5.6. Here, we see a Java program that converts between file formats. The factory methods are used to create decoder and encoder objects suitable for the filenames that have been specified on the command line. The key point to note is that if we subsequently developed encoder and decoder classes for another format—TIFF, say—then we would need to modify the factory methods and recompile the `ImageFile` class but we would *not* need to make any changes to the `Convert` program or recompile it.

LISTING 5.6 A simple image format conversion program.

```
 1  public class Convert {
 2    public static void main(String[] argv) {
 3      if (argv.length > 1) {
 4        try {
 5          ImageDecoder input = ImageFile.createImageDecoder(argv[0]);
 6          BufferedImage image = input.decodeAsBufferedImage();
 7          ImageEncoder output = ImageFile.createImageEncoder(argv[1]);
 8          output.encode(image);
 9        }
10        catch (Exception e) {
11          System.err.println(e);
12          System.exit(1);
13        }
14      }
15      else {
16        System.err.println("usage: java Convert infile outfile");
17        System.exit(1);
18      }
19    }
20  }
```

Source code and bytecode for the classes described in the preceding sections is available on the CD. The classes have been grouped together in a single package, `com.pearsoneduc.ip.io`. You can use them in your own Java programs by inserting the statement

```
import com.pearsoneduc.ip.io.*;
```

at the beginning of the file. (Of course, you will first need to install the package and ensure that Java can find it by specifying a classpath either using the command line arguments of the Java interpreter or via the `CLASSPATH` environment variable.) The `Convert` program can be found in the `Apps` directory.

5.3 Display

5.3.1 Hardware

Images are normally viewed on a monitor employing cathode-ray tube (CRT) technology. In the neck of the tube are three electron guns, emitting narrow beams of electrons which are swept across the front face of the tube by deflection coils. The face is coated with a pattern of dots of three different types of phosphor, which emit varying amounts of red, green and blue light when struck by varying numbers of electrons. The phosphor dots are typically arranged into triangular groups of three: one red, one green, the other blue (Figure 5.8). They are sufficiently small to be unresolvable by the human eye; instead, what we perceive at each point on the screen is a mixture of light from the red, green and blue phosphors of a triplet. Each of the three electron beams is made to strike phosphors of a single colour by means of a 'shadow mask'. The intensities of the beams are modulated by the strength of the red, green and blue components of the colour video signal that is fed into the monitor.

The phosphors in a CRT respond nonlinearly to the electron beam, so doubling the grey level of a pixel will *not* double the intensity of the light emitted from that point on the screen. The transfer characteristic which specifies how screen brightness relates to input grey level is a curve rather than a straight line. The shape of the curve is specified by the **gamma** parameter. If two monitors have different gammas, then a given image will look different on those monitors. Gamma is usually around 2.2 for most CRTs.

Older image processing systems typically employ a separate monitor, dedicated to image display. It is common for newer systems to exploit the graphical user interface of the host computer, displaying images in a separate window on the host's own monitor.

Although a computer's colour monitor has three independent electron guns for the red, green and blue components of a video signal, this does *not* guarantee that we will be able to display 24-bit RGB images. The limiting factor is the graphics hardware of the host computer. PC graphics cards have a fixed quantity of on-board video memory which can be configured for various different combinations of spatial and colour resolution. There is a trade-off between these two parameters; if spatial resolution is increased so that larger images can be displayed on-screen, then colour resolution may need to be reduced—with the result that those images may not be rendered accurately.

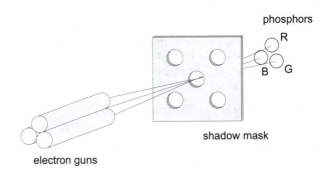

Figure 5.8 Image formation in a CRT monitor.

For example, suppose that we have a graphics card with 2 Mbyte of video RAM. The display of 24-bit colour at a resolution of 800×600 requires $800 \times 600 \times 3 = 1,440,000$ bytes of storage—well within the capacity of the hardware. Now suppose that we wish to increase the resolution to 1024×768, to allow the display of larger images in their entirety. The storage requirements for this would be $1024 \times 768 \times 3 = 2,359,296$ bytes, exceeding the limits imposed by the hardware.

There are two options open to us here: we can continue to drive our display at $800 \times 600 \times 24$ bits, accepting that larger images will not be fully displayed; or we can reduce the number of colours used for display, accepting that this may affect our perception of the image. In this case, $1024 \times 768 \times 16$ bit resolution would be supported by the graphics card, and higher spatial resolutions might be possible (depending on the scanning frequencies supported by the monitor) if we were prepared to tolerate an even more restrictive 8-bit colour palette.

5.3.2   Software: displaying images in Java

Image display is relatively straightfoward in Java. An image can be drawn using methods of the `Graphics` or `Graphics2D` classes. An instance of `Graphics` or `Graphics2D` is known as a *graphics context*. It represents a surface onto which we can draw images, text or other graphics primitives. A graphics context could be associated with an output device such as a printer, or it could be derived from another image (allowing us to draw images inside other images); however, it is typically associated with a GUI component that is to be displayed on the screen.

Image display using the AWT

To display an image using the AWT, we must extend an existing AWT component and override its `paint()` method. In very simple applets or applications, extending `Applet` or `Frame` would be sufficient. However, a more useful solution is to extend `Canvas`, specialising it for image display. `Canvas` is ideal for this because it represents a blank area, on which nothing is drawn by default. Instances of the new class, which we may call `ImageCanvas`, can be aggregrated easily with other GUI components to create interactive image processing applets or applications. Listing 5.7 shows how `ImageCanvas` might be implemented.

The `paint()` method of an `ImageCanvas` is called automatically whenever the display area needs refreshing—e.g., because a window was resized or uncovered. The `Graphics` object that `paint()` receives is the graphics context for the `ImageCanvas`. We must call one of the `drawImage()` methods provided by this graphics context to ensure that the image is painted onto the canvas whenever necessary.

The full method prototype for `drawImage()` on line 13 of Listing 5.7 is

```
public boolean drawImage(Image img, int x,
                         int y, ImageObserver obs)
```

We are free to substitute a `BufferedImage` for the `Image` passed in as the first parameter of the method because `BufferedImage` is a subclass of `Image`. The next two parameters, x and y, represent the location of the image origin on the canvas. Normally, we would use values of zero for these parameters, as in Listing 5.7. The final parameter is an `ImageObserver`:

LISTING 5.7 An AWT component that displays images.

```
1   import java.awt.*;
2
3
4   public class ImageCanvas extends Canvas {
5
6     BufferedImage image; // In Java 1.x this would be an Image object
7
8      public ImageCanvas(BufferedImage img) {
9        image = img;
10     }
11
12     public void paint(Graphics g) {
13       g.drawImage(image, 0, 0, this);
14     }
15
16  }
```

---

an object that will be notified of changes in the status of the image as it is loaded. (This is significant if we are displaying an Image, which may be loading in a separate thread, but not if we are displaying a BufferedImage, for which data are guaranteed to be available.) In Listing 5.7 we pass this, a reference to the ImageCanvas itself. We do this because every AWT component implements the ImageObserver interface and therefore has the capacity to observe delivery of image data and act accordingly. The method returns true if the image can be drawn fully, false otherwise.

There are actually *six* different versions of drawImage() that are provided by a Graphics object. Full details of these can be found in books that explore Java graphics in more detail [55, 27]. Here we consider one other variation:

```
public boolean drawImage(Image img, int x,
                         int y, int w, int h, ImageObserver obs)
```

The extra parameters in this version are the width and height to use for image display. The image will be scaled to fit this area, so this is one way of magnifying or shrinking an image prior to display.

Java 2 provides Graphics2D, a graphics context capable of much more sophisticated operations. It has two additional versions of the drawImage method which can be useful:

```
public void drawImage(Image img, AffineTransform transform,
                      ImageObserver obs)
public void drawImage(BufferedImage img, BufferedImageOp op,
                      int x, int y)
```

The first of these methods transforms an image using the specified AffineTransform object before displaying it. This is a more general solution than the simple rescaling to a new width and height described previously. We will encounter the AffineTransform class again in Chapter 9, when we consider the geometric transformation of images.

The second method applies an image processing operation to the image prior to display. The image itself remains unchanged. The image processing operation is defined in a class that implements the BufferedImageOp interface. We will examine how to implement such a class in Chapter 6. For now, we will simply present in Listing 5.8 an alternative implementation of ImageCanvas that supports processing of the image prior to display. Instances of this new ImageCanvas class are constructed from an image and an image processing operation. The latter can be null if we do not wish to process the image. The paint() method tests whether the operation object is null and, if this is not the case, calls the version of drawImage() that processes the image before displaying it (line 18). Before this can be done, we must obtain a Graphics2D object from the Graphics object, which can be accomplished via a simple cast. If operation is null, the standard version of drawImage() is called (line 21).

LISTING 5.8 An ImageCanvas that can process an image before displaying it.

```
1   import java.awt.*;
2   import java.awt.image.*;
3
4
5   public class ImageCanvas extends Canvas {
6
7     BufferedImage image;
8     BufferedImageOp operation;
9
10    public ImageCanvas(BufferedImage img, BufferedImageOp op) {
11      image = img;
12      operation = op;
13    }
14
15    public void paint(Graphics g) {
16      if (operation != null) {
17        Graphics2D g2 = (Graphics2D) g;
18        g2.drawImage(image, operation, 0, 0);
19      }
20      else
21        g.drawImage(image, 0, 0, this);
22    }
23
24  }
```

Image display using Swing components

In Java 2, we can make use of the Swing GUI components found in the `javax.swing` package. Swing offers improved replacements for AWT components, along with many new and highly sophisticated classes for which there is no equivalent in the rather more primitive AWT. It therefore makes sense to use Swing for the development of new GUI-based applications.

Unfortunately, problems can occur if we try to mix AWT-based components with Swing components. The AWT's 'heavyweight' components depend on peer objects native to the platform on which Java is running [55]; an AWT scrollbar, for instance, is implemented on the Microsoft Windows platform using the code that Microsoft have written to create scrollbars in MS Windows applications. The system-dependent aspects of this are concealed by a peer interface. By contrast, most of the components in Swing are 'lightweight'; that is, they are implemented purely in Java and are therefore independent of any components belonging to the underlying platform. What happens in practice is that heavyweight components are invariably rendered on top of lightweight components, regardless of whether this was intended [14]. We should therefore endeavour to use Swing components only in GUI-based programs written for the Java 2 environment.

There is no direct replacement for `Canvas` in Swing, but Swing does provide the `JLabel` component. A `JLabel` object is typically used to add a short piece of text, an icon or a combination of the two to a user interface. The intention is that the icon should be a small image, but this need not be the case. A `JLabel` can be constructed from an `ImageIcon` object, which, in turn, can be constructed from an `Image` or `BufferedImage` object. So, if we have a `BufferedImage` called image already available, a component to display that image can be created using

```
ImageIcon icon = new ImageIcon(image);
JLabel view = new JLabel(icon);
```

or, more compactly, with

```
JLabel view = new JLabel(new ImageIcon(image));
```

A simple Swing application to load an image from a file and display it is shown in Listing 5.9. We extend Swing's `JFrame` class so that we will have a window in which to display the image. Line 10 invokes the parent class constructor with the image filename as a parameter. This has the effect of placing the filename in the titlebar of the window. Lines 11 and 12 load the image from the file. Line 13 creates a `JLabel` in which the image is drawn. Line 14 adds the `JLabel` to the frame's content pane. Lines 15–19 set up the event handling that will allow us to destroy the frame by clicking on the appropriate button on the titlebar. Finally, lines 25–27 create the frame, resize it to match the size of its contents and then make it visible.

An alternative approach is to create a new component that is dedicated to the task of image display. We can do this by extending `JLabel`. A possible implementation is shown in Listing 5.10. One important difference between this class and `ImageCanvas` from Listing 5.7 is that we must override the `paintComponent()` method, rather than `paint()`. The other features of the class—instance variable `viewSize` and the methods after `paintComponent()`—are there to support scrolling of the component when it is embedded in a `JScrollPane`.

LISTING 5.9 A simple image display application using Swing components.

```
1   import java.awt.*;
2   import java.awt.image.*;
3   import javax.swing.*;
4   import com.pearsoneduc.ip.io.*;
5
6
7   public class Display extends JFrame {
8
9     public Display(String filename) {
10        super(filename);
11        ImageDecoder input = ImageFile.createImageDecoder(filename);
12        BufferedImage image = input.decodeAsBufferedImage();
13        JLabel view = new JLabel(new ImageIcon(image));
14        getContentPane().add(view);
15        addWindowListener(new WindowAdapter() {
16          public void windowClosing(WindowEvent event) {
17            System.exit(0);
18          }
19        });
20      }
21
22      public static void main(String[] argv) {
23        if (argv.length > 0) {
24          try {
25            JFrame frame = new Display(argv[0]);
26            frame.pack();
27            frame.setVisible(true);
28          }
29          catch (Exception e) {
30            System.err.println(e);
31            System.exit(1);
32          }
33        }
34        else {
35          System.err.println("usage: java Display imagefile");
36          System.exit(1);
37        }
38      }
39
40   }
```

LISTING 5.10 A Swing component to display images.

```
1   import java.awt.*;
2   import java.awt.image.*;
3   import javax.swing.*;
4
5
6   public class ImageView extends JLabel implements Scrollable {
7
8     private BufferedImage image;    // image to be displayed
9     private Dimension viewSize;     // size of view, if in a JScrollPane
10
11    public ImageView(BufferedImage img) {
12      image = img;
13      int width = Math.min(256, image.getWidth());
14      int height = Math.min(256, image.getHeight());
15      viewSize = new Dimension(width, height);
16      setPreferredSize(new Dimension(image.getWidth(), image.getHeight()));
17    }
18
19    public void paintComponent(Graphics g) {
20      g.drawImage(image, 0, 0, this);
21    }
22
23    public void setViewSize(Dimension newSize) {
24      viewSize.setSize(newSize);
25    }
26
27    public Dimension getPreferredScrollableViewportSize() {
28      return viewSize;
29    }
30
31    public int getScrollableUnitIncrement(Rectangle rect, int orient, int dir) {
32      return 1;
33    }
34
35    public int getScrollableBlockIncrement(Rectangle rect, int orient, int dir) {
36      if (orient == SwingConstants.HORIZONTAL)
37        return image.getWidth() / 10;
38      else
39        return image.getHeight() / 10;
40    }
41
42    public boolean getScrollableTracksViewportWidth() {
43      return false;
44    }
45
46    public boolean getScrollableTracksViewportHeight() {
47      return false;
48    }
49
50  }
```

The constructor of `ImageView` sets its preferred size to the image dimensions, so that the entire image will be visible if the component is used on its own. The `viewSize` is set to a maximum of 256×256. When an `ImageView` is embedded in a `JScrollPane`, the `viewSize` variable represents the dimensions of the viewport through which we see the image. If the image dimensions exceed `viewSize` then scrollbars will appear automatically at the sides of the image, allowing us to move the view to different parts of the image.

An example: the *ImageViewer* application

We can use the `ImageView` class described above as the basis of a complete image viewing application. This program loads an image from a file using the classes described in Section 5.2 and displays it using an `ImageView` component. The application listens for mouse events occurring within the viewing area and translates cursor coordinates into image coordinates. It then retrieves pixel grey level or colour at those coordinates and displays these data in a panel underneath the image. A final feature of the program is a 'magnifying glass'. Clicking on the magnifier button causes a small window to pop up containing a magnified view of the region surrounding the cursor. The size of this region varies according to the magnification factor that the user selects from a list beneath the magnified view. Figure 5.9 shows the application in action. The code can be found on the CD, in the `Apps` directory.

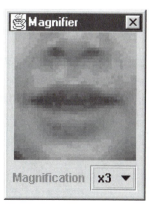

Figure 5.9 An image viewing application.

5.4 Printing

Although it is possible to output digital images direct to photographic film using specialised equipment, it is more common (and less costly) to employ printing technology for the generation of hardcopy. The problem we face when attempting to print an image is that most printers produce a binary output; either a blob of ink is placed on the page, making that part of the page black, or it is not placed on the page, in which case that part of the page remains white. How, then, do we simulate intermediate shades of grey in an 8-bit image? Similarly, how can we use a small number of coloured inks to simulate the huge range of colours possible in a 24-bit image?

5.4.1 Greyscale images

Newspaper photographs simulate a greyscale, despite the fact that they have been printed using only black ink. Close examination reveals how the illusion is achieved; a newspaper picture is, in fact, made up of a pattern of tiny black dots of varying size. The human visual system has a tendency to average brightness over small areas, so the black dots and their white background merge and are perceived as an intermediate shade of grey.

The process of generating a binary pattern of black and white dots from an image is termed **halftoning**. In traditional newspaper and magazine production, this process is carried out photographically by projection of a transparency through a 'halftone screen' onto film. The screen is a glass plate with a grid etched into it. Different screens can be used to control the size and shape of the dots in the halftoned image. A fine grid, with a 'screen frequency' of 200–300 lines per inch, gives the image quality necessary for magazine production, whereas a screen frequency of 85 lines per inch is deemed acceptable for newspapers.

Patterning

A simple digital halftoning technique known as **patterning** involves replacing each pixel by a pattern taken from a 'binary font'. Figure 5.10 shows such a font, made up of ten 3×3 matrices of pixels. This font can be used to print an image consisting of ten grey levels. A pixel with a grey level of 0 is replaced by a matrix containing no white pixels; a pixel with a grey level of 1 is replaced by a matrix containing a single white pixel; and so on. Note that, since we are replacing each pixel by a 3×3 block of pixels, both the width and the height of the image increase by a factor of 3. Figure 5.11 shows an example of halftoning using the binary font depicted in Figure 5.10.

The patterns used in a binary font must be carefully chosen to avoid the generation of prominent stripes or other distracting texture in homogeneous regions of the image.

Dithering

Another technique for digital halftoning is **dithering**. Dithering can be accomplished by thresholding the image against a **dither matrix**. Recursive algorithms are available to compute dither matrices with dimensions that are powers of two [37, 11]. The first two

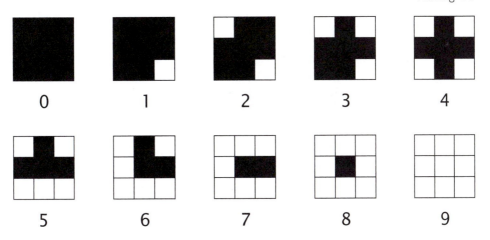

Figure 5.10 A 3 × 3 binary font for printing a greyscale.

(a)   (b)

Figure 5.11 Halftoning with a binary font. (a) 8-bit greyscale image. (b) halftoned image.

dither matrices, rescaled for application to 8-bit images, are

$$\mathbf{D}_1 = \begin{bmatrix} 0 & 128 \\ 192 & 64 \end{bmatrix}, \qquad \mathbf{D}_2 = \begin{bmatrix} 0 & 128 & 32 & 160 \\ 192 & 64 & 224 & 96 \\ 48 & 176 & 16 & 144 \\ 240 & 112 & 208 & 80 \end{bmatrix}.$$

The elements of a dither matrix are thresholds. The matrix is laid like a tile over the entire image and each pixel value is compared with the corresponding threshold from the matrix. The pixel becomes white if its value exceeds the threshold or black otherwise. This approach produces an output image with the same dimensions as the input image, but with less detail visible. To avoid loss of detail, we can enlarge the image first. For a dither matrix $\mathbf{D}_n$, we must enlarge by a factor 2^n, using the approach outlined in Section 5.5. Dithering an enlarged image in this manner is rather like the patterning approach discussed earlier, only the pattern is computed by comparison of pixel grey level with dither matrix elements, rather than being selected from a pre-existing font.

Listing 5.11 shows how application of a dither matrix to an image can be implemented in Java. This particular implementation uses a static method which we assume belongs to some unspecified class. Because the method is static, it can be called without first creating an instance of the class to which it belongs. A more object-oriented approach to implementing image processing operations is described in Chapter 6. Figure 5.12 gives examples of dithering done by this code using matrices $\mathbf{D}_1$ and $\mathbf{D}_2$.

The `Dither` application is provided on the CD. You can run this to experiment with dithering of greyscale images. The program dithers using both the $\mathbf{D}_1$ and $\mathbf{D}_2$ matrices and presents a tabbed display that switches between the input image and the dithered images, allowing comparisons to be made easily.

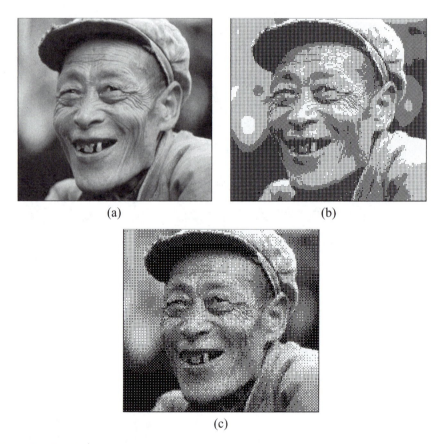

(a)

(b)

(c)

Figure 5.12 Halftoning with dither matrices. (a) Input image. (b) Result of dithering with $\mathbf{D}_1$. (c) Result of dithering with $\mathbf{D}_2$.

LISTING 5.11 Java code to halftone an image using a dither matrix. Indexing the matrix with `[y%n] [x%n]` ensures that thresholds from the matrix are reused in a cyclic manner. This achieves the effect of tiling the image with the matrix.

```
 1   public static BufferedImage ditherByMatrix(BufferedImage image, int[][] matrix) {
 2
 3     int w = image.getWidth();
 4     int h = image.getHeight();
 5     int n = matrix.length;
 6
 7     BufferedImage ditheredImage =
 8      new BufferedImage(w, h, BufferedImage.TYPE_BYTE_BINARY);
 9     Raster input = image.getRaster();
10     WritableRaster output = ditheredImage.getRaster();
11
12     for (int y = 0; y < h; ++y)
13       for (int x = 0; x < w; ++x)
14         if (input.getSample(x, y, 0) > matrix[y%n][x%n])
15           output.setSample(x, y, 0, 1);
16
17     return ditheredImage;
18
19   }
```

Error diffusion

A third halftoning technique is **error diffusion**. This is aims to correct the errors introduced by thresholding. We start by selecting a threshold, typically 128 for images with pixel values in a 0–255 range. Pixels with values less than the threshold will map to 0 (black), whilst those with values greater than or equal to the threshold will map to 255 (white). For pixels whose original values are close to 0 or 255, this mapping is reasonable, but thresholding performs less well for pixels whose values are close to the threshold level. For instance, a grey level of 127 would be mapped onto 0—an 'error' of 127. Similarly, a grey level of 128 would be mapped onto 255—also an error of 127. The idea behind error diffusion is to spread or diffuse this error to neighbouring pixels. The Floyd-Steinberg algorithm for error diffusion distributes the error at any pixel amongst the four neighbours that are ahead of that pixel, assuming a top-to-bottom, left-to-right traversal of the image (Figure 5.13).

Algorithm 5.1 illustrates how Floyd-Steinberg error diffusion is applied to an image. Implementation of the algorithm is fairly straightforward. However, if we wish to keep the original input image, we must be sure to copy it because it will be modified by the error propagation process. Also, we must not attempt to propagate errors beyond the bounds of the image. Finally, we must take care not to allow pixel values to fall below 0 or rise above 255 as a result of error propagation.

Listing 5.12 shows a Java implementation of the algorithm. An image halftoned by error diffusion is shown in Figure 5.14. You can experiment with error diffusion of other greyscale images by running the `ErrorDiffusion` application, provided on the CD. This is similar to the `Dither` application described earlier, in that it can display the greyscale image or the halftoned image, allowing the user to toggle between them.

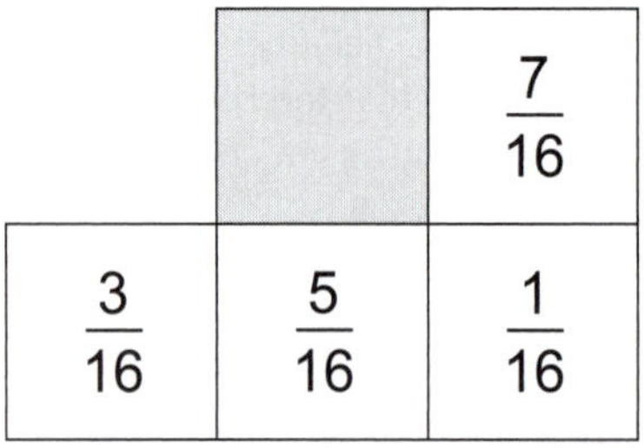

Figure 5.13 Pixels to which quantisation error is dispersed in the Floyd-Steinberg algorithm. The number at each pixel is the proportion of the error that the pixel receives.

ALGORITHM 5.1   Dithering by Floyd-Steinberg error diffusion.

$threshold = (black + white)/2$
for all x and y **do**
  if $f(x, y) < threshold$ **then**
    $g(x, y) = black$
    $\varepsilon = f(x, y) - black$
  else
    $g(x, y) = white$
    $\varepsilon = f(x, y) - white$
  end if
  $f(x + 1, y) = f(x + 1, y) + 7\varepsilon/16$
  $f(x - 1, y + 1) = f(x - 1, y + 1) + 3\varepsilon/16$
  $f(x, y + 1) = f(x, y + 1) + 5\varepsilon/16$
  $f(x + 1, y + 1) = f(x + 1, y + 1) + \varepsilon/16$
end for

5.4.2   Colour images

As we have seen in Section 3.4.2, a CMYK colour model is used for the printing of colour images. The colour printer is equipped with cyan, magenta, yellow and black inks and prints using each of these in turn. Again, the output produced when we print using any one of the four inks is binary: a blob of ink is either present or absent at any point on the page. Consequently, we must use halftoning to represent different proportions of C, M, Y or K in a given colour.

The halftone patterns used to print each of the four inks must be oriented at different angles, as shown in Table 5.4. This ensures that the ink dots form a symmetrical pattern that can be merged by the human eye into a smooth variation of colour. If the orientation of one or more patterns is incorrect, an interference effect known as Moiré fringing can occur, disrupting our perception of smooth colour variation.

LISTING 5.12 Java implementation of Algorithm 5.1.

```
1    public static BufferedImage errorDiffusion(BufferedImage image) {
2
3      // Create a binary output image (0=black, 1=white)
4
5      int w = image.getWidth() - 1;
6      int h = image.getHeight() - 1;
7      outputImage = new BufferedImage(w, h, BufferedImage.TYPE_BYTE_BINARY);
8
9      // Copy input image because error diffusion modifies it
10
11     WritableRaster input = image.copyData(null);
12     WritableRaster output = outputImage.getRaster();
13     final int threshold = 128;
14     int value, error;
15
16     for (int y = 0; y < h; ++y)
17       for (int x = 0; x < w; ++x) {
18
19         // Threshold pixel value and compute error
20
21         value = input.getSample(x, y, 0);
22         if (value < threshold) {
23           output.setSample(x, y, 0, 0);     // set to black
24           error = value;
25         }
26         else {
27           output.setSample(x, y, 0, 1);     // set to white
28           error = value - 255;
29         }
30
31         // Disperse error to pixels that are ahead of us
32
33         value = input.getSample(x+1, y, 0);
34         input.setSample(x+1, y, 0, clamp(value + 0.4375f * error));
35         value = input.getSample(x-1, y+1, 0);
36         input.setSample(x-1, y+1, 0, clamp(value + 0.1875f * error));
37         value = input.getSample(x, y+1, 0);
38         input.setSample(x, y+1, 0, clamp(value + 0.3125f * error));
39         value = input.getSample(x+1, y+1, 0);
40         input.setSample(x+1, y+1, 0, clamp(value + 0.0625f * error));
41
42       }
43
44     return outputImage;
45
46   }
47
48
49   // Rounds a float to the nearest int between 0 and 255
50
51   public static int clamp(float value) {
52     return Math.min(Math.max(Math.round(value), 0), 255);
53   }
```

Figure 5.14   Example of Floyd-Steinberg error diffusion.

Table 5.4   Orientation of halftone patterns for colour printing.

Component	Orientation
C	15°
M	75°
Y	0°
K	45°

5.5   Manipulation of pixel data

5.5.1   Extracting regions of interest

A **region of interest** (ROI) is a rectangular area within the image, defined either by the coordinates of the pixels at its upper-left and lower-right corners or by the coordinates of its upper-left corner and its dimensions. ROIs are commonly used to limit the extent of image processing operations to some small part of the image. Interactive image processing software will often provide the facility to define ROIs of images using the mouse or an equivalent pointing device. An example of this is the MeanROI application, which displays an image, allows the user to draw a ROI on it and then computes mean grey level within that ROI (Figure 5.15). Code for MeanROI can be found below the Apps directory on the CD.

Java's BufferedImage class has three methods that are useful when operating on ROIs:

```
Raster getData(Rectangle rect)
void setData(Raster raster)
BufferedImage getSubimage(int x, int y, int w, int h)
```

The getData() method takes as its sole parameter a Rectangle object that specifies the position and dimensions of the ROI. It returns the data from that ROI as a Raster object. The data stored within the raster are independent of the image on which getData() was called, so subsequent changes to the image will not affect the raster. However, the raster's

Figure 5.15 The MeanROI application in action.

coordinate system is that of the original image. This means that the first pixel in the raster has the same coordinates as the ROI's origin. We must be careful to take this into account when processing raster data.

Instances of Raster are read-only, but we may cast the object returned by getData() to a WritableRaster if we wish to modify the pixel values. The modified raster can then be loaded back into its parent image by invoking the setData() method of the image, with the raster as a parameter.

If in-place processing of a ROI is required, the getSubimage() method of BufferedImage may be more convenient. Given the coordinates and dimensions of the ROI as parameters, this method returns a subimage that shares the same data array as the parent image. This means that changes made to pixel values in the subimage will affect the parent image. The coordinate system of the subimage is *not* that of the parent image, so its pixels are indexed starting from (0, 0).

An example of ROI usage can be seen in Listing 5.13. This shows two versions of a method meanValue(). The first computes the mean pixel value in the supplied image (assumed to be greyscale). The second computes the mean within a ROI specified by a Rectangle object. Note that there is no need to duplicate any code in the second version of the method; all that we need to do is invoke getSubimage() on the image using the ROI parameters contained in the Rectangle object and then pass the image that is returned to the first version of meanValue(). Both of these methods are used in the MeanROI application described earlier.

> **LISTING 5.13** Example of using a ROI in the calculation of mean grey level.
>
> ```
> public static double meanValue(BufferedImage image) {
>   Raster raster = image.getRaster();
>   double sum = 0.0;
>   for (int y = 0; y < image.getHeight(); ++y)
>     for (int x = 0; x < image.getWidth(); ++x)
>       sum += raster.getSample(x, y, 0);
>   return sum / (image.getWidth()*image.getHeight());
> }
>
> public static double meanValue(BufferedImage image, Rectangle roi) {
>   return meanValue(image.getSubimage(roi.x, roi.y, roi.width, roi.height));
> }
> ```

5.5.2 Basic geometric manipulation

Chapter 9 deals with arbitrary geometric transformations of images. Here, we consider some special cases which can be implemented in a much more straightforward manner. These special cases are: enlargement or shrinkage by an integer factor; rotation by a multiple of 90°; and reflection along the x or y axis.

Enlarging or shrinking an image can be accomplished by replicating or skipping pixels. These techniques can be used to magnify small details in an image, or reduce a large image in size so that it fits on the screen. They have the advantage of being fast, but can only resize an image by an integer factor.

To enlarge an image by an integer factor n, we must replicate pixels such that each pixel in the input image becomes an $n \times n$ block of identical pixels in the output image. The most straightforward implementation of this involves iterating over the pixels in the larger output image and computing the coordinates of the input image pixel from which a value must be taken. For a pixel (x, y) in the output image, the corresponding pixel in the input image is at $(x/n, y/n)$. Calculation of the coordinates is done using integer arithmetic. Listing 5.14 shows some code to perform this operation on a BufferedImage object.

To shrink an image by an integer factor n, we must sample every nth pixel in the horizontal and vertical dimensions and ignore the others. Again, this technique is most easily implemented by iterating over pixels in the output image and computing the coordinates of the corresponding input image pixel. Listing 5.15 gives the Java code which performs this operation.

Rotation is relatively simple to implement for the special case where the angle is a multiple of 90° and we are rotating about the image centre. Rotations of 90° or 270° require the creation of a new output image, the dimensions of which are transposed relative to the input image. A rotation of 180° can, if necessary, be performed 'in place' (that is, without the creation of a new image to hold the result of the operation).

Reflection along either of the image axes can also be performed in place. This simply involves reversing the ordering of pixels in the rows or columns of the image. Some Java code to reflect a BufferedImage along the x axis is shown in Listing 5.16.

LISTING 5.14 Java code to enlarge an image by pixel replication.

```java
public static BufferedImage enlarge(BufferedImage image, int n) {

  int w = n*image.getWidth();
  int h = n*image.getHeight();
  BufferedImage enlargedImage =
   new BufferedImage(w, h, image.getType());

  for (int y = 0; y < h; ++y)
    for (int x = 0; x < w; ++x)
      enlargedImage.setRGB(x, y, image.getRGB(x/n, y/n));

  return enlargedImage;

}
```

LISTING 5.15 Java code to shrink an image by skipping pixels.

```java
public static BufferedImage shrink(BufferedImage image, int n) {

  int w = image.getWidth() / n;
  int h = image.getHeight() / n;
  BufferedImage shrunkImage =
   new BufferedImage(w, h, image.getType());

  for (int y = 0; y < h; ++y)
    for (int x = 0; x < w; ++x)
      shrunkImage.setRGB(x, y, image.getRGB(x*n, y*n));

  return shrunkImage;

}
```

LISTING 5.16 Java code for in-place horizontal reflection of an image.

```
public static void xReflectionInPlace(BufferedImage image) {

  int w = image.getWidth();
  int xmax = w/2;

  for (int y = 0; y < image.getHeight(); ++y)
    for (int x = 0; x < xmax; ++x) {

      // swap value at (x,y) with its mirror image

      int value = image.getRGB(x, y);
      image.setRGB(x, y, image.getRGB(w-x-1, y));
      image.setRGB(w-x-1, y, value);

    }

}
```

5.5.3 Arithmetic and logical combination of images

Expressions constructed from numbers and arithmetic or logical operators are easily understood, but what it means to combine images in this manner is less obvious. The key thing to remember is that these operators are applied on pixel-by-pixel basis. So, to add two images together, we add the value at pixel $(0, 0)$ in image 1 to the value at pixel $(0, 0)$ in image 2 and store the result in a new image at pixel $(0, 0)$. Then we move to the next pixel and repeat the process, continuing until all pixels have been visited.

Clearly, this can work properly only if the two images have identical dimensions. If they do not then combination is still possible, but a meaningful result can be obtained only in the area of overlap. If our images have dimensions of $w_1 \times h_1$ and $w_2 \times h_2$ and we assume that their origins are aligned, then the new image will have dimensions $w \times h$, where

$$w = \min(w_1, w_2), \tag{5.1}$$
$$h = \min(h_1, h_2). \tag{5.2}$$

In the case of arithmetic operations, we must also ensure that the representation used for the output image is appropriate for the operation being performed. For example, the values produced when we add two 8-bit greyscale images cannot, in general, be contained in an 8-bit range.

Addition and averaging

If we add two 8-bit greyscale images, then pixels in the resulting image can have values in the range 0–510. We should therefore choose a 16-bit representation for the output image or divide every pixel's value by two. If we do the latter, then we are computing an average of the two images. We may wish to give more emphasis to one image than the other. This can be done by 'alpha blending':

$$g(x, y) = \alpha f_1(x, y) + (1 - \alpha) f_2(x, y). \tag{5.3}$$

When α in Equation 5.3 is 0.5, $g(x, y)$ becomes a simple, evenly-weighted average of the two input images. It is possible for α to vary; in fact, every pixel of an image can have its own α, stored in a separate 'alpha channel'.

The main application of image averaging is noise removal. Every image acquired by a real sensor is afflicted to some degree by random noise. However, the level of noise present in the image can be reduced, provided that the scene is static and unchanging, by the averaging of multiple observations of that scene. This works because the noise distribution can be regarded as approximately symmetrical with a mean of zero. As a result, positive perturbations of a pixel's value by a given amount are just as likely as negative perturbations by the same amount, and there will be a tendency for the perturbations to cancel out when several noisy values are added. If the noise level in one image is σ_1, then it can be shown that the noise level in the average of n images will be approximately

$$\sigma_n = \frac{\sigma_1}{\sqrt{n}}. \tag{5.4}$$

Figure 5.16 shows a synthetic image with Gaussian random noise added, along with averages computed for five and twenty of these images. The noise amplitude in the averaged images is visibly less than in the original image. Listing 5.17 gives some Java code to compute an average of a set of images, supplied as an array of `BufferedImage` objects.

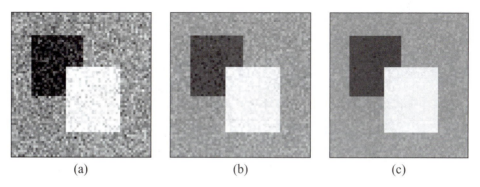

      (a)   (b)   (c)

Figure 5.16 Averaging of multiple observations. (a) Noisy synthetic image. (b) Average of five observations. (c) Average of twenty observations.

LISTING 5.17 Java code to average a set of images.

```
public static BufferedImage average(BufferedImage[] imgArray) {

  int n = imgArray.length;
  int w = imgArray[0].getWidth();    // assume that they all have
  int h = imgArray[0].getHeight();   // the same dimensions
  BufferedImage average =
   new BufferedImage(w, h, BufferedImage.TYPE_BYTE_GRAY);

  for (int y = 0; y < h; ++y)
    for (int x = 0; x < w; ++x) {
      float sum = 0.0f;
      for (int i = 0; i < n; ++i)
        sum += imgArray[i].getRaster().getSample(x, y, 0);
      raster.setSample(x, y, Math.round(sum/n));
    }

  return average;

}
```

Subtraction

Subtracting two 8-bit greyscale images can produce values between -255 and $+255$. This necessitates the use of 16-bit signed integers in the output image—unless sign is unimportant, in which case we can simply take the modulus of the result and store it using 8-bit integers:

$$g(x, y) = |f_1(x, y) - f_2(x, y)|. \tag{5.5}$$

The main application for image subtraction is in **change detection**. If we make two observations of a scene and compute their difference using Equation 5.5, then changes will be indicated by pixels in the difference image which have non-zero values. Sensor noise, slight changes in illumination and various other factors can result in small differences which are of no significance, so it is usual to apply a threshold to the difference image. Differences below this threshold are set to zero. Differences above the threshold can, if desired, be set to the maximum pixel value.

Figure 5.17 shows two frames from a video sequence of a person walking, plus the difference between the frames. The difference image has be thresholded and then inverted, so black pixels represent points in the image where change was detected.

(a)   (b)   (c)

Figure 5.17   Two frames from a video sequence and their difference.

Division

For division of images to produce meaningful results, floating-point arithmetic must be used. The ratio image can be of the floating-point type, or we can rescale and round pixel values to be in a more convenient 0–255 range.

This technique can be useful in remote sensing. Here, multispectral instruments aboard aircraft or satellites produce images that show the surface of the Earth[5] in several spectral bands. The ratio of one band to another can be computed. In a ratio image, the effects of illumination and surface topography on pixel intensity are reduced and the spectral contrasts caused by different surface materials are more prominent [31].

AND & OR

Logical AND and OR operations are useful for the masking and compositing of images. For example, if we compute the AND of a binary image with some other image, then pixels for which the corresponding value in the binary image is 1 will be preserved, but pixels for which the corresponding binary value is 0 will be set to 0 themselves. Thus the binary image acts as a 'mask' that removes information from certain parts of the image.

5.6   Further reading

Various image file formats are described in an encyclopaedic text by Murray and vanRyper [33]. A comparable web resource is the Graphics File Format Page at `http://www.dcs.ed.ac.uk/~mxr/gfx/index-hi.html`.

General issues relating to image display are given a thorough treatment by Glassner [17]. Zukowski [55] describes how images can be displayed using Java's AWT components. Knudsen [27] presents updated information on how instances of `BufferedImage` can be displayed. Eckstein, Loy and Wood [14] give details of Swing components; the sections dealing with `JLabel` and `JScrollPane` are perhaps the most relevant to image display.

---

[5] Or the surfaces of other planetary bodies.

Gomes and Velho [19] give a much more detailed account of digital halftoning techniques. The classic text is by Ulichney [47].

Further information on the applications of image subtraction and image division in remote sensing is given by Mather [31].

5.7 Exercises

1. Write a Java program that will

   (a) Display an image
   (b) Allow the user to select a region of interest (ROI)
   (c) Extract this ROI from the image
   (d) Write the ROI to a user-specified file

   (The easiest way of doing this is probably to modify the MeanROI application described in Section 5.5.1.)

2. Verify by experiment that adding a sequence of noisy observations of a static scene will reduce the noise level in the manner predicted by Equation 5.4.

   You can generate experimental data by writing a program that adds random noise of a given amplitude to an image. You should use a simple synthetic image similar to that in Figure 5.16 for this purpose. To measure noise levels, you will need to compute the standard deviation in grey level within a region of the image. (You could modify the routines in Listing 5.13 for this purpose.) You should try to define a relative homogeneous region in which to make measurements. (Why?)

3. Write a Java program that subtracts two images and thresholds the absolute value of the difference in grey level at each pixel. Test the program with images taken from a sequence of some kind and see if you can identify the limitations of this approach for the detection of change or motion.

Grey level and colour enhancement

This chapter describes various techniques for modifying pixel grey level and colour. These operations are sometimes referred to as 'point processes' because they recalculate the value of each pixel independently of all other pixels. We shall concentrate on the manipulation of grey level here; colour processing will be considered briefly at the end of the chapter.

6.1   Introduction

Some of the simplest, yet most useful, image processing operations involve the adjustment of brightness, contrast or colour in an image. A common reason for manipulating these attributes is the need to compensate for difficulties in image acquisition. For example, in images where an object of interest is backlit, that object can be underexposed almost to the point of being a silhouette. Without the aid of image processing, we might need to reacquire the image several times, adjusting the exposure each time until satisfactory results are obtained. With image processing, however, we can increase the overall brightness of the object of interest and magnify the tiny residual variations in contrast across it, thereby revealing enough detail to allow proper interpretation.

6.2 Grey level mapping

6.2.1 Linear mapping

We can adjust the overall brightness of a greyscale image simply by adding a constant bias, b, to pixel values:

$$g(x, y) = f(x, y) + b. \tag{6.1}$$

If $b > 0$, overall brightness is increased; if $b < 0$, it is decreased. Figure 6.1 shows an example of biasing pixel grey levels in this way. Similarly, we can adjust contrast in a greyscale image through multiplication of pixel values by a constant gain, a:

$$g(x, y) = af(x, y). \tag{6.2}$$

If $a > 1$, contrast is increased, whereas if $a < 1$ it is reduced. An example is given in Figure 6.2.

(a)   (b)

Figure 6.1 Image brightness modification. (a) A dark image. (b) Result of adding 150 to pixel values.

Equations 6.1 and 6.2 can be combined to give a general expression for brightness and contrast modification:

$$g(x, y) = af(x, y) + b. \tag{6.3}$$

Often, we do not want to specify a gain and a bias, but would rather map a particular range of grey levels, $[f_1, f_2]$, onto a new range, $[g_1, g_2]$. This form of mapping is accomplished using

$$g(x, y) = g_1 + \left(\frac{g_2 - g_1}{f_2 - f_1} \right) [f(x, y) - f_1]. \tag{6.4}$$

Figure 6.2 Result of multiplying pixel values of the image in Figure 6.1(a) by 2.5.

It is easy to show that Equations 6.3 and 6.4 are equivalent to a **linear mapping** of pixel grey level. This can be seen clearly if we plot output grey level versus input grey level, as in Figure 6.3(a). When dealing with 8-bit images, the mapping must produce values in the range 0–255. Consequently, a real mapping function may contain horizontal segments, as in Figure 6.3(b).

There are two special cases of linear mapping that are worthy of note. In the first, we increase the gain factor until two adjacent grey levels, f_1 and f_2, are mapped onto the

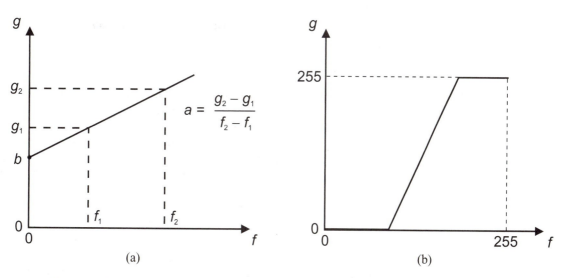

Figure 6.3 Linear grey level mapping. (a) Graphical representation of gain and bias. (b) Forcing output values to lie in a 0–255 range.

extremes of the 8-bit range (Figure 6.4(a)). Consequently, grey levels up to and including f_1 are mapped onto 0, whereas grey levels greater than f_1 are mapped onto 255. We can say that f_1 acts as a *threshold*. The mapping operation is then termed **thresholding**. Figure 6.4(b) shows the result of thresholding the image in Figure 6.2 at a level of 128.

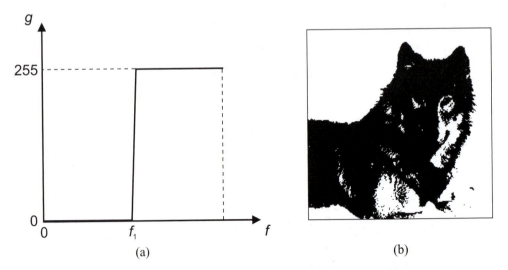

(a) (b)

Figure 6.4 Grey level thresholding. (a) Mapping function for a thresholding operation. (b) Result of thresholding the image of Figure 6.2 at a level of 128.

The second special case of linear mapping is where a, the gain factor applied to grey levels, is negative. Figure 6.5(a) plots the mapping function of Equation 6.2 for $a = -1$ and $b = 255$. Figure 6.5(b) shows the result of applying this mapping to the image of Figure 6.2. This operation is often described as **negation** or **inversion**.

Implementation in Java

It is a simple matter to write Java code that applies Equations 6.3 or 6.4 to an image. Examples appear in Listing 6.1. We follow the approach introduced in Chapter 5, whereby each operation is implemented as a static method. The first method (lines 1–12) implements Equation 6.3. It is overloaded with another version (lines 14–19) that implements Equation 6.4. This version merely computes a gain and a bias from the parameters f_1, f_2, g_1, g_2 of Equation 6.4 and then invokes the primary method to do the rescaling. Some other points to note are

- It is assumed that the input image is an 8-bit greyscale image.
- No validation of parameters f2 and f1 is carried out; there will be an ArithmeticException if they are equal.
- Both methods return a new image; however, we could equally perform the operation in place. This is possible because the remapping of grey level is a point process in which calculations at any pixel are independent of all other pixels.

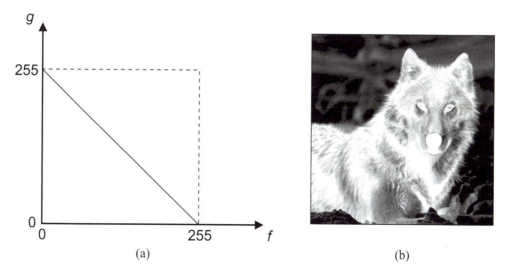

Figure 6.5 Image negation. (a) Mapping function for negation. (b) Negation of image in Figure 6.2.

LISTING 6.1 Java code to do linear rescaling of grey levels in an image.

```java
public static BufferedImage rescale(BufferedImage image, float gain, float bias) {
  int w = image.getWidth();
  int h = image.getHeight();
  BufferedImage rescaledImage =
   new BufferedImage(w, h, BufferedImage.TYPE_BYTE_GRAY);
  WritableRaster input = image.getRaster();
  WritableRaster output = rescaledImage.getRaster();
  for (int y = 0; y < h; ++y)
    for (int x = 0; x < w; ++x)
      output.setSample(x, y, 0, clamp(gain*input.getSample(x, y, 0) + bias));
  return rescaledImage;
}

public static BufferedImage rescale(BufferedImage image, int f1, int f2,
 int g1, int g2) {
  float gain = ((float)(g2 - g1)) / (f2 - f1);
  float bias = g1 - gain*f1;
  return rescale(image, gain, bias);
}


public static int clamp(float value) {
  return Math.min(Math.max(Math.round(value), 0), 255);
}
```

The Java2D API provides a limited range of built-in image processing operations. One of the operations is linear mapping using gain and bias parameters. The operation is implemented in the form of a class named `RescaleOp`. The constructors of `RescaleOp` are

```
public RescaleOp(float gain, float bias, RenderingHints hints)
public RescaleOp(float[] gain, float[] bias, RenderingHints hints)
```

The second constructor is used to create a `RescaleOp` for colour images; it expects an array of three gains and an array of three biases.

Using a `RescaleOp` is straightforward. For example, suppose we wish to brighten an image by a factor of two. This can be accomplished with two lines of code:

```
RescaleOp rescale = new RescaleOp(2.0f, 0, null);
BufferedImage newImage = rescale.filter(image, null);
```

If we already have an image of the correct dimensions and type, we can use it as the second parameter of `RescaleOp`'s `filter` method, instead of `null`. We can also do in-place processing by using the same image for both parameters:

```
RescaleOp rescale = new RescaleOp(2.0f, 0, null);
rescale.filter(image, image);
```

`RescaleOp`, in common with the other image processing operations supported in the Java2D API, implements the `BufferedImageOp` interface. Classes implementing this interface must define the following methods:

```
BufferedImage filter(BufferedImage src, BufferedImage dest)
BufferedImage createCompatibleDestImage(BufferedImage src,
 ColorModel model)
Rectangle2D getBounds2D(BufferedImage src)
Point2D getPoint2D(Point2D srcPoint, Point2D destPoint)
RenderingHints getRenderingHints()
```

The `filter()` method performs the image processing operation. The method `createCompatibleDestImage()` creates an image that is compatible with the given source image and colour model. If `model` is `null`, the colour model of the source image is used. The method `getBounds2D()` returns a `Rectangle2D` indicating how big the destination image would be if the given source image were to be processed. The method `getPoint2D()` specifies what happens to a given point in the source image. For operations which do not affect image geometry, such as those described in this chapter, the method should simply copy `srcPoint` to `destPoint`. The `getRenderingHints()` method returns the rendering hints associated with an operation. Rendering hints help Java's rendering engine to decide how it should display an image. This method can return `null` if there is no guidance to offer the rendering engine.

Writing image processing code as a class that implements the `BufferedImageOp` interface has two advantages. The first is consistency with the predefined operations provided with Java2D. The second benefit is polymorphism; if we create a class that implements this interface, it will automatically work with existing Java code that manipulates `BufferedImageOp` objects. We have already encountered one example of this: the version of `drawImage()` that takes a `BufferedImageOp` as a parameter and applies this operation to an image before drawing it (Section 5.3).

6.2.2   **Non-linear mapping**

We need not restrict ourselves to a linear mapping of grey levels. We may use any function, provided that it gives a one-to-one or many-to-one mapping of input grey level onto output grey level: in other words, the function must be *single-valued*. Figure 6.6 shows a mapping that does not satisfy this requirement, and therefore cannot be used for brightness and contrast modification.

Non-linear mapping functions have a useful property. The gain, a, applied to input grey levels—as measured by the slope of a tangent to the function—can vary. Thus the way in which contrast is modified depends on input grey level. This is illustrated by Figure 6.7, which plots a logarithmic mapping of input grey level onto output grey level. Two ranges of input grey level, Δf_1 and Δf_2, of equal width, are shown. Range Δf_1, which occurs at low grey levels, is mapped onto a *wider* range, Δg_1: thus, contrast is *increased*. However, at the high end of the scale, $\Delta g_2 < \Delta f_2$—so contrast is *reduced* here.

In general, logarithmic mapping is useful if we wish to enhance detail in the darker regions of the image, at the expense of detail in the brighter regions. Figure 6.8 shows a poorly exposed image of a car, whose number plate is difficult to read. It also shows the results of logarithmic and linear mapping applied to that image. Both operations have made

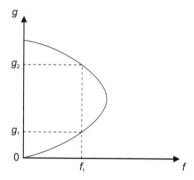

Figure 6.6   An inappropriate function for grey level mapping. Does f_1 map onto g_1 or g_2?

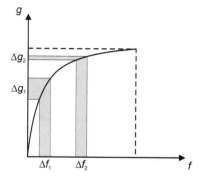

Figure 6.7   A logarithmic mapping function.

Figure 6.8 Example of logarithmic mapping. Top: an underexposed image. Bottom left: result of logarithmic mapping, making the number plate readable. Bottom right: an attempt to achieve similar results with linear mapping.

the number plate readable, but the logarithmic mapping has been less detrimental to the other parts of the image.

An exponential mapping of grey level can also be useful. Here, the effect is the reverse of that obtained with logarithmic mapping; contrast in the brighter parts of an image is increased at the expense of contrast in the darker parts. We can see this in Figure 6.9, where $\Delta g_1 < \Delta f_1$ and $\Delta g_2 > \Delta f_2$.

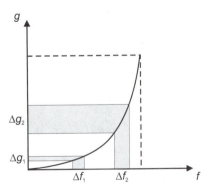

Figure 6.9 An exponential mapping function.

6.2.3   Efficient implementation of mapping

Let us suppose that we wished to carry out a non-linear transformation of grey levels using a square-root function. Algorithm 6.1 shows how we might perform this task for an image quantised using b bits per pixel. Square roots are scaled so that the operation maps zero onto zero and the maximum grey level onto itself. For an image of dimensions $N \times N$, the algorithm performs N^2 multiplications and N^2 square-root calculations. The latter, in particular, are very time-consuming.

ALGORITHM 6.1   An inefficient method for grey level mapping.

Define a scaling factor $a = \sqrt{2^b - 1}$
for all pixel coordinates, x and y, **do**
    $g(x, y) = a\sqrt{f(x, y)}$
end for

For many image types, the approach adopted by Algorithm 6.1 is grossly inefficient. In the case of 8-bit images, there are only 256 possible grey levels, and hence just 256 possible mappings. It makes little sense, therefore, to calculate the mapping many thousands, or even millions, of times; instead, we can perform the calculations 256 times, once for each possible grey level, and store the results in a **look-up table** (LUT). We can then cycle through all the image pixels and carry out the mapping simply by looking up the appropriate result in the table. Algorithm 6.2 demonstrates this new approach.

ALGORITHM 6.2   Efficient grey level mapping using a look-up table.

Define a scaling factor $a = \sqrt{2^b - 1}$
Create an array *table* with space for 2^b elements
for all grey levels, i, **do**
    $table[i] = a\sqrt{i}$
end for
for all pixel coordinates, x and y, **do**
    $g(x, y) = table[f(x, y)]$
end for

We can do some experiments to measure the performance of these two algorithms in real Java programs. Timing can be done using the `currentTimeMillis()` method of the standard `System` class. This method returns the current time in milliseconds since midnight on 1 January 1970. To measure the approximate[1] execution time of a piece of code, we can precede and follow that piece of code with calls to `System.currentTimeMillis()` and compute the difference between the two numbers that are returned. We have created

---

[1]   Timing done this way is approximate because it measures total system time, not the amount of CPU time devoted to this one program.

a class called `IntervalTimer`, available in the `com.pearsoneduc.ip.util` package on the CD, to make this task even easier. Timing a piece of code is as simple as this:

```
IntervalTimer timer = new IntervalTimer();
timer.start();
// some code to be timed
System.out.println(timer.elapsed());   // doesn't stop the clock
// more code to be timed
Sytem.out.println(timer.stop());       // stops clock
```

The program `MapTest1` on the CD uses an `IntervalTimer` to measure the performance of both the direct calculation and LUT approaches to the remapping of grey levels using a square-root function. The program simulates processing of an $N \times N$-pixel image. The value of N is specified as a command line parameter. The image itself is simulated using an array of integers. Some results from this program are plotted in Figure 6.10. These were generated on a 266 MHz Pentium II machine running Windows 95 and JDK 1.2 with just-in-time (JIT) compilation enabled. (Turning JIT compilation off increases all times by a factor of ten or more.)

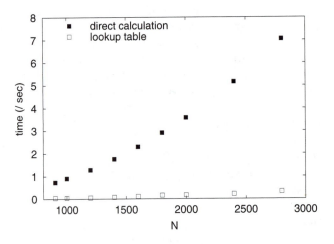

Figure 6.10   Performance of direct calculation and LUT techniques.

The significant improvement in performance that we see when using Algorithm 6.2 occurs because the number of grey levels is much less than the number of pixels being processed, and because the process of table look-up (which, in practice, merely involves accessing an array element) is very much faster than calling a maths library function to calculate a square root. In general, for an $N \times N \times b$-bit image, LUTs are worth using if

$$2^b \ll N^2. \tag{6.5}$$

Essentially, Figure 6.10 compares repeated invocation of a maths library function with the look-up of values in an array. A more realistic performance assessment would involve the use of real `BufferedImage` objects. The program `MapTest2` does this. Results from this program, using the same hardware as before, are summarised in Figure 6.11. The performance gain from using a LUT is not so pronounced with real images, being masked somewhat by the overhead of manipulating BufferedImage objects—but we can still reduce execution times by at least a factor of two if we use a LUT to map grey levels.

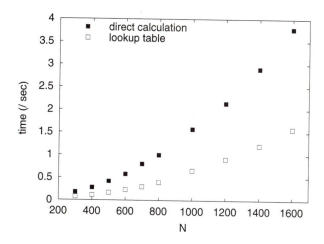

Figure 6.11 Comparison of direct calculation and LUT techniques applied to real images.

Java classes to perform look-up table operations

The Java2D API provides a LookupOp class, implementing the BufferedImageOp interface as discussed in Section 6.2.1. LookupOp objects are constructed as follows:

```
public LookupOp(LookupTable table, RenderingHints hints)
```

LookupTable is an abstract base class used to represent LUTs. LookupOp objects require an instance of one of LookupTable's subclasses: ByteLookupTable or ShortLookupTable from the java.awt.image package. We can pass in null for the RenderingHints parameter.

The following code fragment shows how we can invert an image using ByteLookupTable and LookupOp:

```
byte[] table = new byte[256];
for (int i = 0; i < 256; ++i)
  table[i] = (byte)(255-i);
ByteLookupTable invertTable = new ByteLookupTable(0, table);
LookupOp invertOp = new LookupOp(invertTable, null);
BufferedImage invertedImage = invertOp.filter(image, null);
```

Similar code can be used to threshold an image, apply a non-linear mapping, etc. In each case, the procedure is the same; we set up an array of bytes containing the LUT data, create an instance of ByteLookupTable from these data, create an instance of LookupOp using the ByteLookupTable and then, finally, invoke the filter method of LookupOp to process the image. We can simplify the application of a LookupOp to an image if we develop a class that carries out this common set of tasks. This class can then be extended by subclasses that generate the LUT entries appropriate to particular shapes of mapping function—e.g., linear, square-root, logarithmic, etc.

Figure 6.12 shows the design for a class GreyMapOp that supports grey level mapping operations using look-up tables. The basis for GreyMapOp (and, indeed, for many of the image processing classes described in subsequent chapters) is StandardGreyOp. This class implements the BufferedImageOp interface, thereby providing the basic methods to process an 8-bit greyscale image. The implementations of getBounds2D() and getPoint2D() assume that the operation does not affect the geometry of the image. The implementation of the filter() method merely copies the input image; subclasses must override this method if they are to change the image in any way. StandardGreyOp provides one additional method, checkImage(), which can be called from within the filter() method of a subclass to test whether the input image is suitable for processing. The checkImage() method throws an ImagingOpException if the input image is not of type BufferedImage.TYPE_BYTE_GRAY. Listing 6.2 shows the implementation of the class.

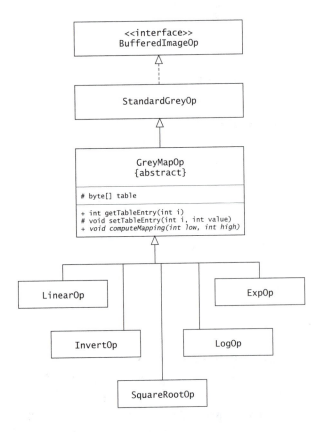

Figure 6.12 UML diagram showing relationships between classes that perform grey level mapping of images.

LISTING 6.2 A Java class to support processing of 8-bit greyscale images.

```java
package com.pearsoneduc.ip.op;

import java.awt.RenderingHints;
import java.awt.geom.*;
import java.awt.image.*;

public class StandardGreyOp implements BufferedImageOp {

  public BufferedImage filter(BufferedImage src, BufferedImage dest) {
    checkImage(src);
    if (dest == null)
      dest = createCompatibleDestImage(src, null);
    WritableRaster raster = dest.getRaster();
    src.copyData(raster);
    return dest;
  }

  public BufferedImage createCompatibleDestImage(BufferedImage src,
   ColorModel destModel) {
    if (destModel == null)
      destModel = src.getColorModel();
    int width = src.getWidth();
    int height = src.getHeight();
    BufferedImage image = new BufferedImage(destModel,
     destModel.createCompatibleWritableRaster(width, height),
     destModel.isAlphaPremultiplied(), null);
    return image;
  }

  public Rectangle2D getBounds2D(BufferedImage src) {
    return src.getRaster().getBounds();
  }

  public Point2D getPoint2D(Point2D srcPoint, Point2D destPoint) {
    if (destPoint == null)
      destPoint = new Point2D.Float();
    destPoint.setLocation(srcPoint.getX(), srcPoint.getY());
    return destPoint;
  }

  public RenderingHints getRenderingHints() {
    return null;
  }

  public void checkImage(BufferedImage src) {
    if (src.getType() != BufferedImage.TYPE_BYTE_GRAY)
      throw new ImagingOpException("operation requires an 8-bit grey image");
  }

}
```

GreyMapOp extends StandardGreyOp, adding an array of bytes to hold LUT data and providing methods to retrieve and modify LUT entries. It also overrides filter() with an implementation that applies the stored LUT to an image. However, it cannot generate entries for the LUT. The method which does this, computeMapping(), is abstract. We therefore cannot create instances of GreyMapOp. To perform a specific operation, we must define a subclass of GreyMapOp that implements the computeMapping() method. The method takes two parameters, both integers, representing the lower and upper limits of the mapping. Grey levels at or below the lower limit should be mapped onto 0 and grey levels at or above the upper limit should be mapped onto 255. An implementation of the method needs access to the LUT itself, so the array of bytes is a protected instance variable of

LISTING 6.3 A Java class to perform mapping of grey levels in an image.

```
1    package com.pearsoneduc.ip.op;
2
3    import java.awt.image.*;
4
5    public abstract class GreyMapOp implements BufferedImageOp {
6
7      protected byte[] table = new byte[256];
8
9      public int getTableEntry(int i) {
10       if (table[i] < 0)
11         return 256 + (int) table[i];
12       else
13         return (int) table[i];
14     }
15
16     protected void setTableEntry(int i, int value) {
17       if (value < 0)
18         table[i] = (byte) 0;
19       else if (value > 255)
20         table[i] = (byte) 255;
21       else
22         table[i] = (byte) value;
23     }
24
25     public void computeMapping() {
26       computeMapping(0, 255);
27     }
28
29     public abstract void computeMapping(int low, int high);
30
31     public BufferedImage filter(BufferedImage src, BufferedImage dest) {
32       checkImage(src);
33       if (dest == null)
34         dest = createCompatibleDestImage(src, null);
35       LookupOp operation = new LookupOp(new ByteLookupTable(0, table), null);
36       operation.filter(src, dest);
37       return dest;
38     }
39
40   }
```

GreyMapOp (as indicated by the # to its left in Figure 6.12). For convenience, LUT entries can also be modified by the setTableEntry() method, which clamps values to a 0–255 range. This is also protected. Listing 6.3 shows the implementation of GreyMapOp.

Figure 6.12 shows five subclasses which implement the different shapes of mapping function described thus far in this chapter. Listing 6.4 shows the implementation of one of these subclasses, LinearOp. All of the classes shown in Figure 6.12 are part of the com.pearsoneduc.ip.op package, available on the CD.

LISTING 6.4 A subclass of **GreyMapOp** that applies a linear grey level mapping function to an image.

```
1   package com.pearsoneduc.ip.op;
2
3
4   public class LinearOp extends GreyMapOp {
5
6     public LinearOp() {
7       computeMapping();
8     }
9
10    public LinearOp(int low, int high) {
11      computeMapping(low, high);
12    }
13
14    public void computeMapping(int low, int high) {
15      if (low < 0 || high > 255 || low >= high)
16        throw new java.awt.image.ImagingOpException("invalid mapping limits");
17      float scaling = 255.0f / (high - low);
18      for (int i = 0; i < 256; ++i)
19        setTableEntry(i, Math.round(scaling*(i - low)));
20    }
21
22  }
```

Grey level mapping applications

GreyMapOp and its subclasses are used in two grey level mapping applications supplied on the CD. The first application, called GreyMap, has a command line interface. It takes filenames for the input image and output image as the first two command line arguments, followed by a string to indicate which operation must be performed, and (optionally) lower and upper limits that will be mapped onto 0 and 255, respectively. If lower and upper limits are not specified, the program scans the input image to find the minimum and maximum grey levels, and uses these as the lower and upper limits. For example, to linearly 'stretch' the range of grey levels in an image, such that the minimum and maximum become 0 and 255, we would simply enter

```
java GreyMap in.jpg out.jpg linear
```

Alternatively, to perform a logarithmic mapping of [10, 220] onto [0, 255], we would type

```
java GreyMap in.jpg out.jpg log 10 220
```

It is sufficient to enter the first few letters of the operation name: `lin` for linear mapping, `inv` for inverted linear, `sq` for square-root, `log` for logarithmic and `exp` for exponential.

The second application, `GreyMapTool`, is an interactive version of `GreyMap`. It presents the user with an interface in which an image is displayed and different grey level mapping operations can be selected and applied to that image. The mapping function is plotted and the lower and upper limits can be adjusted with sliders. Figure 6.13 shows this program in action.

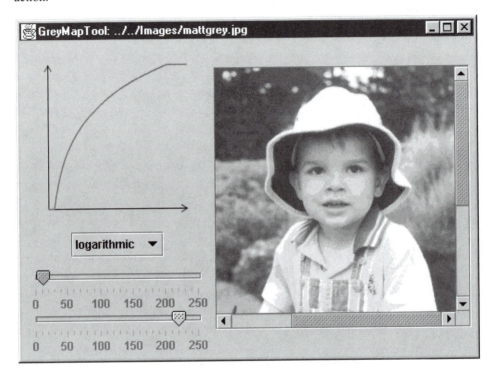

Figure 6.13   An interactive grey level mapping tool.

6.3   Image histograms

The **histogram** of an image records the frequency distribution of grey levels in that image. The histogram of an 8-bit image, for example, can be thought of as a table with 256 entries, or 'bins', indexed from 0 to 255. In bin 0 we record the number of times a grey level of 0 occurs; in bin 1 we record the number of times a grey level of 1 occurs; and so on, up to bin 255. Algorithm 6.3 shows how we can accumulate a histogram from image data. Figure 6.14 shows an image and its histogram computed using this algorithm.

Closely related to the histogram of an image is its **cumulative histogram**, which records the cumulative frequency distribution of grey levels in an image. The cumulative frequency

ALGORITHM 6.3 Calculation of an image histogram.

Create an array *histogram* with 2^b elements
for all grey levels, i, **do**
    histogram$[i] = 0$
end for
for all pixel coordinates, x and y, **do**
    Increment *histogram*$[f(x, y)]$ by 1
end for

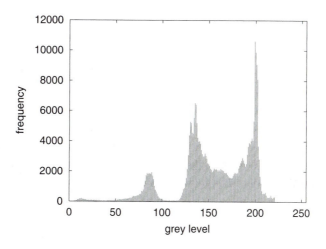

Figure 6.14 An image and its histogram.

of a grey level, i, is the number of times that a grey level less than or equal to i occurs in an image. Cumulative frequencies, c_i, are computed from histogram counts, h_i, using

$$c_j = \sum_{i=0}^{j} h_i.$$ (6.6)

Figure 6.15 plots the cumulative frequency distribution for grey levels in the image of Figure 6.14.

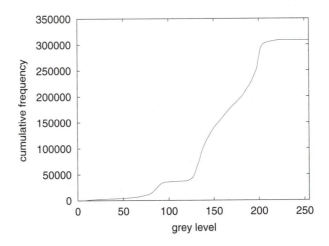

Figure 6.15   Cumulative histogram of the image in Figure 6.14.

We can normalise a histogram by dividing the counts in each bin by the total number of pixels in the image associated with that histogram. This gives us a table of estimated *probabilities*. The entry for any grey level tells us the likelihood of finding that grey level at a pixel selected randomly from the image. Similarly, a normalised cumulative histogram is a table of cumulative probabilities. Here, bin i stores the probability of encountering a pixel grey level less than or equal to i at a randomly selected pixel. Ordinarily, it is sufficient to work with raw frequencies in a histogram. However, probabilities should be used when comparing the histograms of images with different sizes.

The histogram of an image provides a useful indication of the relative importance of different grey levels in an image; indeed, it is sometimes possible to determine whether brightness or contrast adjustment is necessary merely by examining the histogram, and not the image itself. However, we must be wary of overinterpreting histograms. Consider, for example, the histogram of Figure 6.14. There are three distinctive features to be seen: a small peak between 50 and 100; a larger peak between 100 and 150; and an even larger narrow peak close to 200. On examining the image from which this histogram was computed, we see an apparent correspondence between the first peak and the body of the aircraft. Similarly, it appears that the second and third peaks correspond to the sky and the clouds, respectively. However, correspondences between image features and histogram features applies to particular images and *not* to images in general. This is evident from Figure 6.16,

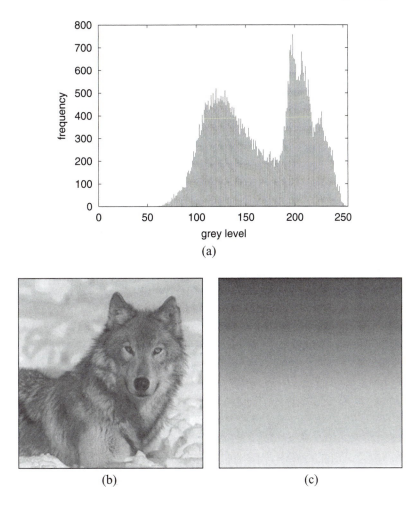

Figure 6.16 Non-uniqueness of a histogram. (a) A histogram. (b) An image with (a) as its histogram. (c) A different image, also with (a) as its histogram.

which shows two very different images that have identical histograms. Although a histogram gives us the frequency distribution of grey levels in an image, it can tell us nothing about the way in which grey levels are distributed spatially.

Grey level mapping operations affect the histogram of an image in predictable ways. For example, adding a constant bias to grey levels will shift a histogram along the grey level axis without changing its shape. Multiplication of grey levels by a constant gain will spread out the histogram evenly if $a > 1$, increasing the spacing between occupied bins, or compress it if $a < 1$, which can have the effect of merging bins. A non-linear mapping of grey levels will stretch some parts of the histogram whilst compressing other parts. This can be seen in Figure 6.17, which plots histograms for the dark car image of Figure 6.8 and the logarithmically-enhanced version of that image.

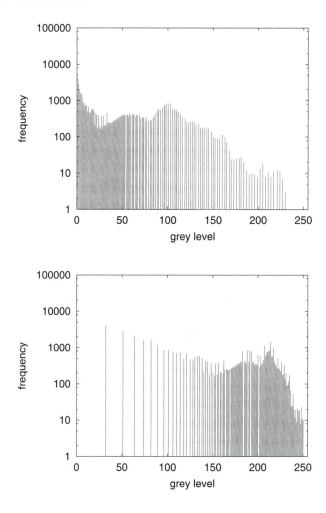

Figure 6.17 Effects of grey level mapping on a histogram. (a) Histogram of original image from Figure 6.8. (b) Histogram of logarithmically-enhanced image.

6.3.1 Computing histograms in Java

The Java2D API does not provide a histogram class; however, it is a simple matter to devise our own. Our basic requirement is for a class that implements Algorithm 6.3. It should also compute cumulative frequencies, using Equation 6.6. It would be useful if the class could handle colour images as well as greyscale images. (This is easily done; we simply need to create three separate histograms—one for the red channel, one for green and one for blue.) Another useful feature would be some form of input/output capability, allowing histogram data to be read from and written to streams.

The `Histogram` class, available on the CD as part of the `com.pearsoneduc.ip.op` package, satisfies these requirements. Selected methods from this class are listed in

Table 6.1   Selected methods of the `Histogram` class.

Method	Description
`Histogram()`	Constructs an empty histogram.
`Histogram(Reader src)`	Constructs a histogram by reading data from the specified source.
`Histogram(BufferedImage img)`	Constructs a histogram from the specified image.
`Object clone()`	Returns a copy of this histogram.
`boolean equals(Object otherHist)`	Compares this histogram with another.
`void computeHistogram(BufferedImage img)`	Computes a histogram of the specified image.
`void read(Reader src)`	Reads histogram data from the specified source.
`void write(Writer dest)`	Writes histogram frequencies to the specified destination.
`void writeCumulative(Writer dest)`	Writes cumulative frequency data to the specified destination.
`boolean sourceIsGrey()`	Indicates whether the data source for this histogram was a greyscale image or not.
`int getNumBands()`	Returns number of bands in histogram: 1 for greyscale images, 3 for colour images.
`int getNumSamples()`	Returns number of samples in histogram, equivalent to the number of pixels in the source image.
`int getFrequency(int value)`	Returns the frequency of occurrence of the specified value.
`int getCumulativeFrequency(int value)`	Returns cumulative frequency for the specified value.
`int getMinFrequency()`	Returns smallest frequency recorded in histogram.
`int getMaxFrequency()`	Returns largest frequency recorded in histogram.
`int getMinValue()`	Returns minimum value for which counts have been recorded.
`int getMaxValue()`	Returns maximum value for which counts have been recorded.
`double getMeanValue()`	Returns mean value of this histogram.

Table 6.1. (This list is not exhaustive; for many of the 'get' methods, there are two versions—one for colour images, in which the band has to be specified as the integer 0, 1 or 2, and one for greyscale images. The table lists only the greyscale version.)

The `Histogram` class forms the basis of two applications included on the CD: `CalcHist` and `HistogramTool`. `CalcHist` accepts two or three command line arguments. The first is the filename of an image; the second is an output filename for the histogram of that image; the third, which is optional, is an output filename for the cumulative histogram of that image. The output data files have a simple text-based format, consisting of a single comment line

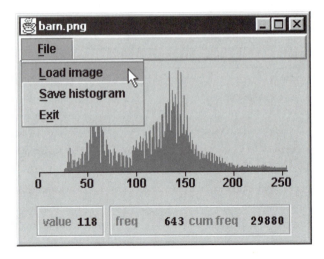

Figure 6.18 The `HistogramTool` application.

(beginning with #) followed by frequency or cumulative frequency data, one value per line. If the image is a colour image, three columns of data are written, corresponding to frequencies (or cumulative frequencies) in the red, green and blue bands of the image.

The `HistogramTool` application is an interactive tool for the display and interrogation of histograms. It can be executed with or without an image filename as a command line argument. A menu is provided, from which you can load a new image from a file, save the histogram data to a file or exit the program. As the cursor is moved over the histogram, an information panel is updated with the grey level, frequency and cumulative frequency at the current cursor position. The program can handle both greyscale and colour images. In the case of colour images, a tabbed display is created, allowing the view to be switched between the red, green and blue bands. Figure 6.18 shows the program in action.

6.4   Histogram equalisation

We can use the histogram of an image to define a non-linear mapping of grey levels, specific to that image, that will yield an optimal improvement in contrast. This technique, known as **histogram equalisation**, redistributes grey levels in an attempt to flatten the frequency distribution. More grey levels are allocated where there are most pixels, fewer grey levels where there are fewer pixels. This tends to increase contrast in the most heavily populated regions of the histogram, and often reveals previously hidden detail.

If we are to increase contrast for the most frequently occurring grey levels and reduce contrast in the less popular part of the grey level range, then we need a mapping function which has a steep slope ($a > 1$) at grey levels that occur frequently, and a gentle slope ($a < 1$) at unpopular grey levels. The cumulative histogram of the image has these properties, as a comparison of Figures 6.14 and 6.15 demonstrates. Indeed, the mapping function we need is obtained simply by rescaling the cumulative histogram so that its values lie in the range 0–255. Algorithm 6.4 shows how this works in practice. From the histogram of the image, we determine the cumulative histogram, c, rescaling the values as we go so that they occupy an 8-bit range. In this way, c becomes a look-up table that can be subsequently applied to the image in order to carry out equalisation.

ALGORITHM 6.4 Histogram equalisation.

Compute a scaling factor, $\alpha = 255$ / number of pixels
Calculate histogram using Algorithm 6.3
$c[0] = \alpha * histogram[0]$
for all remaining grey levels, i, **do**
  $c[i] = c[i-1] + \alpha * histogram[i]$
end for
for all pixel coordinates, x and y, **do**
  $g(x, y) = c[f(x, y)]$
end for

Figures 6.19 and 6.20 show an image and its histogram, before and after equalisation, respectively. The operation has clearly had a significant effect on contrast, yet flattening of the histogram seems not to have been achieved. Why is this?

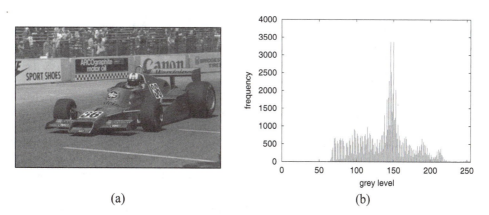

(a)　　　　　　　　　　　　　　　　(b)

Figure 6.19 (a) An unequalised image. (b) Its histogram.

A flat histogram for an $N \times N$, 8-bit image would need to have $N^2/256$ counts in each bin. Adjacent bins in the input histogram which have fewer than $N^2/256$ counts are amalgamated into a single output bin, thereby leaving some bins in the output histogram unoccupied. If we could split bins whose counts were too high into smaller bins to fill these spaces, then the histogram would be literally flattened. However, if we did this, it would no longer be possible to implement equalisation as a straightforward grey level mapping operation using a look-up table. What happens instead is that the gaps between occupied bins vary in size, there being less crowding in the vicinity of bins containing high counts.

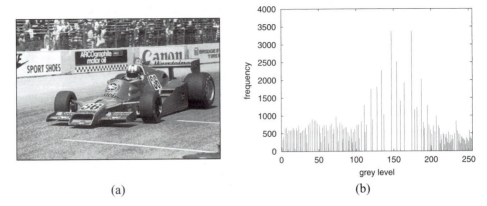

(a)   (b)

Figure 6.20 (a) An equalised image. (b) Its histogram.

This ensures that the cumulative frequency distribution approximates the ideal straight line as closely as possible (Figure 6.21). Thus, rather than saying that equalisation flattens a histogram, it is more accurate to say that it linearises or straightens the cumulative frequency distribution.

A more sophisticated implementation of histogram equalisation might split a single input grey level into several output grey levels, but we would then need some means of choosing one of these output levels. One approach is to make a random selection; another is to select for a pixel the grey level that is most consistent with neighbouring grey levels. The added complexity of these techniques means that they are rarely applied.

Histogram equalisation is used widely in image processing—mainly because it is a completely automatic technique, with no parameters to set. At times, it can improve our ability to interpret an image dramatically. However, it is difficult to predict how beneficial equalisation will be for any given image; in fact, it may not be of any use at all. This is because the improvement in contrast is optimal *statistically*, rather than perceptually. In images with narrow histograms and relatively few grey levels, a massive increase in contrast due to histogram equalisation can have the adverse effect of reducing perceived image quality. In particular, sampling or quantisation artefacts and image noise may become more prominent.

Histogram equalisation becomes **histogram specification** if, instead of requiring a flat histogram, we specify a particular shape explicitly. We might wish to do this in cases where it is desirable for a set of related images to have the same histogram—in order, perhaps, that a particular operation produces the same results for all images.

Histogram specification can be visualised as a two-stage process. First, we transform the input image by equalisation into a temporary image with a flat histogram. Then we transform this equalised, temporary image into an output image possessing the desired histogram. The mapping function for the second stage is easily obtained. Since a rescaled version of the cumulative histogram can be used to transform a histogram with any shape into a flat histogram, it follows that the *inverse* of the cumulative histogram will perform the inverse transformation from a flat histogram to one with a specified shape.

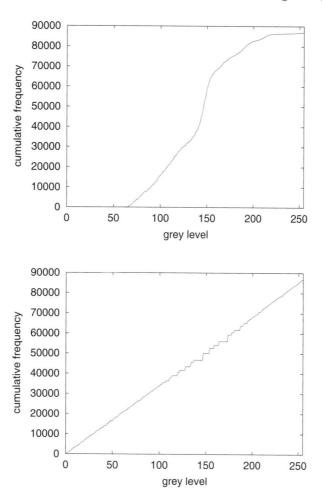

Figure 6.21 Top: cumulative histogram of the unequalised image in Figure 6.19. Bottom: cumulative histogram of the equalised image in Figure 6.20.

6.4.1 Histogram equalisation in Java

Implementing histogram equalisation in Java is trivial if we make use of the classes that we have already developed. Since the operation is performed using a look-up table, we can implement it as a class `EqualiseOp` that extends `GreyMapOp`. All we need to do is add the code that computes look-up table entries. For this, we use the `Histogram` class, which provides us with the cumulative frequency data that are required. Listing 6.5 shows our implementation. Note that the class *must* implement the method `computeMapping()`—even though, in this case, the task that it performs is meaningless.

The following fragment of code shows how we carry out histogram equalisation on a `BufferedImage` using `EqualiseOp`:

LISTING 6.5 A subclass of `GreyMapOp` that performs histogram equalisation.

```
 1    package com.pearsoneduc.ip.op;
 2
 3
 4    public class EqualiseOp extends GreyMapOp {
 5
 6      public EqualiseOp(Histogram hist) throws HistogramException {
 7        float scale = 255.0f / hist.getNumSamples();
 8        for (int i = 0; i < 256; ++i)
 9          table[i] = (byte) Math.round(scale*hist.getCumulativeFrequency(i));
10      }
11
12      public void computeMapping(int low, int high) {
13        // Does nothing - limits are meaningless in histogram equalisation
14      }
15
16    }
```

```
Histogram histogram = new Histogram(image);
EqualiseOp equalise = new EqualiseOp(histogram);
BufferedImage equalisedImage = equalise.filter(image, null);
```

6.5   Colour processing

So far, we have considered how brightness and contrast can be manipulated in greyscale images. But what about colour images? We have already seen that pixel values in a colour image are vectors, typically with three components. These components usually represent the proportions of red, green and blue that make up a colour. Faced with the task of enhancing contrast in such an image, we might be tempted to perform an operation such as histogram equalisation on each of the three components separately. However, if we do this, the intensity distribution of each component is altered in a different way, with the result that both contrast and colour are changed (Plate A). This is probably not what we require.

The problem arises because each component of the RGB model contains both colour and intensity information. If we wish to manipulate colour and intensity independently, we must use a colour model that decouples these attributes. In this respect, the HSI model (Section 3.4.2) is ideal. To manipulate properly the brightness or contrast of an RGB image, we must apply a transformation from RGB space to HSI space, modify the I (intensity) component, then apply the inverse transformation from HSI space to RGB space. Plate A shows histogram equalisation applied to the I component of a colour image; the resulting image has improved contrast and an unchanged balance of colour.

We can achieve other effects by adjusting the H (hue) and S (saturation) components. Plate B shows the effect of a uniform reduction in the hue component at each pixel of the butterfly image in Plate A. (This can be visualised as a $60°$ rotation about the I axis in HSI space.) We can also modify hue selectively—in order to transform red into green without affecting other colours, for example.

Plate C shows the effect of changing the saturation of each pixel in the butterfly image. Increasing saturation increases the apparent purity or 'richness' of the colours in the image; decreasing saturation gives the image a 'washed out', almost grey appearance.

6.5.1 Histograms of colour images

When given the task of computing the histogram of a colour image, our `Histogram` class will, like most image processing software, give us three separate, one-dimensional histograms: one for the R component, one for the G component and one for the B component. Figure 6.22 plots these histograms for the butterfly image of Plate A. It is important to realise, however, that the true histogram of a colour image is *three-dimensional*. We must imagine the RGB colour cube divided up into bins, giving a $256 \times 256 \times 256$ array. There is thus a bin for every possible colour in 24-bit RGB image. The bin at $(0, 0, 0)$ records the number of black pixels in the image; the bin at $(255, 0, 0)$ records the number of pure red pixels in the image; and so on. The three histograms in Figure 6.22 are projections of this 3D histogram onto the R, G and B axes, respectively. Algorithm 6.5 shows how a colour histogram can be computed.

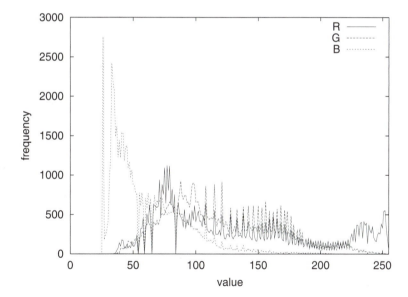

Figure 6.22 Histograms of the R, G and B components of the butterfly image.

One reason for preferring histograms of each component to a single histogram created by Algorithm 6.5 is that the latter demands a great deal of storage space. When $b = 8$, for instance, the array has dimensions $2^8 \times 2^8 \times 2^8$, giving over 16 million bins. If a 32-bit integer is used for bin counts, the total storage requirement for a single colour histogram

ALGORITHM 6.5 Calculation of a colour image histogram.

Create a 3D array *histogram* of dimensions $2^b \times 2^b \times 2^b$
for all red values, r, **do**
  for all green values, g, **do**
    for all blue values, b, **do**
      histogram$[r][g][b] = 0$
    end for
  end for
end for
for all pixel coordinates, x and y, **do**
  Find r, the red component of $f(x, y)$
  Find g, the green component of $f(x, y)$
  Find b, the blue component of $f(x, y)$
  Increment *histogram*$[r][g][b]$ by 1
end for

is a staggering 64 megabytes! However, this type of histogram will invariably be very sparsely populated, so we can reduce storage requirements greatly if we choose a different representation for the histogram that exploits this sparseness[2].

Another disadvantage is that it is difficult to visualise how any quantity varies in a three-dimensional space. As a compromise, we can compute *two-dimensional* histograms, which are much easier to visualise. These can be calculated for R and G, R and B or G and B. The R-G histogram can be thought of as the projection of the 3D histogram onto the $B = 0$ plane. Similar interpretations can be made of the other 2D histograms. The storage requirements for 2D histograms are far more manageable than those of 3D histograms, and they contain more information than a set of one-dimensional histograms. This can be seen in Figure 6.23, which plots the three 2D histograms of the butterfly image. These plots show correlations between the colour components that would not be evident in one-dimensional histograms.

6.6 Further reading

Gonzalez and Woods [20] give a more detailed description of the histogram specification technique.

Adaptive contrast enhancement is discussed by Gonzalez and Woods [20] and by Umbaugh [48]. In this technique each pixel's grey level is mapped to a new value by means of Equation 6.3, the parameters of this mapping being determined from local image statistics.

Lyon [29] describes an adaptive histogram equalisation technique and present a Java implementation of it.

---

[2] A hash table would be a suitable representation.

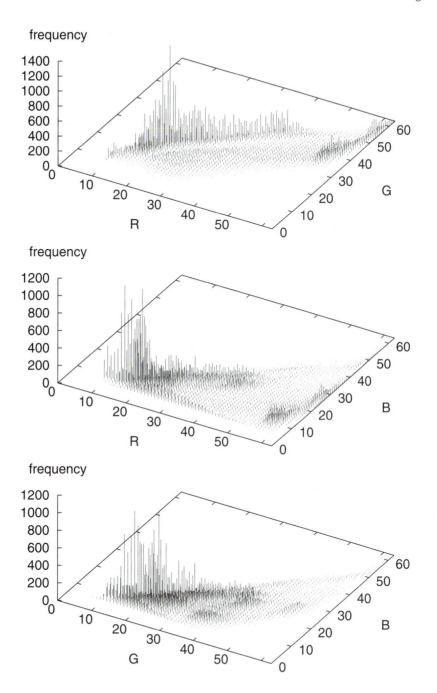

Figure 6.23 Two-dimensional histograms for the butterfly image. (The image was re-quantised to 6 bits per colour component, as this makes the plots somewhat clearer.)

6.7   Exercises

1. Under what circumstances is a grey level mapping reversible? Under what circumstances is the mapping non-reversible?

2. Suppose that we have an image 1000 pixels wide and 1000 pixels high. The image is quantised using 8 bits per pixel, and the full range of grey levels is already in use. A logarithmic mapping of grey level is proposed to improve the appearance of this image. Assuming that the cost of accessing an array element is negligible compared with the cost of calling a logarithm function from the maths library, how much faster is it to use a look-up table than to calculate the mapping pixel by pixel?

   Now suppose that we have a $200 \times 200 \times 16$ bit image. Does the same hold true for this image?

3. An 8-bit image has a minimum grey level of 30 and a maximum grey level of 100. Describe carefully the effect on this image's *histogram* of

   (a) Subtraction of 50 from all pixel grey levels
   (b) Exponential mapping of grey level onto the range 0–255
   (c) Histogram equalisation

4. Modify the code of Listing 6.1 so that an input image and an output image are passed in as method parameters. If `null` is passed in for the output image, the methods should do in-place processing of the input image, rather than creating a new object in which to store the new data.

5. Extend `GreyMapOp` in the `com.pearsoneduc.ip.op` package to create a new class, `PowerLawOp`. This should apply a power-law mapping of grey level, with the power being specified as the sole parameter of the constructor. Then reimplement `SquareRootOp` from `com.pearsoneduc.ip.op` as a simple extension of the `PowerLawOp` class.

6. Create an application similar to `GreyMapTool` in which the mapping applied to an image can be edited using the mouse. The mapping should be shown as a curve or a series of straight line segments. It should be possible to click on points defined on the curve or at the ends of the line segments and drag them to change the shape of the mapping.

Neighbourhood operations

This chapter deals with operations in which the new value calculated for a pixel depends not only on that pixel's original value but also on the values of surrounding pixels. These neighbourhood operations have many applications, including the blurring or sharpening of images, noise reduction and the detection of edges or other features of interest.

7.1   Introduction

A single pixel considered in isolation conveys information on the intensity and possibly the colour at a single location in an image, but it can tell us nothing about the way in which these properties vary spatially. It follows that the point processes described in the preceding chapter, which change a pixel's value independently of all other pixels, cannot be used to investigate or control spatial variations in image intensity or colour. For this, we need to perform calculations over *areas* of an image; in other words, a pixel's new value must be computed from its old value *and* the values of pixels in its vicinity. These **neighbourhood operations** are invariably more costly than simple point processes, but they allow us to achieve a whole range of interesting and useful effects.

In this chapter, we consider two classes of neighbourhood operation: one in which a pixel's new value is a weighted sum of its old value and those of its neighbourhood; and another in which the new value is selected from an ordered sequence of the values found in the neighbourhood. We also assume that these operations are being performed on greyscale images. (Most of them can be extended in a natural way to process colour images.)

7.2 Convolution and correlation

Convolution and correlation are the fundamental neighbourhood operations of image processing. They are *linear* operations. In practice, this means that, for an image f and a scale factor s,

$$C[sf(x, y)] = sC[f(x, y)], \tag{7.1}$$

where C denotes either convolution or correlation. It also means that, for any two images f_1 and f_2,

$$C[f_1(x, y) + f_2(x, y)] = C[f_1(x, y)] + C[f_2(x, y)]. \tag{7.2}$$

The calculations performed in convolution are almost identical to those done for correlation. The two operations differ in a rather subtle way that, in many cases, makes no difference to the result of image processing. Hence you will find that many texts use the term 'convolution' when, strictly, they should be describing the operation as correlation. Here, we shall endeavour to explain carefully the difference between the two operations and the circumstances under which they yield the same results.

The computation performed in convolution or correlation has two main applications. One is the *filtering* of images—e.g., to suppress noise or enhance edges. In this case, it is normal to describe the calculation done at each pixel as a convolution, regardless of what it is in a strict mathematical sense. The other application is in measuring the similarity of two images. This is useful in feature recognition and in registration, where we wish to place one image relative to another at a position of maximum similarity. In these applications, we use the term correlation to describe the calculations.

7.2.1 Calculating a convolution

In convolution, the calculation performed at a pixel is a weighted sum of grey levels from a neighbourhood surrounding a pixel. The neighbourhood includes the pixel under consideration, and it is customary for it to be disposed symmetrically about that pixel. We shall assume this to be the case in our discussion, although we note that it is not a requirement of the technique. Clearly, if a neighbourhood is centred on a pixel, then it must have odd dimensions, e.g., 3×3, 5×5, etc. The neighbourhood need not be square, but this is usually the case—since there is rarely any reason to bias the calculations in the x or y direction.

Grey levels taken from the neighbourhood are weighted by coefficients that come from a matrix or **convolution kernel**. In effect, the kernel's dimensions define the size of the neighbourhood in which calculations take place. Usually, the kernel is fairly small relative to the image—dimensions of 3×3 are the most common. Figure 7.1 shows a 3×3 kernel and the corresponding 3×3 neighbourhood of pixels from an image. The kernel is centred on the shaded pixel. The result of convolution will be a new value for this pixel.

During convolution, we take each kernel coefficient in turn and multiply it by a value from the neighbourhood of the image lying under the kernel. We apply the kernel to the image in such a way that the value at the top-left corner of the kernel is multiplied by the value at the bottom-right corner of the neighbourhood. Denoting the

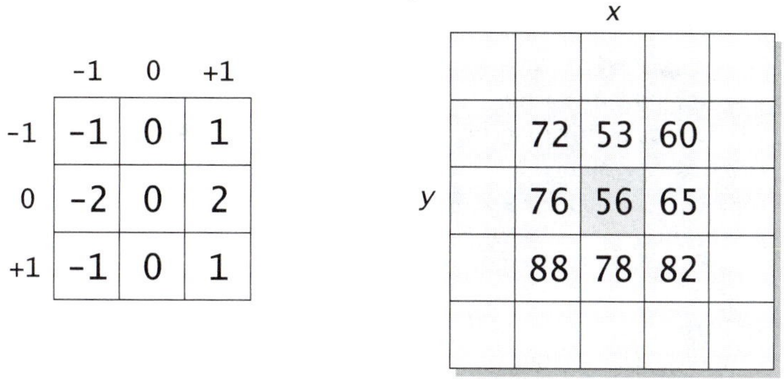

Figure 7.1 A 3 × 3 convolution kernel and the corresponding image neighbourhood.

kernel by h and the image by f, the entire calculation is

$$
\begin{aligned}
g(x, y) = \quad & h(-1, -1) \quad f(x + 1, y + 1) \quad + \\
& h(0, -1) \quad f(x, y + 1) \quad + \\
& h(1, -1) \quad f(x - 1, y + 1) \quad + \\
& h(-1, 0) \quad f(x + 1, y) \quad + \\
& h(0, 0) \quad f(x, y) \quad + \\
& h(1, 0) \quad f(x - 1, y) \quad + \\
& h(-1, 1) \quad f(x + 1, y - 1) \quad + \\
& h(0, 1) \quad f(x, y - 1) \quad + \\
& h(1, 1) \quad f(x - 1, y - 1).
\end{aligned}
\tag{7.3}
$$

This summation can be expressed more succinctly as

$$
g(x, y) = \sum_{k=-1}^{1} \sum_{j=-1}^{1} h(j, k) f(x - j, y - k).
\tag{7.4}
$$

For the kernel and neighbourhood illustrated in Figure 7.1, the result of convolution is

$$
g(x, y) = (-1 \times 82) + (1 \times 88) + (-2 \times 65) + (2 \times 76) + (-1 \times 60) + (1 \times 72) = 40
$$

Note that a new image (denoted g in Equation 7.4) has to be created to store the results of convolution. We cannot perform the operation in place, because application of a kernel to any pixel but the first would make use of values already altered by a prior convolution operation.

Referring to Equation 7.3 and Figure 7.1, we can see that the kernel coefficients are taken in sequence, starting at the top-left corner and ending at the bottom-right corner. The pixels associated with these kernel coefficients are sequenced in precisely the *opposite* direction; that is, starting from the bottom-right corner of the neighbourhood and ending at its top-left corner. Note that if we were to rotate the kernel by 180°, then both sequences would run in the same direction. Each kernel coefficient would then pair with the pixel directly beneath it. This reordering seems more intuitive; indeed, it is assumed in several textbook descriptions of convolution, and in many software implementations of the technique. Strictly speaking, however, these books and programs describe or implement correlation rather than convolution (see Section 7.2.4). The correct definition of convolution requires that we use the counterintuitive pairing of kernel coefficients with pixels. Note that the distinction between convolution and correlation disappears when the kernel is symmetric under 180° rotation. The popular 3×3 kernels

$$\begin{bmatrix} 1 & 1 & 1 \\ 1 & 1 & 1 \\ 1 & 1 & 1 \end{bmatrix} \quad \text{and} \quad \begin{bmatrix} -1 & -1 & -1 \\ -1 & 8 & -1 \\ -1 & -1 & -1 \end{bmatrix}$$

both have this property.

For a kernel of width m and height n, with m and n both odd, Equation 7.4 generalises to

$$g(x, y) = \sum_{k=-n_2}^{n_2} \sum_{j=-m_2}^{m_2} h(j, k) f(x - j, y - k), \tag{7.5}$$

where the kernel half-width, m_2, and half-height, n_2, are given by

$$m_2 = \lfloor m/2 \rfloor, \tag{7.6}$$

$$n_2 = \lfloor n/2 \rfloor, \tag{7.7}$$

and $\lfloor \ \rfloor$ is an operation that rounds its argument down to an integer. The summations therefore go from -1 to 1 for a 3×3 kernel, -2 to 2 for a 5×5 kernel, etc.

Algorithm 7.1 shows how we can compute an $m \times n$ convolution at a single pixel. The only difference between this algorithm and Equation 7.5 lies in the way that kernel coefficients are accessed. The equation assumes that the central coefficient of the kernel has indices $(0, 0)$, but the array that we use to store kernel coefficients has its upper-left corner at these indices. Adding m_2 and n_2 to the kernel indices transforms them into suitable array indices.

ALGORITHM 7.1 Convolution at a single pixel.

Create an array h, indexed from 0 to $m - 1$ horizontally and 0 to $n - 1$ vertically
Fill h with kernel coefficients
$m_2 = \lfloor m/2 \rfloor$
$n_2 = \lfloor n/2 \rfloor$
$sum = 0$
for $k = -n_2$ to n_2 **do**
    for $j = -m_2$ to m_2 **do**
        $sum = sum + h(j + m_2, k + n_2) f(x - j, y - k)$
    end for
end for
$g(x, y) = sum$

Equation 7.5 is somewhat cumbersome. We may avoid writing it out in full by using the shorthand form,

$$g(x, y) = h * f(x, y), \tag{7.8}$$

where h denotes the kernel and $*$ denotes the convolution operation. Note that Equation 7.8 implies the use of Equation 7.5. Note also that these expressions describe convolution *at a single pixel*; we may write

$$g = h * f \qquad (7.9)$$

to indicate that convolution is performed over the entire image.

7.2.2 Computational problems

We must deal with two major computational problems when applying Equation 7.5 to each pixel of an image. The first problem is one of representation. We might assume that the image, g, that we create to hold the results of convolution should have the same pixel data type as the input image, f. However, $g(x, y)$ is computed by a summation over a neighbourhood consisting of several pixels, so it is possible for its value to exceed the range that can be represented by this data type. Moreover, if any of the kernel coefficients are negative, it is possible for $g(x, y)$ to be negative. In such cases, we must use a signed data type for the output image or transform its values in such a way that they no longer fall below zero.

For example, suppose that we are convolving an 8-bit image with a 3×3 kernel whose coefficients are all equal to 1. In this case, convolution is simply a sum over the neighbourhood surrounding a pixel. But all the pixels in a neighbourhood could, in theory, have the maximum value of 255—giving a result of $9 \times 255 = 2295$. We can deal with this by using a 16-bit or 32-bit integer representation; alternatively, we can normalise the result of convolution so that it lies within a range compatible with the input image data type. In this example, dividing $g(x, y)$ by 9 is appropriate[1].

The second major problem concerns the borders of the image. Here, it is not possible to compute a convolution, because part of the kernel lies beyond the image (Figure 7.2). In fact, this is true of *any* neighbourhood operation, not just convolution. The size of the region in which normal convolution is possible is dictated by the dimensions of the convolution kernel. For a 3×3 kernel, one pixel at each border cannot be processed. So if the input image has dimensions $M \times N$, then the region to which Equation 7.5 applies has dimensions $(M - 2) \times (N - 2)$ and an origin of $(1, 1)$. For a 5×5 kernel, two pixels at each border cannot be processed and the region has dimensions $(M - 4) \times (N - 4)$ and an origin of $(2, 2)$. For a general $m \times n$ kernel with kernel half-width and half-height defined by Equations 7.6 and 7.7, the region in which convolution can take place has its origin at (m_2, n_2) and dimensions of $(M - 2m_2) \times (N - 2n_2)$.

A number of different strategies exist to deal with this problem.

1. **No processing at the border**

   The simplest solution is to ignore those pixels for which convolution is not possible. Algorithm 7.2 shows how convolution of an entire image can be performed using this strategy. The dimensions of the output image are the same as those of the input image, and its pixels will normally each be given an initial value of zero; consequently, we will

---

[1] It may be more efficient to incorporate any normalisation factor into the kernel coefficients, since this means that one less multiplication is required at each pixel.

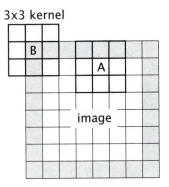

3x3 kernel

image

Figure 7.2 Failure of convolution at the borders of an image. At pixel A, convolution is possible because the kernel fits wholly within the image. Convolution is not possible at pixel B—or, indeed, at any of the shaded pixels.

ALGORITHM 7.2 Convolution of an image, ignoring the borders.

Create a suitable kernel, h, with dimensions $m \times n$
Compute kernel half-width, $m_2 = \lfloor m/2 \rfloor$
Compute kernel half-height, $n_2 = \lfloor n/2 \rfloor$
Create an $M \times N$ output image, g
for all pixel coordinates, x and y, **do**
$\quad g(x, y) = 0$
end for
for $y = n_2$ to $N - n_2 - 1$ **do**
$\quad$ **for** $x = m_2$ to $M - m_2 - 1$ **do**
$\quad\quad$ Compute value of $g(x, y)$ using Algorithm 7.1
$\quad$ **end for**
end for

---

see a black border in the output image. This may cause a significant change in the grey level statistics of the image, which could affect subsequent operations performed on that image.

2. **Copying of input image pixels**

   Another solution is to copy the corresponding pixel value from the input image wherever it is not possible to carry out convolution; consequently, the output image will have a border of unprocessed pixels. For certain convolutions, this may have a less detrimental effect than a black border around the image, but it is not an appropriate solution in all cases.

3. **Truncation of the image**

   A simple way of avoiding a border with very different properties from the rest of the image is to remove those pixels for which convolution is not possible. This results in an output image that is smaller than, and offset relative to, the input image. This may cause problems if we subsequently need to combine the input and output images arithmetically (see Section 5.5.3) or otherwise compare them on a pixel-by-pixel basis.

4. **Truncation of the kernel**

   Another solution is to deal with the borders of the image as a special case, and use a modified kernel to perform convolution in these locations. For example, when convolving with the 3×3 kernel

   $$\begin{bmatrix} 1 & 1 & 1 \\ 1 & 1 & 1 \\ 1 & 1 & 1 \end{bmatrix}$$

   we can use the following truncated versions of this kernel at the corners and sides of the image:

   $$\begin{bmatrix} 1 & 1 \\ 1 & 1 \end{bmatrix} \quad \begin{bmatrix} 1 & 1 \\ 1 & 1 \\ 1 & 1 \end{bmatrix} \quad \begin{bmatrix} 1 & 1 & 1 \\ 1 & 1 & 1 \end{bmatrix}$$

   The effects of these kernels on the image will be similar to the effect of the full-sized kernel.

   This technique adds considerably to the complexity of convolution; moreover, it is not possible to derive sensible truncated versions of many kernels.

5. **Reflected indexing**

   The part of Equation 7.5 that causes problems is the term $f(x - j, y - k)$. For certain values of x and y, one or both of the expressions $x - j$ and $y - k$ will give a value outside the allowed range. (In the case of an $M \times N$ image, the allowed ranges are $[0, M - 1]$ for the x coordinate and $[0, N - 1]$ for the y coordinate.) Therefore, at each stage of the calculation, we can test $x - j$ to see whether it corresponds to a valid pixel x coordinate and, if it doesn't, we can reflect the coordinate back into the image (Figure 7.3). The same

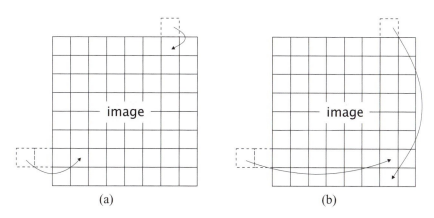

(a) (b)

Figure 7.3 Mapping of invalid x and y coordinates back into an image. (a) Reflected indexing. (b) Circular indexing.

can be done for $y - k$. This simulates mirroring of the image at its borders or, equivalently, reflection of the kernel wherever its coefficients fail to pair with pixels from the image.

Algorithm 7.3 shows how an x coordinate can be reflected back into an image whenever it exceeds the bounds of that image. Algorithm 7.4 demonstrates how this strategy can be incorporated into the convolution of an entire image.

ALGORITHM 7.3 Reflected indexing of an image x coordinate.

Let M be the image width
if $x < 0$ **then**
   $x = -x - 1$
else if $x \geqslant M$ **then**
   $x = 2M - x - 1$
end if

ALGORITHM 7.4 Convolution of an image using reflected indexing.

Create a suitable kernel, h, with dimensions $m \times n$
Compute kernel half-width, $m_2 = \lfloor m/2 \rfloor$
Compute kernel half-height, $n_2 = \lfloor n/2 \rfloor$
Create an $M \times N$ output image, g
for all pixel coordinates, x and y, **do**
   sum $= 0$
   for $k = -n_2$ to n_2 **do**
      for $j = -m_2$ to m_2 **do**
         Reflect $x - j$ using Algorithm 7.3, to give x'
         Reflect $y - k$ by a similar algorithm, to give y'
         sum $=$ *sum* $+ h(j + m_2, k + n_2) f(x', y')$
      end for
   end for
   $g(x, y) =$ *sum*
end for

---

6. **Circular indexing**

The reflected indexing approach described in (5) above is one way of simulating access to pixels beyond the real bounds of the image. Another is to imagine that the image repeats itself endlessly in all directions. This sounds rather odd but, in fact, there are sound theoretical reasons for assuming this to be the case. (We shall return to this point in Chapter 8.) Replicating the image in this way would be costly in terms of time and memory usage, but we can achieve the same effect by means of circular indexing—whereby coordinates that exceed the bounds of the image 'wrap around' to the opposite side (Figure 7.3). Algorithm 7.5 demonstrates circular indexing for the x coordinate. A similar algorithm will perform the task for the y coordinate.

ALGORITHM 7.5 Circular indexing.

Let M be the image width
if $x < 0$ **then**
  $x = x + M$
else if $x \geqslant M$ **then**
  $x = x - M$
end if

To perform convolution of an entire image in this fashion, we can use Algorithm 7.4 again, substituting the circular indexing algorithms for Algorithm 7.3 and its equivalent for y coordinates.

7.2.3 Performance issues

Convolution is very expensive computationally. Evaluation of Equation 7.5 for an $n \times n$ kernel requires n^2 multiplications and the same number of additions *per pixel*, and there are typically 10^5–10^6 pixels per image. We can use software techniques or hardware to speed things up.

A much more efficient algorithm can be used for convolution in the small number of cases where a kernel is *separable*. A separable $n \times n$ kernel can be represented as a vector product of two orthogonal, one-dimensional kernels, each of width n. Convolution with the kernel can be carried out using these one-dimensional components. One of them is applied down the columns of an image, generating an intermediate result. The other kernel is then applied along the rows of the intermediate image, producing the final result. Algorithm 7.6 gives further details of the process.

Note that this is an $O(n)$ operation, compared with $O(n^2)$ for standard, two-dimensional convolution. Convolution with a separable 15×15 kernel requires just 13 percent of the computation necessary when a non-separable kernel is used. The Gaussian kernel discussed in Section 7.3 is the classic example of a separable kernel.

We can benchmark separable versus non-separable convolution in Java using the techniques discussed in Section 6.2.3. Figure 7.4 summarises the results obtained from timing convolution operations on a 512×512 image. The platform used was a Pentium II machine running JDK 1.2 under Windows 95. JIT compilation was enabled. (The slowdown from disabling it was significant, with execution times increasing by a factor of 5–6 for the smaller kernels.)

The data points labelled 'standard kernel' were computed using an implementation of Algorithm 7.2. They lie on an approximately quadratic curve, just as we would expect for an $O(n^2)$ operation. The dataset labelled 'separable kernel' was generated by an implementation of Algorithm 7.6. The improvement in performance achieved when the kernel is separable is significant. The execution times for a 15×15 kernel—just over 8 seconds when it is non-separable, compared with around 1 second when it is separable—agree closely with our earlier observation concerning the relative costs of the two algorithms.

Figure 7.4 plots one further dataset, obtained using the `ConvolveOp` class from the

---

ALGORITHM 7.6 Convolution with a separable kernel.

Decompose the kernel into a pair of one-dimensional kernels, h_x and h_y, each of size n
Compute kernel half-width, $n_2 = \lfloor n/2 \rfloor$
Create an $M \times N$ output image, g
Create an $M \times N$ temporary image, t
for $y = n_2$ to $N - n_2 - 1$ **do**
  for $x = 0$ to $M - 1$ **do**
    $sum = 0$
    for $i = -n_2$ to n_2 **do**
      $sum = sum + h_y(i + n_2) f(x, y - i)$
    end for
    $t(x, y) = sum$
  end for
end for
for $y = 0$ to $N - 1$ **do**
  for $x = n_2$ to $M - n_2 - 1$ **do**
    $sum = 0$
    for $i = -n_2$ to n_2 **do**
      $sum = sum + h_x(i + n_2) t(x - i, y)$
    end for
    $g(x, y) = sum$
  end for
end for

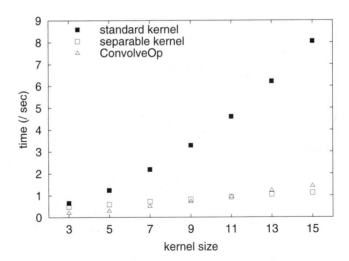

Figure 7.4 Convolution time as a function of kernel size. Curves are plotted for explicit convolution using a standard 2D kernel and a separable kernel, and for convolution using `ConvolveOp`.

Java2D API. This class is discussed further in Section 7.2.5. Here, we simply note that it outperforms our experimental, pure Java implementation significantly and achieves a performance similar to that of the separable algorithm. This occurs because `ConvolveOp` has at its core a native machine code implementation of the critical parts of the algorithm.

Convolution is so fundamental to image processing that specialised hardware exists to perform the operation in real time. We can also use general, high-performance computing architectures to convolve images more efficiently. On multiprocessor machines, for instance, we can split the image into chunks and assign one chunk to each processor. At a lower level, we can allow the multiplication and addition operations that take place in Equation 7.5 to occur in parallel. Without hardware assistance, the cost of spatial convolution with large masks is prohibitive; in such cases, the same effects can be achieved more efficiently by operating in the frequency domain. This is the subject of Chapter 8.

7.2.4   Correlation

A correlation is computed in almost exactly the same way as a convolution. The computation can be expressed as follows:

$$g(x, y) = \sum_{k=-n_2}^{n_2} \sum_{j=-m_2}^{m_2} h(j, k) f(x + j, y + k), \tag{7.10}$$

where m_2 and n_2 are defined as before. This differs from Equation 7.5 only in that kernel indices j and k are added to, rather than subtracted from, pixel coordinates x and y. This has the effect of pairing each kernel coefficient with the image pixel that lies *directly beneath it*. Since the two operations differ only by a 180° rotation of the kernel, we can compute an unnormalised correlation using the same hardware or software that we use for convolution. (By the same token, if we have an implementation of 'convolution' that actually evaluates Equation 7.10, we can obtain a true convolution by rotating the kernel through 180° before computation.)

Correlation is often used in applications where it is necessary to measure the similarity between images or parts of images. For instance, we might need to locate a particular feature in an image. This can be done if we create a small image which acts as a model or template for that feature. We can place the template over the image to be searched and move it around until we find the position of maximum similarity; this we take to be the position of the feature. In such applications, h from Equation 7.10 is our template. We no longer describe it as a kernel because it is usually much larger than typical convolution kernels, and because the values it contains are usually of the same type and range as pixel values in the image. (Convolution kernel coefficients are often real numbers, and can be negative—unlike the pixel values of most images.)

Note that Equation 7.10 implicitly gives higher values for correlation in brighter parts of an image, which can make it difficult to identify the point of maximum similarity. It is therefore customary to normalise $g(x, y)$. One way of doing this is to divide by the sum of grey levels in the image neighbourhood, i.e.,

$$g'(x, y) = \frac{g(x, y)}{\sum_k \sum_j f(x + j, y + k)}. \tag{7.11}$$

Gonzalez and Woods [20] describe a somewhat more sophisticated approach involving computation of a correlation coefficient:

$$\gamma(x, y) = \frac{\sum_k \sum_j [h(j, k) - \bar{h}][f(x + j, y + k) - \bar{f}(x, y)]}{\sqrt{\sum_k \sum_j [f(x + j, y + k) - \bar{f}(x, y)]^2 \sum_k \sum_j [h(j, k) - \bar{h}]^2}}. \quad (7.12)$$

Here, $\bar{h}$, computed once only, is the average pixel value in the template, and $\bar{f}(x, y)$ is the average pixel value in the image neighbourhood. $\gamma(x, y)$ is normalised with respect to both the image and the template, and it always lies in the range $[-1, 1]$.

Figures 7.5 and 7.6 give an example of correlation. In Figure 7.5(a), we see a synthetic image consisting of white text on a grey background. The text has been blurred slightly and a moderate amount of Gaussian random noise has been added to the image. Figure 7.5(b) shows a small template for one of the letters present in the text (the letter 'v'). We can attempt to locate the letter in the text by correlating the image with the template.

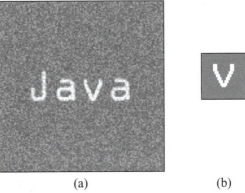

(a)   (b)

Figure 7.5 Correlation of an image with a template. (a) Noisy image containing a feature of interest. (b) Template representing the feature.

Figure 7.6(a) displays correlation in image form, with bright pixels representing points of high correlation between the image and the template. There are partial matches between the template and the other letters in the text, as indicated by the moderately bright pixels in the correlation image. However, the brightest of the pixels is at centre of the letter 'v' in the image, indicating that we have successfully located it. The maximum value of correlation is more prominent in Figure 7.6(b), which plots correlation as a surface.

Correlation works well only if we know the size and the orientation of the feature of interest, and can design an appropriate template. If the size and orientation of the feature can vary, we will need to generate a range of templates and correlate each with the image, at great computational cost. In such cases, it may be better to avoid correlation and, instead, use some measure of similarity that is invariant to scaling and rotation.

The cost of doing correlation using Equation 7.10 becomes prohibitive as template size increases. Fortunately, a more efficient way exists of correlating large templates with images, based in the frequency domain. This is covered in Chapter 8.

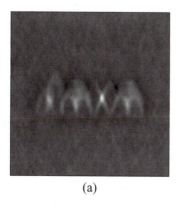
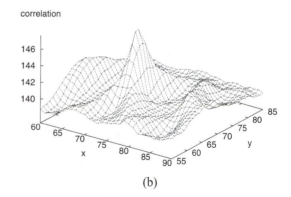

(a)   (b)

Figure 7.6 Results of correlation. (a) Correlation rendered as an image; the brightest spot is the position of maximum similarity. (b) Correlation in the vicinity of the maximum value, plotted as a surface.

7.2.5   Convolution in Java

Java2D provides two classes to support image convolution: `Kernel` and `ConvolveOp`. The `Kernel` class represents convolution kernels. A `Kernel` object is constructed by providing kernel dimensions and a one-dimensional `float` array of coefficients:

```
int width = 3;
int height = 3;
float[] coeff = new float[width*height];
for (int i = 0; i < coeff.length; ++i)
  coeff[i] = 1.0f/coeff.length;
Kernel kernel = new Kernel(width, height, coeff);
```

This example creates a 3×3 kernel whose coefficients are all equal. Note that each coefficient is normalised, such that the sum of coefficients equals 1. We must do this because `ConvolveOp` does not normalise the results of convolution itself.

The `ConvolveOp` class implements `BufferedImageOp` and therefore behaves in much the same way as other classes that implement this interface. An image can be convolved as follows:

```
ConvolveOp op = new ConvolveOp(kernel);
BufferedImage outputImage = op.filter(inputImage, null);
```

The `ConvolveOp` object created in this example performs no processing at the borders of the image, leaving pixels with a value of zero. An additional argument can be supplied to the constructor, specifying this behaviour explicitly or the alternative behaviour of copying pixel values from the source image:

```
ConvolveOp op1 = new ConvolveOp(kernel, ConvolveOp.EDGE_ZERO_FILL);
ConvolveOp op2 = new ConvolveOp(kernel, ConvolveOp.EDGE_NO_OP);
```

An improved kernel class

A useful feature not provided by the Kernel class is the ability to save kernel data to a file (or some other kind of output stream) or create a new kernel from data stored in a file (or from a stream). We can extend Kernel in order to add this capability. This is done in the class StandardKernel, part of the com.pearsoneduc.ip.op package. StandardKernel has a static method createKernel() that takes a Reader object as a parameter and returns a new StandardKernel created with data obtained from the Reader. It also provides write(), a method that outputs kernel data to some destination specified by a Writer object.

A StandardKernel can be constructed using a width, a height and a float array of coefficients. A second constructor takes these parameters plus one additional parameter, representing the number of digits that appear after the decimal point when writing kernel coefficients. This parameter can be inspected and modified subsequently, using the getFractionDigits() and setFractionDigits() methods. By default, four digits appear after the decimal point when coefficients are written.

Listing 7.1 shows a simple program that creates a 5 × 5 kernel and writes it to standard output. It produces the following output on screen:

```
# convolution kernel
5 5 2
 0.04 0.04 0.04 0.04 0.04
 0.04 0.04 0.04 0.04 0.04
 0.04 0.04 0.04 0.04 0.04
 0.04 0.04 0.04 0.04 0.04
 0.04 0.04 0.04 0.04 0.04
```

The first line is a comment, ignored when reading the kernel. The next line contains kernel width, kernel height and the number of fraction digits to use when formatting coefficients,

---

LISTING 7.1 A simple program demonstrating how a convolution kernel can be created and written to an output stream.

```
1    import java.io.OutputStreamWriter;
2    import com.pearsoneduc.ip.op.StandardKernel;
3
4    public class WriteKernel {
5      public static void main(String[] argv) {
6        float[] data = new float[25];
7        float coeff = 0.04f;
8        for (int i = 0; i < 25; ++i)
9          data[i] = coeff;
10       StandardKernel kernel = new StandardKernel(5, 5, data, 2);
11       kernel.write(new OutputStreamWriter(System.out));
12     }
13   }
```

each separated from the other parameters by whitespace. The remainder of the data consists of kernel coefficients, separated from each other by whitespace. If this kernel were stored in a file called `test.ker`, the following code would read data from that file and create a new kernel:

```
Reader input = new FileReader("test.ker");
Kernel kernel = StandardKernel.createKernel(input);
```

The `createKernel()` method has an optional `boolean` parameter that specifies whether kernel coefficients should be normalised on input. By default, no normalisation is done. If this parameter is `true`, kernel coefficients are summed as they are read in and the coefficients are then divided by the sum should it be greater than 1. This facility is useful when reading a kernel file such as this:

```
# convolution kernel
3 3 0
  1 1 1
  1 1 1
  1 1 1
```

When a kernel with these coefficients is used with `ConvolveOp`, the output from convolution at each pixel is likely to exceed 255 in most cases, producing an image in which most of the pixels are white. Reading the kernel using code such as

```
Reader input = new FileReader("test.ker");
Kernel kernel = StandardKernel.createKernel(input, true);
```

solves the problem.

An improved convolution operator

`ConvolveOp` is efficient because it has native code at its core, but it suffers from several limitations. As we have seen, it supports only two of the various ways of dealing with pixels at the borders of an image. Another limitation is that it cannot do separable convolution. Performance is therefore not optimal for kernels that are separable (such as the Gaussian kernel, discussed in Section 7.3.1). A serious flaw in `ConvolveOp` is its handling of kernels containing negative coefficients. As we shall see shortly, many useful kernels possess this characteristic. The result of convolution with such kernels can be a positive or negative number, but when `ConvolveOp` processes an 8-bit greyscale image, it outputs another 8-bit greyscale image, with values in the range 0–255. How, then, are negative values handled?

Figure 7.7 shows an image of a barn and plots grey levels for a short horizontal sequence of pixels taken from the centre of the image. Also plotted are the outputs from `ConvolveOp` and from Equation 7.4 obtained when the 3×3 kernel

$$\begin{bmatrix} -1 & 0 & 1 \\ -1 & 0 & 1 \\ -1 & 0 & 1 \end{bmatrix}$$

is applied to the sequence of pixels. It is quite clear that, when convolution produces a negative result, the output from `ConvolveOp` is zero. Similarly, when convolution produces

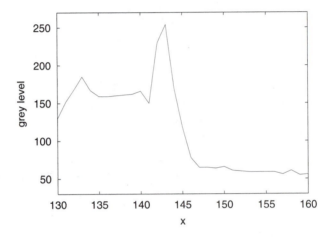

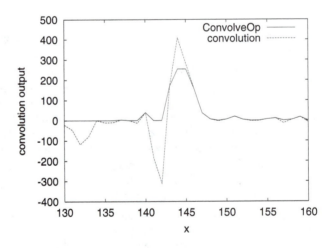

Figure 7.7 Behaviour of `ConvolveOp`. Top: an image. Middle: grey levels for a short sequence of pixels taken from the image. Bottom: results of convolution at these pixels, compared with the output of `ConvolveOp`.

a result exceeding 255, the output from ConvolveOp is fixed at 255. Evidently, ConvolveOp truncates its output to lie in a 0-255 range.

We can implement our own class, ConvolutionOp, that does not suffer from the limitations outlined above. Once again, the StandardGreyOp class described in Chapter 6 forms the basis of the implementation. We define a subclass, NeighbourhoodOp, in order to factor out the characteristics common to all neighbourhood operations, and derive ConvolutionOp from this class. Figure 7.8 shows the structure of NeighbourhoodOp and its relationship to other classes.

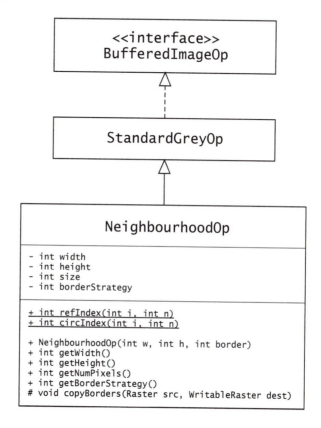

Figure 7.8 A class to support neighbourhood operations on 8-bit greyscale images.

NeighbourhoodOp contains instance variables to hold the width and height of the neighbourhood in which processing is taking place, along with methods to inspect their current values. The class constructor initialises these variables, checking that the supplied integer values are odd and positive. NeighbourhoodOp also contains a variable that records the chosen border processing strategy, which can be one of the values NO_BORDER_OP, COPY_BORDER_PIXELS, REFLECTED_INDEXING or CIRCULAR_INDEXING. Some methods are provided to support these border processing strategies. The two static methods (underlined in Figure 7.8) perform the calculations necessary for reflected and circular indexing;

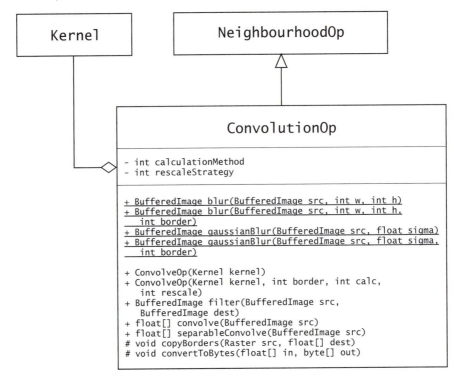

Figure 7.9 Classes involved in convolution.

the protected method, copyBorders(), is used by ConvolutionOp and other neighbourhood operation classes to copy unprocessed pixels at the image borders from the input image to the output image.

ConvolutionOp, illustrated in Figure 7.9, has a Kernel and two other instance variables to record the desired calculation method and rescaling strategy. The calculation method is specified by class constants SINGLE_PASS, signifying that a normal, two-dimensional calculation is to be performed in a single pass; and SEPARABLE, signifying that convolution is a two-pass operation in which the rows and columns of an image are processed separately with a one-dimensional kernel. In the latter case, the kernel supplied to a ConvolutionOp must have a height of 1.

The rescaling strategy determines how the results of convolution are mapped onto the 0–255 range required for an 8-bit greyscale output image. Possible values are: NO_RESCALING, whereby output is truncated, mimicking the behaviour of ConvolveOp; RESCALE_MAX_ONLY, in which a scaling that maps the maximum value in the convolved data onto 255 is used; and RESCALE_MIN_AND_MAX, in which the range of values found in the convolved data is mapped onto a 0–255 range. For the special case of convolved data that contains negative values, RESCALE_MAX_ONLY will transform the data in such a way that 0 maps onto 128.

ConvolutionOp provides constructors similar to ConvolveOp. We can construct a ConvolutionOp object using a Kernel alone—in which case the defaults of no processing at the borders, single-pass calculation and no rescaling of output data are applied—or by using a Kernel, a border handling strategy, a calculation method and a rescaling strategy:

```
ConvolutionOp op1 = new ConvolutionOp(kernel);

ConvolutionOp op2 = new ConvolutionOp(kernel,
   NeighbourhoodOp.REFLECTED_INDEXING,
   ConvolutionOp.SINGLE_PASS,
   ConvolutionOp.RESCALE_MAX_ONLY);
```

Once we have created a ConvolutionOp, it can be used to process a BufferedImage in the normal way:

```
ConvolutionOp op = new ConvolutionOp(kernel);
BufferedImage outputImage = op.filter(inputImage, null);
```

The filter() method does the convolution by calling convolve() or separableConvolve(), as appropriate. The latter is invoked if SEPARABLE was specified as the calculation method. These methods return convolved data in a float array. Data from the array are rescaled in the specified manner and copied to the output image by filter(). Note that convolve() and separableConvolve() are public, so these methods can be used for convolution instead of filter() if rescaling is not appropriate or transfer of the output to a BufferedImage is not required.

The ConvolutionOp class can be viewed as a drop-in replacement for Java2D's ConvolveOp. Its main advantage is greater flexibility. Its performance is generally less impressive than ConvolveOp because its convolve() method has a pure Java implementation. However, for the special case of separable convolution, ConvolutionOp can outperform ConvolveOp when the kernel become moderately sized. ConvolutionOp also provides a small number of static methods to simply the common operation of image blurring by convolution (see Section 7.3.1). These methods delegate processing to ConvolveOp or ConvolutionOp as appropriate, ensuring that blurring is done in the most efficient manner possible.

Example applications

Two convolution applications are provided on the CD. The first, Convolve, has a command line interface. It expects an input image filename, output image filename and kernel filename as command line arguments, along with three integers. The first of these is 1 if kernel coefficients should be normalised on input, 0 otherwise. The second integer parameter specifies a border processing strategy, as indicated in Table 7.1. The third integer specifies rescaling behaviour, as indicated in Table 7.2. Listing 7.2 shows the entire code for Convolve.

The second convolution application, ConvolutionTool, has a graphical user interface. This application reads the image file named on the command line and displays the image on the left-hand side of the application frame. On the right-hand side, the output of a convolution operation is displayed. In the centre is a convolution kernel, whose coefficients

LISTING 7.2 A convolution application with a command line interface.

```
1    import java.awt.image.*;
2    import java.io.*;
3    import com.pearsoneduc.ip.io.*;
4    import com.pearsoneduc.ip.op.*;
5    import com.pearsoneduc.ip.util.IntervalTimer;
6
7
8    public class Convolve {
9      public static void main(String[] argv) {
10       if (argv.length > 5) {
11         try {
12
13           // Parse command line arguments
14
15           ImageDecoder input = ImageFile.createImageDecoder(argv[0]);
16           ImageEncoder output = ImageFile.createImageEncoder(argv[1]);
17           Reader kernelInput = new FileReader(argv[2]);
18           boolean normaliseKernel = (Integer.parseInt(argv[3]) != 0);
19           int borderStrategy =
20            Math.max(1, Math.min(4, Integer.parseInt(argv[4])));
21           int rescaleStrategy =
22            Math.max(1, Math.min(3, Integer.parseInt(argv[5])));
23
24           // Load image and kernel
25
26           BufferedImage inputImage = input.decodeAsBufferedImage();
27           Kernel kernel =
28            StandardKernel.createKernel(kernelInput, normaliseKernel);
29
30           // Create convolution operator and convolve image
31
32           ConvolutionOp convOp = new ConvolutionOp(kernel,
33            borderStrategy, ConvolutionOp.SINGLE_PASS, rescaleStrategy);
34           IntervalTimer timer = new IntervalTimer();
35           timer.start();
36           BufferedImage outputImage = convOp.filter(inputImage, null);
37           System.out.println("Convolution finished [" + timer.stop() + " sec]");
38
39           // Write results to output file
40
41           output.encode(outputImage);
42           System.exit(0);
43
44         }
45         catch (Exception e) {
46           System.err.println(e);
47           System.exit(1);
48         }
49       }
50       else {
51         System.err.println(
52          "usage: java Convolve infile outfile kernel norm border rescale");
53         System.exit(1);
54       }
55     }
56   }
```

Table 7.1 Border processing strategies in the `Convolve` program.

Value	Meaning
1	No border processing (border pixels will be zero)
2	Copy border pixels from input image
3	Reflected indexing
4	Circular indexing

Table 7.2 Rescaling behaviour in the `Convolve` program.

Value	Meaning
1	No rescaling (output truncated to 0–255 range)
2	Rescale using maximum only (symmetrically about 0 if necessary)
3	Rescale so that range maps onto 0–255

can be edited to any desired integer value. Kernel dimensions can be specified on the command line; the default is a 3×3 kernel. A menu bar presents a `File` menu and a `Convolve` menu. The former provides facilities to save the current kernel to a file or load a new kernel; the latter is used to convolve with the current kernel, or reset coefficients to an 'identity kernel' that has no effect on the input image. The `Convolve` menu is also used to set various border processing and output rescaling options. Figure 7.10 shows `ConvolutionTool` in action.

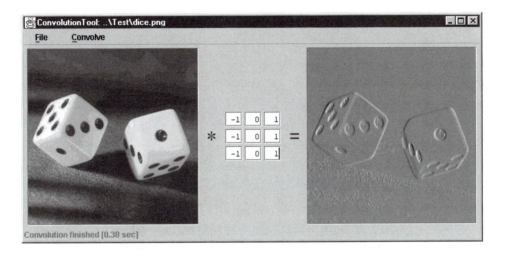

Figure 7.10 A convolution application with a graphical user interface.

7.3   Linear filtering

Convolution can be used to carry out **linear filtering** of an image. The nature of the filter is determined by our choice of kernel coefficients. Standard kernels are available, with which we can accomplish blurring or sharpening of an image. But why are these operations described as 'filtering'? What does the term mean when applied to images?

It may be helpful to consider a more familiar example of filtering. Domestic Hi-Fi equipment is often fitted with filters so that sound quality can be adjusted to suit the listener's

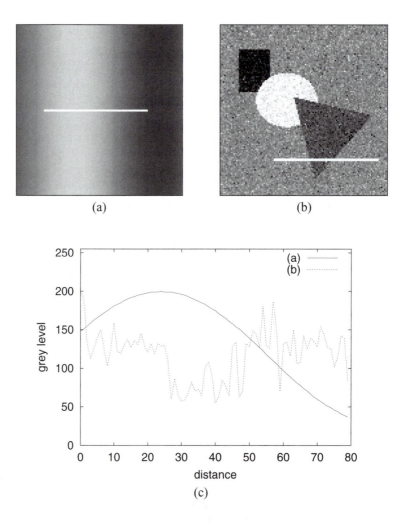

Figure 7.11   Grey level variations and spatial frequency. (a) Image containing low frequency variation only. (b) Noisy image with high frequency components. (c) Grey level profiles across the images in (a) and (b). A white line marks the position of the profile on each image.

preferences. Usually, there are 'bass' and 'treble' controls that alter the proportions of low frequency and high frequency components, respectively, in the audio signal. When we turn down the treble control, we filter out the highest frequencies from the signal; similarly, when we turn down the bass control, we filter out the lowest frequencies.

When we talk of the *frequency* of a sound wave or an audio signal, we are referring to the rate at which the signal changes with *time*. When we talk of the frequencies present in an image, we are referring to changes occurring in *space*. Spatial frequency is a measure of how rapidly brightness or colour varies as we traverse an image. Images in which grey level varies slowly and smoothly are characterised solely by components with low spatial frequencies; images containing sudden grey level transitions, fine detail or strong texture will also contain components with high spatial frequencies (Figure 7.11).

Because an image may be described in terms of spatial frequencies, we can define filtering operations analogous to turning the bass and treble knobs on audio equipment. These operations are termed **low pass filtering** and **high pass filtering**. A low pass filter allows low spatial frequencies to pass unchanged, but suppresses high frequencies. The converse is true of a high pass filter. Applying a low pass filter to an image is analogous to turning down the treble control on your Hi-Fi equipment. The low pass filter *smoothes* or blurs the image. This tends to reduce noise, but also obscures fine detail. High pass filtering is analogous to turning down your Hi-Fi's bass control. It preserves sudden variations in grey level, such as those that occur at the boundaries of objects, but suppresses the more gradual variations. It can have the adverse effect of making noise more prominent, because noise has a strong high frequency component.

7.3.1 Low pass filtering

Any convolution kernel whose coefficients are all positive will act as a low pass filter. In the simplest case, all the coefficients are equal—giving us, for example, the 3×3 and 5×5 kernels

$$
\begin{bmatrix}
0.111 & 0.111 & 0.111 \\
0.111 & 0.111 & 0.111 \\
0.111 & 0.111 & 0.111
\end{bmatrix}
\qquad
\begin{bmatrix}
0.04 & 0.04 & 0.04 & 0.04 & 0.04 \\
0.04 & 0.04 & 0.04 & 0.04 & 0.04 \\
0.04 & 0.04 & 0.04 & 0.04 & 0.04 \\
0.04 & 0.04 & 0.04 & 0.04 & 0.04 \\
0.04 & 0.04 & 0.04 & 0.04 & 0.04
\end{bmatrix}
$$

Note that these kernels are already normalised. Their coefficients sum to 1, so convolution with them will not result in an overall brightening of the image. We can factor out the normalisation like so:

$$
\frac{1}{9}
\begin{bmatrix}
1 & 1 & 1 \\
1 & 1 & 1 \\
1 & 1 & 1
\end{bmatrix}
\qquad
\frac{1}{25}
\begin{bmatrix}
1 & 1 & 1 & 1 & 1 \\
1 & 1 & 1 & 1 & 1 \\
1 & 1 & 1 & 1 & 1 \\
1 & 1 & 1 & 1 & 1 \\
1 & 1 & 1 & 1 & 1
\end{bmatrix}
$$

Now it becomes clear what these kernels do; pixel values from the neighbourhood are summed without being weighted, and the sum is divided by the number of pixels in the neighbourhood. Convolution with these kernels is therefore equivalent to computing the mean grey level over the neighbourhood defined by the kernel. For this reason, these kernels are sometimes described as **mean filters**.

The astute reader may be wondering why the mean filter is specified here as a convolution; after all, the average grey level in an $n \times n$ neighbourhood can be computed simply with n^2 additions and one division, whereas convolution involves n^2 multiplications and n^2 additions. The only real advantage of calculating a mean by convolution is that we can exploit hardware support for convolution, if this is available to us; if it isn't the more direct calculation of the mean in a neighbourhood will be quicker.

An example of noise reduction by low pass filtering is given in Figure 7.12. The filtering operation has suppressed, but has not eliminated, the noise. It has also blurred the objects of interest, making their edges less well defined. The filtering is *non-specific*, in that it reduces the strength of the high spatial frequency components, irrespective of whether they are due to noise or to meaningful structure in the image.

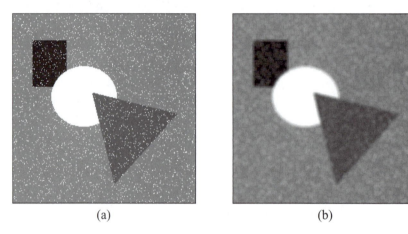

(a)   (b)

Figure 7.12 Noise reduction by low pass filtering. (a) Synthetic image corrupted by 1% impulse noise. (b) Result of applying a 5 × 5 mean filter.

Figure 7.13 gives another example of low pass filtering. Here, we see that larger kernels produce more pronounced smoothing. A high degree of smoothing can also be achieved through repeated application of a small kernel to an image.

Blurring can be done with a uniform kernel, in which the coefficients are all equal, or with a nonuniform kernel. The most common example of the latter is the **Gaussian filter**, in which the coefficients are samples from a two-dimensional Gaussian function,

$$h(x, y) = \exp \left[\frac{-(x^2 + y^2)}{2\sigma^2} \right]. \tag{7.13}$$

This function is plotted as a surface in Figure 7.14. The kernel coefficients diminish in size with increasing distance from the kernel's centre; more weight is therefore given to central pixels than to those in the periphery of the neighbourhood. Larger values of σ produce a wider peak and, consequently, greater blurring. As σ increases, the dimensions of the kernel must also increase if it is to be fully Gaussian in shape.

(a)   (b)

(c)

Figure 7.13   Effect of kernel size on smoothing. (a) Original image. (b) Result of applying a 5 × 5 mean filter. (c) Result of applying a 15 × 15 mean filter.

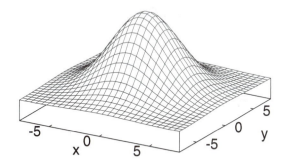

Figure 7.14   A two-dimensional Gaussian function.

There are several advantages to using a Gaussian filter. One is that the kernel is rotationally symmetric, so there will be no directional bias in the amount of smoothing that is carried out. Another is that the Gaussian kernel is separable, which allows for fast computation (Section 7.2.3). Note that, unlike the standard mean filter, a Gaussian kernel's coefficients fall off to (almost) zero at the kernel's edges. We will consider the advantages that this brings in Chapter 8.

7.3.2 High pass filtering

High pass filtering is accomplished using a kernel containing a mixture of positive and negative coefficients. An omnidirectional high pass filter—that is, one whose response is the same, whatever the direction in which grey level varies—should have positive coefficients near its centre and negative coefficients in the periphery of the kernel. The classic 3×3 implementation is

$$\begin{bmatrix} -1 & -1 & -1 \\ -1 & 8 & -1 \\ -1 & -1 & -1 \end{bmatrix}$$

The sum of the coefficients in this kernel is zero. This means that, when the kernel is over an area of constant or slowly varying grey level, the result of convolution is zero or some very small number. However, when grey level is varying rapidly within the neighbourhood, the result of convolution can be a large number. This number can be positive or negative, because the kernel contains both positive and negative coefficients. We therefore need to choose an output image representation that supports negative numbers.

If we wish to display or print the filtered image, we must map the pixel values onto a 0–255 range. This is usually done in such a way that a filter response of 0 maps onto the middle of the range. Thus, negative filter responses will show up as dark tones, whereas positive responses will be represented by light tones. This can be seen in Figure 7.15.

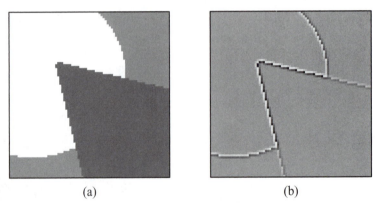

(a)   (b)

Figure 7.15 High pass filtering. (a) Synthetic image. (b) Result of high pass filtering with a 3×3 kernel.

Note that high pass filtering can also be viewed as a process of subtracting from an image a blurred version of that image (thereby removing the low spatial frequencies). This is sometimes referred to as **unsharp masking**.

7.3.3 High frequency emphasis

We can compute a weighted sum of the original image and the output from a high pass filter. The result is an image in which high spatial frequencies are emphasised relative to lower frequencies. The degree of emphasis achieved depends on the weighting given to the original and high pass filtered images. This 'high boost filter' can be used to sharpen an image.

Note that we can perform high boost filtering in a single convolution operation, using the kernel

$$\begin{bmatrix} -1 & -1 & -1 \\ -1 & c & -1 \\ -1 & -1 & -1 \end{bmatrix} \quad (c > 8).$$

When the central coefficient, c, is large, convolution will have little effect on an image. As c gets closer to 8, however, the degree of sharpening increases. If $c = 8$ the kernel becomes the high pass filter described earlier. Figure 7.16 gives examples of high boost filtering with two different values of c.

(a)   (b)

Figure 7.16 High boost filtering of the image in Figure 7.13(a). (a) Result of filtering with central coefficient $c = 12$. (b) Result of filtering with $c = 9$.

7.3.4   Implementations in Java

New kernel classes

The linear filtering operations discussed in the preceding sections can all be implemented by following the same procedure:

1. Create a kernel, an instance of the `Kernel` or `StandardKernel` classes
2. Create an operator, an instance of `ConvolveOp` or `ConvolutionOp`
3. Call the operator's `filter()` method

Initialising the kernel is the most tedious part of the process, particularly if the kernel coefficients have to be calculated (as in the case of Gaussian filters, for example).

We can simplify matters greatly by creating specialised kernel classes for the mean filter, Gaussian filter, Laplacian, etc. The constructors for these new classes determine appropriate values for the kernel coefficients. The classes extend `StandardKernel`, ensuring that kernels can be read from or written to files, and that they can be used by `ConvolveOp` or `ConvolutionOp`. Examples of these classes are

```
MeanKernel
GaussianKernel
SeparableGaussianKernel
HighPassKernel
HighBoostKernel
```

all of which are available in the `com.pearsoneduc.ip.op` package.

Listing 7.3 shows the implementation of `HighPassKernel`. This performs high pass filtering, as described in Section 7.3.2. Kernel dimensions are 3×3, and the coefficients are predefined in a static array. One notable feature in `HighPassKernel` is the presence of a `main()` method, which simply creates an instance of the class and calls its `write()` method to print the kernel on standard output. We can redirect standard output to store the kernel in a file:

```
java com.pearsoneduc.ip.op.HighPassKernel > highpass.ker
```

Because this kernel contains negative coefficients, it cannot be applied properly using `ConvolveOp`. Instead, we should use `ConvolutionOp` as follows:

```
Kernel kernel = new HighPassKernel();
ConvolutionOp op =
  new ConvolutionOp(kernel, NeighbourhoodOp.NO_BORDER_OP,
    ConvolutionOp.SINGLE_PASS, ConvolutionOp.RESCALE_MAX_ONLY);
BufferedImage outputImage = convOp.filter(inputImage, null);
```

LISTING 7.3 A kernel class that performs high pass filtering.

```
 1   package com.pearsoneduc.ip.op;
 2
 3
 4   public class HighPassKernel extends StandardKernel {
 5
 6     private static final float[] data = { -1.0f, -1.0f, -1.0f,
 7                                           -1.0f,  8.0f, -1.0f,
 8                                           -1.0f, -1.0f, -1.0f  };
 9
10     public HighPassKernel() {
11       super(3, 3, data, 0);
12     }
13
14     public static void main(String[] argv) {
15       StandardKernel kernel = new HighPassKernel();
16       kernel.write(new java.io.OutputStreamWriter(System.out));
17     }
18
19   }
```

Any border processing strategy is acceptable, but the rescaling strategy should be RESCALE_MAX_ONLY. This will ensure that 0 maps onto the middle of the range in the output image (i.e., 128).

A somewhat more complex example is GaussianKernel, shown in Listing 7.4. The constructor for this class accepts a single parameter, representing the standard deviation for the Gaussian function. From this, it must compute appropriate kernel dimensions, using static method getSize(), and then sample a Gaussian function in two dimensions, using static method createKernelData(). (Since these methods are declared public and static, we can use them without creating an instance of the kernel, if necessary.) Like HighPassKernel, a main() method is provided to print the kernel to standard output. For $\sigma = 1.0$, the following is produced:

```
# convolution kernel
9 9 4
0.0000 0.0000 0.0000 0.0000 0.0000 0.0000 0.0000 0.0000 0.0000
0.0000 0.0000 0.0002 0.0011 0.0018 0.0011 0.0002 0.0000 0.0000
0.0000 0.0002 0.0029 0.0131 0.0215 0.0131 0.0029 0.0002 0.0000
0.0000 0.0011 0.0131 0.0586 0.0965 0.0586 0.0131 0.0011 0.0000
0.0000 0.0018 0.0215 0.0965 0.1592 0.0965 0.0215 0.0018 0.0000
0.0000 0.0011 0.0131 0.0586 0.0965 0.0586 0.0131 0.0011 0.0000
0.0000 0.0002 0.0029 0.0131 0.0215 0.0131 0.0029 0.0002 0.0000
0.0000 0.0000 0.0002 0.0011 0.0018 0.0011 0.0002 0.0000 0.0000
0.0000 0.0000 0.0000 0.0000 0.0000 0.0000 0.0000 0.0000 0.0000
```

GaussianKernel objects have normalised coefficients, so they can be used with ConvolveOp or ConvolutionOp to do Gaussian blurring of an image. ConvolveOp will be faster. If the kernel is large, however, it may be more efficient to use ConvolutionOp together with SeparableGaussianKernel. This class is much like GaussianKernel, except that a kernel with a height of 1 is created. This can be used with ConvolutionOp if a calculation method of SEPARABLE is selected:

```
Kernel kernel = new SeparableGaussianKernel(2.0f);
BufferedImageOp op = new ConvolutionOp(kernel,
  NeighbourhoodOp.NO_BORDER_OP,
  ConvolutionOp.SEPARABLE,
  ConvolutionOp.NO_RESCALING);
BufferedImage outputImage = op.filter(inputImage, null);
```

For convenience, ConvolutionOp provides a static method gaussianBlur() that carries out these steps. It is called with an image, a value of σ and, optionally, a border processing strategy as parameters. (The latter defaults to NO_BORDER_OP if it is not specified.) An example is

```
BufferedImage outputImage =
  ConvolutionOp.gaussianBlur(inputImage, 3.0f);
```

We have observed that this operation takes just under a second to execute on 266 MHz Pentium II hardware running Windows 95 and JDK 1.2. By comparison, the equivalent convolution using GaussianKernel and Convolve takes just over a second, and a non-separable calculation with ConvolutionOp takes over fifteen seconds.

LISTING 7.4 A kernel class to support Gaussian low pass filtering.

```java
1   package com.pearsoneduc.ip.op;
2
3
4   public class GaussianKernel extends StandardKernel {
5
6     public GaussianKernel() {
7       this(1.0f);
8     }
9
10    public GaussianKernel(float sigma) {
11      super(getSize(sigma), getSize(sigma), createKernelData(sigma));
12    }
13
14    public static int getSize(float sigma) {
15      int radius = (int) Math.ceil(4.0f*sigma);
16      return 2*radius+1;
17    }
18
19    public static float[] createKernelData(float sigma) {
20
21      int n = (int) Math.ceil(4.0f*sigma);
22      int size = 2*n+1;
23      float[] data = new float[size*size];
24
25      double r, s = 2.0*sigma*sigma;
26      float norm = 0.0f;
27      int i = 0;
28      for (int y = -n; y <= n; ++y)
29        for (int x = -n; x <= n; ++x, ++i) {
30          r = Math.sqrt(x*x + y*y);
31          data[i] = (float) Math.exp(-r*r/s);
32          norm += data[i];
33        }
34
35      for (i = 0; i < size*size; ++i)
36        data[i] /= norm;
37
38      return data;
39
40    }
41
42    public static void main(String[] argv) {
43      float sigma = 1.0f;
44      if (argv.length > 0)
45        sigma = Float.valueOf(argv[0]).floatValue();
46      StandardKernel kernel = new GaussianKernel(sigma);
47      kernel.write(new java.io.OutputStreamWriter(System.out));
48    }
49
50  }
```

Example applications

Two complete linear filtering applications are provided on the CD. MeanFilter performs mean filtering of an image, using MeanKernel and ConvolveOp. Its implementation is given in Listing 7.5. GaussianBlur performs Gaussian low pass filtering, using GaussianKernel and ConvolveOp. (We assume here that most Gaussian filtering tasks will involve relatively small filters, for which ConvolveOp is more efficient than separable convolution using ConvolutionOp.)

LISTING 7.5 A mean filtering application.

```
1    import java.awt.image.*;
2    import com.pearsoneduc.ip.io.*;
3    import com.pearsoneduc.ip.op.MeanKernel;
4    import com.pearsoneduc.ip.util.IntervalTimer;
5
6
7    public class MeanFilter {
8      public static void main(String[] argv) {
9        if (argv.length > 3) {
10          try {
11            ImageDecoder input = ImageFile.createImageDecoder(argv[0]);
12            ImageEncoder output = ImageFile.createImageEncoder(argv[1]);
13            int w = Integer.parseInt(argv[2]);
14            int h = Integer.parseInt(argv[3]);
15            BufferedImage inputImage = input.decodeAsBufferedImage();
16            Kernel kernel = new MeanKernel(w, h);
17            ConvolveOp blurOp = new ConvolveOp(kernel);
18            IntervalTimer timer = new IntervalTimer();
19            timer.start();
20            BufferedImage outputImage = blurOp.filter(inputImage, null);
21            System.out.println("Mean filtering finished [" +
22              timer.stop() + " sec]");
23            output.encode(outputImage);
24            System.exit(0);
25          }
26          catch (Exception e) {
27            System.err.println(e);
28            System.exit(1);
29          }
30        }
31        else {
32          System.err.println("usage: java MeanFilter infile outfile w h");
33          System.exit(1);
34        }
35      }
36    }
```

7.4 Edge detection

One of the major applications for convolution is in edge detection. Edges can be defined loosely as locations in an image where there is a sudden variation in the grey level or colour of pixels. The contours of potentially interesting scene elements (solid objects, surface markings, shadows, etc.) all generate intensity or colour edges, so edge enhancement and detection are obvious steps to take when attempting to locate and recognise those scene elements. Location and recognition are far from trivial, because noise and other uninteresting image features can also generate edges.

Given a noisy image, edge detection techniques aim to locate the edge pixels most likely to have been generated by scene elements, rather than by noise. Typically, there are three steps to perform:

1. **Noise reduction**, where we try to suppress as much noise as possible, without smoothing away the meaningful edges.
2. **Edge enhancement**, where we apply some kind of filter that responds strongly at edges and weakly elsewhere, so that edges may be identified as local maxima in the filter's output. Figure 7.15 suggests that some kind of high pass filter is required.
3. **Edge localisation**, where we decide which of the local maxima output by the filter are meaningful edges and which are caused by noise.

Edge detection is a huge field of study, on which it would be possible to write an entire book. In the following sections, we merely consider a few techniques that are representative of the field as a whole.

7.4.1 A simple edge detector

The simplest detectors perform minimal noise smoothing and fairly crude localisation. They are based on the estimation of **grey level gradient** at a pixel. The gradient can be approximated in the x and y directions by

$$g_x(x, y) \approx f(x + 1, y) - f(x - 1, y), \tag{7.14}$$
$$g_y(x, y) \approx f(x, y + 1) - f(x, y - 1). \tag{7.15}$$

We can introduce a small amount of noise smoothing if we compute averages of these gradients over a 3×3 neighbourhood. This also allows us to express gradient calculation as a pair of convolution operations,

$$g_x(x, y) = h_x * f(x, y), \tag{7.16}$$
$$g_y(x, y) = h_y * f(x, y), \tag{7.17}$$

where the kernels are

$$h_x = \begin{bmatrix} -1 & 0 & 1 \\ -1 & 0 & 1 \\ -1 & 0 & 1 \end{bmatrix}, \quad h_y = \begin{bmatrix} -1 & -1 & -1 \\ 0 & 0 & 0 \\ 1 & 1 & 1 \end{bmatrix}.$$

These are known as the **Prewitt kernels**. A similar pair of kernels are the **Sobel kernels**,

$$h_x = \begin{bmatrix} -1 & 0 & 1 \\ -2 & 0 & 2 \\ -1 & 0 & 1 \end{bmatrix}, \quad h_y = \begin{bmatrix} -1 & -2 & -1 \\ 0 & 0 & 0 \\ 1 & 2 & 1 \end{bmatrix}.$$

These give more weight to on-axis pixels.

Figure 7.17 shows the results of convolving the Sobel kernels with an image. Because the kernels contain both positive and negative coefficients, the output can be negative or positive. For display purposes, we map gradients of zero onto a mid-grey tone, with negative and positive gradients appearing darker and lighter, respectively. Clearly, the kernel h_x is sensitive to changes in the x direction, i.e., edges that run vertically, or have a vertical component. Similarly, the kernel h_y is sensitive to changes in the y direction, i.e., edges that run horizontally, or have a horizontal component. But how do we combine the results of convolution with these two kernels to give a single measure of the presence of an edge?

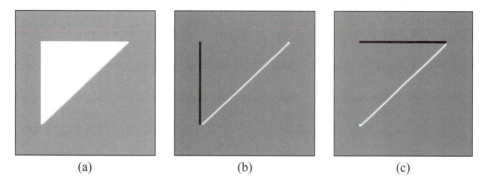

(a)   (b)   (c)

Figure 7.17 Sobel edge detection. (a) Original image. (b) Convolution of image with h_x. (c) Convolution of image with h_y.

The two gradients computed at each pixel by Equations 7.16 and 7.17 can be regarded as the x and y components of a **gradient vector**,

$$\mathbf{g} = \begin{bmatrix} g_x \\ g_y \end{bmatrix}.$$

This vector is oriented along the direction of change, normal to the direction in which the edge runs. Gradient magnitude and direction are given by

$$g = \sqrt{g_x^2 + g_y^2}, \tag{7.18}$$

$$\theta = \tan^{-1}\left(\frac{g_y}{g_x}\right), \tag{7.19}$$

where θ is measured relative to the x axis. The square-root operation in Equation 7.18 is relatively expensive, so gradient magnitude is sometimes approximated by

$$g = |g_x| + |g_y|. \tag{7.20}$$

(a)   (b)

Figure 7.18   (a) The *barn* image. (b) Gradient magnitudes for the *barn* image, scaled to a 0–255 range and displayed as an image.

Gradient magnitude will be large whenever g_x or g_y are large, i.e., whenever there is a big change in grey level within the 3×3 neighbourhood of a pixel. Thus g measures the strength of an edge, irrespective of its orientation. Figure 7.18 shows an image and its gradient magnitudes computed with Sobel kernels and Equation 7.18.

In the localisation step, we must identify the meaningful edges from gradient magnitude data. A typical (though not necessarily correct) assumption is that meaningful edges give rise to the strongest gradients, so a simple approach is to *threshold* the gradient magnitudes computed using Equations 7.18 or 7.20. Thresholding produces an 'edge map'—a binary image in which pixels set to 1 represent meaningful edges. Figure 7.19 shows edge maps created from the gradient magnitude data of Figure 7.18 using two different thresholds.

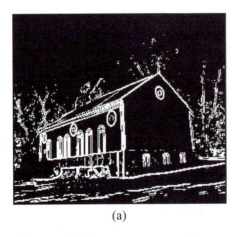 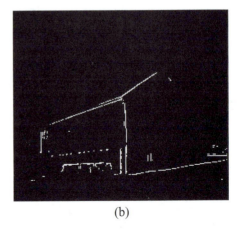

(a)   (b)

Figure 7.19   Edge maps created by thresholding the gradient magnitudes in Figure 7.18. (a) Threshold of 50. (b) Threshold of 150.

There are three problems with this approach. First, the boundaries between scene elements are not always sharp. At sharp boundaries, there is a large change in grey level within a 3 × 3 neighbourhood, so gradient magnitude is high. Diffuse boundaries, however, are characterised by more gradual changes in grey level. The change within a 3 × 3 neighbourhood at a diffuse boundary is likely to be small, so gradient magnitude will be much lower. We can see this in Figure 7.20, which plots profiles of gradient magnitude across slightly blurred and heavily blurred edges. Although both edges are clearly meaningful to the observer, a threshold of 60 would create an edge map in which only the sharper edge was represented.

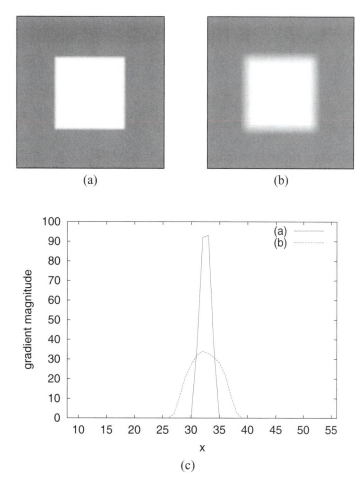

Figure 7.20 Profiles of gradient magnitude across blurred edges. (a) Image of a slightly blurred square. (b) Image of a heavily blurred square. (c) Profiles of gradient magnitude across one edge of the squares in (a) and (b).

A second problem is that noise can sometimes produce gradients as high as, or even higher than, those resulting from meaningful edges. This can be seen in Figure 7.21, which

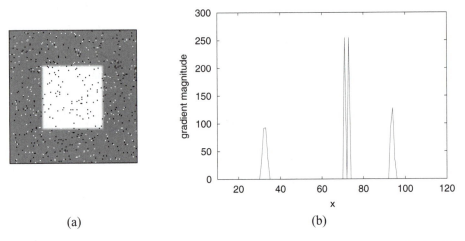

(a)   (b)

Figure 7.21 Sensitivity of gradient magnitude to noise. (a) Noisy image. (b) Profile of gradient magnitude across image.

plots a profile of gradient magnitude across a synthetic image to which impulse noise has been added. The tallest peaks in the profile were produced by a noisy pixel; the two lower peaks correspond to the edges of the square.

The final problem with a simple threshold approach is that the local maximum in grey level gradient associated with an edge lies at the summit of a ridge. Thresholding detects a portion of this ridge, rather than the single point of maximum gradient. The ridge can be rather broad in the case of diffuse edges, resulting in a thick band of pixels in the edge map. This can be seen clearly in Figure 7.19.

7.4.2   The Laplacian

If we imagine an image to be a surface, with height corresponding to grey level, then it is clear that convolution with the Sobel kernels gives us *first-order derivatives* that measure the local slope of this surface in the x and y directions. It is also possible to compute *second-order derivatives*. These measure the rate at which the slope of the grey level surface changes with distance travelled in the x and y directions. These second-order derivatives can be used for edge localisation.

At the top of Figure 7.22 is a profile of grey level across the blurred edge of Figure 7.20(b). Below it, the first derivative of this profile is plotted. A broad peak is produced because the change in grey level is not abrupt. Below the first derivative is the second derivative. On the dark side of the edge, this quantity is positive. On the bright side of the edge, it is negative. It changes sign at the centre of the edge, so we can localise the edge by searching for a **zero crossing** of the second derivative.

The **Laplacian** of an image f combines the second-order derivatives as follows:

$$\nabla^2 f = \frac{\partial^2 f}{\partial x^2} + \frac{\partial^2 f}{\partial y^2}. \tag{7.21}$$

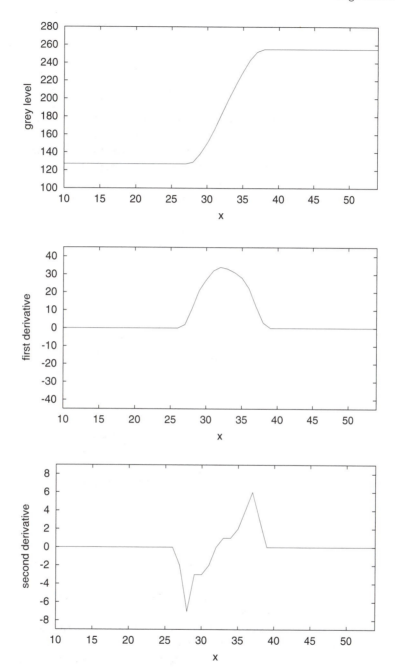

Figure 7.22 Edge detection with first- and second-order derivatives. Note the correspondence between the maximum value of the first derivative, at $x = 32$, and the zero crossing of the second derivative, also at $x = 32$.

A simple, digital approximation to the Laplacian over a 3×3 neighbourhood is given by the kernel

$$\begin{bmatrix} 0 & -1 & 0 \\ -1 & 4 & -1 \\ 0 & -1 & 0 \end{bmatrix},$$

which is very similar to the high pass filter described earlier.

The Laplacian is seldom used on its own for edge detection, because it is unacceptably sensitive to noise. It is more useful as part of the **Laplacian of Gaussian** (LoG) filter. This uses a Gaussian filter to blur the image and a Laplacian to enhance edges. Localisation is done by finding zero crossings.

A radially-symmetric, two-dimensional Gaussian is given by

$$h(r) = \exp\left(\frac{-r^2}{2\sigma^2}\right), \tag{7.22}$$

with $r^2 = x^2 + y^2$. The Laplacian of this is

$$\nabla^2 h = \left(\frac{r^2 - \sigma^2}{\sigma^4}\right) \exp\left(\frac{-r^2}{2\sigma^2}\right). \tag{7.23}$$

This function has a minimum at its origin. However, it is usual to invert the filter such that it has a maximum at its origin, giving it the classic 'mexican hat' shape seen in Figure 7.23.

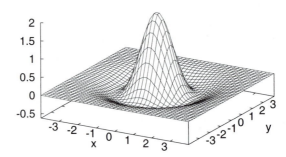

Figure 7.23 The inverted Laplacian-of-Gaussian filter.

The value of σ in Equation 7.23 determines the width of the filter and controls the amount of smoothing produced by its Gaussian component. In effect, σ tunes the filter to detect edges at different scales (Figure 7.24). Note that the kernel used to implement a LoG filter should have a half-width of at least 3σ. LoG filtering is therefore very expensive computationally, even with only a modest amount of smoothing. A good approximation to the LoG filter is formed by subtracting two Gaussians of different widths. Gaussian filters are separable (Section 7.2.3), so this **difference of Gaussians** (DoG) filter is an attractive and efficient alternative to the LoG filter.

In order to form an edge map from LoG filter output, we must locate and mark the zero crossings. In practice, exact values of zero will not be found at many of the pixels in the filtered image; we may therefore need to infer the presence of a zero crossing from the existence of two adjacent pixels with opposite signs. One of these must be marked as the zero—normally the one with the smallest absolute value. Figure 7.24 shows the edge maps created by applying LoG filters to the *barn* image and detecting the zero crossings.

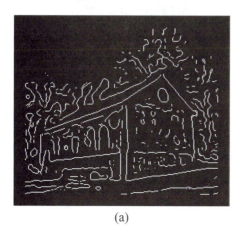 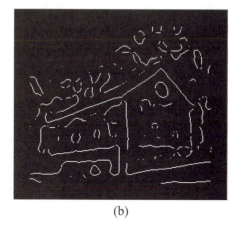

(a)   (b)

Figure 7.24 Edge detection in the *barn* image with a Laplacian-of-Gaussian filter. (a) Edge map for $\sigma = 3.0$. (c) Edge map for $\sigma = 5.0$.

7.4.3   The Canny edge detector

The **Canny edge detector** represents a somewhat more sophisticated approach to the creation of an edge map for an image. It specifically addresses the fact that, for any edge detector, there is a trade-off between noise reduction and edge localisation. Improved noise reduction is typically achieved at the expense of good localisation, and vice versa. The Canny detector can be shown to provide the best possible compromise between these two conflicting requirements[2].

For the smoothing step, the Canny detector employs a Gaussian low pass filter. The standard deviation, σ, determines the width of the filter and hence the amount of smoothing. A filter with large σ will suppress much of the noise but will also smooth away the weakest edges. The edge enhancement step simply involves calculation of the gradient vector at each pixel of the smoothed image, using Equations 7.19 and 7.18, for example. Efficient implementations of the Canny detector combine the smoothing and enhancement steps by convolving the image with a derivative of Gaussian kernel. It is also possible to exploit Gaussian separability, and compute x and y gradients with one-dimensional kernels.

The localisation step has two stages: **non-maximal suppression** and **hysteresis thresholding**. Non-maximal suppression thins the wide ridges around local maxima in gradient magnitude down to edges that are only one pixel wide. Algorithm 7.7 shows

---

[2] The Canny detector is optimal for step edges in the presence of Gaussian noise. Of course, real edges are not simple steps, and real noise is not purely Gaussian in nature. Nevertheless, the Canny detector is observed to give good results with real images.

ALGORITHM 7.7 Non-maximal suppression in the Canny edge detector.

Create an output image, g_s, with the same dimensions as g
for all pixel coordinates, x and y, **do**
    Approximate $\theta(x, y)$ by $\hat{\theta}$, one of the angles $0°$, $45°$, $90°$, $135°$
    if $g(x, y) < g$ at neighbour in direction $\hat{\theta}$ **or** $g(x, y) < g$ at neighbour in direction
    $\hat{\theta} + 180°$ **then**
        $g_s(x, y) = 0$
    else
        $g_s(x, y) = g(x, y)$
    end if
end for

(a)

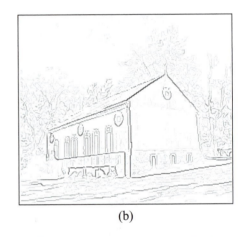
(b)

Figure 7.25 Non-maximal suppression in the Canny edge detector. (a) Gradient magnitudes computed with $\sigma = 1.0$. The image has been inverted for greater clarity. (b) Non-maximal suppression of the gradient data in (a).

how this is done. It assumes that we have already computed gradient magnitude and direction, and that these data are available as two images, g and θ. Figure 7.25 shows gradient magnitudes for the *barn* image, before and after non-maximal suppression using the algorithm.

We have noted already the problems associated with applying a single, fixed threshold to gradient maxima. Choosing a low threshold ensures that we capture the weak yet meaningful edges in the image, but it may also result in an excessive number of 'false positives': gradient maxima caused by noise rather than by interesting scene elements. Too high a threshold, on the other hand, will lead to excessive fragmentation of the chains of pixels that represent significant contours in the image. Hysteresis thresholding offers a solution to these problems. It uses *two* thresholds, T_{low} and T_{high}. The higher of these thresholds is used to mark the best edge pixel candidates. We then attempt to grow these pixels into contours by searching for neighbours with gradient magnitudes higher than T_{low}. In some versions of the technique [such as 25, 36], the search is conducted over all eight neighbours of an edge pixel; in others [46, for example], only the neighbours along a line normal to the gradient orientation at the edge pixel are considered.

This technique can reduce the number of false positives because edges are tracked only if at least one pixel has a gradient magnitude exceeding T_{high}, which can be made quite large. It also reduces the fragmentation of contours in the edge map by allowing significant fluctuations to occur in gradient magnitude on an edge (if T_{low} is suitably small).

Figure 7.26 compares use of a single threshold with use of hysteresis thresholding for gradient magnitudes computed from the *barn* image with $\sigma = 1.0$. Figure 7.27 shows edge maps computed by a Sobel edge detector with the same thresholds.

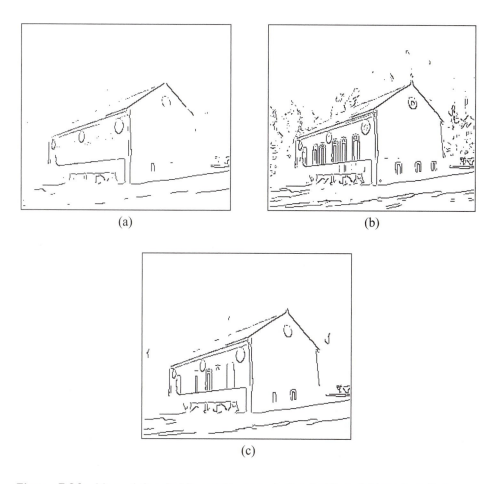

(a)

(b)

(c)

Figure 7.26 Normal thresholding and hysteresis thresholding of thinned gradient magnitude data. (a) Single threshold of 100. (b) Single threshold of 50. (c) Hysteresis thresholding with $T_{low} = 50$ and $T_{high} = 100$.

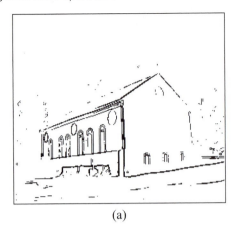
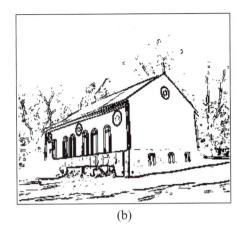

(a)   (b)

Figure 7.27 Sobel edge maps of the *barn* image. (a) Gradient magnitude threshold of 100. (b) Threshold of 50.

7.4.4   Implementations in Java

Kernels

Four kernels that can be used for simple gradient calculation are provided in the `com.pearsoneduc.ip.op` package:

```
HorizontalPrewittKernel
VerticalPrewittKernel
HorizontalSobelKernel
VerticalSobelKernel
```

These should be used with `ConvolutionOp` rather than `ConvolveOp`, because the kernels contain negative coefficients. If the output from convolution is needed for subsequent calculations, the `convolve()` method should be used rather than `filter()`, to avoid any loss of precision caused by rescaling of output data.

Complete edge detectors

Implementations are provided in the `com.pearsoneduc.ip.op` package of the Sobel and Canny edge detectors. A Sobel edge detector application is also available on the CD.

`SobelEdgeOp` implements `StandardGreyOp`. Its default constructor creates an operator that computes gradient magnitude using a square-root, as in Equation 7.18, and performs no thresholding of gradient magnitude data. Other constructors allow a threshold and the alternative gradient magnitude calculation method of Equation 7.20 to be specified. (On the hardware used to develop `SobelEdgeOp`, computing gradient magnitude by Equation 7.20 is about three times faster than computing gradient magnitude by Equation 7.18.) `SobelEdgeOp` overrides the `filter()` method so that it

1. Computes gradient magnitudes using the desired calculation method
2. Rescales gradient magnitudes to a 0–255 range

3. Thresholds gradient magnitudes if required

CannyEdgeOp also implements StandardGreyOp. There are three differents ways of creating a CannyEdgeOp object, illustrated by the following examples:

```
CannyEdgeOp op1 = new CannyEdgeOp(2.0f);
CannyEdgeOp op2 = new CannyEdgeOp(2.0f, 50, 100);
CannyEdgeOp op3 =
  new CannyEdgeOp(2.0f, 50, 100, CannyEdgeOp.ABS_MAGNITUDES);
```

Here, op1 will smooth an image with a Gaussian low pass filter of width $\sigma = 2.0$, compute gradient at each pixel using Equations 7.18 and 7.19 and then perform non-maximal suppression of gradient magnitudes. No thresholding will be done. Operator op2 is essentially the same as op1, except that it performs hysteresis thresholding with $T_{low} = 50$ and $T_{high} = 100$ on the thinned gradient magnitudes. Operator op3 differs from op2 only in that gradient magnitudes are computed by Equation 7.20.

CannyEdgeOp provides methods that can be used to retrieve gradient magnitude and orientation data *after* a call to filter():

```
BufferedImageOp op = new CannyEdgeOp(2.0f, 50, 100);
BufferedImage edgeMap = op.filter(image, null);
BufferedImage magImage = op.getGradientMagnitudeImage();
BufferedImage orientImage = op.getGradientOrientationImage();
```

7.5 Rank filtering

Convolution is not the only way of carrying out spatial filtering. Non-linear techniques also exist. A number of these are known collectively as 'order statistic' filters or **rank filters**. The idea behind rank filtering is simple. We compile a list of the grey levels in the neighbourhood of a given pixel, sort this list into ascending order and then select a value from a particular position in the list to use as the new value for the pixel. The new values must be stored in another image; we cannot perform the operation in place.

As with all neighbourhood operations, special consideration must be given to the borders of the image. The strategies that were discussed for convolution in Section 7.2.1 can also be applied to rank filtering. Rank filters have the advantage of not being kernel-based, so there is no problem with filtering over a smaller neighbourhood at the corners and sides of the image.

7.5.1 Median filter

The most common rank filter is the **median filter**, in which we select the middle-ranked value from a neighbourhood as our output value. For a 3×3 neighbourhood, the middle value is fifth in the list of sorted grey levels; for an $n \times n$ neighbourhood with n odd, the middle value is at position $\lfloor \frac{n^2}{2} \rfloor + 1$.

The median filter is particularly good at removing certain types of noise. Figure 7.28(a) shows a synthetic image in which random *impulse noise* affects 5 per cent of the pixels. Impulse noise forces a pixel's value to one of the extremes of the range—0 or 255 in the

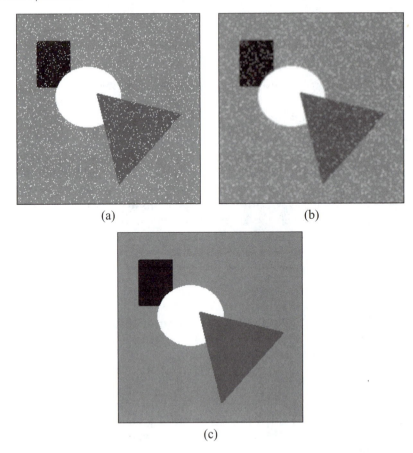

Figure 7.28 Noise suppression by mean and median filtering. (a) Image corrupted by five per cent impulse noise. (b) Result of 3 × 3 mean filtering. (c) Result of 3 × 3 median filtering.

case of 8-bit images[3]. Figure 7.28(b) shows the result of smoothing the noisy image using a 3 × 3 mean filter. The amplitude of the noise has been reduced, but the image still has a distinctly mottled appearance. Furthermore, the main features of interest—the edges—have been blurred. Figure 7.28(c) shows the result of applying a 3 × 3 median filter to the image in (a). The impulse noise has been eliminated completely, and the effect on other features is minimal.

We can see how the median filter is able to eliminate impulse noise by examining the computation that is done in a single 3 × 3 neighbourhood of an image. Figure 7.29 shows a small portion of the image in Figure 7.28(a), with a 3 × 3 neighbourhood outlined. We can guess that the central pixel should have a value of 64, but it has been affected by impulse

---

[3] Here, all noisy pixels have the value 255. Randomly choosing one or the other of the extremes for each noisy pixel gives rise to a pattern often referred to as 'salt and pepper' noise.

64	64	64	64	64	64	64	64
64	64	64	64	64	64	64	64
64	64	64	64	64	255	255	64
64	64	64	255	255	64	64	64
64	64	64	64	255	64	64	255
64	64	64	64	64	255	64	128
64	64	64	64	64	64	128	128
64	64	64	64	255	128	128	128

Figure 7.29 A 3 × 3 neighbourhood within a portion of the noisy image in Figure 7.28(a).

noise. The new value obtained for this pixel using a 3 × 3 mean filter is

$$\frac{64 + 64 + 64 + 64 + 255 + 255 + 64 + 64 + 255}{9} = 128$$

(rounding to the nearest integer)

so mean filtering has not removed the noise completely. To apply a median filter, we place the grey levels from the neighbourhood in a list,

$$\{64, 64, 64, 64, 255, 255, 64, 64, 255\},$$

and sort the list into ascending order, producing

$$\{64, 64, 64, 64, \mathbf{64}, 64, 255, 255, 255\}.$$

The median from this set of values is 64. The noisy values have migrated to the end of the list and therefore do not affect the selection of a new pixel value.

Clearly, median filtering can eliminate impulse noise only if the noisy pixels occupy less than half the area of the neighbourhood. We can see this in Figure 7.30, which shows the effects of median filtering on an image corrupted by 20% impulse noise. In Figure 7.30(b), a 3 × 3 median filter has been applied. The noise density is high enough that, in a few locations, a 3 × 3 neighbourhood contains more than four noisy pixels. Consequently, some noise remains in the filtered image. In Figure 7.30(c), a 9 × 9 median filter has been applied. With a larger neighbourhood, local noise density stays closer to the global average of 20%, with the result that no noisy pixels pass through the filter.

It is evident from Figure 7.30(c), and from the magnified views shown in Figure 7.31, that features of interest do not necessarily survive median filtering unscathed. It is important to remember that median filtering is non-specific; any structure that occupies less than half of the filter's neighbourhood will tend to be eliminated. The damage seen in Figure 7.31 is, in part, a result of the *shape* of the filter. Figure 7.32 shows how a square neighbourhood erodes the corners of a rectangular object and how a cross-shaped neighbourhood leaves them unaffected.

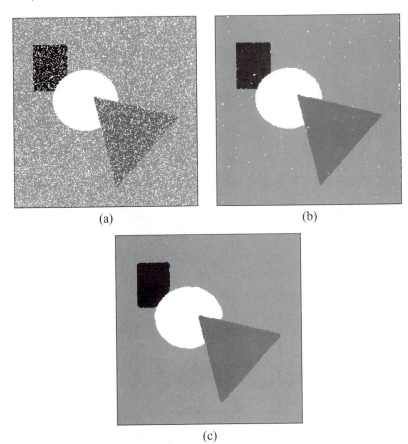

(a)   (b)

(c)

Figure 7.30 Median filtering of very noisy images. (a) Image with 20% impulse noise. (b) Result of 3 × 3 median filtering. (c) Result of 9 × 9 median filtering.

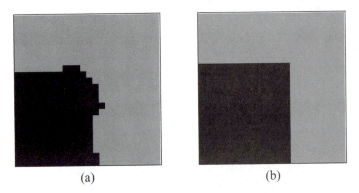

(a)   (b)

Figure 7.31 (a) Magnified portion of Figure 7.30(c), showing damage to the rectangle's corners. (b) Same portion of the original image, before the addition of noise and median filtering.

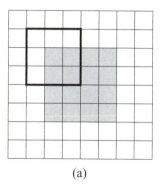 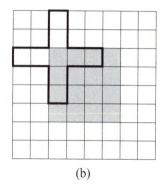

(a) (b)

Figure 7.32 Effect of neighbourhood shape on the results of median filtering. (a) Square neighbourhood contains 5 background pixels and 4 object pixels, so central pixel takes on the background value. (b) Cross-shaped neighbourhood contains 4 background pixels and 5 object pixels, so central pixels remains unchanged.

Performance

The sorting of neighbourhood grey levels into ascending order is a significant computational burden, particularly when the neighbourhood is large. Consequently, we must select a sorting algorithm carefully. Relatively small differences in performance can be magnified because sorting is done many thousands, or even millions, of times to process a single image. Quicksort is widely acknowledged to be, on average, the best general-purpose sorting algorithm [43], and an efficient implementation is available in Java 2 as a static method of the java.util.Arrays class, so this is an obvious choice for an implementation of median filtering in Java. However, Quicksort is known to perform poorly, relative to certain other sorting algorithms, on small lists. This point is significant, because a 3×3 neighbourhood, the most common that we use in spatial filtering, yields a small list consisting of only nine values. Figure 7.33 bears this out. It shows that (in this particular environment, at least) insertion sort performs slightly better than Quicksort for 3×3 filters. Quicksort is marginally better for 5×5 filters, and far superior to insertion sort for larger filters.

But do we really need to use a sorting algorithm? An alternative approach is possible, in which we calculate the histogram of grey levels in a neighbourhood and then search this histogram to find the median. The median will be the grey level at which the cumulative frequency equals or exceeds half the neighbourhood size. Figure 7.33 shows execution times for a median filter that implements this approach. For a 3×3 median filter, the sorting approach is clearly faster; for a 5×5 filter, there is very little difference in performance; for neighbourhoods larger than 5×5, sorting becomes more expensive than computing and searching the histogram.

The histogram technique can be improved if we exploit the fact that the neighbourhoods of adjacent pixels overlap to a large degree. Rather than computing a completely new histogram for the neighbourhood surrounding a pixel at (x, y), we can simply adjust the histogram that we computed at $(x - 1, y)$. If the neighbourhood has dimensions $n \times n$, then the histogram must lose counts for the n pixels no longer in the neighbourhood and gain counts for the n pixels that have moved into the neighbourhood. The median, likewise, can be updated from the previous estimate.

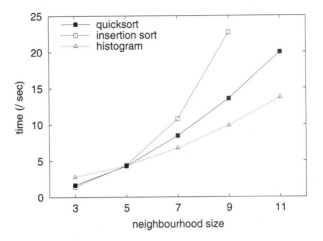

Figure 7.33 Execution times for median filtering of a 512×512 image, using two different sorting techniques and a histogram-based technique. Times were obtained using JDK 1.2 with JIT compilation enabled, on a 266 MHz Pentium II running Windows 95.

7.5.2 Minimum and maximum filters

The **minimum filter** is a rank filter in which we select the bottom-ranked grey level from the neighbourhood (i.e., the minimum grey level) as the output value. The **maximum filter** performs similarly, except that we select the top-ranking grey level from the neighbourhood (i.e., the maximum grey level) as the output value.

Figures 7.34 and 7.35 show the results of minimum and maximum filtering, respectively, in 3×3 and 7×7 neighbourhoods. Minimum filtering causes the darker regions of an image to swell in size and dominate the lighter regions, whereas maximum filtering has the converse effect. Both operations have a non-linear blurring effect on an image.

(a)　　　　　　　　　　　　　　　　　(b)

Figure 7.34 Effect of minimum filtering on the *barn* image of Figure 7.13. (a) 3×3 neighbourhood. (b) 7×7 neighbourhood.

 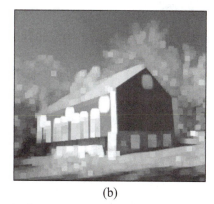

(a) (b)

Figure 7.35 Effect of maximum filtering on the *barn* image. (a) 3×3 neighbourhood. (b) 7×7 neighbourhood.

Performance

The general idea of a rank filter is that we sort grey levels from the neighbourhood into ascending order[4]. An implementation of a minimum or maximum filter might well use this generic approach, but determining the minimum or maximum of a set of values does *not* require that they be sorted. In fact, we can determine the minimum or maximum of a set of n values by making $n - 1$ comparisons—whereas the average cost of Quicksort is on the order of $n \log_2 n$. This is borne out in Figure 7.36, which plots execution time versus neighbourhood size for two implementations of a minimum filter: one using Quicksort

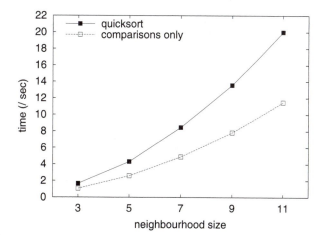

Figure 7.36 Execution times for minimum filtering of a 512×512 image, using sorting and straight comparison. Benchmarking was carried out using the software and hardware described earlier.

---

[4] Although, as we have seen, algorithms that do not involve sorting can be devised.

and the other simple comparisons. Clearly, there is no compelling reason to use sorting in a minimum or maximum filter—unless some other order statistic like the median is also required.

We will encounter minimum and maximum filters once again, in a different guise, in Chapter 11.

7.5.3 Range filter

The range filter simply outputs the difference between the maximum and minimum grey levels in a neighbourhood centred on a pixel. Essentially, it is an omnidirectional, non-linear edge detector. An example can be seen in Figure 7.37. Note, however, that edges detected by this filter are not well-localised, particularly when the neighbourhood is large.

Figure 7.37   Non-linear edge detection by range filtering.

7.5.4 Implementation of rank filters in Java

When developing a Java implementation of convolution in Section 7.2.5, we took care to factor out those aspects of the calculation that apply generally to all neighbourhood operations and not merely to convolution. This code exists in the NeighbourhoodOp class, which we can extend into a new class that performs rank filtering. A design for this class, RankFilterOp, is shown graphically in Figure 7.38. Three constructors are provided to create RankFilterOp objects. All three require that the rank of the filter be specified. The dimensions of the neighbourhood in which filtering takes place can optionally be specified. (A default of 3×3 is used if they are not.) We can also specify a particular border processing strategy. (The default is NO_BORDER_OP.) The filter() method performs rank filtering, using the sort() method of java.util.Arrays to place neighbourhood grey levels in ascending order.

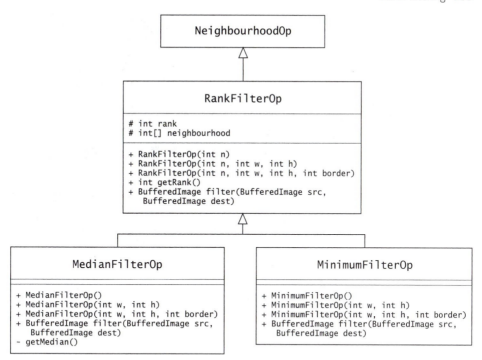

Figure 7.38   Classes for rank filtering.

We have already noted that sorting values from each pixel's neighbourhood is not necessarily the optimal approach to use in rank filtering. The solution adopted here is to subclass RankFilterOp and override filter() with a more efficient implementation. This is done in classes MedianFilterOp, MinimumFilterOp and MaximumFilterOp, two of which are shown in Figure 7.38. Creation of instances of these classes is similar to creation of a RankFilterOp, except that the rank of the filter is now implicit and need not be specified. MedianFilterOp implements a histogram-based approach to finding the median. MinimumFilterOp and MaximumFilterOp determine the minimum and maximum, respectively, by means of comparisons rather than sorting.

Example applications

A number of rank filtering applications are provided on the CD. RankFilter uses a RankFilterOp to carry out generalised rank filtering in neighbourhoods of arbitrary dimensions. MedianFilter, MinFilter and MaxFilter use their associated operators to perform more efficient median, minimum and maximum filtering, respectively, in neighbourhoods of arbitrary dimensions. Each of these programs is controlled from the command line.

You can experiment more readily with the performance of different rank filtering algorithms by running the MedianTest and MinTest programs.   The former uses

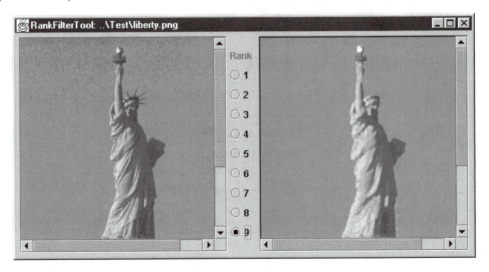

Figure 7.39 A GUI-based tool for rank filtering.

`RankFilterOp` and `MedianFilterOp` to compare execution times for median finding techniques based on sorting and histogram searching; the latter uses `RankFilterOp` and `MinimumFilterOp` to compare execution times for minimum finding by sorting and by comparisons only.

Finally, the `RankFilterTool` application provides a graphical user interface to display an image and the results of applying a 3×3 rank filter to that image. The rank of the filter is selected via a set of radiobuttons. Figure 7.39 shows this program in action.

7.6 Hybrid filters

Some spatial filters are hybrids of linear and non-linear filters. The classic example is the **α-trimmed mean filter**. This filter sorts values from a neighbourhood into ascending order, discards a certain number of these values from either end of the list and outputs the mean of the remaining values. If the ordered set of values is $f_1 \leqslant f_2 \leqslant \ldots \leqslant f_{n^2}$, then the α-trimmed mean is

$$\frac{1}{n^2 - 2\alpha} \sum_{i=\alpha+1}^{n^2-\alpha} f_i. \tag{7.24}$$

The parameter α is the number of values removed from each end of the list. It can vary between 0 and $\frac{n^2-1}{2}$. When $\alpha = 0$, no values are removed from the list and the filter behaves as a straightforward mean filter; when $\alpha = \frac{n^2-1}{2}$, all values are removed but the middle one, and the filter behaves exactly like a median filter; for intermediate values of α, the filter acts as a compromise between a mean filter and a median filter.

The value of the α-trimmed mean lies in the fact that mean filters suppress additive Gaussian noise reasonably well but perform poorly on impulsive noise, whereas the opposite is true of median filters. In images afflicted by both types of noise, the α-trimmed mean filter performs better than a pure mean or pure median filter.

7.7   Adaptive filters

The spatial filters described in this chapter all perform the same calculation at almost every pixel in an image. However, the properties of an image can vary spatially; thus, a filter that performs well in one part of an image is not guaranteed to perform well in another part of that image. For example, in an image corrupted by Gaussian random noise, a mean filter will be effective in those parts of the image that are supposed to be homogeneous, but will have an adverse blurring effect in regions that are meant to be heterogeneous due to the presence of edges. Problems of this nature can be minimised by using an **adaptive filter**—a filter whose behaviour changes in response to variations in local image properties.

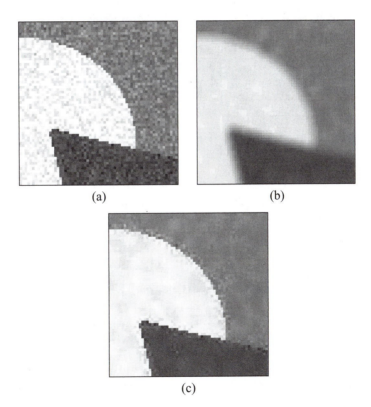

(a)   (b)

(c)

Figure 7.40 Minimal mean squared error filtering of noisy images. (a) Synthetic image corrupted by Gaussian random noise, $\sigma = 20$. (b) Results of 5×5 mean filtering. (c) Output from a 5×5 MMSE filter.

Most adaptive filters compute local grey level statistics within the neighbourhood of a pixel and base their behaviour on this information. The classic example is the **minimal mean square error filter**, or MMSE filter. This filter computes

$$g(x, y) = f(x, y) - \frac{\sigma_n^2}{\sigma^2(x, y)}[f(x, y) - \bar{f}(x, y)], \qquad (7.25)$$

where σ_n^2 is an estimate of noise variance, $\sigma^2(x, y)$ is the grey level variance computed for the neighbourhood centred on (x, y) and $\bar{f}(x, y)$ is the mean grey level in that neighbourhood.

In supposedly homogeneous regions of an image, noise will be the sole cause of variations in grey level; thus, $\sigma^2(x, y) = \sigma_n^2$ and Equation 7.25 reduces to

$$g(x, y) = \bar{f}(x, y).$$

In the vicinity of edges, we expect $\sigma^2(x, y)$ to dominate local noise variance, resulting in a small ratio of variances and a value for $g(x, y)$ that is close to the original value at that pixel, $f(x, y)$. This behaviour can be seen in Figure 7.40, which shows a portion of a synthetic image to which Gaussian random noise has been added, along with the output from mean and MMSE filters applied to that image. The mean filter has suppressed the noise but has also blurred the edges significantly; the MMSE filter has preserved the edges, and also the noise in the immediate vicinity of the edges.

An implementation of the MMSE filter is provided as the class `MMSEFilterOp` in the `com.pearsoneduc.ip.op` package. A program called `MMSEFilter` that uses this operator can also be found on the CD.

7.8   Further reading

The technique of circular indexing and its role in convolution are discussed further by Lyon [29] and by Umbaugh [48], amongst others.

Umbaugh [48] discusses the performance of mean filters based on statistics other than the standard arithmetic mean.

There is a vast literature on the subject of edge detection. An article by Prewitt [40] gives a perspective on early work in this field. The Laplacian of Gaussian filter was first described by Marr and Hildreth [30]. (In fact, it is sometimes referred to as the Marr–Hildreth filter.) Further information on the Canny edge detector can be found in the original paper by Canny [8]. Parker [36] presents a thorough experimental comparison of the Canny edge detector with another optimal edge detector due to Shen and Castan [44].

The 'running median' technique mentioned in Section 7.5 was introduced by Huang et al. [24] and has been revisited by Astola and Campbell [3]. Pitas [37] gives an implementation in C. Pitas also presents implementations of fast minimum and maximum filters.

Crane [11] considers how blurring, sharpening and median filtering operations might be performed on colour images. Sangwine and Horne [41] present further information on this topic.

7.9 Exercises

1. Convolution can produce an image which has a narrow border of black pixels. What effect will this have on an operation such as histogram equalisation?

2. Use the classes described in this chapter to create applications that perform high pass and high boost filtering.

3. Convolve the Sobel x and y kernels with the following 3×3 neighbourhood:

$$\begin{array}{ccc} 10 & 15 & 17 \\ 11 & 100 & 101 \\ 20 & 103 & 97 \end{array}$$

   Then compute the magnitude and direction of the gradient vector.

4. Modify the `GaussianBlur` application from the CD so that it switches to separable convolution when filter size gets sufficiently large.

5. The mean filter is a linear filter but the median filter is not. Explain why this is the case.

6. Given the 3×3 neighbourhood

$$\begin{array}{ccc} 176 & 177 & 172 \\ 174 & 2 & 170 \\ 171 & 172 & 170 \end{array}$$

   calculate a new value for the central pixel using the mean and median filters. Compare and comment on your results.

7. "Median filtering may reduce the number of occupied bins in a histogram. It will never increase the numbers of occupied bins." Is this true? Explain your reasoning.

8. Improve the histogram-based `MedianFilter` class so that it exploits overlapping neighbourhoods. (Consult the references [3, 24, 37] for guidance if required.) Perform benchmark testing of this improved class with other implementations based on the quicksort routine provided with Java 2 and your own implementation of insertion sort. (See Shaffer [43] or other texts on algorithms for details.) Use the results of benchmarking to create a hybrid median filter that uses the quickest technique for any given neighbourhood size.

9. Implement an alpha trimmed mean filter. (Inherit from `RankFilterOp` and use the `filter()` implementation in that class as the basis of your new `filter()` method.)

CHAPTER 8

The frequency domain

Images represent variations of brightness or colour in space. We saw in Chapter 7 how these spatial variations can be manipulated by operations such as convolution. But we are not restricted to processing images in the spatial domain. There exists an alternative representation of an image based on the frequencies of brightness or colour variation in that image. We can convert an image into a spectrum of different frequency components and convert this spectral representation back into a spatial representation without any loss of information. We can also process the image in the frequency domain by manipulating its spectrum. In this chapter, we shall explore the nature of the frequency domain, consider the computational techniques used to move between domains and examine the ways in which images can be changed by manipulating their spectra.

8.1 Spatial frequency

We noted in Section 7.3 that areas of an image in which grey level varies rapidly with distance travelled contain high spatial frequencies; conversely, areas in which grey level varies slowly contain only low spatial frequency components. But what, precisely, do we mean by the term 'spatial frequency'?

Frequency has a precise meaning when we consider periodic functions. A periodic function such as the sinusoid in Figure 8.1 consists of a fixed pattern or cycle that repeats endlessly in both directions. The length of this cycle, L, is known as the **period** of the function. The frequency of variation is the reciprocal of the period. If the variation is spatial and L is a distance, then $1/L$ is termed the **spatial frequency** of the variation. A

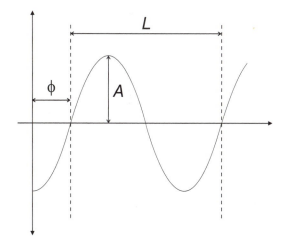

Figure 8.1 A sinusoidal function, characterised by a period (L), an amplitude (A) and a phase (ϕ).

periodic variation is characterised by two further parameters: an **amplitude** and a **phase**. The amplitude (labelled A in Figure 8.1) is the size of the variation—the height of a peak or depth of a trough. The phase (ϕ in Figure 8.1) is the position of the start of a cycle, relative to some reference point (e.g., the origin). A sine function has $\phi = 0$, whereas a cosine function has $\phi = \frac{\pi}{2}$.

What does a sinusoidal variation of image intensity look like? We investigate this by defining a sinusoidal function and rendering it as an image. A suitable function is

$$f(x, y) = 128 + A \sin\left(\frac{2\pi u x}{N - 1} + \phi\right). \tag{8.1}$$

This function generates a sinusoidal variation along the x axis, about a mean grey level of 128. (This offset is necessary because 8-bit greyscale images cannot represent the negative values produced by a sine function.) Amplitude, A, is a value in the range [1, 127]. N is the width of the image, in pixels. The parameter u is a dimensionless spatial frequency, corresponding to the number of complete cycles of the sinusoid that fit into the width of the image. (Dividing by N would give the spatial frequency in units of cycles per pixel.) Lastly, ϕ is the phase.

Figure 8.2 shows the image generated by Equation 8.1 with parameter values $N = 100$, $u = 3$, $A = 127$ and $\phi = 0$. As expected, there are three complete cycles of variation visible in the image (equivalent to a spatial frequency of 0.03 cycles per pixel), and the variation in image brightness spans the full range of 0–255. Figure 8.3 shows images generated by varying each of the parameters u, A and ϕ in turn. In Figure 8.3(a), $u = 6$, producing six cycles of variation in the image. We have doubled the spatial frequency, with the result that grey level fluctuates more rapidly as we move across the image. In 8.3(b), we have reduced A by 60%, resulting in weaker fluctuations in grey level—although the rate of change in grey level remains unchanged. In 8.3(c), we have introduced a phase shift of $\frac{\pi}{2}$ (i.e., 90°),

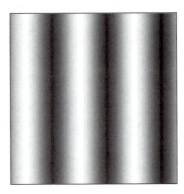

Figure 8.2   An image with a horizontal sinusoidal variation in grey level.

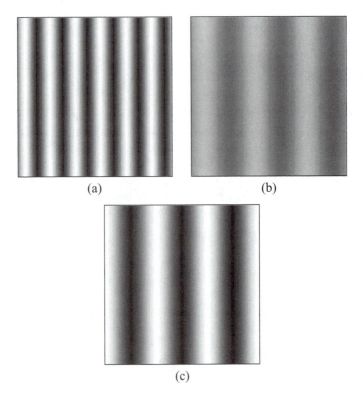

(a)   (b)

(c)

Figure 8.3   Effect of changing frequency, amplitude and phase for the sinusoid in Figure 8.2. (a) Doubling of frequency. (b) 60% reduction in amplitude. (c) 90° phase shift.

turning the sine wave of Figure 8.2 into a cosine pattern without affecting the strength or the frequency of the variation in grey level.

Of course, we can also have sinusoidal variation in the y direction, or in both the x and the y directions simultaneously. We can introduce a second spatial frequency parameter, v,

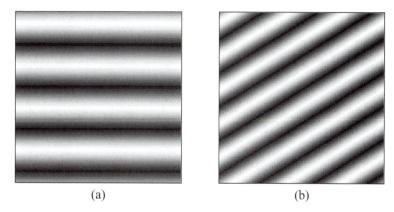

Figure 8.4   More images of sinusoids. (a) $u = 0$, $v = 4$. (b) $u = 3$, $v = 5$.

representing the number of cycles of variation that span the height of the image, to deal with this. Figure 8.4(a) shows a sinusoidal image generated with $u = 0$ and $v = 4$; Figure 8.4(b) shows an image generated with $u = 3$ and $v = 5$.

Evidently, it is possible to determine the frequencies present in images with a very simple, periodic pattern of grey level variation; for sinusoids like those of Figures 8.3 and 8.4, we can simply count peaks and troughs. However, such images are highly artificial. It is not at all obvious how we can measure spatial frequency in real images; indeed, real images often seem to lack any strong periodicity, leading us to question whether the notion of spatial frequency has any meaning. Fortunately, **Fourier theory**, discussed in the following section, comes to our rescue, providing us with the means of analysing an image and measuring the frequencies that are present.

8.2   Fourier theory

8.2.1   Basic concepts

Techniques for the analysis and manipulation of spatial frequency are based on the work of the eighteenth century French physicist Jean Baptiste Joseph Fourier. Fourier developed a representation of functions, based on frequency, that is of considerable importance in many branches of science and engineering. Fourier's theory considers sinusoidal variations (i.e., sine and cosine waves), of the kind depicted in Figure 8.1. The key idea is that any periodic function, however complex it might appear, can be represented as a sum of these simpler sinusoids. This solves the problem of whether it is meaningful to think of spatial frequency in a real, highly complicated image. Although there may be little regularity apparent in such an image, it can be decomposed into a set of sinusoidal components, each of which has a well-defined frequency.

A set of sine and cosine functions having particular frequencies are chosen for the representation. These are termed the **basis functions** of the representation. A weighted sum of these basis functions is called a **Fourier series**. The weighting factors for each sine and cosine function are known as the **Fourier coefficients**. We can write the summation as follows:

$$f(x) = \sum_{n=0}^{\infty} a_n \cos\left(\frac{2\pi nx}{L}\right) + b_n \sin\left(\frac{2\pi nx}{L}\right)$$

$$= a_0 + \sum_{n=1}^{\infty} a_n \cos\left(\frac{2\pi nx}{L}\right) + b_n \sin\left(\frac{2\pi nx}{L}\right). \tag{8.2}$$

The index n in this equation is the number of cycles of the sinusoid that fit within one period of $f(x)$. Thus, n can be considered as a dimensionless measure of the frequency of a basis function. Equation 8.2 indicates that a function with period L can be represented by two infinite sequences of coefficients.

Newcomers to these concepts may need convincing that a summation of smoothly varying functions such as sinusoids can synthesise the sharp discontinuities and relatively homogeneous regions that might be found in an image. A simple example will illustrate that a Fourier series has this capability. Consider a summation of sine functions obtained from Equation 8.2 with $a_0 = 0$, $a_n = 0$ for all n and

$$b_n = \begin{cases} \frac{1}{n} & \text{for } n \text{ odd,} \\ 0 & \text{for } n \text{ even.} \end{cases}$$

Figure 8.5 shows the effect of increasing the number of terms in the series. With only one term, we see a simple sine wave. With fifteen terms, it is clear that the summation is approaching a square wave. We can surmise that it *is* possible for a sum of sinusoids to produce regions of no change and regions of sudden change in an image.

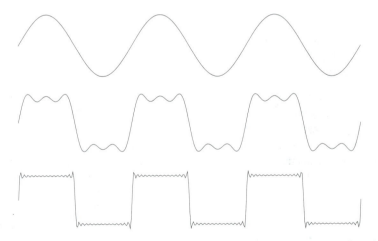

Figure 8.5 Examples of a Fourier series consisting only of sine functions. Top: one term. Middle: three terms. Bottom: fifteen terms.

8.2.2 Extension to two dimensions

The notion of a Fourier series is equally valid in two dimensions. Now, the basis functions are two-dimensional sine and cosine functions. Figure 8.6 plots one of these basis functions as a surface. A Fourier series representation of a two-dimensional function, $f(x, y)$, having a period L in both the x and the y directions, can be written

$$f(x, y) = \sum_{u=0}^{\infty} \sum_{v=0}^{\infty} a_{u,v} \cos \left[\frac{2\pi(ux + vy)}{L} \right] + b_{u,v} \sin \left[\frac{2\pi(ux + vy)}{L} \right]. \quad (8.3)$$

Here, u and v are the number of cycles fitting into one horizontal and vertical period, respectively, of $f(x, y)$. We can regard the Fourier series representation of $f(x, y)$ as a pair of two-dimensional arrays of coefficients, each of infinite extent.

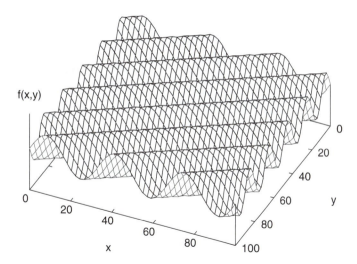

Figure 8.6 Example of a two-dimensional sinusoidal basis function with $u = 3, v = 5$.

The Fourier series in Equation 8.3 can be used to represent any image. We can visualise the basis functions as 'basis images'—rather like the sinusoidal images that we used to explore the idea of spatial frequency in Section 8.1. Figure 8.7 shows the first few basis images for the sine component of the series; a similar set of cosine basis images is also used. The basis image for $u = 0$, $v = 0$ is constant, with a value of $a_{0,0}$. It represents the mean grey level of the image. Higher terms in u and v introduce the fluctations about this mean level that are needed to represent changes in grey level across the image. The coefficients $a_{u,v}$ and $b_{u,v}$ determine the relative contributions of each basis image to the representation. They provide useful information on the spatial frequencies that are present in the image.

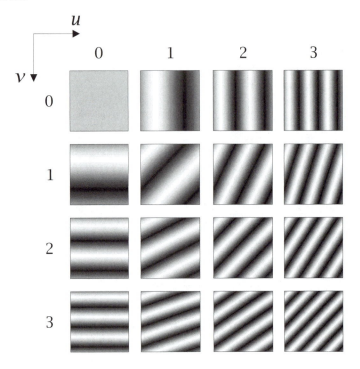

Figure 8.7   Some of the basis images used in a Fourier representation of an image.

8.3   The discrete Fourier transform

Fourier theory provides us with a means of determining the contribution made by any basis function to the representation of some function $f(x)$. The contribution is determined by projecting $f(x)$ onto that basis function. This procedure is described as a **Fourier transform**. When applying the procedure to images, we must deal explicitly with the fact that an image is

- Two-dimensional
- Sampled
- Of finite extent

These considerations give rise to the **discrete Fourier transform** (DFT). The DFT of an $N \times N$ image can be written

$$F(u, v) = \frac{1}{N} \sum_{x=0}^{N-1} \sum_{y=0}^{N-1} f(x, y) \left[\cos\left(\frac{2\pi(ux + vy)}{N} \right) + j \sin\left(\frac{2\pi(ux + vy)}{N} \right) \right], \quad (8.4)$$

or, noting that $\cos\theta + j\sin\theta$ can be written in exponential form,

$$F(u, v) = \frac{1}{N}\sum_{x=0}^{N-1}\sum_{y=0}^{N-1} f(x, y)e^{-j2\pi(ux+vy)/N}. \tag{8.5}$$

Note that $F(u, v)$ is a complex number; we are now dealing with a set of complex coefficients, rather than two sets of real coefficients, as was the case with the Fourier series in Equation 8.3.

For any particular spatial frequency specified by u and v, evaluating Equation 8.5 gives us the contribution that the corresponding pair of basis images makes to a Fourier representation of the image f; in essence, it tells us how much of that particular frequency is present in the image. Of course, to build up a complete picture of the relative importance of different frequencies, we must evaluate the equation for all u and v. It is usual to apply the term 'Fourier transform' to the process of calculating all the values of $F(u, v)$—or, indeed, to the values themselves.

There also exists an **inverse Fourier transform** that converts a set of Fourier coefficients into an image. It has a form very similar to the forward transform:

$$f(x, y) = \frac{1}{N}\sum_{x=0}^{N-1}\sum_{y=0}^{N-1} F(u, v)e^{j2\pi(ux+vy)/N}. \tag{8.6}$$

The only material difference is the sign of the exponent. Comparing Equations 8.5 and 8.6, it is clear that the forward transform of an $N \times N$ image yields an $N \times N$ array of coefficients. Since the inverse transform reconstructs the original image from this set of coefficients, they must constitute a complete representation of the information present in the image. When we manipulate $F(u, v)$, we say that we are processing the image in the **frequency domain**; conversely, when we manipulate pixel values $f(x, y)$, we are processing the image in the spatial domain. Although these manipulations may result in the loss of information from the image, the transformation from one domain to the other via a forward or inverse Fourier transform does not, in itself, result in any information loss.

8.3.1 The spectra of an image

We have already noted that $F(u, v)$ is a complex number. Its real and imaginary parts are not particularly informative in themselves; it is far more useful to think of the magnitude and phase of $F(u, v)$. We note that

$$F(u, v) = R(u, v) + jI(u, v) = |F(u, v)|e^{j\phi(u,v)}, \tag{8.7}$$

where $R(u, v)$ and $I(u, v)$ are the real and imaginary parts, respectively, of $F(u, v)$, $|F(u, v)|$ is the magnitude and $\phi(u, v)$ is the phase. Magnitude and phase are given by

$$|F(u, v)| = \sqrt{R^2(u, v) + I^2(u, v)}, \tag{8.8}$$

$$\phi(u, v) = \tan^{-1}\left[\frac{I(u, v)}{R(u, v)}\right]. \tag{8.9}$$

Equations 8.8 and 8.9 allow us to decompose an array of complex coefficients into an array of magnitudes and an array of phases. The magnitudes correspond to the amplitudes of the basis images in our Fourier representation. The array of magnitudes is termed the **amplitude spectrum** of the image. Likewise, the array of phases is termed the **phase spectrum**. When the term 'spectrum' is used on its own, the amplitude spectrum is normally implied. This is because the phases are generally less significant for the purposes of interpretation. Another term that is used is **power spectrum**, or spectral density. The power spectrum of an image is simply the square of its amplitude spectrum, i.e.,

$$P(u, v) = |F(u, v)|^2 = R^2(u, v) + I^2(u, v). \tag{8.10}$$

We can render the spectra of an image as images themselves, for the purposes of visual-isation and interpretation. Section 8.4 gives further details of how this is done. Figure 8.8 shows examples of an amplitude spectrum and a phase spectrum of an image. Looking at these examples, it is tempting to think that the amplitude spectrum contains all the use-ful information. The phase spectrum appears to be somewhat random and noisy. This is deceptive; if we attempt to reconstruct the image with an inverse Fourier transform after de-stroying either the phase information or the amplitude information, then the reconstruction will fail. This is illustrated by Figure 8.9. The amplitude spectrum is clearly sensitive to the

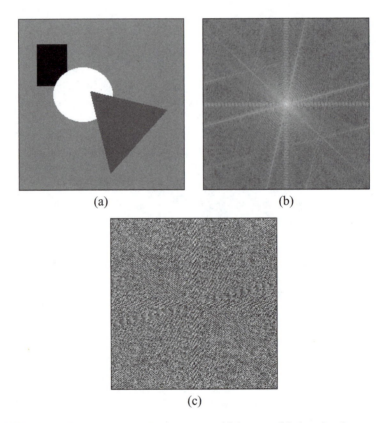

(a)   (b)

(c)

Figure 8.8 A synthetic image and its spectra. (a) Image. (b) Amplitude spectrum. (c) Phase spectrum.

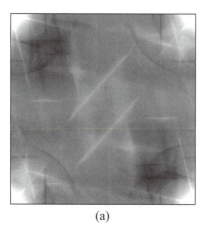 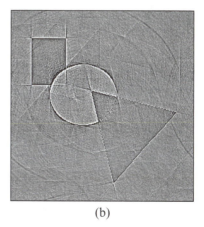

(a)   (b)

Figure 8.9 Reconstructions of an image from its spectra. (a) After destroying phase information. (b) After destroying amplitude information.

presence of particular features in an image, but the phase spectrum encodes their location in that image. Without phase information, the spatial coherence of the image is disrupted and it becomes impossible to recognise features of interest; without amplitude information, we can no longer determine the relative brightnesses of those features, but we can at least see the boundaries between them, which aids recognition. Because phase is so crucial to maintaining image integrity, most image processing operations leave the phase spectrum untouched and manipulate only the amplitude spectrum.

8.3.2   The fast Fourier transform

Calculating a single value of $F(u, v)$ by Equation 8.5 involves a summation over all pixels in the image. If the image has dimensions $N \times N$, then this is an $O(N^2)$ operation. However, there are N^2 values of $F(u, v)$ to calculate, so the overall complexity of a DFT is $O(N^4)$. This is very costly; Crane [11] cites execution times of 71 minutes for the DFT of a 256×256 image and 12 days for the DFT of a 1024×1024 image, assuming that the multiplication of a complex number consumes 1 microsecond of CPU time. Clearly, it is not practical to compute the DFT in this manner.

Fortunately, a much faster method exists, known as the **fast Fourier transform** (FFT). The classic two-dimensional FFT algorithm takes advantage of the separability of the Fourier transform, which allows us to perform a one-dimensional FFT along each row of the image to generate an intermediate array, followed by another one-dimensional FFT down each column of this array to produce the final result. The one-dimensional FFT algorithm uses another trick to speed up calculations. It so happens that a Fourier transform of length N can be written as the sum of two Fourier transforms, each of length $N/2$. If N is a power of two, this decomposition can be applied recursively until we reach the point where we are computing transforms of length 2. The overall cost of this procedure is $O(N \log_2 N)$, compared with $O(N^2)$ for a directly calculated one-dimensional transform.

Exploiting separability alone reduces the complexity of a two-dimensional Fourier trans-

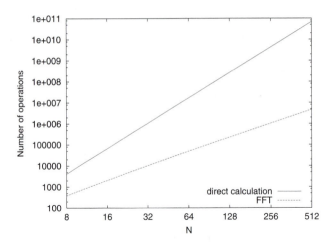

Figure 8.10 Cost of calculating the Fourier transform of an image.

form from $O(N^4)$ to $O(N^3)$. When we introduce the one-dimensional FFT, the cost of transforming an $N \times N$ image becomes $O(N^2 \log_2 N)$. Figure 8.10 compares the cost functions graphically. Note that the y axis is logarithmic; the difference in performance is therefore huge. We can see that, for a 512×512 image, a two-dimensional FFT is roughly 30,000 times faster than direct calculation.

The classic two-dimensional FFT requires that both image dimensions are powers of two. If necessary, we must enforce this by either cropping the image or by padding it out to the appropriate dimensions with zero-valued pixels[1]. Cropping the image discards data and may significantly change the spectrum of that image, but it reduces the time required to calculate the transform; padding with zeros does not affect the spectrum, but it will increase computation time.

The input to standard implementations of the FFT is an array of values. If a complex data type is available, the array may be of this type. Some implementations specify two floating-point arrays, one for the real part of the data and one for the imaginary part; others expect data to be passed into the routine in a single floating-point array, with real and imaginary values interleaved. Since an image consists of real, rather than complex, numbers, we must copy the pixel values to the storage used for the real part of the data, however it may be specified, and set the imaginary part to zero. Because the forward and inverse transforms are so similar, a single FFT routine is usually provided to compute both transforms. A flag of some kind indicates the direction of the transform. Since the only difference in the calculations is the sign of the exponent ($e^{j\theta}$ for the forward transform, $e^{-j\theta}$ for the inverse transform), the sign itself is often used to specify the direction. The FFT routine may store its output in a separate array; however, many implementations use the array that provided the input data, overwriting its values with the results of the transform.

---

[1] Actually, there is a third option; we can use other, more complex algorithms that do not require the dimensions to be powers of two.

8.3.3   Properties of the Fourier transform

Periodicity and conjugate symmetry

The DFT of an image has some rather unusual properties. One is *periodicity*. $F(u, v)$ repeats itself endlessly in both directions, with a period of N. This means that

$$F(u, v) = F(u + N, v) = F(u, v + N) = F(u + N, v + N). \qquad (8.11)$$

The $N \times N$ block of coefficients that we compute from an $N \times N$ image with our two-dimensional FFT algorithm is a single period from this infinite sequence. Another property, arising because the image is real-valued whereas the DFT operates on complex numbers, is *complex conjugate symmetry*. This means that

$$|F(u, v)| = |F(-u, -v)|. \qquad (8.12)$$

In other words, there exist negative frequencies, which (as far as the amplitude spectrum is concerned) are mirror images of the corresponding positive frequencies.

The periodicity and conjugate symmetry properties of the DFT give rise the situation depicted in Figure 8.11. Here we see a portion of an infinite, periodic $F(u, v)$, along with the single period that is computed by a DFT (shown as a square with a thick black border). We can infer that, for our computed values of $F(u, v)$, frequency increases up to $u = N/2$ and decreases thereafter; the half of the spectrum for which $u > N/2$ is a 'double reflection'

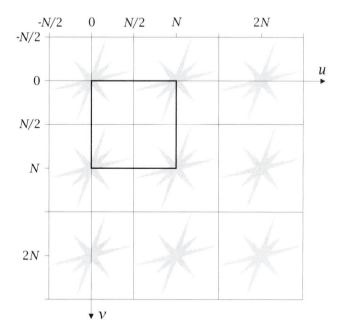

Figure 8.11   A portion of an infinite, periodic spectrum exhibiting complex conjugate symmetry, and the sample of the spectrum that is computed by the DFT.

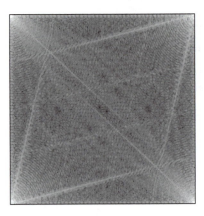

Figure 8.12 Unshifted amplitude spectrum of an image. Frequency increases from the corners towards the centre of the spectrum.

of the half with $u \leq N/2$. The same applies to frequencies either side of $v = N/2$. This can be seen clearly in the spectrum of Figure 8.12.

The interpretation of spectra is made much easier if we centre the results of the DFT on the point $u = 0$, $v = 0$, such that frequency increases as we move in any direction away from the origin. We can do this by a circular shifting of the four quadrants of the array; alternatively, we can exploit the shift theorem of the Fourier transform, which tells us that we can achieve the same result by making the input values alternately positive and negative in both the x and y directions prior to computing the transform. Multiplying $f(x, y)$ by $(-1)^{x+y}$ will achieve this. The effect of shifting can be seen by comparing Figure 8.12 with Figure 8.8(b).

Windowing

We have seen that the Fourier transform is periodic, but there is also an implied periodicity in the image. Fourier theory assumes that the array of pixels supplied as input to the DFT is merely one period of an image that repeats itself infinitely in the x and y directions (Figure 8.13). An equivalent way of thinking about this is to regard the image as being wrapped around on itself, such that the left side touches the right and the top touches the bottom. (This is exactly the assumption made when using circular indexing to deal with the problem of convolution at the borders of an image. The justification for this strategy is therefore that it makes convolution consistent with operations in the frequency domain, which make the same assumption.) If there is any mismatch between the left and right sides of the image, or its top and bottom, then the Fourier transform sees this as an abrupt change in the image that can be accommodated only through distortion of the spectrum.

The problem of spatial discontinuity at the borders of the image can be minimised, if desired, by **windowing** the data prior to computing the DFT. Windowing involves modulating pixel values in such a way that they fall smoothly to zero at the edges of the image. Multiplying the data by a **windowing function** will accomplish this. There are a number

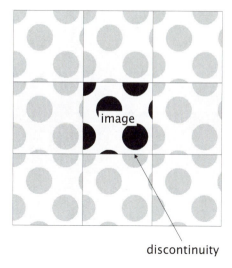

discontinuity

Figure 8.13 Spatial discontinuities caused by considering an image to be periodic.

of standard windows. The Bartlett window, for instance, is defined in two dimensions by

$$w(r) = \begin{cases} 1 - (r/r_{\max}) & r \leq r_{\max}, \\ 0 & r > r_{\max}, \end{cases} \tag{8.13}$$

where r is the distance from the centre of the image and $r_{\max}$ is its maximum value. It has a conical shape. The Hanning window, defined for $r \leq r_{\max}$ by

$$w(r) = 0.5 - 0.5 \cos\left[\pi\left(1 - \frac{r}{r_{\max}}\right)\right], \tag{8.14}$$

is somewhat smoother. The Blackman window,

$$w(r) = 0.42 - 0.5 \cos\left[\pi\left(1 - \frac{r}{r_{\max}}\right)\right] + 0.08 \cos\left[2\pi\left(1 - \frac{r}{r_{\max}}\right)\right], \tag{8.15}$$

has a similar shape but is narrower than the Hanning window. Figure 8.14 plots these windowing functions as they would be applied to a 128×128 image.

Figure 8.15 shows a simple, synthetic image exhibiting discontinuity at its borders, together with the spectrum computed from unmodified data and the spectrum computed after applying the Hanning window. The unwindowed spectrum contains a bright horizontal line and a bright vertical line, both passing through the origin. These features are the direct result of the mismatch between opposite sides of the image. The windowed spectrum lacks these artefacts and, consequently, the features caused by genuine structure in the image can be seen more clearly.

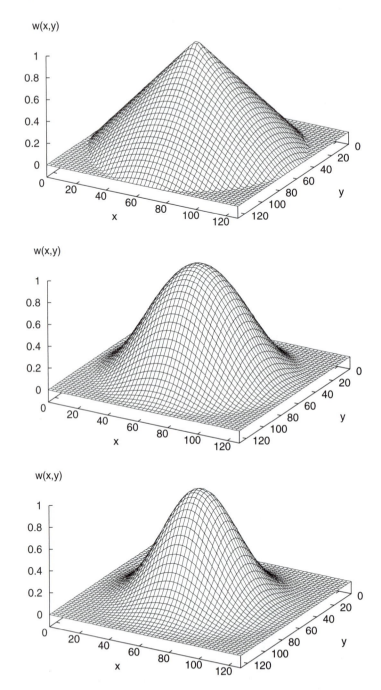

Figure 8.14 Windowing functions for a 128×128 image. Top: Bartlett window. Middle: Hanning window. Bottom: Blackman window.

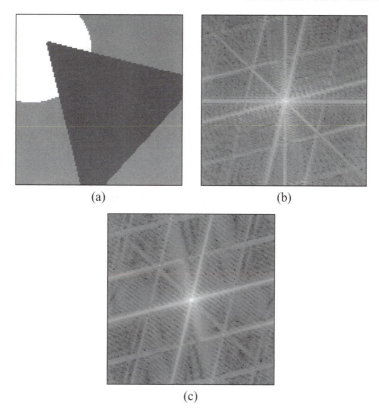

Figure 8.15 Spectral distortion and its reduction by windowing. (a) An image. (b) Its spectrum, computed without windowing. (c) Spectrum computed using a Hanning window.

8.3.4 Java implementation

The com.pearsoneduc.ip.op package provides a single class called ImageFFT to support operations in the frequency domain. Instances of this class can

- Compute the forward and inverse Fourier transform using an FFT algorithm
- Manage the complex data used as the input and output of the FFT
- Allow the results of a Fourier transform to be inspected and manipulated in a controlled manner

Unlike many of the classes described so far, the ImageFFT class does not lend itself to implementation as a BufferedImageOp; instead, it provides a set of methods that can be used to implement operations in the frequency domain as BufferedImageOp classes. Some of these methods are listed in Table 8.1.

To illustrate the use of the ImageFFT class, we present two simple examples, in the form of static methods belonging to some unspecified class. The first example, shown in Listing 8.1, computes the spectrum of an image using a Hanning window and returns the

Table 8.1 Selected methods of the `ImageFFT` class.

Method	Description
`ImageFFT(BufferedImage img)`	Creates an `ImageFFT` for the specified image, without windowing the image data.
`ImageFFT(BufferedImage img, int win)`	Creates an `ImageFFT` for the specified image, with the specified windowing function (see Table 8.2).
`String toString()`	Returns a string describing the object.
`int getWidth()`	Returns the width of the dataset. (This will be greater than the width of the input image if its width is not a power of two.)
`int getHeight()`	Returns the height of the dataset. (This will be greater than the height of the image if its height is not a power of two.)
`int getWindow()`	Returns an integer indicating the current windowing function.
`boolean isSpectral()`	Returns `true` if the data are spectral (i.e., last transform was in the forward direction), `false` if the data are spatial.
`void transform()`	Computes a forward or inverse Fourier transform, as appropriate.
`BufferedImage toImage(BufferedImage img)`	Converts stored data into an image, using the supplied image as a destination or creating a new image and returning it.
`BufferedImage toImage(BufferedImage img, int bias)`	Converts stored data into an image, using the supplied image as a destination or creating a new image and returning it. The specified bias level will be added to the results.
`BufferedImage getSpectrum()`	Returns the amplitude spectrum in image form, shifted such that a frequency of zero is at the centre and scaled logarithmically.
`BufferedImage getUnshiftedSpectrum()`	Returns the amplitude spectrum in image form, scaled logarithmically.
`float getMagnitude(int u, int v)`	Returns the magnitude of the Fourier transform at the specified spectral coordinates.
`float getPhase(int u, int v)`	Returns the phase of the Fourier transform at the specified spectral coordinates.
`void setMagnitude(int u, int v, float mag)`	Changes the magnitude of the Fourier transform at the specified spectral coordinates.
`void setPhase(int u, int v, float phase)`	Changes the phase of the Fourier transform at the specified spectral coordinates.

Table 8.2 Constants defined by the `ImageFFT` class.

Name	Value
NO_WINDOW	1
BARTLETT_WINDOW	2
HAMMING_WINDOW	3
HANNING_WINDOW	4

LISTING 8.1 Use of `ImageFFT` to compute the amplitude spectrum of an image.

```
1   public static BufferedImage computeSpectrum(BufferedImage image)
2     throws FFTException {
3       ImageFFT fft = new ImageFFT(image, ImageFFT.HANNING_WINDOW);
4       fft.transform();
5       return fft.getSpectrum();
6   }
```

spectrum as another image. Line 3 creates an instance of `ImageFFT` to perform this task. An exception is thrown if the image is not an 8-bit greyscale image. When an `ImageFFT` object is created, the following things happen:

- Image data are copied into the internal storage of the `ImageFFT` object.
- The data are padded with zeros in the appropriate dimension if that dimension is not a power of two.
- The data are windowed, if a second integer parameter has been passed to the constructor and its value specifies a known windowing function.

Line 4 computes a forward Fourier transform, via a call to the `transform()` method. Line 5 retrieves and returns the spectrum in the form of a `BufferedImage` object. Note that a Fourier transform must always be requested explicitly when using `ImageFFT`. If line 4 had been omitted, then `getSpectrum()` would have thrown an `FFTException`.

The second example, shown in Listing 8.2, is a routine that synthesises a sinusoidal image by direct manipulation of its spectrum. A 128×128 image of the appropriate type is created in lines 2 and 3. By default, all its pixels will have a value of zero. Line 4 creates an `ImageFFT` associated with this image, and Line 5 computes its Fourier transform. Since all pixels were zero in the input image, the spectrum of this image will be blank. Line 7 adds a spike to the spectrum, representing a sinusoid with $u = 20$, $v = 8$. Line 8 adds the complex conjugate reflection of this spike. Line 9 returns us to the spatial domain by performing an inverse Fourier transform. Finally, line 10 copies the data stored inside the `ImageFFT` back into the original image. A bias of 128 is added to values as they are copied, to offset the sinusoidal variation such that it lies within a 0–255 range. Note that the `toImage()` method can also be called with `null` in place of an image—in which case, a new image is created and passed to the caller as the return value of the function.

LISTING 8.2 Use of `ImageFFT` to synthesise a sinusoidal pattern.

```
1   public static BufferedImage createSinusoid() throws FFTException {
2     BufferedImage image =
3      new BufferedImage(128, 128, BufferedImage.TYPE_BYTE_GRAY);
4     ImageFFT fft = new ImageFFT(image);
5     fft.transform();
6     final float mag = (float) 1.0e6;
7     fft.setMagnitude(20, 8, mag);
8     fft.setMagnitude(108, 120, mag);
9     fft.transform();
10    fft.toImage(image, 128);
11    return image;
12  }
```

8.4   Investigating spectra

8.4.1   Display

Amplitude spectra are normally visualised as 8-bit greyscale images. In order to do this, we must scale the magnitudes computed from Equation 8.8 to lie in a 0–255 range. The obvious approach of multiplying by a scaling factor

$$\frac{255}{|F(u, v)|_{\max}}$$

will be of little use, because the spectrum is typically dominated by a few values that are very much larger than all the others. These values tend to be found at the low frequencies, towards the centre of the spectrum; indeed, $|F(0, 0)|$ is usually the largest value of all, so one approach is to scale values linearly but to exclude $|F(0, 0)|$ from the determination of $|F(u, v)|_{\max}$. A more common approach is a logarithmic mapping of the data, analogous to that performed on images to enhance dark features (see Chapter 6). We calculate

$$|F(u, v)|' = C \log[|F(u, v)| + 1], \tag{8.16}$$

where C is chosen so that the results occupy the full 8-bit range. We add one to $|F(u, v)|$ because the spectrum can be zero in places, and the logarithm of zero is undefined. Note that Equation 8.16 is applied for display purposes only; we retain a copy of the original spectrum and it is this that we modify if we wish to process the image.

Three Java programs that visualise spectra are provided on the CD. The first of these, `Spectrum`, has a command line interface. It takes an input filename and an output filename as arguments, plus an optional integer parameter specifying the window to be applied to the data. Meaningful values for this parameter are those given in Table 8.2. If some other value is specified, or no value is given, no windowing will be carried out. The input file is an image and the output file is the shifted spectrum of that image, rendered as an image itself. The `Spectrum` program was used to generate all of the amplitude spectra that appear in this chapter.

The second program, `SpectrumViewer`, has a graphical user interface. It loads an image from a file named on the command line, computes the FFT of that image and then displays the image and its spectrum, side by side. The spectrum will be computed from windowed data if a window is specified as a command line parameter. Meaningful parameter values are those given in Table 8.2. The spectrum can be toggled between its shifted or unshifted forms. The user can interact with the spectrum by moving the cursor over it. As the cursor moves, the information panel beneath the spectrum is updated with

- The spatial frequency parameters u and v for the point under the cursor
- The magnitude of $F(u, v)$ at that point
- The phase of $F(u, v)$ at that point

Figure 8.16 shows `SpectrumViewer` in action.

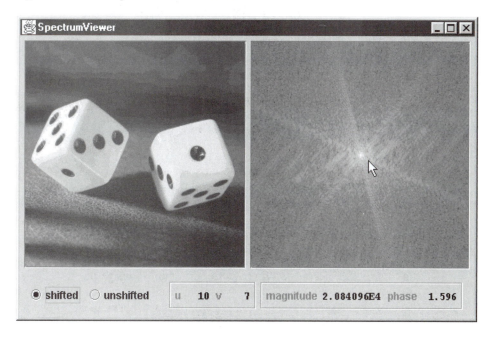

Figure 8.16 The `SpectrumViewer` application.

The third program, `SpectralProbe`, resembles `SpectrumViewer`, in that it displays an image and a spectrum computed from that image. However, the spectrum is derived from a small, square region, rather than the entire image. This makes it possible to investigate variations in the spatial frequency content of the image by comparing the spectra obtained at different locations. The region can be centred on a given location by clicking at that point on the image. A control panel is provided, from which the user can set region dimensions to 16×16, 32×32 or 64×64 and select a windowing function from the options listed in Table 8.2. Figure 8.17 shows the application's interface.

Figure 8.17 The SpectralProbe application.

8.4.2 Interpretation

We can gain insight into the the relationship between the spatial and frequency domains by comparing simple images with their corresponding amplitude spectra.

Spectra of simple periodic patterns

A purely sinusoidal pattern of varying grey level, such as that of Figure 8.18(a), is, from the perspective of the Fourier transform, the simplest image possible. This is because it corresponds to a single basis image. We might therefore expect its spectrum to be featureless apart from a bright spot at one point, corresponding to the frequency of the sinusoid. What we actually see is three bright spots [Figure 8.18(b)]. One of these spots occurs at precisely the position we would expect, from the frequency of the pattern. A 'mirror image' of this spot is also present, due to the complex conjugate symmetry of the Fourier transform. The third bright spot is at the origin. This point represents a zero-frequency, i.e., constant, component of the image. It is needed in Fourier analysis because sines and cosines can only represent variation about a mean of zero, whereas images have a mean grey level that is non-zero.

The spectrum of the pattern in Figure 8.18(a) is relatively simple because the image is reasonably well sampled. The spectrum becomes more complicated if the pattern is undersampled. Figure 8.18(c) simulates undersampling of the sinusoid by averaging over 4×4 blocks of pixels and assigning the average value to each pixel in the block. Aliasing artefacts are clearly visible in the new image, and in its spectrum, also [Figure 8.18(d)].

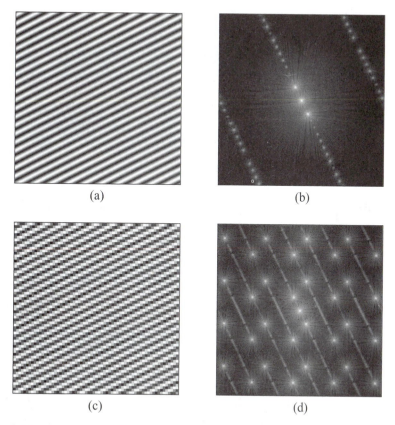

Figure 8.18 Spectra of simple sinusoidal patterns. (a) Sinusoid with $u = 10, v = 20$. (b) Corresponding spectrum, showing complex conjugate symmetry and a constant component at $(0, 0)$. (c) Simulated undersampling of the sinusoid in (a). (d) Corresponding spectrum, showing aliasing.

Spectra of edges

We have observed that points of sudden change in an image are characterised by high spatial frequencies. This is evident if we use the `SpectralProbe` application to compare the spectrum of a homegeneous region near an edge with the spectrum of a region that includes the edge. Figure 8.19 gives examples of these spectra. The spectrum of the homogeneous region contains a bright spot at its centre, indicating that the region is dominated by low frequencies. The spectrum of the region containing the edge is spanned by a stripe of high values, indicating the presence of a wide spread of frequencies.

The sharpness of an edge determines the balance of spatial frequencies that are present. Blurred edges are not characterised by as wide a range of spatial frequencies as sharp edges. We can see this in Figure 8.20, which shows the spectra for sharp and blurred edges. Amplitudes diminish rapidly as we move away from the centre of the spectrum for a blurred edge, but the spectrum for a sharp edge has large amplitudes spanning its entire width.

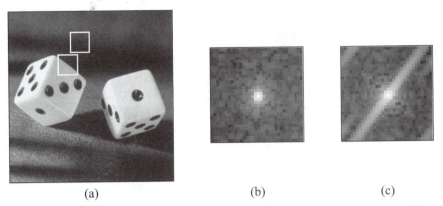

(a)   (b)   (c)

Figure 8.19 Effect of an edge on a spectrum. (a) Image, showing a uniform 32×32 region and a 32×32 region containing an edge. (b) Windowed spectrum of the uniform region. (c) Windowed spectrum of the region containing the edge.

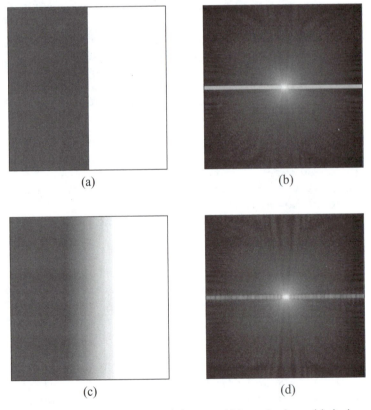

(a)   (b)

(c)   (d)

Figure 8.20 Spectral characteristics of sharp and blurred edges. (a) A sharp edge. (b) Spectrum of a sharp edge. (c) A blurred edge. (d) Spectrum of a blurred edge.

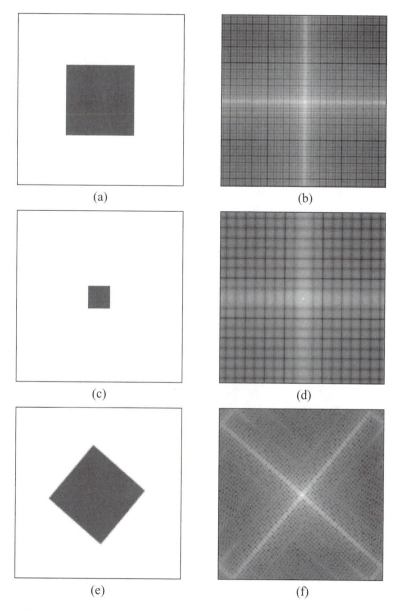

(a)

(b)

(c)

(d)

(e)

(f)

Figure 8.21 A square, transformed versions of that square, and their corresponding spectra.

Spectra of simple shapes

Finally, we consider the spectra of two simple shapes: a square and a circular disc. A square (Figure 8.21(a)) has a pair of edges running horizontally and a pair of edges running vertically. Its spectrum (Figure 8.21(b)) has a vertical stripe produced by the horizontal edges and a horizontal stripe produced by the vertical edges. (Other features in the spectrum are produced by the corners.) Translating the square to a different part of the image will have no effect on its amplitude spectrum, although it will change the phase spectrum. Scaling the square does have an effect on the amplitude spectrum, however. When the square is smaller (Figure 8.21(c)), features in the spectrum become larger (Figure 8.21(d)), and vice versa. When the square is rotated (Figure 8.21(e)), its spectrum undergoes the same rotation (Figure 8.21(f)).

Figure 8.22 shows a disc and its spectrum. The spectrum has the same circular symmetry as the disc itself. We can understand how this comes about by considering a line passing through the centre of the disc. This line crosses two edges, just like a horizontal or vertical line crossing the sides of the square in Figure 8.21(a). These two edges will contribute a single bright stripe to the spectrum, rather like the horizontal or vertical stripe in the spectrum of the square, but with the same orientation as that of the line. We can define any number of these lines, having any orientation we choose—so the spectrum of the disc will be a superposition of the spectra all of these lines, giving the structure seen in Figure 8.22(b). Another way of thinking about this is to imagine the spectrum of Figure 8.21(d) rotated through 360°; the structure that this 'sweeps out' as it rotates will resemble that of Figure 8.22(b).

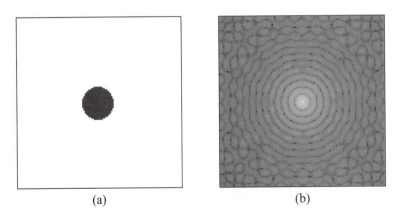

(a)   (b)

Figure 8.22   (a) Circular disc. (b) Spectrum.

8.5   Filtering of images

We saw in Chapter 7 that images can be filtered in the spatial domain by operations such as convolution. Convolution with the appropriate kernel can blur or sharpen an image. We can infer from this that the operation suppresses or enhances certain spatial frequencies relative to others, but we cannot quantify the effect that it has, because the operation takes place in the spatial domain. The frequency domain is the more natural domain for filtering, because we specify precisely the effect that a filter has on the spatial frequencies present in an image. Moreover, filtering in the frequency domain is simpler, computationally, than convolution in the spatial domain.

Filtering can be expressed generally as the point-by-point multiplication of the spectrum by a **filter transfer function**. We can write

$$G(u, v) = F(u, v)H(u, v), \qquad (8.17)$$

where F is the spectrum of the image, H is the filter transfer function and G is the filtered spectrum. An inverse Fourier transform of G must be computed in order to see the results of filtering as an image. Remember that we are dealing with complex numbers here, so the multiplication in Equation 8.17 could, in theory, affect both the magnitude and phase of $F(u, v)$. In practice, most filters are **zero-phase-shift filters**; that is, they affect magnitude rather than phase. We will assume that this is the case in the remainder of this section.

There is a fundamental relationship between filtering done by convolution in the spatial domain and filtering done by multiplication in the frequency domain. This is expressed by the **convolution theorem**, which states that

$$f * h \Leftrightarrow FH. \qquad (8.18)$$

The left-hand side of this expression represents the convolution of an image, f, with a kernel, h. The right-hand side of the expression represents the product of the Fourier transform of the image, F, and the Fourier transform of the kernel, H. The symbol $\Leftrightarrow$, which links the two sides, indicates that they form a 'Fourier transform pair'; the left-hand side can be converted into the right-hand side by a Fourier transform, whereas the right-hand side can be converted into the left-hand side by an inverse Fourier transform.

Equation 8.18 tells us that convolving an image with a given kernel has the *same effect* on an image as multiplying the spectrum of that image by the Fourier transform of the kernel. Any result achievable by convolution in the spatial domain can also be obtained by a multiplication in the frequency domain, and vice versa. This means that we always have two different ways of carrying out linear filtering operations. Given a kernel, we can convolve that kernel with the image, or we can filter in the frequency domain via the following procedure:

1. Compute the Fourier transform of the image
2. Compute the Fourier transform of the kernel
3. Multiply the two transforms together
4. Compute the inverse Fourier transform of the product

In step 3, the multiplication is done on a point-by-point basis, which means that the transforms of the kernel and the image must have the same dimensions. We accomplish this by padding out the kernel with zeros prior to computing its transform.

Although it may seem strange to perform this rather complicated sequence of operations when we have a kernel that can be used directly for convolution, significant computational benefits can accrue from working in the frequency domain. Consider, for example, an $N \times N$ image filtered by an $n \times n$ mask. In the spatial domain, filtering requires approximately $N^2 n^2$ multiplications and a similar number of additions. In the frequency domain, however, filtering (step 3 above) requires only N^2 multiplications. Of course, there is a significant cost associated with FFT computation, but if n is large enough the total cost of filtering in the frequency domain falls below that of operating in the spatial domain.

8.5.1 Low pass filtering

A low pass filter suppresses high spatial frequencies. Recalling that frequency increases outward from the centre of a shifted spectrum, we can see that a low pass filter must force $F(u, v)$ to zero at some distance from the centre. Decreasing this distance will result in more frequencies being suppressed, increasing the blurring effect of the filter.

The simplest type of low pass filter is the **ideal low pass filter**. (The term 'ideal filter' comes from electrical engineering and refers to the fact that such filters cannot be implemented using real electronic components; it does *not* imply that such filters are the best choices for filtering.) The filter has a sharp cut-off at some distance from the centre of the spectrum. Frequencies below this critical radius pass through unaffected and all other frequencies are blocked. The filter transfer function is

$$H(u, v) = \begin{cases} 1, & r(u, v) \leqslant r_0, \\ 0, & r(u, v) > r_0, \end{cases} \tag{8.19}$$

where r_0 is the filter radius and $r(u, v)$ is the distance from the centre of the spectrum,

$$r(u, v) = \sqrt{u^2 + v^2}. \tag{8.20}$$

Figure 8.23 plots Equation 8.19 as a surface, showing clearly the cylindrical shape of the ideal low pass filter and the sharp cutoff in response at the filter radius. Figure 8.24 gives an example of the application of Equation 8.19. It shows an image, its spectrum before and after filtering, and the image generated by an inverse Fourier transform of the filtered spectrum.

Application of an ideal low pass filter has the expected effect of blurring the image, but it also introduces ripple-like artefacts. This phenomenon, known as **ringing**, is a direct

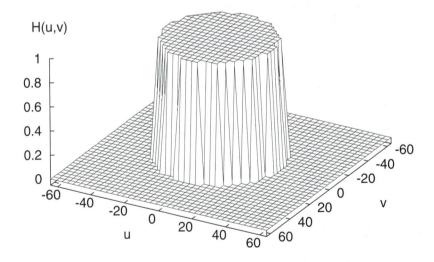

Figure 8.23 Transfer function of an ideal low pass filter.

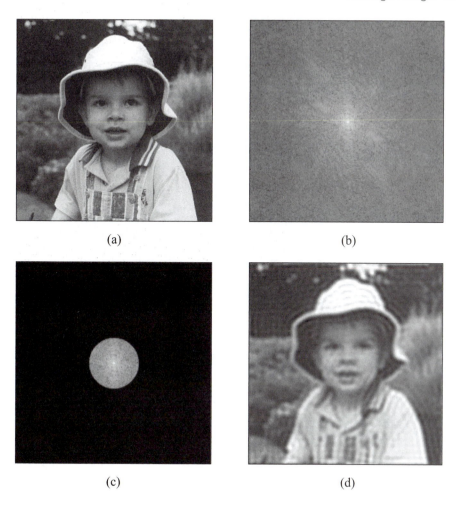

(a)   (b)

(c)   (d)

Figure 8.24 Example of ideal low pass filtering. (a) Input image. (b) Spectrum of input image. (c) Spectrum after ideal low pass filtering with r_0 set to 25% of spectrum's radius. (d) Output image.

consequence of the sharp cutoff in response of the ideal low pass filter. But how does this give rise to a ripple-like effect in the image? According to the convolution theorem (Equation 8.18), multiplication of the spectrum by a filter has the same effect as a convolution of the image with a kernel that is the inverse Fourier transform of that filter. The inverse Fourier transform of the sharply defined ideal low pass filter has the shape depicted in Figure 8.25. The radial variation is that of a 'sinc function', $\sin(r)/r$. We must imagine a convolution kernel whose coefficients are samples from this function. Such a kernel will have large positive coefficients at its centre, producing the expected smoothing effect, but these will be surrounded by a ring of smaller, negative coefficients. This kernel would

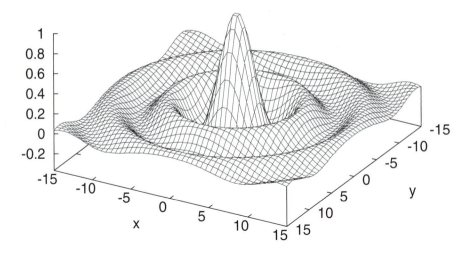

Figure 8.25 Shape of the spatial convolution kernel that corresponds to an ideal low pass filter in the frequency domain.

interact with edges in the image to produce a rippled effect.

To avoid ringing, we can use a low pass filter with a transfer function that falls smoothly to zero. A classic example is the **Butterworth low pass filter** of order n, defined by

$$H(u, v) = \frac{1}{1 + [r(u, v)/r_0]^{2n}}. \tag{8.21}$$

Here, filter radius r_0 no longer defines a sharp cutoff frequency; instead, it represents the distance at which $H(u, v)$ has fallen to one-half of its maximum value. Figure 8.26 plots the transfer functions of order-1 and order-3 Butterworth low pass filters. As the order of the filter increases, the 'rolloff' in filter response with frequency becomes steeper and the filter becomes more like an ideal low pass filter. Figure 8.27 shows the results of applying an order-1 Butterworth low pass filter to the image of Figure 8.24(a). The filter radius r_0 is again set to 25% of the spectrum's radius. Comparing the results with those from a low pass filter, we can see that the filter has a less pronounced blurring effect, and also that ringing is absent from the filtered image.

Many other types of filter transfer function will perform low pass filtering. A notable example is a Gaussian function. The Fourier transform of a Gaussian is another Gaussian. A Gaussian filter is smooth and well-behaved spectrally whether we apply it in the spatial domain, by convolution, or in the frequency domain, by multiplication. We can contrast this with the case of filters shaped like rectangular or cylindrical boxes. Applying a filter of this type in the frequency domain induces a ripple-like distortion of the filtered image; similarly, applying a box-shaped filter in the spatial domain induces ripples in the spectrum of the filtered image.

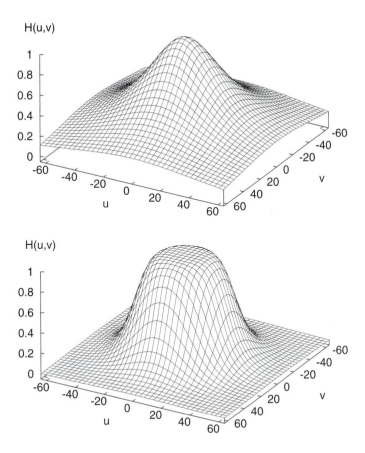

Figure 8.26 Transfer functions of the Butterworth low pass filter. Top: $n = 1$. Bottom: $n = 3$.

Figure 8.27 Result of Butterworth low pass filtering.

8.5.2   High pass filtering

We can define an **ideal high pass filter**, too. Frequencies up to the cutoff frequency are suppressed, whereas frequencies beyond this point pass through unchanged. The transfer function is

$$H(u, v) = \begin{cases} 0, & r(u, v) < r_0, \\ 1, & r(u, v) \geqslant r_0. \end{cases} \tag{8.22}$$

This filter has an inverted cylindrical shape, as seen in Figure 8.28. As with the ideal low pass filter, the sharp cutoff leads to ringing in the filtered image. This effect can be avoided by using a filter with a smooth rolloff in response, such as the **Butterworth high pass filter**,

$$H(u, v) = \frac{1}{1 + [r_0/r(u, v)]^{2n}}. \tag{8.23}$$

Figure 8.29 plots the transfer functions of order-1 and order-3 Butterworth high pass filters. As the filter order increases, the filter increasingly resembles an ideal high pass filter.

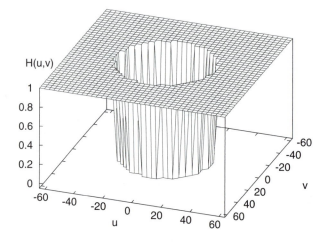

Figure 8.28   Transfer function of an ideal high pass filter.

8.5.3   Band pass and band stop filtering

A **band pass filter** passes a specific range of frequencies whilst suppressing others. A **band stop filter** (or 'band reject' filter) has the opposite effect, suppressing a particular range of frequencies whilst passing all other frequencies. A band stop filter is, in effect, a combination of a low pass filter of radius r_{low} and a high pass filter of radius r_{high}, with $r_{\text{high}} > r_{\text{low}}$.

We can specify a band pass or band stop filter using a pair of radii or, more usefully, using the radius of the band centre and its width. The transfer function of a Butterworth

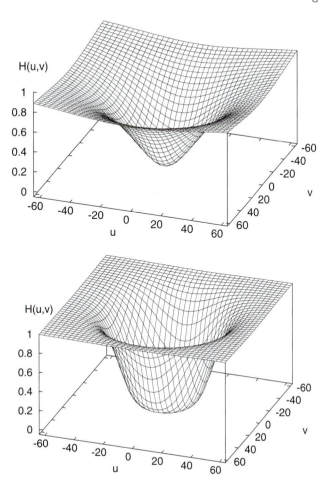

Figure 8.29 Transfer functions of the Butterworth high pass filter. Top: $n = 1$. Bottom: $n = 3$.

band stop filter specified in this manner is

$$H_s(r) = \frac{1}{1 + \left[\Omega r / (r^2 - r_0^2)\right]^{2n}},$$
(8.24)

where $r = \sqrt{u^2 + v^2}$, r_0 is the radius of the band centre and Ω is the band width. The corresponding band pass filter is given by

$$H_p(r) = 1 - H_s(r).$$
(8.25)

An order-1 Butterworth band pass filter is plotted in Figure 8.30.

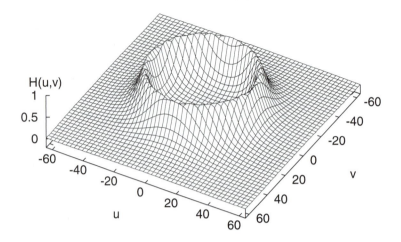

Figure 8.30 A Butterworth band pass filter with $n = 1$, $r_0 = 32$ and $\Omega = 10$.

8.5.4 Removal of periodic noise

More selective filtering is possible by 'editing out' specific frequencies from the spectrum. This approach can be used to remove structured, periodic noise from an image. An example is the interference patterns sometimes observed when electromechanical devices are operated close to video equipment. An electric motor will cause interference with a characteristic frequency that is related to the speed of the motor. This interference manifests itself in the image as a superimposed periodic pattern of varying brightness. If the pattern is sinusoidal in nature, the spectrum of the image will have a pair of narrow spikes that can be removed by zeroing amplitudes in the area of each spike. If possible, there should be a smooth transition from the zeroed area to the surrounding spectrum. Figure 8.31 shows an example of noise removal using this technique.

8.5.5 Implementations of filters in Java

The `ImageFFT` class provides support for low pass, high pass, band pass and band stop filtering operations using the ideal or Butterworth filter types. For example, an order-2 Butterworth low pass filter can be applied to an image using the following Java code:

```
ImageFFT fft = new ImageFFT(inputImage);
fft.transform();
fft.butterworthLowPassFilter(2, r);
fft.transform();
BufferedImage outputImage = fft.toImage(null);
```

The parameter `r` is the filter radius, normalised to lie in the range [0, 1]. A radius of 1 represents the maximum radius attainable by a filter that fits wholly within the spectrum. To apply a different filter, we need only replace the third line of this code fragment with the appropriate method call, from the options listed in Table 8.3.

(a) (b)

(c)

Figure 8.31 Removal of periodic noise. (a) Image corrupted by a periodic noise pattern. (b) Central part of the image's spectrum, showing spikes caused by the noise pattern. (c) Image produced after removing noise spikes from the spectrum.

Table 8.3 Filters supported in ImageFFT. Parameter r is the filter radius. For band pass and band stop filters, w is the band width. For Butterworth filters, n is the order of the filter.

```
void idealLowPassFilter(double r)
void idealHighPassFilter(double r)
void idealBandPassFilter(double r, double w)
void idealBandStopFilter(double r, double w)
void butterworthLowPassFilter(double r)
void butterworthLowPassFilter(int n, double r)
void butterworthHighPassFilter(double r)
void butterworthHighPassFilter(int n, double r)
void butterworthBandPassFilter(double r, double w)
void butterworthBandPassFilter(int n, double r, double w)
void butterworthBandStopFilter(double r, double w)
void butterworthBandStopFilter(int n, double r, double w)
```

The filters provided by `ImageFFT` can be incorporated easily into the `filter()` method of classes that implement `BufferedImageOp`. One example of this, called `ButterworthLowPassOp`, is provided in the `com.pearsoneduc.ip.op` package.

Other filters can be implemented by using the `setMagnitude()` method of `ImageFFT` to modify particular frequencies in the spectrum. For example, the routine in Listing 8.3 zeros an $m \times n$ region of a spectrum centred on coordinates (u, v). This code could be used to remove periodic noise from an image (Section 8.5.4). Note that spectral data are maintained by `ImageFFT` in unshifted form. Thus, for an $N \times N$ spectrum, frequency increases up to $u = N/2$ and decreases thereafter, and similarly for v.

LISTING 8.3 Java code to zero a rectangular region of a spectrum.

```
1   public static void zeroRegion(ImageFFT fft, int u, int v, int m, int n) {
2     try {
3       int m2 = m/2;
4       int n2 = n/2;
5       for (int k = -n2; k <= n2; ++k)
6         for (int j = -m2; j <= m2; ++j)
7           fft.setMagnitude(u+j, v+k, 0.0f);
8     }
9     catch (FFTException e) {
10      // do nothing if not in frequency domain
11    }
12  }
```

8.6   Deconvolution

Real images suffer from a variety of defects. For example, imaging devices generally add a certain amount of random noise to an image. Sometimes, as in the case of impulse noise, this can have a pronounced effect on the appearance of the image. We have already looked at several techniques for the suppression or removal of random noise from images.

But noise is not the only type of defect found in images. Other forms of degradation are possible. Some sources of degradation are essentially environmental; examples are the blurring that can occur when a moving object is imaged, or the distortion induced by atmospheric turbulence in astronomical images obtained from ground-based telescopes. Other defects are introduced by the imaging device; misfocusing of a camera lens, for instance, can blur an image significantly.

In many cases, the degraded image can be modelled as a perfect image that has been blurred by filtering and then further corrupted by the addition of noise. Thus, we may write

$$\hat{f}(x, y) = f(x, y) * h(x, y) + \epsilon(x, y), \tag{8.26}$$

where $\hat{f}$ is the observed image, f is the undegraded image, h is a convolution kernel that models the blurring and ϵ is the noise term. This expression is quite general, allowing both h and ϵ to vary spatially. We can simplify matters by assuming that degradation is spatially invariant. If we can further assume that the noise is negligible, then we have

$$\hat{f}(x, y) = f(x, y) * h, \tag{8.27}$$

which is a simple convolution. Clearly, it would be advantageous to reverse the effect of this convolution via some **deconvolution** technique—but it is not obvious how this might be achieved.

8.6.1   Point spread functions

The convolution kernel h in Equation 8.27, which models the net effect of blurring from all sources in the scene and imaging system, is known as the **point spread function** (PSF). The term is an apt one, for the PSF describes how energy from a point source is 'smeared out' by the imaging process. If the system were perfect, a point source would produce an image consisting of a single bright pixel, surrounded by zero-valued pixels; instead, what we see is an area of non-zero pixels. A profile of grey level across this area will have the same shape as the PSF.

If we are to deconvolve an image, we must know the form of its PSF. This can sometimes be determined from theoretical considerations, or by careful examination of the circumstances of image acquisition. Suppose, for example, that an object in an image is blurred as a result of uniform motion along the x axis. If we know its speed and the exposure time for the image, we can calculate the distance that it travelled in the scene during imaging. If we also know the distance in the image represented by a single pixel, we can determine the width in pixels of the PSF, and hence create an appropriate kernel.

If the PSF cannot be derived, it must be estimated from measurements of the image. It helps in this case if we can see points or lines whose properties are known—e.g., a star of known size in an astronomical image, or the (presumably sharp) edge of a building in an image of an outdoor scene.

8.6.2   The inverse filter

It becomes clear how Equation 8.27 might be inverted if we move to the frequency domain. Applying the convolution theorem, the expression becomes

$$\hat{F}(u, v) = F(u, v)H(u, v).$$

$\hat{F}$ is the spectrum of the observed image and F is the spectrum of the unobserved, undegraded image. H, the Fourier transform of the PSF, is known as the **modulation transfer function** (MTF). Rearranging the previous expression, we get

$$F(u, v) = \frac{\hat{F}(u, v)}{H(u, v)} = \hat{F}(u, v)\left[\frac{1}{H(u, v)}\right]. \tag{8.28}$$

The term $1/H(u, v)$ is an **inverse filter** that will remove the degradation.

In practice, there are numerous problems with inverse filtering. These become apparent if we consider the example of motion blur. The PSF for uniform linear motion is a rectangular pulse with a width correspdonding to the distance travelled during the time it took to acquire the image. Its MTF, plotted in Figure 8.32, contains zeros, so division by zero may occur

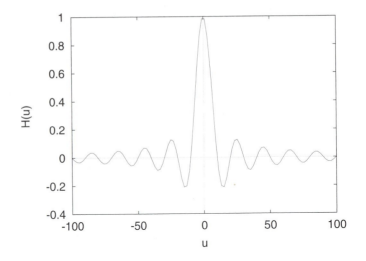

Figure 8.32 MTF for uniform linear motion.

at some point in frequency space. If the assumption of no noise is correct, the spectrum of the degraded image will have corresponding zeros, giving an indeterminate ratio of $0/0$ in Equation 8.28. But what if noise *is* present? In this case, the zeros will not coincide, and the image restored by the inverse filter will be obscured by the contribution of the noise term. We can see this if we assume a degradation model of the form

$$\hat{f}(x, y) = f(x, y) * h + \epsilon(x, y),$$

with $\epsilon(x, y)$ modelling the noise. In the frequency domain, this becomes

$$\hat{F}(u, v) = F(u, v)H(u, v) + E(u, v).$$

Applying the inverse filter to both sides, we get

$$\frac{\hat{F}(u, v)}{H(u, v)} = F(u, v) + \frac{E(u, v)}{H(u, v)}.$$

Looking at the right-hand side of this expression, we can see that, as $H(u, v)$ nears zero, the second term becomes large and dominates $F(u, v)$ (which is what we are trying to recover).

One empirical solution to these problems is to set a threshold on $H(u, v)$, below which the corresponding value of $F(u, v)$ is set to zero. Another idea is to limit inverse filtering to a certain distance from the origin of the spectrum—the 'restoration cutoff frequency'. Figure 8.33 shows this approach applied to the deconvolution of a blurred image to which a small amount of noise has been added. A cutoff frequency of 20 has been used, which excludes over 90% of the area of the spectrum from the analysis. This limits the amount of blurring that can be removed, and the sharp cutoff causes ringing in the output image. Nevertheless, the output image is clearly an improvement over the input.

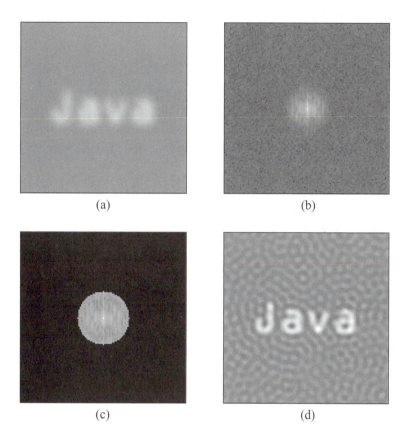

(a) (b)

(c) (d)

Figure 8.33 Deconvolution of a blurred, noisy image. (a) Input image. (b) Spectrum of input image. (c) Deconvolved spectrum, with a cutoff frequency of 20. (d) Deconvolved image.

8.6.3 The Wiener filter

A more rigorous solution to the problem of noise affecting deconvolution is the **Wiener filter**. A simplified version of this filter is applied as follows:

$$F(u, v) = \left[\frac{1}{H(u, v)} \frac{|H(u, v)|^2}{|H(u, v)|^2 + K} \right] \hat{F}(u, v), \tag{8.29}$$

where K is a constant value proportional to the variance of the noise present in the image. If $K = 0$, this expression reduces to a simple inverse filter. If K is large compared with $H(u, v)$, then the second term inside the brackets will be small, thereby balancing out the large value of the first term.

8.7 Further reading

Various image processing texts [5, 11, 36, 48] give accessible introductions to Fourier transforms and the frequency domain. Gonzalez and Woods [20] and Castleman [9] give the subject a fairly thorough treatment. A comprehensive survey of Fourier techniques and their applications is given by Bracewell [7].

The original source of the FFT algorithm is a classic paper by Cooley and Tukey [10]. Crane [11] gives an implementation in C. Pitas [37] describes this and other types of FFT algorithm and gives implementations, again in C. Porting these examples to Java should be a straightforward matter.

Deconvolution techniques are described by Parker [36] and by Umbaugh [48]. For even more detail, consult the classic text by Andrews and Hunt [2]. Note that other filters exist besides the simple inverse filter and Wiener filter discussed here; examples include the constrained least squares filter, the power spectrum equalisation filter and the geometric mean filter. Umbaugh [48] gives some practical examples of these filters at work. It has been shown [2] that, under conditions of limited blurring and moderate noise, the inverse filter produces the least desirable results, and that the Wiener filter produces images that are more blurred than we would like. The geometric mean filter seems to produce results that are more pleasing visually.

The discrete Fourier transform is just one of a number of discrete linear transformations that are useful in image processing. For example, there is the discrete cosine transform, used in image compression (see Chapter 12). Other transforms have basis functions that are rectangular, rather than sinusoidal, waves; examples are the Hadamard, Walsh and Haar transforms. Discrete image transforms are reviewed by Castleman [9] and by Gonzalez and Woods [20]; a less mathematical treatment is given by Umbaugh [48].

8.8 Exercises

1. Follow up the references given above on other discrete image transforms. Compile a list of their strengths and weaknesses and compare with those of the Fourier transform.

2. Investigate alternative algorithms for FFTs and modify the `ImageFFT` class to accommodate them.

3. Implement a version of `ImageFFT` that uses a native method to compute the Fourier transform, and benchmark it against the pure Java version described in this chapter.

4. A video camera has been operated near some unshielded electrical machinery and, as a result, each frame of the video signal is corrupted by a superimposed sinusoidal noise pattern. Images digitised from the video signal have dimensions 640 × 480. A student is asked to outline the steps involved in computing the spectrum of one of these images, displaying it and then modifying it to remove the noise pattern. The student makes the following observations:

    (a) "You take the image and just do a Fourier transform on it. This gives you the spectrum—which is just an array of numbers that tells you how much of each frequency is present in the image."

(b) "If the image has dimensions $N \times N$, then the spectrum also has dimensions $N \times N$— but half of the numbers are duplicated, and you can throw these away."

(c) "When you display the spectrum as an image, it will be too dark; you can make more detail visible by taking the logarithm of each amplitude in the spectrum, and scaling this to lie in the range 0–255."

(d) "There will be a bright spot visible in the spectrum, at a position corresponding to the frequency of the noise pattern. If you set amplitudes to zero at this point and do an inverse Fourier transform, the resulting image will have lost the noise pattern."

Comment on each of these statements, correcting any errors and omissions that you find.

5. Implement an interactive tool that

(a) Displays an image and its spectrum
(b) Allows the spectrum to be edited by blanking out regions selected with the mouse
(c) Displays the inverse Fourier transform of the spectrum, allowing the user to see the effects of their editing

6. Many photo editing software packages provide a facility to simulate motion blur. Use this to simulate a known amount of motion blur in an image or, if you have no access to such a package, write a Java application to do the same. Create another version of the blurred image, to which a *small* amount of noise has been added. (You can use the GaussianNoise application on the CD for this.) Then implement the inverse filter and the Wiener filter in Java and experiment with deconvolution of the images using these filters.

CHAPTER 9

Geometric operations

Geometric operations change image geometry by moving pixels around in a carefully constrained way. We might do this to remove distortions inherent in the imaging process, or to introduce a deliberate distortion that matches one image with another. There are three elements common to most geometric operations: transformation equations that move a pixel to a new location, a procedure for applying these equations to an image, and some way of computing a value for the transformed pixel. In this chapter, we will look at each of these elements in turn. We will consider simple operations such as rotation or scaling first, before moving on to more complex operations such as warping and morphing.

9.1   Introduction

Every image has its own set of geometric properties. This geometry is visible in the form of spatial relationships that exist between the groups of pixels representing particular features of interest in the image. Two images of the same scene, containing the same features, can have different geometries—if, for example, the distance between a pair of features is greater in one image than in the other, or if a particular group of features lie on a straight line in one image but not in the other.

It is sometimes necessary to transform image geometry, moving pixels around to change the relationships between image features. We may wish to do this for images that suffer from some form of **geometric distortion**. In modern cameras having standard lenses and CCD sensors, distortion is usually very small, and correction of any distortion is necessary only if we wish to make precise measurements of the sizes and shapes of features in an image. However, cases arise where we must use special optics (such as a fisheye lens) or an unusual type of sensor (of the log-polar type discussed in Chapter 3, for example); in these cases, geometric correction may be essential. Geometric processing is also essential in situations where there are distortions inherent in the imaging process—such as remote sensing from aircraft or spacecraft.

Consider, for example, the line scanner instruments flown aboard aircraft for remote sensing purposes. A line scanner's sensor is a one-dimensional array of photosites. A two-dimensional image is built up by the motion of the aircraft, which sweeps the sensor across an area of the ground below—hence the term 'pushbroom imaging', which is sometimes used to describe the mode of image acquisition for these devices. While a sweep is taking place, the aircraft may be experiencing changes in altitude, attitude or velocity—each of which can cause a particular type of distortion in the image. An increase in altitude, for instance, means that the first row of pixels spans a smaller distance on the ground than the last row of pixels.

In images that have not suffered geometric distortion, we may nonetheless wish to modify geometry in some way. To use the example of remote sensing once again, cartographers frequently need to distort images of terrestrial or planetary surfaces deliberately, so that they conform to a particular map projection [9]. We might also need to *register* two or more images of the same scene, obtained from slightly different viewpoints or acquired with different instruments. **Image registration** matches up the features that are common to two or more images. A typical application is change detection, where we quantify the changes in a scene by subtracting an image obtained at one time from an image obtained at a later time. Registration also finds applications in medical imaging, where it can help doctors to improve their diagnoses by allowing them to combine data obtained using different imaging techniques (e.g., x-ray CT and nuclear magnetic resonance imaging).

9.2   Simple techniques and their limitations

In Chapter 5, we encountered some very basic techniques for manipulating image geometry. We saw that an image can be enlarged by an integer factor, n, simply by copying each pixel to an $n \times n$ block of pixels in the output image. This technique is fast, and has been a standard feature of specialised image processing hardware. An obvious disadvantage is that it cannot be used to expand an image by some arbitrary, non-integer factor. Another problem is that greatly enlarged images have a very 'blocky' appearance. This may not bother us in applications where we merely wish to examine pixels more closely, but is of serious concern otherwise.

There are similar problems with the technique of shrinking an image by subsampling its array of pixels. First, the technique cannot be used to reduce image dimensions by an arbitrary factor. Second, subsampling can eliminate information from the image completely, as Figure 9.1 illustrates. One solution to this latter problem is to turn an $n \times n$ block of pixels in the input image into a single pixel in the output image. The value of each output pixel must be representative of the corresponding block in the input image. The mean grey level of the block can be used (Figure 9.2). Crane [11] also suggests the median, but Figure 9.2

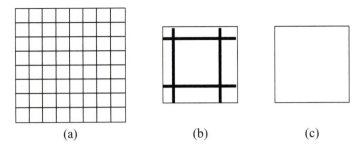

(a)   (b)   (c)

Figure 9.1 Problems with shrinking a simple image by subsampling. (a) Input image. (b) Image generated by sampling every fifth pixel, magnified for easier viewing. (c) Image generated by sampling every sixth pixel.

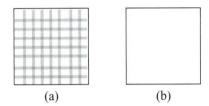

(a)   (b)

Figure 9.2 Shrinking the image of Figure 9.1(a) by using the mean or median of an $n \times n$ block. (a) Mean. (b) Median.

shows that this can suffer from the same problem as subsampling, given the right type of image.

Figure 9.3 compares subsampling with the $n \times n$ mean and $n \times n$ median approaches for a real image of a face. In this case, there is little to choose between the mean and median images. The subsampled image is clearly inferior, with data loss leading to an apparent change in facial expression.

9.3   Affine transformations

An arbitrary geometric transformation will move a pixel at coordinates (x, y) to a new position, (x', y'), given by a pair of transformation equations,

$$x' = T_x(x, y),$$ (9.1)
$$y' = T_y(x, y).$$ (9.2)

T_x and T_y are typically expressed as polynomials in x and y. In their simplest form, they are linear in x and y, giving us an **affine transformation**,

$$x' = a_0 x + a_1 y + a_2,$$ (9.3)
$$y' = b_0 x + b_1 y + b_2.$$ (9.4)

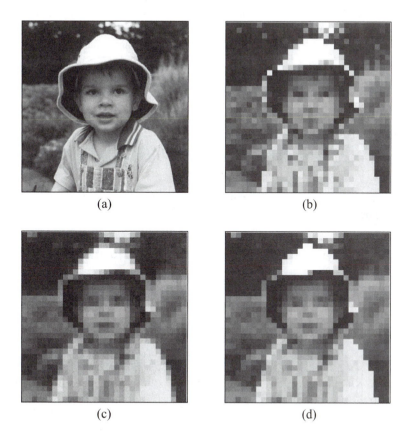

(a)

(b)

(c)

(d)

Figure 9.3 Shrinking a real image by a factor n. (a) Original image. (b) Subsampling. (c) Mean of $n \times n$ block. (d) Median of $n \times n$ block.

This can be expressed in matrix form as

$$
\begin{bmatrix} x' \\ y' \\ 1 \end{bmatrix} = \begin{bmatrix} a_0 & a_1 & a_2 \\ b_0 & b_1 & b_2 \\ 0 & 0 & 1 \end{bmatrix} \begin{bmatrix} x \\ y \\ 1 \end{bmatrix}.
\tag{9.5}
$$

Note the use of *homogeneous coordinates*; the two-dimensional points (x, y) and (x', y') are represented using three-dimensional vectors, with the third dimension equal to 1. This is a convenient trick that allows us to represent the entire transformation as a single 3×3 matrix. We could represent points as 2D vectors, but then our transformation would consist of multiplication by a 2×2 matrix followed by addition of a vector, i.e.,

$$
\begin{bmatrix} x' \\ y' \end{bmatrix} = \begin{bmatrix} a_0 & a_1 \\ b_0 & b_1 \end{bmatrix} \begin{bmatrix} x \\ y \end{bmatrix} + \begin{bmatrix} a_2 \\ b_2 \end{bmatrix}.
$$

This is less compact and more difficult to manipulate than the homogeneous representation.

Under an affine transformation, straight lines are preserved and parallel lines remain parallel. Translation, scaling, rotation and shearing are all special cases of Equations 9.3 and 9.4. For example, a translation of 3 pixels down and 5 pixels to the right is

$$x' = x + 5,$$
$$y' = y + 3.$$

The corresponding affine transformation matrix is

$$\begin{bmatrix} 1 & 0 & 5 \\ 0 & 1 & 3 \\ 0 & 0 & 1 \end{bmatrix}.$$

Table 9.1 specifies how the elements of the transformation matrix are computed for selected special cases of affine transformation.

Table 9.1 Transformation coefficients for some simple affine transformations.

Transformation	a_0	a_1	a_2	b_0	b_1	b_2
Translation by Δx, Δy	1	0	Δx	0	1	Δy
Scaling by a factor s	s	0	0	0	s	0
Clockwise rotation through angle θ	$\cos\theta$	$-\sin\theta$	0	$\sin\theta$	$\cos\theta$	0
Horizontal shear by a factor s	1	s	0	0	1	0

Note that any combination of the transformations listed in Table 9.1 is also an affine transformation. Thus, it is usual to express an arbitrary affine transformation as some combination of these simpler transformations, performed in sequence. This is generally more meaningful than specifying values for the elements of the transformation matrix in Equation 9.5. Alternatively, we can specify an affine transformation in terms of the effect it has on points in the xy plane. Given the coordinates of three points before transformation, and the corresponding coordinates of those points after transformation, we can write down six simultaneous equations in x and y. These can be solved to find the six transformation coefficients. The three points in each image can be regarded as the vertices of a triangle; the affine transformation can therefore be viewed as the mapping of one triangle onto another (Figure 9.4).

9.3.1 Affine transformations in Java

The Java2D API supports affine transformations of images and other graphic objects. A transformation is specified by an instance of the class java.awt.geom. AffineTransform. An AffineTransform can be created in various ways, using the constructors listed in Table 9.2. For example,

```
AffineTransform transform = new AffineTransform();
```

creates an identity transformation, i.e., a transformation that will leave an image unchanged. This can be changed subsequently by calling various methods of AffineTransform. Transformation objects can also be created from a set of coefficients, supplied in an array or as

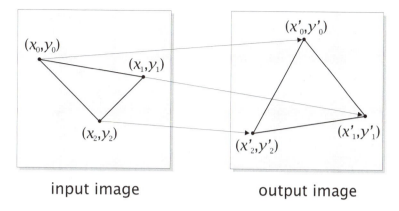

input image   output image

Figure 9.4 Mapping of one triangle onto another by an affine transformation.

Table 9.2 Constructors provided by Java's `AffineTransform` class.

```
AffineTransform()

AffineTransform(AffineTransform t)

AffineTransform(double[] coeff)

AffineTransform(float[] coeff)

AffineTransform(double a0, double b0, double a1, double b1, double a2,
double b2)

AffineTransform(float a0, float b0, float a1, float b1, float a2, float b2)
```

separate parameters. Data types of `float` and `double` are supported. When an array with at least six elements is provided, it is assumed that the first six elements are the coefficients $a_0, b_0, a_1, b_1, a_2, b_2$. If the array has four or five elements, the first four are assumed to be the coefficients a_0, b_0, a_1, b_1.

For simple transformations, it is more convenient to use the factory methods listed in Table 9.3. For example, a transformation object that will increase image size by 50% can be created with

```
AffineTransform scale = AffineTransform.getScaleInstance(1.5, 1.5);
```

Similarly, a transformation that will rotate an image 45° about its centre can be created thus:

```
double angle = Math.PI/4.0;
double x = image.getWidth()/2.0;
double y = image.getHeight()/2.0;
AffineTransform rotate =
  AffineTransform.getRotateInstance(angle, x, y);
```

Note that `AffineTransform` expects angles to be expressed in radians. Note also that the `getScaleInstance()` and `getShearInstance()` permit us to specify different degrees of scaling or shearing in the x and y directions.

Table 9.3 Factory methods provided by Java's `AffineTransform` class.

```
AffineTransform getTranslateInstance(double tx, double ty)

AffineTransform getScaleInstance(double sx, double sy)

AffineTransform getRotateInstance(double theta)

AffineTransform getRotateInstance(double theta, double x, double y)

AffineTransform getShearInstance(double sx, double sy)
```

LISTING 9.1 Java code to analyse the properties of an `AffineTransform`.

```
1   public static boolean bitSet(int flags, int mask) {
2     return (flags & mask) != 0;
3   }
4
5   public static void checkTransform(AffineTransform transform) {
6     System.out.println("Transformation involves:");
7     int flags = transform.getType();
8     if (bitSet(flags, AffineTransform.TYPE_TRANSLATION))
9       System.out.println("translation");
10    if (bitSet(flags, AffineTransform.TYPE_MASK_SCALE))
11      System.out.println("scaling");
12    if (bitSet(flags, AffineTransform.TYPE_MASK_ROTATION))
13      System.out.println("rotation");
14    if (bitSet(flags, AffineTransform.TYPE_FLIP))
15      System.out.println("reflection");
16  }
```

The state of an existing `AffineTransform` can be probed by calling its `getType()` method. The integer returned by this method will have various bits set to indicate the properties of the transformation. The Java code shown in Listing 9.1 illustrates how these bits can be checked. Note that there are, in fact, two types of scaling: uniform scaling, indicated by the bit value `AffineTransform.TYPE_UNIFORM_SCALE`; and scaling by different amounts in the x and y directions, indicated by the bit value `AffineTransform.TYPE_GENERAL_SCALE`. A bit mask called `AffineTransform.TYPE_MASK_SCALE` is provided to test for either type of scaling. Similarly, there are two types of rotation: rotation by a multiple of 90° (`AffineTransform.TYPE_QUADRANT_ROTATION`) and rotation through some arbitrary angle (`AffineTransform.TYPE_GENERAL_ROTATION`). The bit mask `AffineTransform.TYPE_MASK_ROTATION` can be used to test for either type of rotation.

Be warned that `getType()` has a flaw. If we create an `AffineTransform` that performs a 90° rotation and check the value returned by `getType()`, we find that the scaling bit is set, despite the fact the transformation is merely a rotation! (Presumably, `getType()` is not taking account of the fact that matrix elements a_0 and b_1 can have values other than 1 without there being any scaling.)

An existing `AffineTransform` can be modified in five different ways. It can be

- Replaced with a simple transformation
- Replaced with an arbitrary transformation
- Concatenated with a simple transformation
- Concatenated with an arbitrary transformation
- Preconcatenated with an arbitrary transformation

Methods that replace the existing transformation are listed in Table 9.4. The concatenation methods, listed in Table 9.5, update the transformation matrix with an additional transformation, rather than replacing it. The following example illustrates how these methods work.

```
AffineTransform t = new AffineTransform();
t.setToTranslation(10, 20);
t.rotate(30.0*Math.PI/180.0);
AffineTransform translate =
  AffineTransform.getTranslateInstance(5, 0);
t.concatenate(translate);
AffineTransform scale = AffineTransform.getScaleInstance(0.3, 0.3);
t.preConcatenate(scale);
```

The first line creates t as an identity transformation. This is then replaced by a translation of 10 units to the right and 20 units down. Next, a 30° rotation is added—so the transformation is now a translation, followed by a rotation. The fourth and fifth lines create another `AffineTransform` that performs a translation and concatenate it with t—with the result that t is now a translation, followed by a rotation, followed by another translation. The last two lines create a transformation object that scales by a factor 0.3 in both directions and *pre*concatenate it with t. At this stage, t consists of a scaling, a translation, a rotation and another translation. We should emphasise that this sequence of operations is merely a convenient way to visualise the transformation. As far as an `AffineTransform` is concerned, they are aggregated into a single transformation matrix.

Table 9.4 Methods to replace the current transformation of an `AffineTransform` with a different transformation.

```
void setToIdentity()
void setToTranslation(double tx, double ty)
void setToScale(double sx, double sx)
void setToRotation(double angle)
void setToRotation(double angle, double x, double y)
void setToShear(double sx, double sy)
void setTransform(AffineTransform newTransform)
```

Table 9.5 Methods to concatenate the current transformation of an AffineTransform with an additional transformation.

```
void translate(double tx, double ty)

void scale(double sx, double sy)

void rotate(double angle)

void rotate(double angle, double x, double y)

void shear(double sx, double sy)

void concatenate(AffineTransform extraTransform)

void preConcatenate(AffineTransform firstTransform)
```

AffineTransform has a small number of other methods that may prove useful: getMatrix() copies the elements of the current transformation matrix to the double array provided as a parameter; getDeterminant() returns the determinant of the current transformation matrix; createInverse() returns an AffineTransform object representing the inverse of the current transformation.

An enhanced transformation class

Although AffineTransform is very useful, it lacks one feature: the ability to create a transformation that maps one triangle onto another, as illustrated in Figure 9.4. We provide a class called AffineTransformation to do this, as part of the com.pearsoneduc. ip.util package. AffineTransformation extends AffineTransform, duplicating its constructors and adding one more. This new constructor takes two arrays of type Point2D as parameters. The first specifies the vertices of the input triangle and the second the corresponding vertices of the output triangle.

9.4   Transformation algorithms

How do we apply an affine transformation—or any kind of transformation, for that matter—to an image? One approach, described as **forward mapping**, involves iterating over each pixel of the input image, computing new coordinates for it using Equation 9.5 and copying its value to the new location. Suppose, for example, that we wish to rotate an image by an angle θ about the origin. Referring to Table 9.1, we see that this is accomplished with the transformation matrix

$$\begin{bmatrix} \cos\theta & -\sin\theta & 0 \\ \sin\theta & \cos\theta & 0 \\ 0 & 0 & 1 \end{bmatrix}.$$

Now let us consider what happens to

1. The pixel at (0, 100) after a 90° rotation
2. The pixel at (50, 0) after a 35° rotation

In case 1, $\cos 90°$ is 0 and $\sin 90°$ is 1, so the pixel moves to coordinates $(-100, 0)$. This is clearly a problem, since pixels cannot have negative coordinates. Case 2 illustrates a different problem. Here, we calculate that

$$x' = x \cos \theta - y \sin \theta = 50 \cos(35°) = 40.96,$$

$$y' = x \sin \theta + y \cos \theta = 50 \sin(35°) = 28.68.$$

The coordinates calculated by the transformation equations are not integers, and therefore do not index a pixel in the output image.

The first problem can be solved by testing coordinates to check that they lie within the bounds of the output image before attempting to copy pixel values. A simple solution to the second problem is to find the nearest integers to x' and y' and use these as the coordinates of the transformed pixel. Algorithm 9.1 incorporates both of these solutions into a procedure for rotating an $M \times N$ image by forward mapping. An implementation of this algorithm is shown in Listing 9.2. This code can be found in the application ForwardRotation, available on the CD.

The forward mapping approach is clearly wasteful, as it potentially calculates many coordinates that do not lie within the bounds of the output image. Furthermore, each output pixel may be addressed several times—or, worse still, not at all. We can see this in Figure 9.5, which shows an image and the results of a 25° rotation anticlockwise about the origin, produced using the ForwardRotation program. The rotated image contains numerous 'holes' where no value was computed for a pixel.

To guarantee that a value is generated for every pixel in the output image, we must consider each output pixel in turn and use the *inverse* transformation to determine the position in the input image from which a value must be sampled. This is known as the **backward**

ALGORITHM 9.1 Image rotation by forward mapping.

Create an output image, g, of dimensions $M \times N$
for all pixel coordinates x, y in g **do**
$\quad g(x, y) = 0$
end for
$a_0 = \cos \theta$
$b_0 = \sin \theta$
$a_1 = -b_0$
$b_1 = a_0$
for all pixel coordinates x, y in input image f **do**
$\quad x' = round(a_0 x + a_1 y)$
$\quad y' = round(b_0 x + b_1 y)$
$\quad$ **if** (x', y') is inside g **then**
$\quad\quad g(x', y') = f(x, y)$
$\quad$ **end if**
end for

LISTING 9.2 Java implementation of Algorithm 9.1.

```
 1  public static BufferedImage rotate(BufferedImage input, double angle) {
 2
 3    int width = input.getWidth();
 4    int height = input.getHeight();
 5    BufferedImage output = new BufferedImage(width, height, input.getType());
 6
 7    double a0 = Math.cos(angle*Math.PI/180.0);
 8    double b0 = Math.sin(angle*Math.PI/180.0);
 9    double a1 = -b0, b1 = a0;
10
11    int rx, ry;
12    for (int y = 0; y < height; ++y)
13      for (int x = 0; x < width; ++x) {
14        rx = (int) Math.round(a0*x + a1*y);
15        ry = (int) Math.round(b0*x + b1*y);
16        if (rx >= 0 && rx < width && ry >= 0 && ry < height)
17          output.setRGB(rx, ry, input.getRGB(x, y));
18      }
19
20    return output;
21
22  }
```

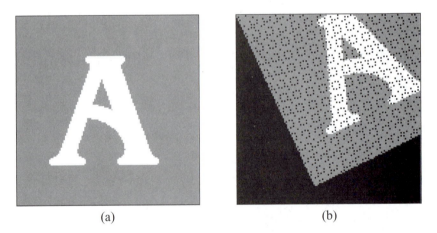

(a)   (b)

Figure 9.5 Rotation by forward mapping. (a) Input image. (b) Output image, showing holes where there was no mapping of an input pixel to an output pixel.

mapping approach. Algorithm 9.2 shows the procedure for rotation by an angle θ using backward mapping. Notice that we must still contend with the two problems mentioned earlier, namely that the calculated coordinates are real numbers, and that they might lie outside the bounds of the image (in this case, the input image).

ALGORITHM 9.2   Image rotation by backward mapping.

Create an output image, g, of dimensions $M \times N$
$a_0 = \cos\theta$
$a_1 = \sin\theta$
$b_0 = -a_1$
$b_1 = a_0$
for all pixel coordinates x', y' in g **do**
   $x = round(a_0x' + a_1y')$
   $y = round(b_0x' + b_1y')$
   if (x, y) is inside f **then**
      $g(x', y') = f(x, y)$
   else
      $g(x', y') = 0$
   end if
end for

9.5   Interpolation schemes

9.5.1   Zero-order interpolation

The rounding of calculated coordinates (x', y') to their nearest integers is a strategy known as **zero-order** (or *nearest-neighbour*) **interpolation**. This is illustrated in Figure 9.6. Zero-order interpolation is simple computationally, but can degrade the appearance of the transformed image. Images may look very 'blocky' when scaled up in size by a large factor, and horizontal or vertical lines may have a very jagged appearance when rotated through angles that are not multiples of 90°—as in Figure 9.8(b).

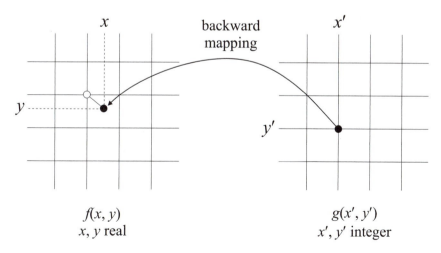

Figure 9.6   Zero-order (nearest-neighbour) interpolation.

9.5.2 First-order interpolation

First-order (or *bilinear*) **interpolation** computes output pixel grey level as a distance-weighted function of the grey levels of the four pixels surrounding the calculated point in the input image. This is illustrated in Figure 9.7. For a calculated point (x', y') surrounded by pixels with coordinates (x_0, y_0), (x_1, y_0), (x_0, y_1) and (x_1, y_1), the first-order interpolation function can be written

$$
\begin{aligned}
f(x', y') = f(x_0, y_0) &+ [f(x_1, y_0) - f(x_0, y_0)]\Delta x \\
&+ [f(x_0, y_1) - f(x_0, y_0)]\Delta y \\
&+ [f(x_1, y_1) + f(x_0, y_0) - f(x_0, y_1) - f(x_1, y_0)]\Delta x \Delta y,
\end{aligned}
\tag{9.6}
$$

where $\Delta x = x' - x_0$ and $\Delta y = y' - y_0$. This formula requires ten additions or subtractions (including those needed to compute Δx and Δy) and four multiplications. A slightly more efficient approach breaks the computation down into three interpolation steps, as in Algorithm 9.3. This requires eight additions or subtractions and three multiplications. The saving in computation, though small, may become significant when transforming large images, since interpolation must be performed every time that there is a mapping to an output pixel from a point inside the input image.

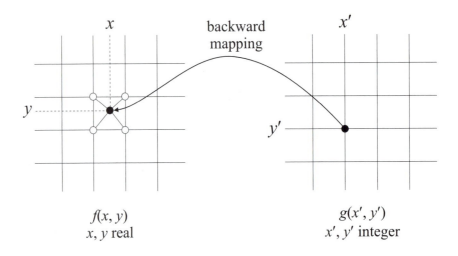

$f(x, y)$
x, y real

$g(x', y')$
x', y' integer

Figure 9.7 First-order (bilinear) interpolation.

ALGORITHM 9.3 First-order interpolation of pixel grey level.

$\Delta x = x' - x_0$
$\Delta y = y' - y_0$
$p = f(x_0, y_0) + [f(x_1, y_0) - f(x_0, y_0)]\Delta x$
$q = f(x_0, y_1) + [f(x_1, y_1) - f(x_0, y_1)]\Delta x$
$f(x', y') = p + (q - p)\Delta y$

Although first-order interpolation is more demanding, computationally, than zero-order interpolation, it produces results that are smoother and more pleasing than zero-order interpolation. This can be seen clearly in Figure 9.8(c).

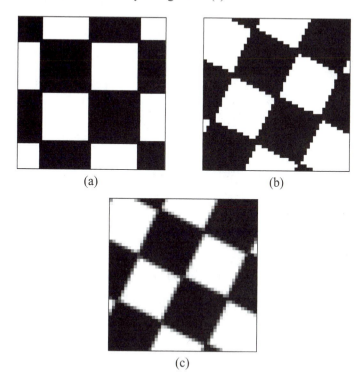

Figure 9.8 Interpolation of pixel grey level. (a) Input image. (b) Rotation with zero-order interpolation. (c) Rotation with first-order interpolation.

9.5.3   Higher-order interpolations

Higher-order interpolation schemes are sometimes used. A third-order, or *bicubic*, interpolation uses a 16×16 neighbourhood of pixels surrounding the calculated point to compute its value. The calculation can be viewed as the convolution of a 16×16 neighbourhood with a cubic function, so this method of interpolation is sometimes described as cubic convolution. In fact, any interpolation scheme can be viewed as the convolution of image data with an interpolation function.

Figure 9.9 plots one-dimensional functions representing nearest-neighbour, linear and cubic interpolation. The discontinuity in the nearest-neighbour function models the jump that occurs from one pixel to a neighbouring pixel when a calculated coordinate x' is no longer closest to that first pixel. This sudden jump is the cause of the blockiness or jaggedness visible in images that are transformed in this manner. The other two interpolation functions have widths greater than one pixel, so convolution with these functions computes a weighted average of grey level over a neighbourhood, rather than selecting the grey level

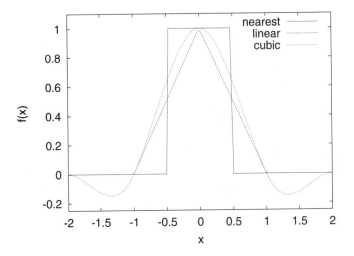

Figure 9.9 Nearest-neighbour, linear and cubic interpolation functions.

of one particular neighbour. Both functions act as low pass filters. One difference between the cubic and linear functions is that the cubic function has a continuous derivative, whereas the linear function exhibits sudden changes in slope. Also, the cubic function has negative lobes. Thus, a value interpolated using this function will be a weighted sum of nearby pixel values, minus some contribution from pixels slightly further away. This reduces the low pass filtering effect, so bicubic interpolation will produce results a little sharper than those from bilinear interpolation.

Higher-order interpolation is very costly, so it is generally used only if the smoothing from first-order interpolation is excessive or the slope discontinuities of first-order interpolation have an undesirable effect on the image.

9.6   Affine image transformation in Java

The Java2D API provides a `BufferedImageOp` class called `AffineTransformOp` to perform affine transformations on images. Before creating an `AffineTransformOp`, we must first specify the transformation by creating an appropriate `AffineTransform` (see Section 9.3.1). An `AffineTransformOp` is constructed from this transformation object and an integer specifying the type of interpolation to be used. This should have one of the values

```
AffineTransformOp.TYPE_NEAREST_NEIGHBOR
AffineTransformOp.TYPE_BILINEAR
```

signifying zero-order or first-order interpolation, respectively. For example, suppose that we wish to rotate a `BufferedImage` called `inputImage` 30° anticlockwise using first-order interpolation. This is accomplished with

```
AffineTransform rotation =
 AffineTransform.getRotateInstance(-Math.PI/6);
BufferedImageOp rotateOp =
 new AffineTransformOp(rotation, AffineTransformOp.TYPE_BILINEAR);
BufferedImage rotatedImage = rotateOp.filter(inputImage, null);
```

The program `Rotate1` on the CD uses similar code to rotate an image about its centre coordinates or about a specified point. Figure 9.10(b) shows typical output generated when the program rotates an image about the origin. Notice that some of the image has been lost because the rotation has moved pixels outside the allowed coordinate space of $0 \leqslant x \leqslant M - 1$ and $0 \leqslant y \leqslant N - 1$, M and N being image width and height, respectively. The solution to this problem is to enlarge the coordinate space and translate the image, either before or after rotation. To determine coordinate space dimensions and the translation parameters, we can apply the transformation to the corners of the image and compute a bounding box for these four points. The width and height of this bounding box are the required dimensions of the output image. The upper-left corner of the box must be translated to $(0, 0)$ in order for all of the rotated pixels to lie within the output image.

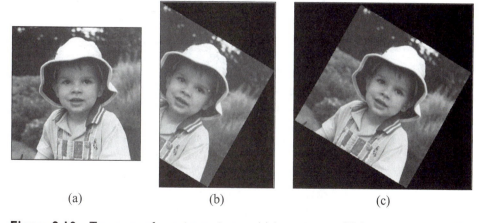

(a)   (b)   (c)

Figure 9.10 Two ways of rotating an image. (a) Input image. (b) Image transformed by `Rotate1`, without special measures to deal with pixels outside the coordinate space. (c) Image transformed by `Rotate2` in such a way that all rotated pixels are visible.

Listing 9.3 shows a Java method `getBoundingBox()` that computes the bounding box of an image under a given affine transformation. This method is part of the `GeomTools` class in package `com.pearsoneduc.ip.util`. The program `Rotate2` provided on the CD uses `getBoundingBox()` to find the bounds of an image following a specified rotation. It then modifies the transformation, creates storage for the output image and performs the rotation in the following manner:

```
AffineTransform rotation =
 AffineTransform.getRotateInstance(angle);
Rectangle2D box = GeomTools.getBoundingBox(image, rotation);
AffineTransform translation =
```

LISTING 9.3 A method to calculate the bounding box of a transformed image.

```
1  public static Rectangle2D getBoundingBox(
2    BufferedImage image, AffineTransform transformation) {
3
4    // Apply transformation to image corners
5
6    int xmax = image.getWidth()-1;
7    int ymax = image.getHeight()-1;
8    Point2D[] corners = new Point2D.Double[4];
9    corners[0] = new Point2D.Double(0, 0);
10   corners[1] = new Point2D.Double(xmax, 0);
11   corners[2] = new Point2D.Double(xmax, ymax);
12   corners[3] = new Point2D.Double(0, ymax);
13   transformation.transform(corners, 0, corners, 0, 4);
14
15   // Calculate bounding box of transformed corner points
16
17   Rectangle2D boundingBox = new Rectangle2D.Double();
18   for (int i = 0; i < 4; ++i)
19     boundingBox.add(corners[i]);
20
21   return boundingBox;
22
23  }
```

```
AffineTransform.getTranslateInstance(-box.getMinX(),
  -box.getMinY());
rotation.preConcatenate(translation);

int width = (int) Math.round(box.getWidth());
int height = (int) Math.round(box.getHeight());
BufferedImage rotatedImage =
  new BufferedImage(width, height, image.getType());
BufferedImageOp rotateOp =
  new AffineTransformOp(rotation, interpolation);
rotateOp.filter(image, rotatedImage);
```

Figure 9.10(c) shows output from the Rotate2 program. We can see that the image has become larger in order to accommodate all of the rotated pixels.

Two further programs that perform affine transformations are provided on the CD. Scale enlarges or shrinks an image uniformly by an arbitrary factor, or non-uniformly using different factors for the x and y directions. As with Rotate1 and Rotate2, zero-order and first-order interpolation schemes are supported.

Also available is `AffineTransformTool`. This has a graphical user interface, showing an image before and after affine transformation. A control panel provides sliders to scale the image in the x and y directions by factors in the range $[0.1, 2.0]$. Another slider can be used to rotate the image through the range $[-90°, 90°]$. Radiobuttons allow the user to toggle between zero-order and first-order interpolation. Figure 9.11 is a screen dump showing `AffineTransformTool` in action.

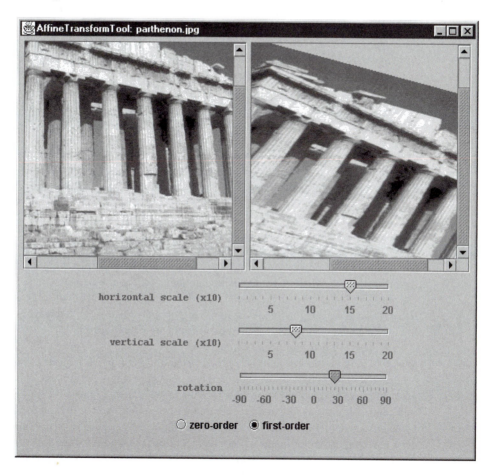

Figure 9.11 The `AffineTransformTool` application.

9.7 Warping and morphing

We noted in Section 9.3 that the transformation equations mapping (x, y) to (x', y') can be expressed as polynomials in x and y. For example, we can write

$$x' = a_0 x^2 + a_1 y^2 + a_2 xy + a_3 x + a_4 y + a_5, \tag{9.7}$$

$$y' = b_0 x^2 + b_1 y^2 + b_2 xy + b_3 x + b_4 y + b_5. \tag{9.8}$$

The twelve coefficients in these equations specify a **quadratic warp**. This can introduce more complex distortions into an image than an affine transformation—warping straight lines into curves, for example. Cubic warps, with twenty warp coefficients, are also used—e.g., to remove the pincushion and barrel distortions caused by camera lenses. Increasing the order of the warp increases both the complexity of the distortions introduced into the image and the time required to compute the transformation.

The only practical way of specifying polynomial warps of second order or higher is by means of the effect they have on a set of **control points**. Consider the quadratic warp, for example. Here, there are twelve coefficients to be determined. We can specify the coordinates and displacements of six control points and substitute this information into Equations 9.7 and 9.8. This gives a set of twelve simultaneous equations that can be solved exactly for the twelve coefficients using standard numerical techniques. A cubic warp can likewise be determined from the coordinates and displacements of ten control points.

These operations are useful in image registration, where we wish to warp one image so that it matches another image as closely as possible. Registration typically involves marking the locations of key features in the image to be warped (e.g., the corners of objects), along with the corresponding locations of these features in the reference image. More points than the minimum required for determination of the warp are usually specified, to minimise the effect of placement errors. This means that it is not possible to solve exactly for the warp coefficients; instead, a least-squares technique is used to compute the coefficients of a warp that best fits the specified displacements.

In many cases, polynomial warping is too smooth and simple to model the complex distortions that we wish to introduce into an image. An alternative technique is 'piecewise warping', in which we apply a simple transformation locally but allow that transformation to vary across the image. An advantage of this approach is that we can leave some areas of the image unchanged whilst warping others to a significant degree.

In a piecewise warping operation, the user of the warping software will typically define a **control grid** on the image to be warped. This grid is drawn as a mesh of horizontal and vertical lines lying on top of the image. The intersections of the grid lines represent control points that can be dragged to new locations using the mouse. Figure 9.12 shows an example of a control grid drawn on an image, before and after modification by the user.

When calculating the warp, we imagine that the control grid marks out a set of quadrilaterals covering the entire image. The intersections of the grid lines are the corners of these quadrilaterals. For every quadrilateral in the original, unwarped grid, there is a corresponding quadrilateral in the warped grid. A **bilinear transformation** can be specified that will map the former onto the latter:

$$x' = a_0 xy + a_1 x + a_2 y + a_3, \qquad (9.9)$$
$$y' = b_0 xy + b_1 y + b_2 y + b_3. \qquad (9.10)$$

This is rather like the affine transformation, but with an extra term in xy. There are eight coefficients to be determined, but the four corner points are sufficient to solve for them exactly. We can also write down similar equations for the inverse transformation, expressing x and y each as bilinear functions of x' and y', and determine their coefficients in the same manner.

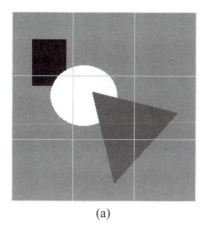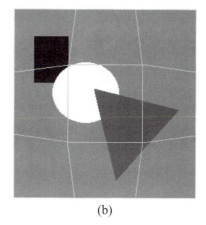

(a)   (b)

Figure 9.12 Piecewise warping with a control grid. (a) Original, regular control grid drawn over an image. (b) Irregular grid indicating the desired warp.

ALGORITHM 9.4 A simple piecewise warping technique.

for all rectangles of the unwarped grid **do**
    Find corresponding quadrilateral of warped grid
    Solve for coefficients $\{a_i, b_i : i = 0, 3\}$ of the inverse transformation
    Store rectangle's corners and its transformation coefficients in a list
end for
Create an output image, g, with same dimensions as f
for all pixel coordinates x', y' in g **do**
    Search list to find the rectangle containing (x', y')
    Use its coefficients to compute x and y
    Determine value of $f(x, y)$ by interpolation
    $g(x', y') = f(x, y)$
end for

Algorithm 9.4 sketches the steps involved in piecewise warping of an image. It assumes that the input image exists, and that the coordinates of control points from the original control grid and the warped control grid have already been determined. Figure 9.13 shows the results of piecewise warping using the grids of Figure 9.12. The image in Figure 9.13(a) was generated by warping from the regular grid to the irregular grid; the image of Figure 9.13(b) was produced by a warp in the opposite direction.

Morphing is a technique for transforming one image into another in an incremental fashion. It has found favour as a special effect in the TV and film industries, although it has few—if any—serious applications. Morphing incorporates the ideas of piecewise warping and registration. It requires an initial image and a final image, onto which the initial image will be warped. In most morphing algorithms, the user must define matched pairs of control points on the two images to specify the warp. A mesh of some kind—

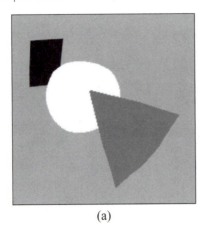
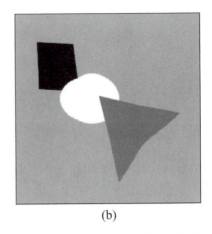

(a) (b)

Figure 9.13 Examples of piecewise warping. (a) Warp specified in Figure 9.12. (b) Reverse of the transformation in (a).

triangular, for example—is then generated from the control points of the initial image, and another mesh is generated in the same way from the control points of the final image. In the case of triangular meshes, an affine transformation relates one triangle of the initial mesh to the corresponding triangle of the final mesh. The remainder of the algorithm is much like the piecewise warping technique discussed previously, with the important difference that the warp is computed incrementally, as a sequence of smaller warps. It is also necessary to 'dissolve' from the initial image to the final image by interpolating pixel grey level or colour; without this operation, morphing would merely provide an animated registration of the two images, rather than the smooth transition between them that is required.

An alternative warping technique that does away with the triangular or quadrilateral mesh is *fields-based morphing* [6]. In this technique, pairs of reference lines are drawn on the initial and final images. Then, for each pixel, a perpendicular distance to each control line is calculated. Distance and relative position along the line are used to place the pixel in the correct position in the final image. All control lines have an influence on what happens to a pixel, although that influence is much lower for distant lines than it is for lines near to the pixel.

9.8 Further reading

Castleman [9] gives a good introduction to geometric operations on images. Particularly noteworthy is the discussion of how spacecraft images can be transformed geometrically so as to conform to various cartographic projections.

Lyon [29] describes affine and bilinear transformations in some detail and presents examples in Java.

The definite guide to image warping and morphing techniques is the book by Wolberg [52]. Crane [11] provides a good introduction to these techniques, complete with source code in C. Fields-based warping and morphing were introduced by Beier and Neely [6].

Crane gives a useful summary of the technique, again with source code. The book by Gomes et al. [18] gives a broader perspective on warping and morphing, describing their application not only to images but also to curves, surfaces and volumetric objects.

9.9   Exercises

1. Consult the appropriate references [6, 11] and then implement a fields-based morphing technique in Java. The program should have a graphical user interface, displaying the initial and final images side by side in a tabbed pane and allowing the user to draw matching pairs of lines on the two images. Selecting the other tab on the tabbed pane should bring up an animated display of the morph. There should be some way of writing the morph sequence out to a set of image files.

Segmentation

If we are to analyse or interpret an image automatically, we must have a way of identifying unambiguously the pixels that correspond to particular features of interest. The process of identifying these pixels is known as segmentation. In this chapter, we consider a simple segmentation technique based on the thresholding operation described in Chapter 6 and compare it with a more sophisticated technique that seeks to group similar pixels into connected regions corresponding to objects of interest. We also consider the different types of information that can be used in segmentation: pixel grey level, pixel colour and texture in the neighbourhood of a pixel.

10.1   Introduction

Thus far, our discussion of image processing has examined techniques that can be used to correct defects in images or enhance features of interest. We have not yet considered the issues of image analysis and interpretation. **Segmentation** is generally the first stage in any attempt to analyse or interpret an image automatically. Segmentation partitions an image into distinct regions that are meant to correlate strongly with objects or features of interest in the image. Segmentation can also be regarded as a process of grouping together pixels that have similar attributes. For segmentation to be useful, the regions or groups of pixels that we generate should be meaningful.

Segmentation bridges the gap between low-level image processing, which concerns itself with the manipulation of pixel grey level or colour to correct defects or enhance certain characteristics of the image, and high-level processing, which involves the manipulation and analysis of groups of pixels that represent particular features of interest. Some kind of segmentation technique will be found in any application involving the detection, recognition and measurement of objects in images. Examples of such applications include

- Industrial inspection
- Optical character recognition (OCR)
- Tracking of objects in a sequence of images
- Classification of terrains visible in satellite images
- Detection and measurement of bone, tissue, etc., in medical images

The role of segmentation is crucial in most tasks requiring image analysis. The success or failure of the task is often a direct consequence of the success or failure of segmentation. However, a reliable and accurate segmentation of an image is, in general, very difficult to achieve by purely automatic means.

Segmentation techniques can be classified as either *contextual* or *non-contextual*. Non-contextual techniques ignore the relationships that exist between features in an image; pixels are simply grouped together on the basis of some *global* attribute, such as grey level. Contextual techniques, on the other hand, additionally exploit the relationships between image features. Thus, a contextual technique might group together pixels that have similar grey levels *and* are close to one another.

10.2   A simple non-contextual technique: thresholding

The technique of **thresholding** is used in a variety of different image processing operations, some of which we have already encountered. Thresholding transforms a dataset containing values that vary over some range into a new dataset containing just two values. It does this by applying a threshold to the input data. Input values that fall below the threshold are replaced by one of the output values; input values at or above the threshold are replaced by the other output value.

Image thresholding is a segmentation technique because it classifies pixels into two categories: those at which some property measured from the image falls below a threshold, and those at which that property equals or exceeds the threshold. Because there are two possible output values, thresholding creates a binary image. The nature of this image depends on the property being thresholded. For example, we saw in Chapter 7 that thresholding was a part of simple edge detection algorithms. Here, the thresholded quantity is some measure of the strength of an edge—typically the grey level gradient at a pixel. We output a value of 0 if the gradient falls below the threshold, to indicate that this pixel is not considered to be a 'proper' edge; we output any non-zero value (commonly 1 or, if the output image is to be displayed, 255) if the gradient matches or exceeds the threshold, to indicate that this pixel is a proper edge.

10.2.1   Thresholding of pixel grey level

The most common form of image thresholding makes use of pixel grey level. Grey level thresholding applies to every pixel the rule

$$g(x, y) = \begin{cases} 0, & f(x, y) < T, \\ 1, & f(x, y) \geqslant T, \end{cases} \tag{10.1}$$

where T is the threshold. This equation specifies 0 and 1 as output values, giving a true binary image, but it is common to use 0 and 255 so that pixels appear black or white if the output image is displayed. Note that thresholding can be performed in place; this means that we can replace $g(x, y)$ in Equation 10.1 by $f(x, y)$ if we wish. A variation of Equation 10.1 is

$$g(x, y) = \begin{cases} 0, & f(x, y) < T_1, \\ 1, & T_1 \leqslant f(x, y) \leqslant T_2, \\ 0, & f(x, y) > T_2. \end{cases} \tag{10.2}$$

This uses two thresholds to define a range of acceptable grey levels. Equations 10.1 and 10.2 can be visualised as mappings of input grey level onto output grey level, as illustrated in Figure 10.1.

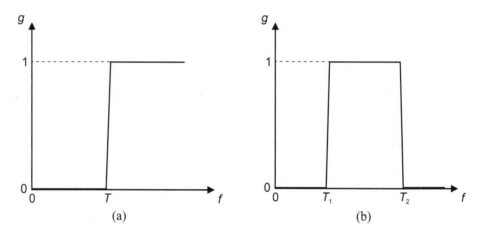

(a)   (b)

Figure 10.1   (a) Thresholding with a single threshold. (b) Thresholding with a pair of thresholds.

Thresholding can be implemented in two ways. We can iterate over every pixel, applying Equations 10.1 or 10.2 to each grey level; alternatively, we can apply these equations once for all grey levels and store the results in a look-up table, which we use subsequently to map the grey level of each pixel onto 0 or 1. The latter approach is marginally more efficient, becoming more so as we increase the number of threshold levels.

In thresholded images, we usually regard the non-zero value as 'interesting' and a value of 0 as having no significance. Hence, Equations 10.1 and 10.2 assume that bright pixels are of interest and dark pixels are not. If the goal of segmentation is to detect features that are brighter than everything else in the image then this quite reasonable; if, however, we are aiming to detect the darker features, then Equation 10.1 should be

$$g(x, y) = \begin{cases} 1, & f(x, y) \leqslant T, \\ 0, & f(x, y) > T, \end{cases} \tag{10.3}$$

and similarly for Equation 10.2.

The success or otherwise of thresholding depends critically on the selection of an appropriate threshold. To understand this point fully, let us consider a hypothetical example. Imagine that we are involved in the development of a robot that will play the game of poker with a human. This robot uses a video camera to view its hand of cards. Images from the camera must be analysed to determine the suits and values of the cards in a hand. Segmentation is an essential part of this process. Now suppose that we decide to use thresholding as the segmentation technique. Figure 10.2 shows a typical image, along with the results of thresholding that image using three different values of T. Clearly, only one of the thresholds gives an acceptable result. But how do we arrive at this correct threshold?

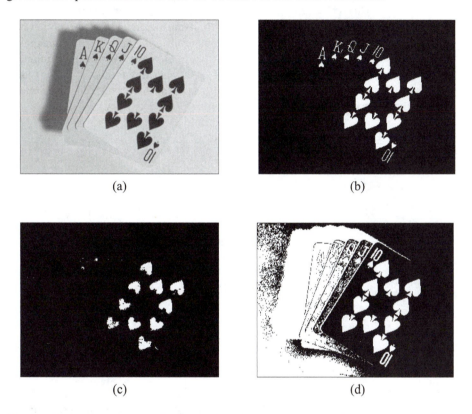

(a)   (b)

(c)   (d)

Figure 10.2 Importance of accurate threshold selection. (a) Input image. (b) Correct choice of threshold ($T = 90$). (c) Threshold too low ($T = 40$). (d) Threshold too high ($T = 215$).

An obvious solution is to rely on intervention by a human operator, who can vary the threshold until acceptable results are achieved. However, this is not possible in cases where fully automatic segmentation is required. Alternatively, we might be able to determine in advance a single, fixed threshold that will always give good results. In practice, this is feasible only in highly constrained imaging scenarios, where we have control over lighting conditions and the degree of contrast that exists between different image features. An example would be industrial inspection.

Another approach is to make T equal to the mean grey level of the image. The idea here is that the mean lies between two extremes of grey level, one representing the features of interest and the other everything else. Clearly, this is only going to work well for images containing bright objects on a simple, dark background, or vice versa.

A more subtle technique involves choosing T so that a fixed proportion of pixels are detected (i.e., set to 1) by the thresholding operation. This is likely to work only in cases where we know, in advance, the proportion of image pixels associated with the features of interest—which may be true in certain OCR or industrial inspection applications.

A more general approach to threshold selection involves analysing the histogram of an image. This is based on the assumption, true only in certain situations, that different features in an image give rise to distinct peaks in its histogram. If the assumption holds true, then we may distinguish between two features of differing grey level by thresholding at a point between the histogram peaks corresponding to those two features. Figure 10.3 shows the histogram of the image in Figure 10.2(a), annotated with the thresholds used to generate the images in Figures 10.2(b)–(d). The best of the three thresholds is the one lying between the peaks of the histogram.

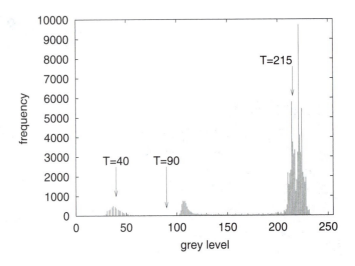

Figure 10.3 Histogram of the image in Figure 10.2(a), showing thresholds that are too low (40), correct (90) and too high (215).

In general, the histogram peaks corresponding to two features will overlap. The degree of overlap will depend on peak separation and peak width. Consider an image showing an object on top of a contrasting background. The separation of the peaks produced by the object and the background is determined by the difference in their mean grey levels. The overlap of the peaks is determined by the uniformity of object pixels and background pixels. A flat object with no discernable surface texture and no colour variation will give rise to a relatively narrow histogram peak; an object with pronounced surface relief or significant variations of texture or colour across its surface will produce a much broader peak that may overlap with the peak generated by the background. Note that we may still choose a threshold in the valley between two overlapping peaks, but that, inevitably, some pixels will be detected or rejected falsely by the thresholding operation. The optimal threshold minimises the numbers of false detections and rejections. It does not, in general, occur at the lowest point in the valley between two overlapping peaks (Figure 10.4).

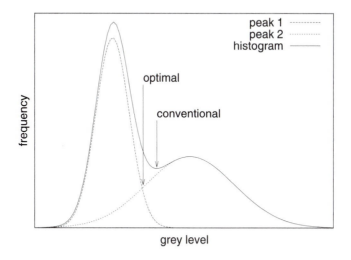

Figure 10.4 Optimal threshold between two overlapping peaks of a histogram.

Sonka et al. [45] and Parker [36] give details of an iterative method for automatic threshold selection, summarised in Algorithm 10.1. The method starts with an initial guess at the threshold and refines this estimate by successive passes through the image. The initial guess can be the mean grey level of the image [36] or an average of the mean grey level of the corner pixels and the mean grey level of all other pixels in the image [45]. The latter assumes that the corner pixels represent the background, rather than objects of interest. Four to ten iterations are usually sufficient for the algorithm to converge.

ALGORITHM 10.1 Iterative threshold determination.

Compute μ_1, the mean grey level of the corner pixels
Compute μ_2, the mean grey level of all other pixels
$T_{old} = 0$
$T_{new} = (\mu_1 + \mu_2)/2$
while $T_{new} \neq T_{old}$ **do**
    μ_1 = mean grey level of pixels for which $f(x, y) < T_{new}$
    μ_2 = mean grey level of pixels for which $f(x, y) \geqslant T_{new}$
    $T_{old} = T_{new}$
    $T_{new} = (\mu_1 + \mu_2)/2$
end while

10.2.2   Thresholding of colour

Colour images contain more information than greyscale images, which can make segmentation easier. But how do we carry out thresholding of a colour image? The simplest approach is to define independent thresholds for each component of the colour model used by the image. Thus, for an RGB image, we must define a red threshold, a green threshold and a blue threshold (or a pair of thresholds for each colour component). Colours in an RGB image can be visualised as points in a three-dimensional colour space. Thresholding can likewise be visualised as a *partitioning* of this space (Figure 10.5). The three (or six) thresholds are orthogonal planes that carve up RGB space, isolating a cuboid in which the colours of interest lie. Plate D shows a colour image and two examples of thresholded images generated from it using this technique. In the first example, three thresholds were chosen to isolate one corner of RGB space in which pixels belonging to the sign reside. In the second example, six thresholds were used to detect sky pixels.

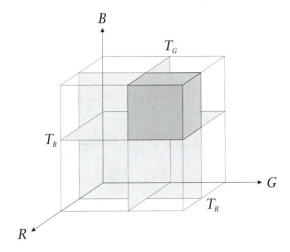

Figure 10.5   Thresholding in RGB space.

It may be simpler, conceptually, to define a threshold on the distance of any colour from some reference colour in RGB space. If this reference colour is (R_0, G_0, B_0), then our thresholding rule becomes

$$g(x, y) = \begin{cases} 1, & d(x, y) \leqslant d_{\max}, \\ 0, & d(x, y) > d_{\max}, \end{cases} \tag{10.4}$$

where

$$d(x, y) = \sqrt{[f_R(x, y) - R_0]^2 + [f_G(x, y) - G_0]^2 + [f_B(x, y) - R_0]^2}. \tag{10.5}$$

In effect, this thresholding rule defines a sphere in RGB space, centred on the reference colour. Any pixel with a colour that lies inside or on the surface of the sphere will be set to 1; all other pixels will be set to 0. Plate E shows an example of thresholding using this technique. Here, the *Hollywood* image of Plate D(a) has been thresholded to detect vegetation. The reference colour was chosen to be representative of vegetation and the distance threshold was selected by trial and error.

Note that we can generalise Equations 10.4 and 10.5 by specifying independent distance thresholds for the red, green and blue components. These define an ellipsoidal volume in RGB space, within which pixels are set to 1 by thresholding.

We have seen that a suitable threshold for a greyscale image can sometimes be estimated by inspection of its histogram. The same idea applies in the case of colour images. As noted in Chapter 6, 3D colour histograms are difficult to manipulate and visualise, and a 2D projection of the colour histogram may be more convenient. Figure 10.6 shows the histogram of the *Hollywood* image projected onto the *R-B* plane. Three distinct peaks can be identified. One peak is produced by the sign, another by the sky and the third by the remaining pixels of the image. It is a simple matter to identify on this histogram and the

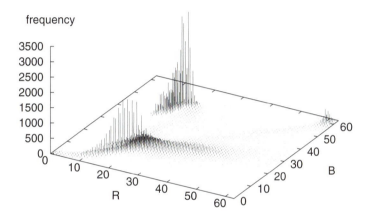

Figure 10.6   2D histogram of the red and blue components of the *Hollywood* image.

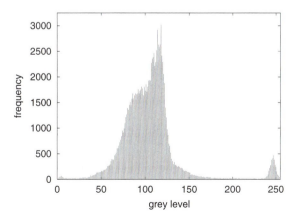

Figure 10.7   Histogram of a greyscale version of the *Hollywood* image.

other 2D projections pairs of thresholds—or a reference colour and distance thresholds—that will detect the sky only, or the sign only. Given a greyscale version of the *Hollywood* image, with the histogram shown in Figure 10.7, it is possible to isolate the sign from the rest of the image by thresholding but the peaks produced by the sky and the vegetation overlap, making isolation of these features impossible.

10.2.3 Java tools for thresholding of grey level and colour

We have noted in this chapter and in Chapter 6 that grey level thresholding can be viewed as a grey level mapping operation, implemented using a look-up table. We can therefore

LISTING 10.1 A Java class to perform grey level thresholding.

```
 1   package com.pearsoneduc.ip.op;
 2
 3
 4   public class ThresholdOp extends GreyMapOp {
 5
 6     public ThresholdOp(int threshold) {
 7       computeMapping(threshold, 255);
 8     }
 9
10     public ThresholdOp(int low, int high) {
11       computeMapping(low, high);
12     }
13
14     public void setThreshold(int threshold) {
15       computeMapping(threshold, 255);
16     }
17
18     public void setThresholds(int low, int high) {
19       computeMapping(low, high);
20     }
21
22     public void computeMapping(int low, int high) {
23       if (low < 0 || high > 255 || low >= high)
24         throw new java.awt.image.ImagingOpException("invalid thresholds");
25       int i;
26       for (i = 0; i < low; ++i)
27         table[i] = (byte) 0;
28       for (; i <= high; ++i)
29         table[i] = (byte) 255;
30       for (; i < 256; ++i)
31         table[i] = (byte) 0;
32     }
33
34   }
```

create a thresholding operator in Java by extending the GreyMapOp class described in Chapter 6. The resulting class, ThresholdOp, is shown in Listing 10.1. This class is used in two applications provided on the CD: Threshold and GreyMapTool. GreyMapTool was discussed in Chapter 6. Its thresholding option allows the user to experiment with thresholding of an image using Equation 10.2. The two thresholds T_1 and T_2 can be varied interactively using the sliders on the application's control panel.

The Threshold application has no GUI, being driven instead by parameters supplied on the command line. It can be used to threshold both greyscale and colour images. For a greyscale image, one or two thresholds must be specified, e.g.,

```
java Threshold grey.jpg thresholded.pbm 175
java Threshold grey.jpg thresholded.pbm 92 140
```

For a colour image, three or six thresholds must be specified, e.g.,

```
java Threshold colour.jpg thresholded.pbm 200 75 128
```

Two further thresholding applications are provided on the CD. IterativeThreshold thresholds a greyscale image with a threshold determined automatically using Algorithm 10.1. Mean grey levels are computed from the histogram of the image, rather than the image itself, since this is more efficient. The second program, DistanceThreshold, thresholds a colour image using a reference colour and either the radius of a sphere centred on that colour or the three radii of an ellipsoid centred on that colour.

10.3   Contextual techniques

Thresholding groups together pixels according to some global attribute, such as grey level. Two pixels at opposite corners of an image will both be detected if they both have grey levels above the threshold, even though they are probably not related in any meaningful way. It is possible to distinguish between these two pixels if we additionally take into account their separation. This is the basis of contextual segmentation techniques. Contextual techniques can be more successful at isolating individual objects in an image because they take into account the fact that pixels belonging to a single object are close to one another.

Approaches to contextual segmentation are based on the concept of discontinuity or the concept of similarity. Techniques based on discontinuity attempt to partition the image by detecting abrupt changes in grey level. Edge detection techniques, discussed in Section 7.4, fall into this category. However, an edge detector will perform a proper segmentation only if it generates complete boundaries that enclose relatively uniform regions. Techniques based on similarity attempt to create these uniform regions directly, by grouping together connected pixels that satisfy predefined similarity criteria. The results of segmentation may depend critically on these criteria and on our definition of connectivity.

Note that approaches based on discontinuity and similarity mirror one another, in the sense that completion of a boundary is equivalent to breaking one region into two.

10.3.1 Pixel connectivity

Pixel connectivity is a central concept of both edge- and region-based approaches to segmentation. In an image with a normal, rectangular sampling pattern, we may define two types of neighbourhood surrounding a pixel. A **4-neighbourhood** contains only the pixels above, below, to the left and to the right of the central pixel. An **8-neighbourhood** contains all the pixels of a 4-neighbourhood, plus four diagonal neighbours (Figure 10.8).

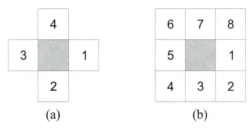

(a)　　　　　　　　(b)

Figure 10.8 (a) The 4-neighbours of a pixel. (b) The 8-neighbours of a pixel.

A 4-connected path from a pixel p_1 to another pixel p_n is the sequence of pixels $\{p_1, p_2, \ldots, p_n\}$, where p_{i+1} is a 4-neighbour of p_i for all $i = 1, \ldots, n-1$. The path is said to be 8-connected if p_{i+1} is an 8-neighbour of p_i.

If we have a set of pixels and we can identity at least one 4-connected path between any pair of pixels from that set, we can say that the set is a 4-connected region. An 8-connected region can be defined similarly. The distinction between 4-connectivity and 8-connectivity is important. The set of shaded pixels in Figure 10.9, for instance, can be interpreted either as one 8-connected region or as two 4-connected regions.

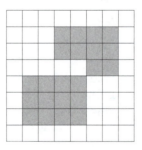

Figure 10.9 A set of connected pixels.

Armed with these definitions of connectivity, we can solve the problem with thresholding noted earlier, namely that it groups together pixels with grey levels above the threshold, despite the fact that they may not be connected. What we must do is find each connected region of pixels that were detected by thresholding and give all the pixels in that region their own unique label. One of the simplest and most common labelling algorithms scans the image pixel-by-pixel, invoking a recursive labelling procedure whenever a non-zero pixel is found. This procedure implements the 'grassfire' concept. We imagine that a 'fire' is started at the pixel, and that it propagates to any of the pixel's 4- or 8-neighbours that were also detected by thresholding. Wherever a fire is started, the pixel is 'burnt away' from the input image (i.e., has its value set to zero) so that it cannot be visited again by the labelling procedure. At the end of the procedure, all pixels belonging to the region have been set to 0 in the input image, making them indistinguishable from the background, and the corresponding pixels in the output image have been assigned a region number. The region number is then incremented, ready for the next connected region.

A class called `RegionLabelOp` that implements this algorithm is provided in the `com.pearsoneduc.ip.op` package. The `filter()` method of this class and the associated recursive labelling method are shown in Listing 10.2. Lines 7 and 8 assign image dimensions

---

LISTING 10.2 Java code to perform connected region labelling, taken from the `RegionLabelOp` class.

```
 1   public BufferedImage filter(BufferedImage src, BufferedImage dest) {
 2
 3     checkImage(src);
 4     if (dest == null)
 5       dest = createCompatibleDestImage(src, null);
 6
 7     width = src.getWidth();
 8     height = src.getHeight();
 9     WritableRaster in = src.copyData(null);
10     WritableRaster out = dest.getRaster();
11
12     int n = 1;
13     for (int y = 0; y < height; ++y)
14       for (int x = 0; x < width; ++x)
15         if (in.getSample(x, y, 0) > 0) {
16           label(in, out, x, y, n);
17           ++n;
18           if (n > MAX_REGIONS)
19             return dest;
20         }
21
22     return dest;
23
24   }
25
26
27   private void label(WritableRaster in, WritableRaster out, int x, int y, int n) {
28     in.setSample(x, y, 0, 0);
29     out.setSample(x, y, 0, n);
30     int j, k;
31     for (int i = 0; i < connectivity; ++i) {
32       j = x + delta[i].x;
33       k = y + delta[i].y;
34       if (inImage(j, k) && in.getSample(j, k, 0) > 0)
35         label(in, out, j, k, n);
36     }
37   }
38
39
40   private final boolean inImage(int x, int y) {
41     return x >= 0 && x < width && y >= 0 && y < height;
42   }
```

to instance variables `width` and `height`. These variables are used subsequently by the method `inImage()`, which determines whether a pixel's coordinates are valid. Line 9 creates a raster that is a copy of the input image. Copying is necessary because input pixels are erased by the grassfire algorithm. Line 12 initialises the region number to 1. The first non-zero pixel found in the image will be labelled with this number, as will all other non-zero pixels connected to it. Lines 13–20 scan the image from top to bottom and left to right. When a non-zero pixel is found (line 15), the recursive labelling method is invoked (line 16) and, when this has finished, the region number is incremented. Since the output image is an 8-bit greyscale image, there can be no more than 255 different labels assigned to regions. Lines 18 and 19 terminate the labelling procedure if this limit is exceeded.

The `label()` method burns away the input pixel (line 28) and sets the corresponding output pixel to the region number (line 29). It then examines each of the pixel's neighbours. Neighbours are located by adding to pixel coordinates x and y a displacement vector from array `delta` (lines 32 and 33). This array has four or eight elements, depending on the connectivity that has been specified. Each element is an instance of the `Point` class. If the coordinates calculated for the neighbour lie within the image *and* that neighbour has a non-zero value (line 34), `label()` invokes itself on that neighbouring pixel.

An application called `RegionLabel` that uses `RegionLabelOp` can be found on the CD. It requires an input filename, an output filename and the desired pixel connectivity as command line arguments.

10.3.2 Region similarity

The uniformity or otherwise of a connected region of pixels may be indicated by a **uniformity predicate**, a logical statement that is true only if pixels in the region are sufficiently similar in terms of grey level, colour or some other property. A common uniformity predicate is

$$P(R) = \begin{cases} \text{TRUE} & \text{if } |f(j, k) - f(m, n)| \leqslant \Delta, \\ \text{FALSE} & \text{otherwise,} \end{cases} \tag{10.6}$$

where (j, k) and (m, n) are the coordinates of neighbouring pixels in region R. This predicate states that a region R is uniform if (and only if) any two neighbouring pixels differ in grey level by no more than Δ. A common misconception is that this restricts the grey level variation within a region to a range of width Δ. In fact, small changes in grey level from neighbour to neighbour that satisfy Equation 10.6 can accumulate, resulting in a big difference in grey level between opposite sides of a large region.

A similar predicate is

$$P(R) = \begin{cases} \text{TRUE} & \text{if } |f(j, k) - \mu_R| \leqslant \Delta, \\ \text{FALSE} & \text{otherwise,} \end{cases} \tag{10.7}$$

where $f(j, k)$ is the grey level of a pixel from region R with coordinates (j, k) and μ_R is the mean grey level of all pixels in R except the pixel at (j, k).

Equations 10.6 and 10.7 are easily generalised to cope with colour images. Now, instead of computing a difference in grey level, we compute the distance in RGB space between the colours of neighbouring pixels, or between the colour of a pixel and the mean colour for the region.

10.3.3   Region growing

Region growing is a bottom-up procedure that starts with a set of seed pixels. The aim is to grow a uniform, connected region from each seed. A pixel is added to a region if and only if

- It has not been assigned to any other region
- It is a neighbour of that region
- The new region created by addition of the pixel is still uniform

The procedure is outlined in Algorithm 10.2, assuming the uniformity predicate of Equation 10.7. The progress of region growing in a very simple image is illustrated in Figure 10.10. Here, 8-connectivity is assumed. The uniformity predicate is that given in Equation 10.7, with $\Delta = 3$.

ALGORITHM 10.2 Region growing.

Let f be an image for which regions are to be grown
Define a set of regions, $R_1, R_2, \ldots R_n$, each consisting of a single seed pixel
repeat
   for $i = 1$ to n **do**
      for each pixel, p, at the border of R_i **do**
         for all neighbours of p **do**
            Let x, y be the neighbour's coordinates
            Let μ_i be the mean grey level of pixels in R_i
            if the neighbour is unassigned **and** $|f(x, y) - \mu_i| \leqslant \Delta$ **then**
               Add neighbour to R_i
               Update μ_i
            end if
         end for
      end for
   end for
until no more pixels are being assigned to regions

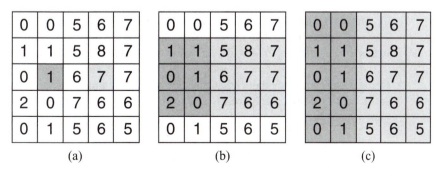

Figure 10.10   Region growing. (a) Seed pixels. (b) First iteration. (c) Final iteration.

Java implementation of region growing

An implementation of Algorithm 10.2 is provided in the class `RegionGrower`, part of the `com.pearsoneduc.ip.op` package. A `RegionGrower` object is created from an image, a list of seed pixel coordinates, a connectivity and a uniformity threshold. The image can be a greyscale or colour image. Seed pixel coordinates are specified as instances of `java.awt.Point`, stored in a `List` object—either a `Vector` or an instance of one of the newer collection classes, `ArrayList` and `LinkedList`. An optional fifth parameter is a Boolean flag, specifying whether a `RegionGrower` should create and update a special 'status image' that can be used to monitor the progress of a region growing operation. If no fifth parameter is specified, then no monitoring will be done.

The simplest way to use `RegionGrower` is to invoke its `growToCompletion()` method. This iterates until no more pixels can be assigned to regions. The `getRegionImage()` method can then be called to retrieve a greyscale image in which pixels are labelled by their region number or have a value of zero to indicate that they were not assigned to any region. The following example shows how a `RegionGrower` can be created and used in this manner. First, we create a list containing two seeds and then a `RegionGrower` that will grow these seeds into regions with 8-connectivity, using a uniformity threshold of 25. The `growToCompletion()` method is called to grow the two regions, and the number of iterations performed is reported on the standard output stream. Finally, the region image is written to a file.

```
List seeds = new ArrayList();
seeds.add(new Point(128, 128));
seeds.add(new Point(75, 30));
RegionGrower grower = new RegionGrower(image, seeds, 8, 25);
grower.growToCompletion();
System.out.println(grower.getNumIterations() + " iterations");
ImageEncoder output = ImageFile.createImageEncoder("regions.png");
output.encode(grower.getRegionImage());
```

More control is possible using the `grow()` method, which performs a single iteration of the region growing algorithm. The `isFinished()` or `isNotFinished()` methods, both of which return Boolean values, can be used to check whether region growing has completed. After each call to `grow()`, `getRegionImage()` can be invoked to retrieve the current set of regions. Alternatively, `getStatusImage()` can be used (provided that the status monitoring parameter was supplied and set to `true` when the `RegionGrower` was created). This method returns a colour image with an alpha channel. Unassigned pixels are transparent in this image, allowing it to be drawn on top of the input image if required. Pixels assigned to regions are opaque, with a colour specified by the `setAssignedColour()` method. Border pixels with neighbours that have not yet been examined are given a different colour, specified by `setBorderColour()`. The following code fragment shows how all these methods can be used.

```
RegionGrower grower = new RegionGrower(image, seeds, 8, 25, true);
grower.setAssignedColour(Color.blue);
grower.setBorderColour(Color.cyan);
BufferedImage status;
```

Plate A Histogram equalisation of a colour image. Top: original image. Middle: effect of equalising R, G, and B components separately. Bottom: effect of equalising the intensity component in HSI space.

Plate B Effect of modifying the hue of the butterfly image.

Plate C Effect of modifying the saturation of the butterfly image. Top: Saturation reduced to 60% of its original value. Bottom: Saturation increased by 60%.

(a)

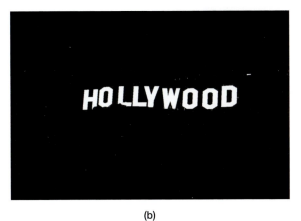

(b)   (c)

Plate D Examples of RGB thresholding. (a) Colour image. (b) Result of thresholding
with $T_R = T_G = T_B = 200$. (c) Result of threshold with a range of [50, 100] for
the red component, [100, 150] for green and [150, 200] for blue.

Plate E Image in Plate D (a), threshold to detect all colours within a distance of 50
from the colour (80, 100, 50).

Plate F The RegionGrowingTool program.

```
while (grower.isNotFinished()) {
  grower.grow();
  status = grower.getStatusImage();
  // do something with status image...
}
```

Two applications that use RegionGrower are provided on the CD. The first, RegionGrow, reads an image from a file named on the command line and grows a single region from a seed with the specified *x* and *y* coordinates. Connectivity and the uniformity threshold must also be specified on the command line. An example of use is

```
java RegionGrow test.jpg region.pbm 100 100 4 35
```

which reads the image test.jpg, grows a region from the point (100, 100) using 4-connectivity and a threshold of 35 and then writes the resulting region image to the file region.pbm.

The second application, RegionGrowingTool, is a fully-interactive program with a graphical user interface. It displays an image read from a file named on the command line and allows the user to define seed pixels on that image using the mouse. A menu option is provided to initiate region growing from those seeds. The growing regions are drawn on top of the image, making it easy to monitor the progress of the operation. Once regions have been grown, they can be saved to a file as an image. The user also has the option of starting again from the same seeds (adding more if necessary) or of starting again with a completely new set of seeds. This makes it possible to experiment with different connectivities and uniformity thresholds. Menu options permit switching between 4- and 8-connectivity, and a threshold can be specified in a text field beneath the image. Plate F shows the program in action.

Limitations of region growing

Region growing isn't a particularly stable operation. For example, Figure 10.9 indicates that 4-connected region growing may produce different results from 8-connected region growing. Also, the results obtained can be very sensitive to our choice of uniformity predicate. This can be seen in Figure 10.11, which shows attempts to segment the *dice* image by region growing. Both regions were grown using 8-connectivity from the same seed, on the upper-left face of the die. The only difference is in the choice of a value for Δ in Equation 10.7—41 for the region in (a), 42 for the region in (b).

Note that a complete segmentation of an image must satisfy a number of criteria:

1. All pixels must be assigned to regions.
2. Each pixel must belong to a single region only.
3. Each region must be a connected set of pixels.
4. Each region must be uniform.
5. Any merged pair of adjacent regions must be non-uniform.

Region growing satisfies the third and fourth of these criteria, but not the others. It fails to satisfy the first and second criteria because, in general, the number of seeds defined by the user will not be sufficient to create a region for every pixel. The fifth criterion is not

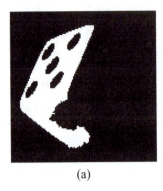 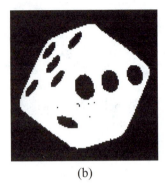

(a)   (b)

Figure 10.11 Sensitivity of region growing to the uniformity threshold, Δ. (a) Region grown with $\Delta = 41$. (b) Region grown with $\Delta = 42$.

satisfied because the regions grown from two nearby seeds are always regarded as distinct, even if those seeds are defined in a part of the image that should be segmented as a single region.

10.3.4 The split and merge algorithm

A complete segmentation is possible if we adopt a top-down approach, in which the entire image is considered initially to be a single region. Inevitably, the uniformity predicate will be false for this region, so we divide it into subregions. These subregions are then split or merged in an attempt to meet the uniformity criteria. The procedure iterates until all regions are uniform or until the desired number of regions have been established.

A common splitting strategy for a square image is to divide it recursively into smaller and smaller quadrants until, for any region R, $P(R)$ is true. In other words, if $P(\text{image})$ is false, we divide the image into four quadrants; if $P(\text{quadrant})$ is false, we divide that quadrant into subquadrants; and so on. If region splitting alone were used to segment the image, the final partition would be likely to contain many small, adjacent regions with identical properties. We therefore alternate splitting with a merging stage, in which two adjacent regions R_i and R_j are combined into a new, larger region if the uniformity predicate for the union of these two regions, $P(R_i \cup R_j)$, is true.

10.4 Segmentation using other image properties

Pixel grey level and colour are not the only image properties that can be used for segmentation. In Chapter 5, for instance, we saw that a difference in pixel grey level for two images acquired at different times could be thresholded to detect change in a scene. Many edge detection techniques also rely on the thresholding of differences in grey level—although here it is a spatial, rather than a temporal, difference that is is thresholded.

Segmentation techniques based on grey level or colour are often unsuccessful when applied to complex, highly-textured images. Consider the image in Figure 10.12(a), for example. This is a square containing a random texture superimposed on a background with

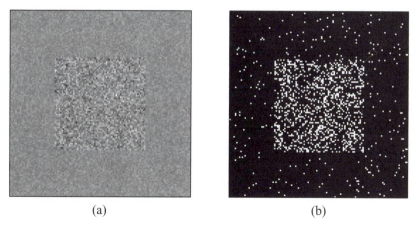

(a)   (b)

Figure 10.12 Performance of grey level thresholding on textured images. (a) Image of a square. (b) Result of thresholding the image in (a).

a different random texture. The mean grey levels of the square and the background in this image are identical and their grey level ranges overlap—suggesting that thresholding on grey level will fail to distinguish the features. This is confirmed by Figure 10.12(b). To achieve a good segmentation, we would need to make use of texture measures rather than grey level.

Grey level is an attribute associated with a single pixel; texture, on the other hand, is a property of groups of pixels. A local measure of texture must therefore be computed over a neighbourhood. For random textures, such as those of Figure 10.12, statistical measures may be appropriate. One of the simplest is the *variance* of grey levels in an $n \times n$ neighbourhood

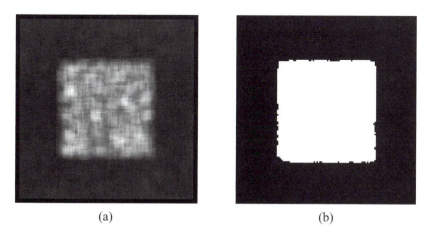

(a)   (b)

Figure 10.13 Texture segmentation using grey level variance. (a) Variance image. (b) Result of thresholding the image in (a).

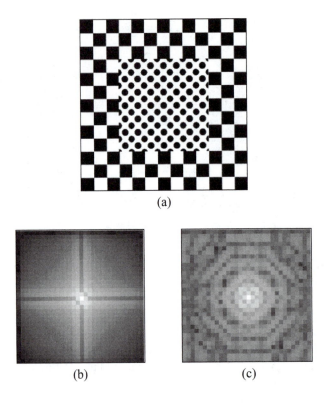

Figure 10.14 (a) An image consisting of two repeating patterns. (b) Spectrum of a 32 × 32 sample of the background pattern. (c) Spectrum of a 32 × 32 sample of the smaller patterned region.

centred on a pixel. For n odd, this is given by

$$\sigma^2 = \frac{1}{n^2} \sum_{j=-n/2}^{n/2} \sum_{k=-n/2}^{n/2} [f(x+j, y+k) - \mu]^2, \tag{10.8}$$

where μ, the mean grey level in the neighbourhood, is

$$\mu = \frac{1}{n^2} \sum_{j=-n/2}^{n/2} \sum_{k=-n/2}^{n/2} f(x+j, y+k). \tag{10.9}$$

Figure 10.13(a) is an image of grey level variance in 7 × 7 regions of the textured image in Figure 10.12(a). Bright pixels in this image signify regions with high variance. Figure 10.13(b) shows the result of applying a threshold to the variance data. The square has been detected adequately because local variance at its pixels is significantly greater than the variance at background pixels.

For other types of texture, simple statistical measures are of little use. In the image of Figure 10.14(a), for instance, the square and the background have similar variances, so we must turn to some other kind of texture measure in order to segment the image adequately. The periodic nature of the two patterns visible in the image suggests that they might be distinguishable in the frequency domain. This can be investigated by using the SpectralProbe application described in Chapter 8 to compare the spectra of small (e.g., 32×32) samples taken from the two patterns. Examples of these spectra are shown in Figure 10.14. As expected, there are significant differences in the spectra.

Spectral techniques for texture segmentation typically use the power spectrum of a region in an image rather than its amplitude spectrum. Radial or angular integration of the power spectrum is often performed. Radial integration basically sums power within a ring of radius r and width Δr. Angular integration sums power within a sector defined by a radius, r, an orientation, θ, and an angular width, $\Delta \theta$ (Figure 10.15). The ring-based measurement provides information on the scale of the texture; high power at small radii signifies coarse texture, whereas a concentration of power at large radii indicates fine texture. The sector-based measurement provides information on the orientation of the texture; a texture that is oriented in a direction indicated by an angle ϕ will result in high power for a sector at angle $\theta = \phi + \frac{\pi}{2}$.

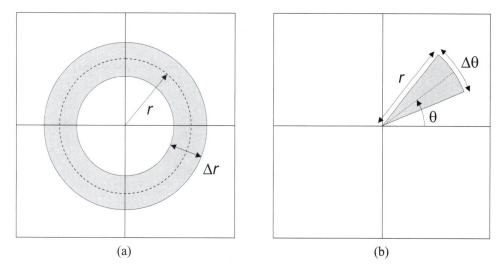

(a)   (b)

Figure 10.15 Texture measures derived from the power spectrum. (a) Radial power is measured by integrating over a ring-shaped region of the spectrum. (b) Angular power is measured by integrating over a sector of the spectrum.

10.5   Further reading

Jain et al. [25] and Parker [36] describe a number of techniques for threshold selection. Parker also compares the performance of each of these techniques [36].

Pitas [37] presents implementations of region growing, region splitting and the split and merge algorithm. These techniques are also described by Parker [36]. Lyon [29] describes how regions can be segmented by means of a heuristic edge searching technique.

Parker [36] discusses a variety of approaches to texture measurement. Some discussion can also be found in the book by Jain et al. [25].

10.6 Exercises

1. A biscuit factory has installed an image processing system for quality control. The system uses a camera to acquire images of biscuits moving on a conveyor belt. The biscuits are somewhat brighter than the conveyor belt, and hence are represented by higher grey levels. Grey level thresholding is used to detect the biscuits, and the resulting binary images are analysed to determine biscuit size.

    What would happen to estimates of biscuit size if the threshold were too low? What would happen to size estimates if the threshold were too high?

2. It was stated in Section 10.3 that region-based and boundary-based segmentation techniques mirror one another. Is it reasonable, therefore, to assume that region growing gives the same results as edge detection?

3. What disadvantages might there be to a quadtree representation of regions, from the viewpoint of image analysis? (Hint: think about what happens to an object that straddles the boundary between regions.)

4. Implement in Java the 'split and merge' algorithm described previously.

Morphological image processing

The binary images produced by simple segmentation techniques such as thresholding may contain numerous imperfections caused by noise, texture or the inaccurate specification of a threshold. Morphological image processing techniques can remove these imperfections and provide us with information on the form and structure of the image. Morphological techniques are also applicable to greyscale images, where they can be used for non-linear smoothing and feature enhancement. In this chapter, we start by considering the basic concepts of morphological image processing before moving on to consider the standard operations performed on binary images. We conclude the chapter with a brief examination of morphological operations on greyscale images.

11.1   Introduction

The term 'morphological image processing' describes a range of non-linear image processing techniques that deal with the shape or morphology of features in an image. Most morphological techniques operate on binary images; in fact, they are often used to remove noise or other artefacts in the binary images produced by an imperfect segmentation process. (This is why we are considering these techniques now, after the chapter on segmentation, rather than earlier, in the chapter on neighbourhood operations.) Morphological operations can also be applied to greyscale images; we shall present some examples of this at the end of the chapter, but most of our attention will be devoted to binary morphology.

Morphological techniques typically probe an image with a small shape or template known as a **structuring element**. The structuring element is positioned at all possible locations in the image and it is compared with the corresponding neighbourhood of pixels. Morphological operations differ in how they carry out this comparison. Some test whether the structuring element 'fits' within the neighbourhood; others test whether it 'hits' or intersects the neighbourhood. These concepts are illustrated in Figure 11.1. (Precise definitions of fitting and hitting will follow shortly.) A morphological operation on a binary image creates a new binary image in which a pixel has a non-zero value only if the test is successful at that location in the input image.

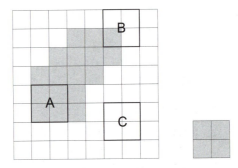

Figure 11.1 Probing of an image (left) with a structuring element (right). At A, the structuring element fits the image; at B, it hits (or intersects) the image; at C, it neither fits nor hits the image.

11.2 Basic concepts

11.2.1 Structuring elements

The structuring element applied to a binary image can be represented as a small matrix of pixels, each with a value of 1 or 0. The dimensions of the matrix determine the overall size of the structuring element, and its shape is determined by the pattern of ones and zeros. For example, we can define a 5×5 structuring element that is square, diamond-shaped or cross-shaped:

$$\begin{bmatrix} 1 & 1 & 1 & 1 & 1 \\ 1 & 1 & 1 & 1 & 1 \\ 1 & 1 & 1 & 1 & 1 \\ 1 & 1 & 1 & 1 & 1 \\ 1 & 1 & 1 & 1 & 1 \end{bmatrix} \quad \begin{bmatrix} 0 & 0 & 1 & 0 & 0 \\ 0 & 1 & 1 & 1 & 0 \\ 1 & 1 & 1 & 1 & 1 \\ 0 & 1 & 1 & 1 & 0 \\ 0 & 0 & 1 & 0 & 0 \end{bmatrix} \quad \begin{bmatrix} 0 & 0 & 1 & 0 & 0 \\ 0 & 0 & 1 & 0 & 0 \\ 1 & 1 & 1 & 1 & 1 \\ 0 & 0 & 1 & 0 & 0 \\ 0 & 0 & 1 & 0 & 0 \end{bmatrix}.$$

A structuring element also has an origin. Note that the origin can be outside the structuring element, although this is uncommon; usually, one of its pixels acts as the origin. Strictly, this should be indicated when representing the structuring element—by displaying the value of that pixel in a bold font, for example:

$$\begin{bmatrix} \mathbf{1} & 1 & 1 \\ 1 & 1 & 1 \\ 1 & 1 & 1 \end{bmatrix} \qquad \begin{bmatrix} 1 & 1 & 1 & 1 & 1 \\ 1 & 1 & 1 & 1 & 1 \\ 1 & 1 & \mathbf{1} & 1 & 1 \\ 1 & 1 & 1 & 1 & 1 \\ 1 & 1 & 1 & 1 & 1 \end{bmatrix}$$

As with convolution kernels, it is common for structuring elements to have odd dimensions. This allows the origin to be defined as the centre of the matrix. We shall assume this to be case throughout this chapter.

11.2.2 Fitting and hitting

When we place a structuring element in a binary image, each of its pixels is associated with the corresponding pixel of the neighbourhood under the structuring element. In this sense, a morphological operation resembles a 'binary correlation'. However, the operation is logical rather than arithmetic in nature. The structuring element is said to *fit* the image if, for each of its pixels that is set to 1, the corresponding image pixel is also 1. (We assume here that the image has values of 0 and 1—although we could allow a different non-zero value and simply test whether the image is non-zero at points where the structuring element is 1.) Structuring element pixels that are 0 define points where the corresponding image value is irrelevant.

For example, suppose we have two 3×3 structuring elements

$$s_1 = \begin{bmatrix} 1 & 1 & 1 \\ 1 & 1 & 1 \\ 1 & 1 & 1 \end{bmatrix}, \qquad s_2 = \begin{bmatrix} 0 & 1 & 0 \\ 1 & 1 & 1 \\ 0 & 1 & 0 \end{bmatrix}.$$

Now let us imagine that these structuring elements are positioned over the 3×3 neighbourhoods labelled A, B and C in the image of Figure 11.2. Both s_1 and s_2 fit the image at

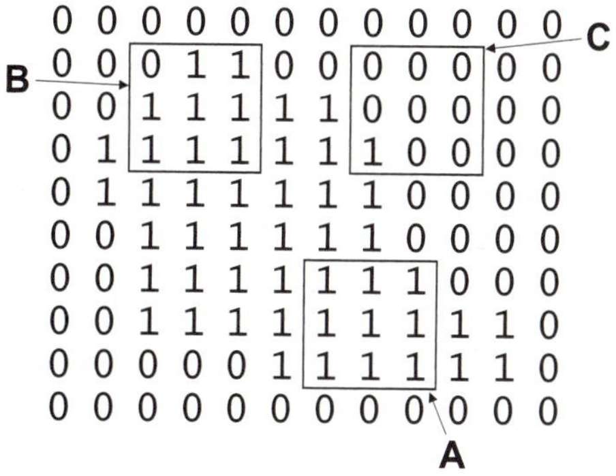

Figure 11.2 Binary image used to test fitting and hitting of structuring elements s_1 and s_2 (see text).

A. (Remember that structuring element pixels set to 0 are ignored when testing for a fit.) However, only s_2 fits the image at B, and neither s_1 nor s_2 fit at C.

Similarly, a structuring element is said to intersect, or *hit*, an image if, for any of its pixels that is set to 1, the corresponding image pixel is also 1. Again, we ignore image pixels for which the corresponding structuring element pixel is 0. Referring again to Figure 11.2, we can see that both s_1 and s_2 hit the image in neighbourhood A. The same holds true at B. At C, however, only s_1 hits the image.

11.2.3   Java classes to represent structuring elements

Figure 11.3 is a class diagram showing how structuring elements and the operations they perform can be represented in Java. The basis for this design is an abstract class called StructElement. Structuring elements that apply to binary images are represented by BinaryStructElement, a class that inherits from StructElement. (This seems a complicated way of doing things; it begins to make sense when you consider that it is possible to have structuring elements that apply to greyscale images. The StructElement class specifies the attributes and behaviour common to both types of structuring element.) StructElement provides a structuring element with dimensions, an origin and storage for its pixel values. It also provides various methods that inspect the values of these attributes. Methods to set the values of structuring element pixels or write structuring element data to an output stream of some kind are declared abstract, so implementations must be provided in derived classes.

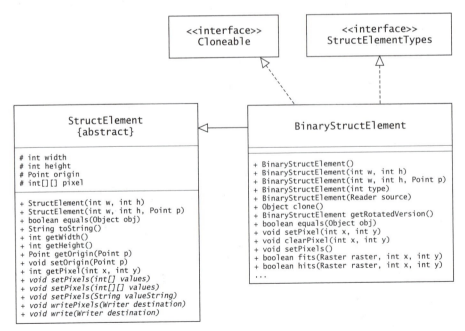

Figure 11.3   Java classes for the representation of structuring elements.

A BinaryStructElement can be created in a variety of ways. The default constructor creates a 3 × 3 square structuring element with its origin at the centre. Two other constructors allow the dimensions or the dimensions and the origin to be specified explicitly. Again, structuring element pixels are all set to 1 by default. A fourth constructor accepts a single integer specifying one of a range of standard structuring elements. These standard structuring elements are specified by constants defined in the StructElementTypes interface:

```java
public interface StructElementTypes {
    int CROSS_3x3 = 1;
    int CROSS_5x5 = 2;
    int DIAMOND_5x5 = 3;
    int DIAMOND_7x7 = 4;
    int DISK_5x5 = 5;
    int DISK_7x7 = 6;
}
```

The fifth and final constructor creates a BinaryStructElement using a Reader object as a data source. The data read from this source must conform to a specific format. A 5 × 5 cross-shaped structuring element with a central origin, for example, should look like this:

```
# binary structuring element
# width=5
# height=5
# xorigin=2
# yorigin=2
00100
00100
11111
00100
00100
```

The write() method will output a BinaryStructElement in this format to a Writer that represents the destination for the data.

Once a BinaryStructElement has been created, its pixels can be modified on an individual basis using setPixel()—which sets the pixel at the specified coordinates to 1—and clearPixel()—which sets a pixel at the specified coordinates to 0. The setPixels() method with no parameters sets all pixels to 1. Other versions of this method accept new pixel values stored in one- or two-dimensional int arrays, or stored as the characters "1" and "0" in a String object.

Two key methods of BinaryStructElement are fits(), which returns true if the element fits in an image (specified by its raster) at particular coordinates, and hits(), which returns true if the element hits an image at particular coordinates. An example of some Java code that calls these methods is shown below.

```java
BufferedReader input =
  new BufferedReader(new InputStreamReader(System.in));
Raster raster = image.getRaster();
```

```
while (true) {
  try {
    String line = input.readLine();
    StringTokenizer parser = new StringTokenizer(line);
    int x = Integer.parseInt(parser.nextToken());
    int y = Integer.parseInt(parser.nextToken());
    if (element.fits(raster, x, y))
      System.out.println("SE fits at (" + x + "," + y + ")");
    else if (element.hits(raster, x, y))
      System.out.println("SE hits at (" + x + "," + y + ")");
  }
  catch (Exception e) { return; }
  }
}
```

This code assumes the existence of a BufferedImage object called image and a BinaryStructElement called element. It reads continually from the standard input, expecting x and y coordinates as integers typed on a single line, separated by whitespace. The loop terminates if this is not the case. Once coordinates have been obtained, the code invokes the fits() and hits() methods and indicates whether the structuring element fits or merely hits the image at those coordinates by printing an appropriate message on the standard output stream.

StructElement and BinaryStructElement are both part of the com.pearsoneduc. ip.op package on the CD.

11.3 Fundamental operations

11.3.1 Erosion

The **erosion** of an image f by a structuring element s is denoted $f \ominus s$. To compute the erosion, we position s such that its origin is at image pixel coordinates (x, y) and apply the rule

$$g(x, y) = \begin{cases} 1 & \text{if } s \text{ fits } f, \\ 0 & \text{otherwise,} \end{cases} \tag{11.1}$$

repeating for all x and y. Thus, erosion creates a new image that marks all the locations of a structuring element's origin at which it fits the input image.

Remember that the origin can be external to the structuring element; thus, it is possible that the comparison of structuring element pixels with image pixels takes place some distance from (x, y). In fact, at certain coordinates, a structuring element's pixels may lie beyond the bounds of the input image, making comparison impossible. For the simplest case of a structuring element with odd dimensions and an origin at the centre of the matrix, this problem becomes identical to that which we encountered when considering convolution and rank filtering in Chapter 7, and it can be dealt with in a similar manner.

What effect does erosion have on an image? Figure 11.4 shows erosions of a binary image using 3×3 and 5×5 square structuring elements. For added clarity, we have inverted these images, so you should think of the black pixels as having the value 1 and the white background as having the value 0. We can see from these examples that erosion is an apt term, because the operation seems to strip away a layer of pixels from an object, shrinking it in the process. Pixels are eroded from both the inner and outer boundaries of regions, so erosion will enlarge the holes enclosed by a single region as well as making the gap between different regions larger. Erosion will also tend to eliminate small extrusions on a region's boundaries. For example, in Figure 11.4(b), we can see that the hole inside the character has become larger, and in Figure 11.4(c) we can see that the serifs at the top and bottom of the character have disappeared.

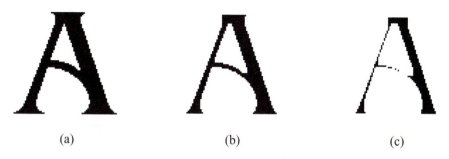

(a)   (b)   (c)

Figure 11.4   Examples of binary erosion. (a) Input image. (b) Erosion by a 3×3 square structuring element. (c) Erosion by a 5×5 square structuring element. Black represents a pixel value of 1, white a pixel value of 0.

Figure 11.4 demonstrates that the result of erosion depends on structuring element size, with larger structuring elements having a more pronounced effect. Note that the result of erosion with a large structuring element is similar to the result obtained by iterated erosion using a smaller structuring element of the same shape. For example, if s_1 and s_2 are a pair of structuring elements identical in shape, with s_2 twice the size of s_1, then

$$f \ominus s_2 \approx (f \ominus s_1) \ominus s_1.$$

An obvious application of erosion is in the removal of unwanted, small-scale features from a binary image. An unfortunate side-effect of this is a reduction in the size of features that we want to preserve. (We will encounter shortly a similar operation that does not suffer from this problem.)

Another application of erosion is boundary finding. Suppose we have an image containing various connected regions of pixels. We wish to remove pixels inside these regions, leaving only the pixels at the boundary of each region. We know already that the eroded image contains regions lacking these boundary pixels, so we can find the boundaries by subtracting the eroded image from the original image, i.e.,

$$g = f - (f \ominus s), \tag{11.2}$$

Figure 11.5 A region boundary detected by subtracting an eroded image from an uneroded image.

where f is an image of the regions, s is a 3×3 square structuring element and g is an image of the region boundaries. Figure 11.5 shows boundaries of the *letter A* image, found in this manner.

11.3.2 Dilation

The **dilation** of an image f by a structuring element s is written $f \oplus s$. To compute the dilation, we position s such that its origin is at pixel coordinates (x, y) and apply the rule

$$g(x, y) = \begin{cases} 1 & \text{if } s \text{ hits } f, \\ 0 & \text{otherwise,} \end{cases} \tag{11.3}$$

repeating for all pixel coordinates. Dilation creates a new image showing all the locations of a structuring element's origin at which that structuring element hits the input image. As with erosion, we must deal with the possibility that there are no image pixels corresponding to structuring element pixels for certain positions of its origin.

Figure 11.6 shows dilations of the *letter A* image by 3×3 and 5×5 square structuring elements. We can see that dilation has the opposite effect to erosion. It seems to add a layer of pixels to an object, thereby enlarging it. Pixels are added to both the inner and

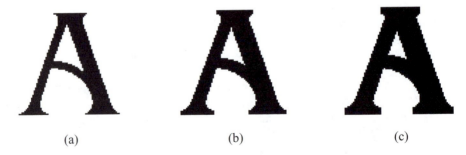

(a) (b) (c)

Figure 11.6 Examples of binary dilation. (a) Input image. (b) Dilation by a 3×3 square structuring element. (c) Dilation by a 5×5 square structuring element.

outer boundaries of regions, so dilation will shrink the holes enclosed by a single region and make the gaps between different regions smaller. Dilation will also tend to fill in any small intrusions into a region's boundaries.

The results of dilation (or erosion, for that matter) are influenced not just by the size of a structuring element but by its shape, also. This can be seen in Figure 11.7, which shows the *letter A* image dilated by a large square and a large disc. Dilation by the square has thickened the character without changing its shape; dilation by the disc, on the other hand, has rounded the character's corners. Why does this happen?

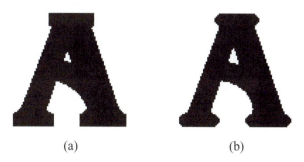

(a)   (b)

Figure 11.7 Effect of structuring element shape on dilation. (a) Square. (b) Disc.

Let us suppose that we are performing dilation on an image of a cross-shaped object, using structuring elements that are square and disc-shaped. A pixel in the output image will be set to 1 whenever the structuring element intersects the object. This will occur at points where the structuring element is just touching the object, but it will no longer occur if we move the structuring element away from the object. We can therefore imagine sliding the structuring element around the boundary of the object, such that it is always touching the object. The closed path marked out by the structuring element's origin as it slides around the boundary represents the limit of the dilation; pixels inside this path are set to 1 in the output image, but pixels outside it remain at 0. When a square slides around the boundary of the cross-shaped object, it encounters concave and convex right-angled corners. In either case, the path marked out as it moves around the corner has the same shape as the corner, so dilation by the square enlarges the object but does not change its shape (Figure 11.8).

Now, consider what happens when we dilate the image with a disc instead of a square. When a disc sliding around the outside of the object encounters a concave right-angled corner, the path traced by its origin is also right-angled. But when the disc slides around a convex corner, the path traced by its origin is curved (Figure 11.9). Hence, dilation by the disc enlarges the object and smoothes its convex corners.

We can visualise erosion in the same manner, only now we must imagine that we are sliding the structuring element around the boundary on the *inside* of the object. The path traced out by the structuring element's origin represents the limit of the erosion; pixels inside this path are set to 1 in the output image but pixels outside it remain at 0. A corner that is concave to a structuring element sliding around the outside of the object will appear convex to a structuring element sliding around the inside of the object, and vice versa. Consequently, we can expect erosion to have the opposite effect to dilation; erosion by a

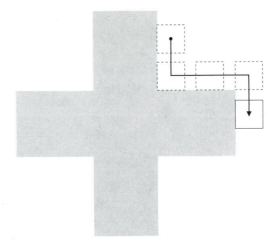

Figure 11.8 Effect of dilation by a square structuring element on concave and convex corners.

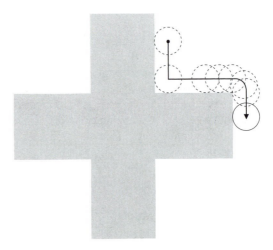

Figure 11.9 Effect of dilation by a disc-shaped structuring element on concave and convex corners.

disc will shrink the object and smooth its concave corners, but will leave the convex corners unaffected (Figure 11.10).

Dilation is said to be the dual of erosion. This is merely a more precise way of saying that the two operations have opposite effects. Formally, we can write that

$$f \oplus s = (f^c \ominus \hat{s})^c, \tag{11.4}$$

where the superscript c denotes the complement of an image, i.e., the image produced by replacing 1 with 0 and vice versa, and $\hat{s}$ is the structuring element s rotated by 180°. Many

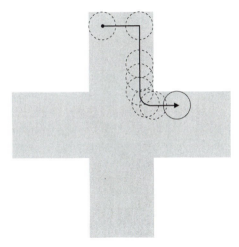

Figure 11.10 Effect of erosion by a disc-shaped structuring element on concave and convex corners.

structuring elements are symmetrical with respect to rotation, allowing us to replace $\hat{s}$ with s in Equation 11.4. This equation tells us that, to dilate an image by a structuring element s, we can erode the complement of the image by s (or, if necessary, a rotated version of s) and then take the complement of the eroded image. In practice, this means that both dilation and erosion can be carried out by a single piece of code that performs an erosion—provided that we also have a routine that computes the complement of an image.

If we consider a binary image to be a collection of connected regions of pixels set to 1 on a background of pixels set to 0, then erosion can be viewed as the fitting of a structuring element into these regions and dilation can be viewed as the fitting of a structuring element into the background, followed by inversion of the result. This explains why erosion by a disc has the effect of smoothing the concave corners of an object and why dilation by a disc has the effect of smoothing its convex corners.

11.3.3 Implementations of erosion and dilation in Java

In the com.pearsoneduc.ip.op package on the CD are the classes BinaryErodeOp and BinaryDilateOp. These behave like any other BufferedImageOp class. Both extend BinaryMorphologicalOp. This class extends StandardGreyOp and overrides its checkImage() method with a new version that tests whether an image is suitable for binary morphological operations. True binary images, of type BufferedImage.TYPE_BYTE_BINARY, are suitable for processing, as are 8-bit greyscale images with only two grey levels, one of which is zero. An ImagingOpException will be thrown if an attempt is made to erode or dilate any other type of image. BinaryMorphologicalOp contains one instance variable, nonZeroValue. This is set to 1 by checkImage() if the input image is a true binary image, or 255 if it is a two-level greyscale image.

When creating a BinaryErodeOp or a BinaryDilateOp, an instance of a

BinaryStructElement must be supplied as a parameter to the constructor. For example, to create an operator that erodes an image using a 5×5 diamond-shaped structuring element, we would use the following code:

```
BinaryStructElement structElement =
  new BinaryStructElement(StructElementTypes.DIAMOND_5x5);
BufferedImageOp erosion = new BinaryErodeOp(structElement);
```

We then simply need to invoke the `filter()` method of `BinaryErodeOp` in the usual manner to perform the erosion. This method is shown in Listing 11.1. Lines 17–23 use the dimensions of the input image together with the dimensions and origin of the structuring

---

LISTING 11.1 BinaryErodeOp's `filter()` method.

```
 1   package com.pearsoneduc.ip.op;
 2
 3
 4   public BufferedImage filter(BufferedImage src, BufferedImage dest) {
 5
 6     checkImage(src);
 7     if (dest == null)
 8       dest = createCompatibleDestImage(src, null);
 9
10     int w = src.getWidth();
11     int h = src.getHeight();
12     Raster srcRaster = src.getRaster();
13     WritableRaster destRaster = dest.getRaster();
14
15     // Determine range of pixels for which operation can be performed
16
17     Point origin = structElement.getOrigin(null);
18     int xmin = Math.max(origin.x, 0);
19     int ymin = Math.max(origin.y, 0);
20     int xmax = origin.x + w - structElement.getWidth();
21     int ymax = origin.y + h - structElement.getHeight();
22     xmax = Math.min(w-1, xmax);
23     ymax = Math.min(h-1, ymax);
24
25     // Fit structuring element into source image
26
27     for (int y = ymin; y <= ymax; ++y)
28       for (int x = xmin; x <= xmax; ++x)
29         if (structElement.fits(srcRaster, x, y))
30           destRaster.setSample(x, y, 0, nonZeroValue);
31
32     return dest;
33
34   }
```

element to determine bounds within which the image and the structuring element can be compared. Lines 27–30 iterate between these bounds, invoking the `fits()` method of the `BinaryStructElement` object at each pixel and setting the corresponding output pixel to the non-zero value (1 or 255) if there is a fit.

The `BinaryDilateOp` class is almost identical to `BinaryErodeOp`. Its `filter()` method looks very much like that in Listing 11.1; the only difference is line 29—which, for `BinaryDilateOp`, invokes the `hits()` method of the structuring element rather than the `fits()` method.

Two applications are provided on the CD to perform binary erosion and dilation. They are called, unsurprisingly, `BinaryErode` and `BinaryDilate`. Both take an input image filename, an output image filename and the name of a file containing a structuring element as command line argument. The format for the structuring element is that described in Section 11.2.3.

11.4   Compound operations

Many different types of morphological operation can be represented as combinations of erosion, dilation and various other simple operations that will be familiar to anyone versed in the language of set theory. One operation that we have mentioned already is calculation of the complement of a binary image, which involves application of the rule

$$g(x, y) = \begin{cases} 1 & \text{if } f(x, y) = 0, \\ 0 & \text{if } f(x, y) = 1, \end{cases} \tag{11.5}$$

to all pixels of the image. Another operation is *intersection*. The intersection of two binary images f and g is the set of non-zero pixels common to both images. Intersection is denoted by the expression

$$h = f \cap g$$

and is computed by applying the rule

$$h(x, y) = \begin{cases} 1 & \text{if } f(x, y) = 1 \text{ and } g(x, y) = 1, \\ 0 & \text{otherwise,} \end{cases} \tag{11.6}$$

to all pixels. A third operation is *union*. The union of two binary images f and g is denoted by the expression

$$h = f \cup g$$

and is computed by applying the rule

$$h(x, y) = \begin{cases} 1 & \text{if } f(x, y) = 1 \text{ or } g(x, y) = 1, \\ 0 & \text{otherwise,} \end{cases} \tag{11.7}$$

to all pixels. The effects of these operations are illustrated in Figure 11.11.

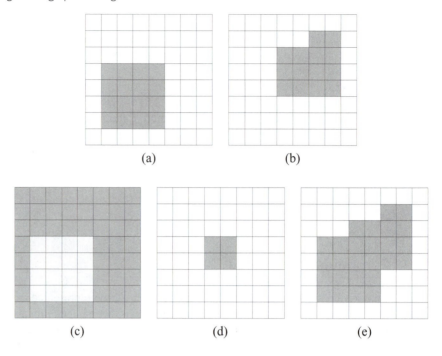

Figure 11.11 Set operations on binary images. (a) A binary image. (b) Another binary image. (c) Complement of (a). (d) Intersection of (a) and (b). (e) Union of (a) and (b).

11.4.1 Opening

The **opening** of an image f by a structuring element s is denoted $f \circ s$ and is defined as an erosion followed by a dilation, i.e.,

$$f \circ s = (f \ominus s) \oplus s. \tag{11.8}$$

Figure 11.12 shows openings of the *letter A* image using square structuring elements of various sizes. Opening by a 3×3 square eliminates the serifs that protrude from the boundary at the top and bottom of the character. Opening by a 5×5 square breaks the bridge of pixels that joins the two upright parts of the character. Opening by a 9×9 square has an even more dramatic effect, eradicating everything but the thicker of the two upright parts of the character.

Opening is so called because it can open up a gap between objects that have been fused into a single region via a thin bridge of pixels. Sometimes, segmentation will produce a result of this kind, rather than an image containing distinct objects. In such cases, opening can be applied to the segmented image to separate the joined objects. Of course, erosion will also do this, but it will shrink regions as well. The advantage of opening is that it follows an erosion with a dilation. Any regions that have survived the erosion will be restored to their original size by the dilation.

Opening can be visualised using the analogy introduced earlier, of sliding a structuring element around the boundary of an object. First, we slide the structuring element around

(a)   (b)   (c)

Figure 11.12 Openings of the *letter A* image by square structuring elements of various sizes. (a) 3 × 3. (b) 5 × 5. (c) 9 × 9.

the inside of the boundary. The path traced by its origin defines a new boundary for the object. The new boundary is inside the old one, so the object shrinks. Depending on the shape of the structuring element, concave corners may be smoothed. Also, extruding parts of the original boundary into which the structuring element cannot fit will be removed. Next, we slide the structuring element around the outside of the new boundary. The path traced by the structuring element's origin defines the final boundary for the object. The final boundary will usually be similar to the original boundary. There may be additional changes to the corners of the object as a result of this dilation stage, and any small extrusions that disappeared after the first stage will not be restored. However, the overall size of the object will be relatively unaffected by the operation.

Another way of visualising opening is to imagine that the structuring element is a kind of paintbrush applied to an entirely black output image. The input image is used to guide the application of white paint to the output image. We slide the paintbrush around inside an object in the input image and, everywhere it fits, a blob of white paint with the same size and shape as the structuring element is transferred to the output image. For example, suppose that we open an image of a rectangular object using a disc-shaped structuring element. The disc fits inside the object at most locations but it cannot fill the corners of the rectangle—so the corresponding feature painted onto the output image has rounded corners, rather than sharp corners (Figure 11.13).

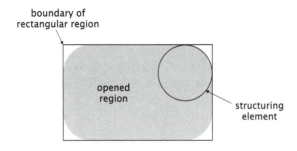

Figure 11.13 Opening of a rectangle with a disc.

Opening is said to be **idempotent**. This means that, once an image has been opened, subsequent openings with the same structuring element have no further effect on that image. This property can be expressed more formally as follows:

$$(f \circ s) \circ s = f \circ s. \tag{11.9}$$

11.4.2 Closing

The **closing** of an image f by a structuring element s is denoted $f \bullet s$ and is defined as a dilation followed by an erosion, i.e.,

$$f \bullet s = (f \oplus \hat{s}) \ominus \hat{s}. \tag{11.10}$$

Note the use of $\hat{s}$ rather than s; strictly, we should dilate and erode by a rotated version of the structuring element. We generally need not concern ourselves with this subtle point, because most structuring elements are symmetrical with respect to 180° rotation.

Figure 11.14 shows the *letter A* image closed by square structuring elements of different sizes. It now becomes obvious why the operation is termed 'closing'. Its sole effect on this image is to fill the hole enclosed by the character. The degree of filling relates to the size of the structuring element, with larger structuring elements having a more pronounced effect. Dilation alone will fill holes, but it enlarges regions as well. The advantage of closing is that it follows a dilation with an erosion. The dilation fills any holes enclosed by a region and the erosion restores the region to its original size.

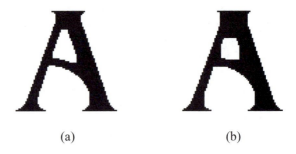

(a)   (b)

Figure 11.14 Closing of the *letter A* image by square structuring elements. (a) 5 × 5. (b) 9 × 9.

Closing can be visualised in much the same way as opening. We can consider changes to an object caused by first sliding the structuring element around the outside of its boundary and then sliding it around the inside of the new boundary generated by the first stage of the process. Alternatively, we can use the simpler analogy of the paintbrush once again. Here, we imagine a structuring element as a paintbrush moving around *outside* the object. The output image is, at first, completely covered in white paint. At all locations where the brush misses the object and remains wholly within the background of the input image, we transfer a blob of black paint to the output image.

Like opening, closing is idempotent; once an image has been closed, further attempts at closing with the same structuring element are fruitless. Formally, we can say that

$$(f \bullet s) \bullet s = f \bullet s. \qquad (11.11)$$

Closing is the dual operation of opening, and vice versa. We may summarise this as follows:

$$f \bullet s = (f^c \circ s)^c, \qquad (11.12)$$

$$f \circ s = (f^c \bullet s)^c. \qquad (11.13)$$

These equations are merely a concise way of saying that closing of a binary image may be accomplished by taking the complement of that image, opening with the structuring element and taking the complement of the result. Similarly, opening may be accomplished by taking the complement of an image, closing and then taking the complement of the result. The practical implication of this is that we can carry out both operations using code that implements only one of the operations (if we also have code available to compute the complement of an image).

11.4.3   Hit and miss transform

Rather than simply probing the inside or the outside of objects in a binary image, it can be fruitful to probe both at the same time, to derive information on how objects are related to their surroundings. We can accomplish this using the **hit and miss transform**. This operation requires a matched pair of structuring elements, $\{s_1, s_2\}$, that probe the inside and outside, respectively, of objects in the image. The transform may be written

$$f \circledast \{s_1, s_2\} = (f \ominus s_1) \cap (f^c \ominus s_2). \qquad (11.14)$$

A pixel belonging to an object is preserved by the hit and miss transform if and only if s_1 translated to that pixel fits inside the object *and* s_2 translated to that pixel fits outside the object. (It is assumed that s_1 and s_2 do not intersect, otherwise it would be impossible for both fits to occur simultaneously.)

The hit and miss transform can be used for shape detection. Consider, for example, an image obtained by scanning a paper document. Figure 11.15(a) shows some text in a portion of this image. Now let us suppose that, for some reason, we wish to count occurrences of the character 'n'. We might think that erosion is an appropriate morphological technique for this purpose. Erosion marks locations where there is a perfect fit of a structuring element to regions of pixels in the image, so if the structuring element has the same shape as the character we are seeking, then erosion should mark the locations of that character. We should then be able to determine the number of occurrences by counting the number of non-zero pixels in the output image. Figure 11.15(b) shows the results of erosion by a structuring element with the shape of the character 'n'. Although the text contains only two instances of this character, four pixels have been marked by the erosion: two corresponding to 'n' and a further two corresponding to 'h'. This occurs because instances of 'n' and 'h' in the image are so similar that the structuring element fits inside both characters.

The hit and miss transform solves the problem. To detect the character 'n', we define the pair of structuring elements shown in Figure 11.16. structuring element s_1 is the one

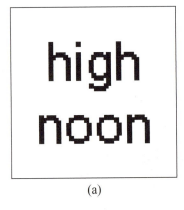 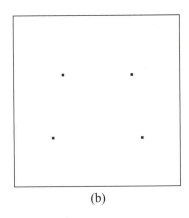

(a)   (b)

Figure 11.15 'False positives' generated when erosion is used for shape detection. (a) Image of some text. Black and white pixels have values of 1 and 0, respectively. (b) Result of erosion by a structuring element with the shape of the character 'n'. Four pixels have been marked.

$$
s_1 = \begin{matrix}
1\ 1\ 0\ 1\ 1\ 1\ 1\ 0\ 0 \\
1\ 1\ 1\ 1\ 1\ 1\ 1\ 1\ 0 \\
1\ 1\ 1\ 0\ 0\ 0\ 1\ 1\ 1 \\
1\ 1\ 0\ 0\ 0\ 0\ 1\ 1 \\
1\ 1\ 0\ 0\ 0\ 0\ 1\ 1 \\
1\ 1\ 0\ \mathbf{0}\ 0\ 0\ 1\ 1 \\
1\ 1\ 0\ 0\ 0\ 0\ 1\ 1 \\
1\ 1\ 0\ 0\ 0\ 0\ 1\ 1 \\
1\ 1\ 0\ 0\ 0\ 0\ 1\ 1 \\
1\ 1\ 0\ 0\ 0\ 0\ 1\ 1 \\
1\ 1\ 0\ 0\ 0\ 0\ 1\ 1
\end{matrix}
\qquad
s_2 = \begin{matrix}
1\ 1\ 1\ 1\ 1\ 1\ 1\ 1\ 1\ 1 \\
1\ 0\ 0\ 1\ 0\ 0\ 0\ 0\ 1\ 1\ 1 \\
1\ 0\ 0\ 0\ 0\ 0\ 0\ 0\ 0\ 1\ 1 \\
1\ 0\ 0\ 0\ 1\ 1\ 1\ 0\ 0\ 0\ 1 \\
1\ 0\ 0\ 1\ 1\ 1\ 1\ 0\ 0\ 1 \\
1\ 0\ 0\ 1\ 1\ 1\ 1\ 1\ 0\ 0\ 1 \\
1\ 0\ 0\ 1\ 1\ \mathbf{1}\ 1\ 1\ 0\ 0\ 1 \\
1\ 0\ 0\ 1\ 1\ 1\ 1\ 1\ 0\ 0\ 1 \\
1\ 0\ 0\ 1\ 1\ 1\ 1\ 1\ 0\ 0\ 1 \\
1\ 0\ 0\ 1\ 1\ 1\ 1\ 1\ 0\ 0\ 1 \\
1\ 0\ 0\ 1\ 1\ 1\ 1\ 1\ 0\ 0\ 1 \\
1\ 1\ 1\ 1\ 1\ 1\ 1\ 1\ 1\ 1\ 1
\end{matrix}
$$

Figure 11.16 A pair of structuring elements suitable for detecting the character 'n' in the image of Figure 11.15 by a hit and miss transform. The origin of each structuring element is indicated with a bold font. s_1 probes inside the character and s_2 probes its surroundings.

that we used to erode the image in Figure 11.15. Although it fits inside the character 'n', it also fits inside 'h'. The structuring element s_2 probes outside the character. It is designed specifically to fit the surroundings of an 'n'—or, equivalently, to miss an 'n'. It will not miss 'h', and this ensures that there are no false positives generated by the hit and miss transform.

11.4.4 Java implementations

The package com.pearsoneduc.ip.op contains classes BinaryOpenOp and BinaryCloseOp to perform opening and closing, respectively, on binary images. Both classes simply apply BinaryErodeOp and BinaryDilateOp, in the appropriate order. The filter() method of BinaryOpenOp is shown in Listing 11.2. Note that BinaryCloseOp follows the strict definition of closing and rotates the structuring element before performing the dilation and erosion.

LISTING 11.2 `filter()` method of `BinaryOpenOp`.

```
public BufferedImage filter(BufferedImage src, BufferedImage dest) {
  BinaryErodeOp erodeOp = new BinaryErodeOp(structElement);
  BinaryDilateOp dilateOp = new BinaryDilateOp(structElement);
  if (dest == null)
    dest = createCompatibleDestImage(src, null);
  return dilateOp.filter(erodeOp.filter(src, null), dest);
}
```

The applications `BinaryOpen` and `BinaryClose` on the CD employ these two operators to carry out opening and closing. Both programs take the same command line arguments as the `BinaryErode` and `BinaryDilate` applications described earlier. Thus, the command to open an image `foo.pbm` with a 3 × 3 square structuring element and write the result to a new file `bar.pbm` is

```
java BinaryOpen foo.pbm bar.pbm sq3x3.bse
```

where `sq3x3.bse` is a file containing the following text:

```
# binary structuring element
# width=3
# height=3
# xorigin=1
# yorigin=1
111
111
111
```

The hit and miss transform is implemented by the program `HitAndMiss`, also on the CD. This program reads a binary image and a pair of structuring elements from files, performs the hit and miss transform and then outputs the results to a new file as a list of all the pixel coordinates where the inner structuring element fits the image and the outer structuring element misses the image.

Finally, we must mention `BinaryMorphologyTool`. This application has a graphical user interface, allowing the user to view the input to and output from a morphological operation. The pixels of the structuring element are displayed and each value can be toggled between 0 and 1 by clicking on that pixel. A menu provides a choice of erosion, dilation, opening or closing of the input image by this structuring element. The output can be copied to the input, allowing a sequence of morphological operations to be carried out. Figure 11.17 shows `BinaryMorphologyTool` at work.

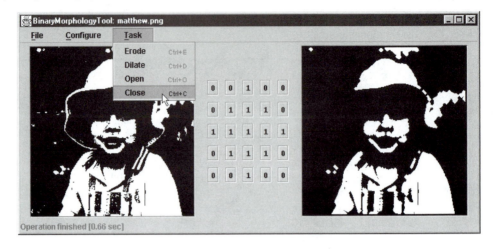

Figure 11.17 `BinaryMorphologyTool` in action.

11.5   Morphological filtering

We can regard operations such as opening and closing as morphological filters. They act as filters of shape; opening with a disc, for example, smooths corners from the inside, and closing with a disc smooths corners from the outside. However, there is another sense in which opening and closing act as filters. We can regard them as operations that filter out from an image any features that are smaller in size than the structuring element.

Let us consider a simple, hypothetical example. Suppose we are analysing the images generated by an industrial inspection system operating in a cookie factory. The system consists of a video camera mounted above a dark, moving conveyor belt, upon which lighter-coloured cookies lie. Images from the camera are fed to a computer, which performs segmentation using a simple thresholding technique. The aim is to measure cookie size and shape from the resulting binary images, but image noise and cookie crumbs on the conveyor belt lead to images such as that shown in Figure 11.18(a). If we open this image with a 9 × 9 disc, we get the image shown in Figure 11.18(b). The noise and other artefacts surrounding the cookie have been eliminated completely, and the irregularities on the edge of the cookie have been reduced to some degree.

In this example, opening is filtering the binary image at a scale defined by the size of the structuring element. Only those portions of the image into which the structuring element can be fitted are passed by the filter; smaller structure is blocked, and does not appear in the output image. The blobs of noise, in particular, are eliminated, because the structuring element will not fit inside any of them.

Now let us suppose that the manufacturer adds chocolate chips to its cookies. Being dark, these are not detected by thresholding, but they can be seen in the binary image as holes inside the cookie. Figure 11.19(a) shows an example. The opening operation fails to remove these holes because it erodes (thereby enlarging the holes) before it dilates, as in Figure 11.19(b). We remedy the problem by closing the opened image. Closing, which dilates and then erodes, fills the holes—as Figure 11.19(c) demonstrates.

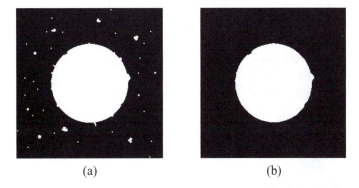

(a)   (b)

Figure 11.18 Example of morphological filtering. (a) Input image, a cookie surrounded by crumbs. (b) Result of opening the cookie image.

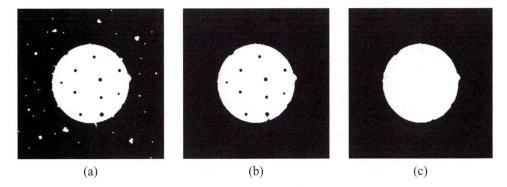

(a)   (b)   (c)

Figure 11.19 Dealing with holes. (a) Input image. (b) Result of opening by a 9 × 9 disc. (c) Result of closing the opened image, again using a 9 × 9 disc.

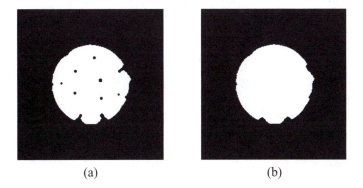

(a)   (b)

Figure 11.20 Damage caused by the excessive size of a structuring element. (a) Image of Figure 11.19(a) opened by a 17 × 17 disc. (b) Result of closing the opened image using the same structuring element.

The size of the structuring element is very important here. If it is too large, the holes will prevent it from fitting into the object properly during the initial opening, with the result that the object is degraded by the operation. Figure 11.20(a) shows the result of opening the chocolate chip cookie image with a 17 × 17 disc; the noise blobs have disappeared, but the cookie has been damaged. Figure 11.20(b) shows that a subsequent closing operation with this structuring element cannot repair the damage.

11.6 Greyscale morphology

11.6.1 Erosion and dilation

Morphological image processing is not restricted to binary images; morphological operations on greyscale images can also be defined. The definitions of these operations are similar to those for binary images, but they additionally take into account the extra dimension provided by pixel grey level. The image must be visualised as a landscape, with the height at any point representing the grey level at that point. The structuring element, sometimes referred to as a structuring function, is also three-dimensional. Structuring element pixels can take on any integer value—even a negative value, or zero. Because a value of zero is now significant, we must flag pixels that don't participate in morphological operations by some other means.

Greyscale erosion is a process of placing the structuring element beneath the grey level landscape of an image and pushing it up as far as it will go without any part of it rising above the landscape. The new value recorded at the origin of the structuring element is this maximum distance. Note that this distance will be negative if any of the structuring element's pixel values is greater than the grey level at the corresponding image pixel. The distance could also exceed the maximum of an 8-bit range if any of the structuring element pixels have negative values. Thus, we must either truncate distances to a 0–255 range or compute all the distances and then rescale to a 0-255 range.

Another way of formulating greyscale erosion is as a calculation of the minimum difference between pixel grey level and the corresponding value from the structuring element over the domain defined by the structuring element. Denoting an image by f and a structuring element by s, the greyscale erosion $f \ominus s$ at a pixel (x, y) is

$$(f \ominus s)(x, y) = \min_{j,k}[f(x + j, y + k) - s(j, k)], \tag{11.15}$$

where j and k index the pixels of s. If s is a 3 × 3 structuring element with its centre as the origin, j and k will range from -1 to $+1$; if it is a 5 × 5 structuring element with its centre as the origin, they will range from -2 to $+2$; and so on.

For the special case of a flat structuring element, this calculation has the same effect as the minimum filter described in Chapter 7; in fact, if all the structuring element's pixels are set to 0, the calculation that is performed is exactly that of the minimum filter. Figure 11.21 shows the *dice* image and its erosion by a 3 × 3 flat structuring element.

Greyscale dilation is defined in a dual manner to erosion. Instead of pushing the structuring element up by the maximum amount from beneath the grey level landscape of the image, we flip the structuring element upside down and find the minimum distance it needs to be

(a)   (b)   (c)

Figure 11.21 Greyscale erosion and dilation. (a) Input image. (b) Result of erosion by a 3 × 3 flat structuring element. (c) Result of dilation by the same structuring element.

pushed up to be above the landscape. It can be shown that this is equivalent to computing

$$(f \oplus s)(x, y) = \max_{j,k}[f(x - j, y - k) + s(j, k)], \qquad (11.16)$$

where j and k vary as before. For a flat structuring element, this is equivalent to the maximum filter discussed in Chapter 7. Figure 11.21 shows an example of dilation by a flat structuring element.

11.6.2 Opening and closing

The definitions of opening and closing for greyscale images are essentially the same as those for binary images. As in the binary case, opening and closing with an appropriate structuring

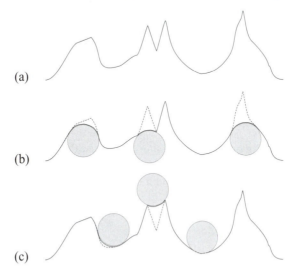

Figure 11.22 Geometric interpretation of greyscale opening and closing. (a) Grey level topography, shown in cross-section. (b) Effect of opening with a sphere. (b) Effect of closing with a sphere.

element can have a smoothing effect on the image; however, now it is the topography of the grey level landscape that is smoothed, rather than the contours of shapes in a 'flat' binary image. The three-dimensional analogue of a disc-shaped binary structuring element is spherical in shape. Opening an image with this 3D structuring element can be visualised as rolling the sphere across the underside of the grey level landscape. The sphere cannot be pushed up inside narrow peaks in this landscape, so opening tends to smooth away the small-scale bright structure in an image (Figure 11.22(b)). Closing can be visualised in a similar manner, only now we roll the sphere over the top of the landscape. The sphere cannot be pushed down into narrow valleys, so closing tends to smooth away the small-scale dark structure in an image (Figure 11.22(c)).

Figure 11.23 shows examples of opening and closing with a 5×5 flat structuring element. Greyscale opening and greyscale erosion differ in a manner similar to the corresponding binary operations. Erosion will shrink bright features but it will also enlarge dark features; opening, on the other hand, will remove small, bright structure without enlarging dark features. Similar considerations apply to dilation and closing.

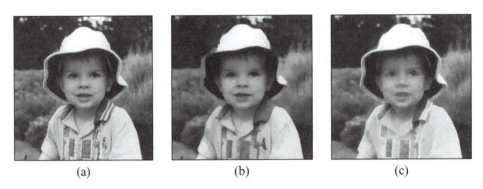

(a)   (b)   (c)

Figure 11.23 Examples of greyscale opening and closing. (a) Input image. (b) Result of opening by a 5×5 flat structuring element. (c) Result of closing by the same structuring element.

11.6.3   Other compound operations

An iteration of opening and closing on a greyscale image is termed **morphological smoothing**. This operation has the effect of removing small-scale bright and dark structure from an image. The non-linear smoothing effect resembles that produced by certain extreme forms of the median filter. Figure 11.24 gives an example.

Another compound operation is the **top-hat transform**, defined for an image f and a structuring element s as

$$g = f - (f \circ s). \tag{11.17}$$

Recall that $f \circ s$ removes small-scale bright structure from an image. It follows that subtracting $f \circ s$ from f leaves us with this small-scale bright structure. The top-hat transform therefore acts as a detector of peaks and ridges of the grey level surface. Figure 11.25 shows

Figure 11.24 Result of morphological smoothing with a 5 × 5 flat structuring element.

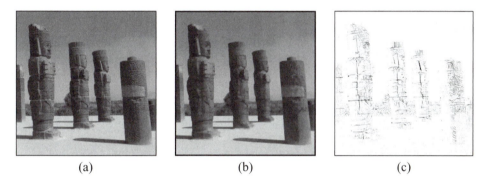

| (a) | (b) | (c) |

Figure 11.25 The top-hat transform. (a) Input image. (b) Result of opening by a 3 × 3 flat structuring element. (c) Result of subtracting (b) from (a), inverted for clarity.

an example. The dual of the top-hat transform is

$$g = (f \bullet s) - f. \tag{11.18}$$

This acts as detector of pits and valleys in the grey level surface.

11.6.4 Java implementations of greyscale operations

Greyscale morphological operations are supported in the `com.pearsoneduc.ip.op` package by classes equivalent to those implemented for binary operations. `GreyStructElement` represents the structuring elements applied to greyscale images. Instances of this class behave in almost exactly the same way as binary structuring elements. The main difference is that there is no restriction on the values of structuring element pixels. Also, the format for structuring element data written to or read from files is slightly different, with pixel values being separated by spaces. Instead of `fits()` and `hits()`, `GreyStructElement` has `below()` and `above()`. The former returns the maximum distance that the structuring element can be pushed up whilst remaining below the image; the latter returns the minimum distance that the structuring element must be pushed up to be above the image.

Erosion and dilation are supported by the classes `GreyErodeOp` and `GreyDilateOp`. These operate very much like their binary counterparts. The main difference is the need to deal with results that lie outside the 0–255 range required for 8-bit images. Both classes can truncate out-of-range values or compute the results and then rescale them so that they occupy a 0–255 range. The required behaviour is indicated by a Boolean instance variable, the value of which can be set when a `GreyErodeOp` or `GreyDilateOp` is created. For example, the operators defined by

```
GreyStructElement element = new GreyStructElement(5, 5);
...
GreyErodeOp op1 = new GreyErodeOp(element, true);
GreyErodeOp op2 = new GreyErodeOp(element, false);
```

differ in that op1 will rescale output values to lie in the required range, whereas op2 will truncate output values. The Boolean parameter can be omitted if desired. The default behaviour in this case is to truncate output values.

Opening and closing are supported by the classes `GreyOpenOp` and `GreyCloseOp`. As in the binary case, these merely apply the erosion and dilation operators in the appropriate order.

Four applications that use these classes are provided on the CD. They are: `GreyErode`, `GreyDilate`, `GreyOpen` and `GreyClose`. Each behaves in a similar manner to the corresponding applications written for binary images. Each truncates output values to a 0–255 range by default. Rescaling to a 0–255 range is requested by supplying the word 'rescale' as a fourth command line parameter.

11.7 Further reading

Dougherty [12] discusses morphological operations on both binary and greyscale images in considerable detail. Lyon [29] provides some examples of morphological operations on colour images. Parker [36] gives some practical examples of applications, and some code. Parker's book also contains a detailed discussion of skeletonisation. This is a 'thinning' process whereby we remove pixels that are not essential for communicating the shape of a region of pixels. Pitas [37] also discusses skeletonisation and presents an implementation in C.

11.8 Exercises

1. Calculate the erosion, dilation, opening and closing of the image below by a 3×3 square structuring element.

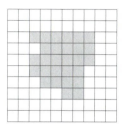

2. A bank is developing a machine that can recognise the handwritten signatures of its customers. Binary images of the signatures are produced by scanning a document and thresholding the scanned image. In these binary images, pen strokes should appear as chains of connected pixels; however, image quality is often so poor that these chains are broken in many places.

   Suggest a technique that will join up the broken pen strokes in these binary images. Draw diagrams to illustrate the different stages of the technique.

3. Why can't we test for existence of a particular shape by erosion with a single structuring element having a border of zeros, rather than using the more complicated hit and miss transform?

4. Using the classes described in this chapter, write a Java program to perform the top-hat transform.

Image compression

It is important that we store and transport images efficiently, given their increasing importance in the network-oriented, multimedia computing environments that we use today. Image compression techniques make efficient storage and transmission possible by reducing the amount of data needed to represent an image. These techniques are either lossless, meaning that they exploit redundancy already present in the image, or lossy, meaning that the image is modified in subtle ways to create redundancy, which is then removed to achieve compression. In this chapter, we look at examples of both types of compression technique.

We start by reviewing the basic concepts and considering how the performance of compression techniques can be measured. We then move on to consider four lossless techniques that achieve compression by exploiting different kinds of redundancy in the image. This is followed by discussion of two different lossy techniques: JPEG compression and fractal compression. The chapter concludes with the brief description of the MPEG standard for the compression of video data.

12.1   Introduction

The storage requirements for images can be excessive, particularly if true colour and a high perceived image quality are desired. Suppose, for example, that we wish to create a digital family photo album; the raw data for a hundred pictures might occupy a gigabyte or more of disk space, if we require images comparable in quality to conventional photographic prints. Storage problems are particularly acute in remote sensing applications; the scenes imaged by Earth-orbiting satellites typically have widths and heights of several thousand pixels, and there may be several bands representing the different wavelengths in which images are acquired. The raw data for a single scene therefore requires several hundred megabytes of storage space. Video presents perhaps the most serious storage problems of all. A one minute sequence of full colour video data occupies over 1.5 gigabytes when in digital form.

Another issue is image communication. The prodigious size of many images leads to long, costly transmission times. Cost is not the only reason for speeding up transmission, however. The emergence of the World-Wide Web has resulted in a huge increase in the exchange of images via the Internet. Rapid transfer of these data is essential if the Web is to remain usable as an interactive information-gathering tool.

Image compression addresses the problem of reducing the amount of data required to represent a digital image, so that it can be stored or transmitted more efficiently. We must make a clear distinction between *data* and *information*. Data are the means by which information is conveyed. Various amounts of data can be used to convey the same amount of information. Consider, for example, Figure 12.1. This shows ways of representing the number five using different amounts of data. The quantity of data used varies by four orders of magnitude. Clearly, the binary integer representation is vastly more efficient than the pictorial representation.

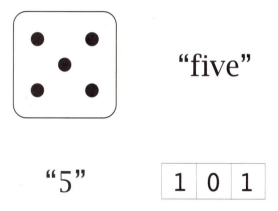

Figure 12.1 Four different representations of the same information. From left to right and top to bottom: a picture (101,632 bits); a word, spelled in English using the ASCII character set (32 bits); a single ASCII digit (8 bits); a binary integer (3 bits).

If more data are used than is strictly necessary, then we say that there is *redundancy* in the dataset. **Lossless compression** techniques are designed to remove this redundancy when data are stored or transmitted and then replace it when the image is reconstructed from those data. The reconstructed image is identical to the original, i.e., all of the information originally present in the image has been preserved by compression.

Many 'real' images contain only a small amount of redundant data. Lossless techniques give only moderate compression of such images. Higher compression is possible using **lossy compression** techniques, which discard some of the information present in the image. This is not as drastic as it might seem. An image can be changed in many ways that are almost undetectable by the human visual system. If these changes lead to highly redundant data, then the image can be greatly compressed. The reconstructed image will *not* be identical to the original image, although the difference need not be clearly visible to the human eye.

12.2   Redundancy

Three basic types of redundancy can be identified in a single image. **Coding redundancy** arises when the representation chosen for the pixel values of an image is not the most efficient that is possible. Remember that the value at a pixel in a typical greyscale image relates to the intensity of light detected by the camera that acquired the image. We cannot represent the actual intensity measurements; instead, we quantise the data and represent intensities by a discrete set of what, in the language of information theory, are termed **codewords**. Image quantisation uses a standard binary coding scheme in which the codewords are the set of values that can be represented with a fixed number of bits (typically eight). Furthermore, the codewords are ordered in the same way as the intensities that they represent; thus, the bit pattern 00000000, corresponding to the value 0, represents the darkest points in an image and the bit pattern 11111111, corresponding to the value 255, represents the brightest points.

An 8-bit coding scheme has the capacity to represent 256 distinct levels of intensity in an image. But what if there are only 16 different grey levels in a particular image? Such an image exhibits coding redundancy because it could, in theory, be represented using a 4-bit coding scheme. (In fact, as we shall see shortly, coding redundancy can also arise due to the use of fixed-length codewords.)

A second type of redundancy often present in images is **interpixel redundancy**. This arises because the values of a pixel and its immediate neighbours are often strongly correlated. This means that the value at a pixel can be predicted with a reasonable degree of accuracy from values of its neighbours. Consequently, the amount of information conveyed by an individual pixel is relatively small, and the amount of data that is needed to represent that pixel is correspondingly small.

The third type of redundancy is **psychovisual redundancy**. This arises because not all the information present in an image is of equal importance to the human visual system. For example, there are upper limits on the number of quantisation levels that can be easily distinguished by eye, and on the spatial frequencies that can be detected by the eye.

When video data are available, there is a fourth type of redundancy: **interframe redundancy**. This is the temporal equivalent of interpixel redundancy. Video frame rates are sufficiently high that the change in a pixel's value from frame to frame is typically very small over the majority of the frame. Data compression can be achieved by encoding the relatively small number of changes that occur from frame to frame, rather than each frame in its entirety.

12.3   Performance characterisation

How do we characterise the performance of a compression algorithm? The obvious answer is to measure the degree to which it has compressed the image data. There are various ways of expressing the amount of compression that has been achieved. One way is to compute the **compression ratio**, defined as

$$C = \frac{n}{n_c},$$

(12.1)

where n is the number of information-carrying units used in the uncompressed dataset and n_c is the number of units in the compressed dataset. The same units should be used for n and n_c; bits or bytes are typically used. Larger values of C indicate better compression.

A less obvious performance measure is the time required for compression or decompression of the data. In certain applications where time is at a premium, we might favour quicker algorithms over algorithms that achieve a better compression ratio. The *symmetry* of the technique may also be important. A symmetrical technique will require similar amounts of time to compress and decompress data. This is what we desire in applications where images are compressed as frequently as they are decompressed. Some compression techniques are highly asymmetrical in time, taking much longer to compress images than to decompress them. (This is part of the price paid for the very high compression ratios that these techniques can achieve.) This asymmetry is not a problem if compression takes place infrequently relative to decompression.

Consider, for example, the storage of images from a multimedia encyclopedia on a CD-ROM. In this application it is important that high compression ratios are achieved, to maximise the number of images that can be stored in the fixed space available on the CD-ROM. It is also important that decompression is quick, so that the interactive feel of the encyclopedia is preserved. Provided that these requirements are satisfied, the technique can be highly asymmetrical, with compression taking orders of magnitude longer than decompression. This is because the set of images from the encyclopedia are compressed once only, when the CD-ROM is mastered. In a different application, such as the storage of images acquired at regular intervals from a security camera, this technique might be totally inappropriate.

When lossy techniques are employed, the decompressed image will not be identical to the original image. In such cases, we can define **fidelity criteria** that measure the difference between the decompressed and original images. An example of an objective criterion is the root-mean-square (RMS) error, defined for an $M \times N$ image by

$$\varepsilon = \left[\frac{1}{MN} \sum_{y=0}^{N-1} \sum_{x=0}^{M-1} [\hat{f}(x, y) - f(x, y)]^2 \right]^{1/2},$$

(12.2)

where f and $\hat{f}$ are the original and decompressed images, respectively. Smaller values of RMS error indicate that the decompressed image is closer to the original. Note, however, that this measure does not necessarily correlate with how we perceive the image. It does not follow that one technique is better than another just because it results in a lower RMS error; it may be the case that a decompressed image from the technique with the higher error is closer, visually, to the original image. For this reason, subjective fidelity measures based on human perception are sometimes used to characterise the performance of lossy techniques.

12.4   Lossless compression techniques

12.4.1   Delta compression

Delta compression (also known as differential coding) is a very simple, lossless technique in which we recode an image in terms of the difference in grey level between each pixel and the previous pixel in the row. The first pixel, of course, must be represented as an absolute value, but subsequent values can be represented as differences, or 'deltas'. Most of these differences will be very small, because gradual changes in grey level are more frequent than sudden changes in the majority of images. These small differences can be coded using fewer bits. Thus, delta compression exploits interpixel redundancy to create coding redundancy, which we then remove to achieve compression.

Figure 12.2 shows an image along with a histogram of the grey level differences for this image. Note that the frequency axis of this histogram is logarithmic. Large differences are relatively infrequent; differences close to zero are orders of magnitude more common. Reasonable compression of this image should therefore be possible by encoding grey level differences.

(a)

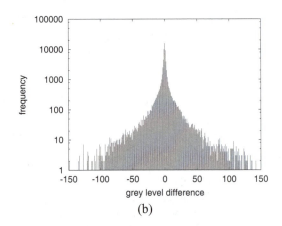

(b)

Figure 12.2   Suitability of an image for delta compression. (a) An image. (b) Histogram of grey level differences for adjacent pixels in this image.

We can compress the image of Figure 12.2(a) by using four bits to code differences in the range -7 to $+7$. Four bits give us $2^4 = 16$ codewords, but there are only 15 values in the range. The remaining codeword can be used to flag pixels for which the grey level difference exceeds the range. The values of these pixels are output using the full eight bits. Using this scheme, the storage requirements for a completely homogenous image would be almost halved by delta compression. For the image of Figure 12.2(a), the actual compression ratio achieved using the technique is 1.52.

You can experiment with delta compression yourself by running the `DeltaEncoder` application on the CD. This reads an image from a named file and performs delta compression of it. If a second filename is supplied on the command line, the compressed datastream is written to this file; otherwise, it is written to memory and the compression ratio achieved by the technique is calculated.

12.4.2   Run length encoding

The technique of **run length encoding** (RLE) exploits the high interpixel redundancy that exists in relatively simple images. In RLE, we look for grey levels that repeat along each row of the image. A 'run' of consecutive pixels whose grey levels are identical is replaced with two values: the length of the run and the grey level of all pixels in the run. Hence, the sequence {50, 50, 50, 50} becomes {4, 50}. RLE can be applied on a row-by-row basis, or we can consider the image to be a one-dimensional datastream in which the last pixel in a row is adjacent to the first pixel in the next row. This can lead to slightly higher compression ratios if the left and right-hand sides of the image are similar.

For the special case of binary images, we don't need to record the value of a run, unless it is the first run of the row (or, if we regard the image as one-dimensional, the first run of the image). This is because there are only two values possible for a pixel in a binary image. If the first run has one of these values, the second run implicitly has the other value, the third run implicitly has the same value as the first, and so on.

Note that, if the run is of length 1, RLE replaces one value with a pair of values. It is therefore possible for RLE to *increase* the size of the dataset in images where runs of length 1 are numerous. This might be the case in noisy or highly textured images. For this reason, RLE is most useful for the compression of binary images or very simple greyscale images.

The main practical application of RLE is the compression of binary images of documents prior to transmission by fax machine. Here, the algorithm is an extension of RLE into two dimensions, known as READ (relative element address designate) coding.

You can experiment with run length encoding yourself by running the RunLengthEncoder application on the CD. This reads an image from a named file and performs run length encoding of it. If a second filename is supplied on the command line, the compressed datastream is written to this file; otherwise, it is written to memory and the compression ratio achieved by the technique is calculated.

12.4.3   Statistical coding

Statistical coding techniques remove the coding redundancy in an image. This redundancy exists because fixed-length (typically 8-bit) codewords are used to represent pixel values. Information theory tells us that the amount of information conveyed by a codeword relates to its probability of occurrence. Codewords that occur rarely convey more information than codewords that occur frequently in the data. An optimal coding scheme will use more bits for the rare codewords and fewer bits for the frequent codewords.

Basic concepts

To quantify how effectively an image is coded by a fixed-length scheme, we can compute its **entropy**. For an image coded using b bits, this is given by

$$H = -\sum_{i=0}^{2^b-1} p_i \log_2 p_i, \tag{12.3}$$

where $p(i)$ is the probability of occurrence for a grey level i. Probability can be estimated from the histogram of an image using

$$p_i = \frac{h_i}{n},\qquad(12.4)$$

where h is the frequency of occurrence of grey level i and n is the total number of pixels in the image. Figure 12.3 shows two very different images and gives their entropies, calculated using the program `Entropy` on the CD. The synthetic image contains just a few distinct grey levels, and the background grey level is much more numerous than the other grey levels. Clearly, this image is not coded effectively by the standard 8-bit binary scheme. This observation is supported by the image's entropy, which is very much lower than that of the real image.

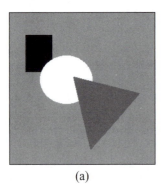

(a)   (b)

Figure 12.3 Two images and their entropies. (a) A synthetic image, with an entropy of 1.1. (b) A real image, with an entropy of 5.4.

The units of entropy are 'bits per pixel'; in fact, the entropy of an image is an estimate of the average number of bits per pixel that are required to code that image. If more bits are used, there is coding redundancy. If b is the smallest number of bits needed to generate the number of quantisation levels observed in an image, then the information redundancy of that image is defined as

$$r = b - H.\qquad(12.5)$$

We can also write down an expression for the compression ratio that can be achieved by the removal of all coding redundancy. This ratio is

$$C_{\max} = \frac{b}{H}.\qquad(12.6)$$

Note that this is *not*, in general, the maximum compression ratio achievable by lossless techniques, because it does not take into account interpixel redundancy.

A statistical coding technique must analyse an image in order to estimate the probability of occurrence for each value in that image. This is done simply by computing the histogram and normalising. The task is then to construct a set of codewords to represent each pixel value. These codewords must have the following properties:

1. Different codewords must have different lengths (numbers of bits).
2. Codewords for infrequent values must be longer than codewords for frequently occurring values.
3. It must not be possible to mistake a particular sequence of concatenated codewords for any other sequence.

The performance of a coding scheme can be assessed by computing the average bit length of its codewords. This is given by

$$\bar{l} = \sum_{i=0}^{2^b-1} l_i p_i, \tag{12.7}$$

where l_i is the length of the codeword used to represent the grey level i. The upper limit for $\bar{l}$ is b, the number of bits used in the fixed-length codewords representing image intensities. The lower limit for $\bar{l}$ is the entropy.

Huffman coding

Huffman coding is simply a particular way of choosing the codewords, such that $\bar{l}$ is as close as possible to the entropy of the image. We can illustrate how the technique works with a simple example. Figure 12.4 shows an image coded with 3 bits per pixel and its histogram. Grey levels range from 0 to 7. The probabilities associated with each of these grey levels are listed in Table 12.1. We start by ranking pixel values in decreasing order of their probability. We then pair the two values with the lowest probabilities, labelling one of them with 0 and the other with 1. Their probabilities are summed to give the probability of either value from the pair occurring in the image. We then identify the next two lowest probabilities from the current set of individual values or paired values. These are then paired, with one member of the pair labelled 0 and the other 1, and so on. The process continues, building up a tree-like structure of paired values (Figure 12.5).

(a)

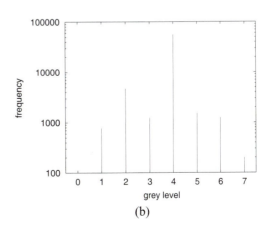

(b)

Figure 12.4 (a) Image to be compressed by Huffman coding. (b) Histogram of this image.

Table 12.1 Codewords produced by Huffman coding of the image in Figure 12.4(a).

grey level	p	codeword	l	lp
0	0.000	111111	6	0.000
1	0.012	11110	5	0.060
2	0.071	10	2	0.142
3	0.019	1101	4	0.076
4	0.853	0	1	0.853
5	0.023	1100	4	0.092
6	0.019	1110	4	0.076
7	0.003	111110	6	0.018
				1.317

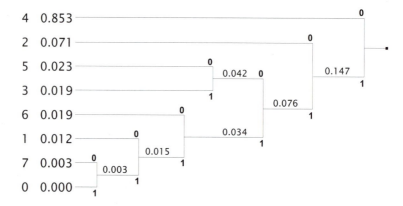

Figure 12.5 Huffman tree for the image in Figure 12.4.

Following this tree from each leaf node to the root gives a sequence of bits that, when reversed, represent the codeword for the value at the leaf node. Table 12.1 lists the codewords determined by traversing the tree in Figure 12.5. Also listed here are the lengths of each codeword, and the product of codeword length and probability. Summing this column gives us an average bit length of 1.317. Since the original image was coded using 3 bits, the compression ratio achieved by Huffman coding is $3/1.317 = 2.28$.

12.4.4 Dictionary-based coding

Statistical coding techniques such as Huffman coding represent individual symbols in a datastream using codewords of variable length. Dictionary-based compression adopts a completely different approach, encoding variable-length strings of symbols as single codewords. Compression occurs because these codewords are shorter than the strings of symbols that they replace.

Following Nelson and Gailly [34], we can illustrate how dictionary-based compression works using the example of English text and a conventional printed dictionary. Let us suppose that we wish to compress the phrase

"Image compression is important and fun"

using the dictionary. One way of doing this is to encode a word using the number of the dictionary page on which it occurs, along with its position on that page. If we use the seventh edition of Chambers English Dictionary, the phrase above becomes the string of codes

710–14, 293–13, 756–18, 715–37, 48–26, 573–16.

The first number of each pair is the page number and the second is the position of the word on that page. Assuming that one byte is the fundamental unit of storage, page numbers can be stored in two bytes and word positions in one byte; hence, the total storage required for the string of codes is 18 bytes. This compares with 38 bytes required for storage of the original phrase.

Although this simple example illustrates the basic concept, it uses an existing dictionary to perform the compression. With an arbitrary image, no such dictionary of 'phrases' exists, so we must construct it from the image data.

Most dictionary-based techniques have their origins in work by Ziv and Lempel in the late 1970s [53, 54]. These researchers developed two techniques that have come to be known as LZ77 and LZ78. The deflation algorithm used by Zip archiving tools on the PC platform and by the gzip compression program on Unix systems is based on LZ77. A variant of LZ78 known as the LZW algorithm forms the basis of compression techniques used by modems and in the GIF image format. The LZW technique is patented, and attempts by the patent owner Unisys to collect licence fees led directly to the development of the PNG image format, with patent-free compression based on LZ77. We shall focus here on LZ77 because it features in the PNG format and because there is direct support for this type of compression in Java, via the classes of the java.util.zip package. Readers interested in LZ78 and its derivatives should consult other texts [34, 37].

Sliding window compression

LZ77 is what is known as a **sliding window compression** technique. The dictionary is a window of previously seen data that slides along the datastream. This window is usually thousands or tens of thousands of bytes in size. (In the deflation algorithm used by Zip tools, gzip, the PNG format, etc, it is 32 kilobytes long.) at the leading end of the window is a look-ahead buffer, typically a few hundred bytes long. The algorithm tries to match strings of bytes in the look-ahead buffer with strings of bytes in the dictionary. When a match is found, the algorithm replaces the string of bytes with the distance to the match (which can be no larger than the size of the window) and its length. In the deflation algorithm based on LZ77, strings of unreplaced bytes and the match lengths are Huffman coded using one tree and the match distances are Huffman coded using another. Compressed data are output in blocks, and the algorithm can use different pairs of Huffman trees for each block if it deems that this would be beneficial.

Sliding window compression exploits recency in the input data. When a string of bytes has been seen recently enough to still be within the window, it can be compressed by the algorithm; however, if it was seen earlier in the datastream, it will not be replaced by much shorter tokens. This limits the effectiveness of the technique in image compression. We can envisage a scenario in which a sequence of pixel values near the top of an image is duplicated near the bottom of the image. If the image is large compared with the size of the window, the sequence of pixel values will no longer be in the dictionary when it is encountered for the second time.

Another problem when using this technique for image compression is that it seeks exact matches between strings in the look-ahead buffer and strings in the dictionary. Unfortunately, in many images, sequences of pixels that appear to be identical to the human eye may differ enough to prevent compression. For example, suppose that an image contain the two nearby sequences

    100,101,100,99,101 ...
    101,101,99,100,100 ...

The second sequence would look the same as the first but it would not be recognised as a duplicate by a dictionary-based algorithm.

Dictionary-based compression in Java

Java provides a range of classes in the `java.util.zip` package to support compression via the deflation algorithm described above. Full details can be found in reference books describing Java version 1.1 onwards [21, for example]. We shall restrict ourselves here to showing some Java code that can be used to experiment with dictionary-based compression of images.

The `java.util.zip` provides a class called `DeflaterOutputStream` that can be used to write data to a stream in compressed form. Compressing an array of bytes named `data` can be as simple as

```
DeflaterOutputStream output =
  new DeflaterOutputStream(new FileOutputStream("compressed.dat"));
output.write(data, 0, data.length);
```

A `DeflaterOutputStream` uses an internal `Deflater` object as the compression engine. If more control over compression is required, a custom `Deflater` can be created and used:

```
Deflater deflater = new Deflater();
// change deflater parameters here...
DeflaterOutputStream output =
  new DeflaterOutputStream(new FileOutputStream("compressed.dat"),
    deflater);
output.write(data, 0, data.length);
```

When the `Deflater` has done its job, we can query it to find out how many bytes of compressed data were generated and then compute a compression ratio:

```
int n = deflater.getTotalOut();
System.out.println(n + " bytes written");
float ratio = (float) data.length / n;
System.out.println("Compression ratio = " + ratio);
```

Similar code is used in the program `DeflateTest` on the CD. This program reads an 8-bit greyscale image from a file and gains access to the byte array used to store pixel values. The bytes are compressed using a `Deflater` that has been configured with a compression level specified by the user (or with the default compression level if none has been specified). Valid compression levels range from 1 (fast, low compression) to 9 (slow, high compression). Since we are interested only in the compression ratio and not in keeping the data, `DeflateTest` uses the memory-based `ByteArrayOutputStream` as the destination for the compressed data. This is neater and more efficient than outputting to a temporary file.

Note that the `Deflater` class also allows different compression strategies to be selected. One of these, specified by the constant `Deflater.HUFFMAN_ONLY`, disables the dictionary and uses Huffman coding only to achieve compression. We can therefore use a `Deflater` to create a Huffman coding program and compare its results with those from `DeflateTest`. `HuffmanTest` on the CD is such a program.

12.4.5   Comparison of techniques

Table 12.2 compares the compression ratios achieved when the lossless techniques described in this chapter are applied to the two images of Figure 12.3. The programs used were those described previously: `DeltaEncoder`, `RunLengthEncoder`, `HuffmanTest` and `DeflateTest`. We can see that delta compression is a fairly consistent performer, achieving a compression ratio close to the theoretical maximum of 2 for the synthetic image and a slightly lower ratio for the real image. The other techniques perform very much better on the synthetic image than on the real image. This is precisely what we expect, given that there is considerable coding redundancy and interpixel redundancy in the synthetic image and much less in the real image.

Table 12.2 Compression ratios achieved by various lossless compression techniques. The synthetic image is the image shown in Figure 12.3(a); the real image is the image shown in Figure 12.3(b).

image	delta	RLE	Huffman	deflate
synthetic	1.97	60.24	6.14	84.89
real	1.80	1.15	1.61	2.57

Run length encoding gives excellent compression of the synthetic image; the technique is ideal for this type of image, in which there are few grey levels and, therefore, relatively long runs of the same grey level. However, RLE is bettered by deflation, which combines sliding window compression with Huffman coding. RLE is a poor performer on the real image, relative to the other techniques. (Actually, this is a good result for RLE; it is common for the technique to increase the amount of storage required for real images.) The most effective compression technique for the real image is deflation, but the compression ratio is thirty times smaller than that achieved on the synthetic image.

12.5 Lossy compression techniques

Lossy compression techniques rely on the fact that the human visual system is insensitive to the loss of certain kinds of information. Consider, for example, one of the sequences of pixel values from the hypothetical example discussed earlier:

> 100,101,100,99,101 ...

This is similar to the sequence

> 100,100,100,100,100 ...

allowing for a random fluctuation of ± 1 in each value. A fluctuation this small will be imperceptible, so we could replace the first sequence by the second without affecting the appearance of the image to any significant degree. The advantage of this is that the second sequence is highly redundant. The compression techniques described in Section 12.4 could be used to store this sequence very compactly.

12.5.1 JPEG compression

The Joint Photographic Experts Group (JPEG) have specified a lossy algorithm based on **transform coding**. Techniques of this kind create a frequency-based representation of the image and discard some of the high frequencies to create redundancy and hence achieve compression. The basis for the JPEG algorithm is the **discrete cosine transform** (DCT). This is rather like a Fourier transform; the main difference is that it is performed on real, rather than complex, data, and it yields a set of real-valued coefficients. The DCT is preferred to the Fourier transform for transform coding because it packs a given amount of information into fewer coefficients [20].

Although we could, in theory, perform a transform on an entire image, there are two disadvantage to this. First, it is demanding computationally. Second, discarding high frequencies from the spectrum generated by the transform will have the effect of a low pass filter, blurring all parts of the image to the same degree (see Chapter 8). This runs counter to our aim of achieving high compression ratios whilst minimising perceptible information loss. The solution is to perform the transform on small areas of the image. Compression techniques that operate on blocks of pixels in this manner are often described as **block coding** techniques. Block coding allows compression to be adaptive. In areas where information loss can be tolerated, we can discard many of the high frequency components; in other areas where the loss of these components would be very noticeable, we can leave the transform coefficients unaltered.

The transform of a block of pixels may suffer from discontinuity effects of the kind discussed in Chapter 8, resulting in the presence of **blocking artefacts** in the image after it has been decompressed. This is a further reason to prefer the DCT to the DFT; the symmetry of the DCT is such that it is inherently less susceptible to discontinuity effects.

The stages of JPEG compression for an 8-bit greyscale image are outlined in Algorithm 12.1. The image is broken up into non-overlapping 8×8 blocks, which are processed in left to right, top to bottom order. Padding can be done if the image dimensions are not multiples of eight; the padding is discarded on decompression. The DCT of each block is computed, generating an 8×8 block of coefficients. Since transforms like the DCT

ALGORITHM 12.1 JPEG compression of an 8-bit greyscale image.

Split image up into 8×8 blocks of pixels
for all blocks of pixels **do**
    Shift pixel values by subtracting 128
    Compute a discrete cosine transform (DCT) of the block
    Quantise the DCT coefficients
    Arrange coefficients into a one-dimensional sequence
    Delta encode the first (zero frequency) coefficient
    Compress zero-valued coefficients by run length encoding
    Perform Huffman coding of the coefficients
    Output coded coefficients for the block
end for

---

produce real numbers, a block of coefficients would normally occupy much more space than the corresponding block of pixels. To avoid this problem, we quantise the coefficients. A particular DCT coefficient $T(u, v)$ is quantised by calculating

$$T'(u, v) = \text{round} \left[\frac{T(u, v)}{Q(u, v)} \right],$$ (12.8)

where u and v are spatial frequency parameters each ranging from 0 to 7, $Q(u, v)$ is a value from a quantisation table and 'round' denotes rounding to the nearest integer. The values in the quantisation table tend to increase as u and v increase. This has the effect of giving greater precision to the lower frequency components of the transform, for which accuracy is more important, and reduced precision to the higher frequency components. In fact, this approach implicitly discards components above a certain frequency by setting their coefficients to zero.

A typical quantisation table is shown in Figure 12.6. The values in this table can be scaled to produce other quantisation tables. Scaling up has the effect of increasing the number of coefficients in a given block that are set to zero by Equation 12.8; scaling down has the opposite effect. This gives us a way of controlling the compression ratio.

$$\begin{bmatrix} 16 & 11 & 10 & 16 & 24 & 40 & 51 & 61 \\ 12 & 12 & 14 & 19 & 26 & 58 & 60 & 55 \\ 14 & 13 & 16 & 24 & 40 & 57 & 69 & 56 \\ 14 & 17 & 22 & 29 & 51 & 87 & 80 & 62 \\ 18 & 22 & 37 & 56 & 68 & 109 & 103 & 77 \\ 24 & 35 & 55 & 64 & 81 & 104 & 113 & 92 \\ 49 & 64 & 78 & 87 & 103 & 121 & 120 & 101 \\ 72 & 92 & 95 & 98 & 112 & 100 & 103 & 99 \end{bmatrix}$$

Figure 12.6 Example of a JPEG quantisation table.

Most JPEG implementations allow the user to specify a quality parameter that is used to generate an appropriate quantisation table. A high value for this quality parameter produces a quantisation table that sets relatively few coefficients to zero, resulting in a relatively modest compression ratio; a low value for the quality parameter produces a quantisation table that sets many coefficients to zero, resulting in a much higher compression ratio.

Note that the effect of quantisation using a particular table depends on image content. In places where grey level is varying slowly and smoothly, an 8×8 block of pixels will be relatively homogeneous and many of the DCT coefficients will be small enough to be set to zero by quantisation. At edges, where grey level is varying much more rapidly, fewer of the DCT coefficients will have small values, and so fewer will be discarded as a result of quantisation. In effect, the JPEG algorithm blurs the image most in places where the blurring won't be noticed and tries to preserve information in the more interesting parts of the image.

After quantisation, the DCT coefficients are reordered into a one-dimensional sequence by following a zigzag path from the lowest frequency component to the highest (Figure 12.7). The first value in the sequence is the zero-frequency coefficient. It is usually much larger than the other coefficients, and can be stored more efficiently by delta encoding—i.e., by storing the difference between its value and the value from the previous block. The remainder of the sequence typically contains several long runs of zeros which may be compressed by run length encoding. Finally, a Huffman coding scheme can be applied to compress the coefficients still further.

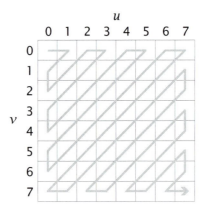

Figure 12.7 Reordering of DCT coefficients.

To decompress a JPEG-compressed image, we follow the procedure in reverse. The Huffman coded bit sequence is decoded and runs of zeros are expanded, giving sequences of 64 values per block. These are written back into an 8×8 array in zigzag fashion and dequantised. Dequantisation simply involves multiplication by values in the quantisation table. An inverse DCT of this array of coefficients followed by addition of 128 yields an 8×8 block of pixels with values that are similar to those in that same part of the original, uncompressed image.

JPEG compression in Java

Java provides a variety of classes to handle JPEG image compression and decompression in the com.sun.image.codec.jpeg package. JPEGImageEncoder encodes an image as a JPEG datastream, the process being controlled by the parameters in JPEGEncodeParam. Similarly, JPEGImageDecoder decodes a JPEG datastream and reconstructs an image, the process being controlled by parameters in JPEGDecodeParam. Note that these four classes are specified as interfaces, which means that they cannot be instantiated directly; instead, the factory class JPEGCodec provides methods that manufacture instances of objects implementing these interfaces. For example, to compress a BufferedImage object named image, writing the results to a file called test.jpg, we can do

```
JPEGImageEncoder output =
  JPEGCodec.createJPEGEncoder(new FileOutputStream("test.jpg"));
output.encode(image);
```

If we wish to control the process, we must use JPEGCodec to manufacture a set of encoding parameters, which we may then modify. For example, to compress an image with a quality factor of 0.25, we would do the following:

```
JPEGEncodeParam parameters =
  JPEGCodec.getDefaultJPEGEncodeParam(image);
parameters.setQuality(0.25, true);
JPEGImageEncoder output =
  JPEGCodec.createJPEGEncoder(new FileOutputStream("test.jpg"),
    parameters);
output.encode(image);
```

The first line of this example manufactures a parameter object suitable for encoding the specified image. The parameters are at default values that can be modified by invoking methods such as setQuality(). This method takes two parameters, the first being the desired quality (0.0–1.0) and the second a Boolean flag indicating whether the baseline quantisation tables specified by the JPEG standard are to be used.

The quantisation tables used in JPEG compression are represented as instances of the class JPEGQTable. A static method of this class allows us to access the standard quantisation table:

```
int[] data = JPEGQTable.StdLuminance.getTable();
```

The array data contains the quantisation values $Q(u, v)$ arranged in zigzag order. We can also retrieve a JPEGQTable from a JPEGEncodeParam. This allows us to investigate the relationship between the quality parameter and the quantisation table used to encode an image:

```
JPEGEncodeParam parameters =
  JPEGCodec.getDefaultJPEGEncodeParam(image);
parameters.setQuality(0.25, true);
int[] data = parameters.getQTable(0).getTable();
```

This approach is used in the program `JPEGQuantTable` on the CD. This program takes a quality parameter specified on the command line and writes to standard output the quantisation table associated with that parameter.

One further application, `JPEGTool`, is provided on the CD as a practical example of how to use Java's JPEG classes. This program reads an image from a named file and displays it in a tabbed pane. Also displayed is a version of the input image that has been subjected to one cycle of JPEG compression and decompression. The quality parameter can be varied between 0.0 and 1.0 using a slider beneath the tabbed display. The compression ratio and RMS error (Equation 12.2) for this quality setting are displayed beneath the slider. A menu is provided, allowing the output image or the difference between the input and output images to be saved. Figure 12.8 shows the application in action.

Figure 12.8   `JPEGTool` in action.

Examples

The JPEGTool application was used to compress the synthetic and real images of Figure 12.3. Figure 12.9 shows part of the real image compressed using a quality parameter of 0.8. The compression ratio achieved here is 12.88, five times greater than that achieved using deflation, and there are no significant differences between this image and the original. Also shown in Figure 12.9 is the same image compressed with a quality parameter of 0.2. This results in a compression ratio of 32.4, roughly twelve times greater than that achieved using deflation. Here, the artefacts of compression are much more obvious—although this image is still adequate for many purposes.

Figure 12.9   The image of Figure 12.3(b), compressed using the lossy JPEG technique. Top: quality of 0.8, giving a compression ratio of 12.88 and an RMS error of 1.64. Bottom: quality of 0.2, giving a compression ratio of 32.4 and an RMS error of 3.84.

The lossy JPEG algorithm is not well-suited to the compression of very simple images. This can be seen in Figure 12.10(b), which shows how a portion of the synthetic image in Figure 12.3(a) looks after a cycle of JPEG compression and decompression. Compression artefacts are significant in this image, and yet the compression ratio that has been achieved here—42.83—is inferior to that obtained using the error-free techniques of deflation or

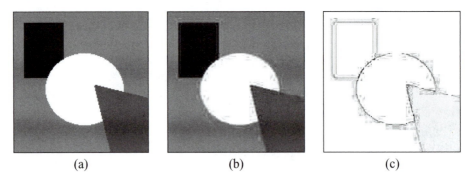

(a)	(b)	(c)

Figure 12.10 JPEG compression of simple, synthetic images. (a) Portion of the original image. (b) Corresponding portion of the compressed image. (c) Difference between the original and compressed images, inverted and equalised.

run length encoding (see Table 12.2). Figure 12.10(c) shows the difference between the compressed image and the original image, inverted and equalised for added clarity. We can see that the differences between the images occur in blocks that straddle sharp boundaries between image features. In each of these blocks, many of the DCT coefficients are being discarded—and yet most of them are needed to represent a sharp edge adequately. This leads to highly visible artefacts. The artefacts in real images are often less obvious to the eye because they lie embedded within the complex textures that exist in these images.

12.5.2   Fractal compression

Fractal geometry is capable of creating some striking images—a classic example being the Mandelbrot set depicted in Figure 12.11. Fractal shapes appear to be incredibly complex, and yet they are generated by simple rules. In the case of the Mandelbrot set, repeated evaluation of a very simple equation generates a fractal with infinite levels of detail. We can zoom in on the domain of the Mandelbrot set and see the same structure repeating itself again and again. Another example is the Koch curve. This is generated by the recursive application of a very simple rule. We start with a straight line and divide it into three segments of equal size. The middle segment is then replaced with two sides of an outward-facing equilateral triangle. This procedure is then repeated for each line segment. Figure 12.12 shows the results. Application of this rule to an equilateral triangle generates a shape that resembles a snowflake.

Fractals share the property of *self-similarity*; parts of the shape look like transformed copies of other parts. This self-similarity is a kind of redundancy. It allows complex shapes to be described by very simple transformational rules. Fractal image compression takes this idea and applies it to images. The assumption is that we can represent one group of pixels in an image as a transformed copy of some other group of pixels. If the transformation can be represented more compactly than the pixel data, compression is achieved. Of course, for real images, is it unlikely that two different regions differ only by some geometric transformation. The pixel values themselves are likely to differ. We can approximate the difference by incorporating a simple, linear transformation of grey level. Any residual

Figure 12.11   Part of the Mandelbrot set.

Figure 12.12   First five iterations in the generation of the Koch curve.

difference not explained by this transformation of grey level will be lost; hence, fractal compression is a lossy technique.

In practical fractal image compression algorithms, we partition the input image into a set of non-overlapping square 'ranges'. For each range, we must search for a larger square region of the image, called the domain, that is most similar to the range. The domain is typically restricted to be twice the size of the range, and domains can, in theory, overlap[1]. Compression is achieved by encoding the parameters of the affine transformation that maps the chosen domain onto the range. Affine transformations were discussed in Chapter 9. The main difference here is that the transformation is three-dimensional, taking into account not only the geometric relationship between domain and range but also the relationship between grey levels in the two regions.

The geometric part of the transformation is specified by six numbers, and the mapping of grey level is represented by a further two numbers—corresponding to the brightness and contrast parameters of Equation 6.3. The scaling and translation elements of the geometric transformation are already known; the scale factor is 0.5, and the translation parameters are simply the offsets of the upper-left corner of the range relative to the domain. Because the domain and the range are both square, there are only eight possible differences in orientation between them (allowing for both rotation and reflection). For each orientation, we must determine the grey level mapping parameters by a least-squares procedure. We then store the best set of translation, orientation and grey level mapping parameters. The orientation parameter can be stored very compactly, using only three bits; the brightness and contrast parameters can each be quantised and stored using fewer than eight bits.

Figure 12.13 shows an image and two fractally-compressed versions of that image. These images were compressed using an implementation of the algorithm that attempts to use 16×16 ranges, subdividing these into 4×4 ranges if no domain can be found for which the RMS error lies below an error tolerance parameter. This parameter acts as a quality factor for the compression. When it is high, suitable domains can be found for many 16×16 ranges, so fewer ranges are required to cover the image and fewer transformations need to be stored. When the error tolerance is low, most of the ranges in the image will be 4×4 pixels in size, so there will be more of them and more transformations will need to be stored. Figure 12.13(b) was produced using an error tolerance of 8, resulting in a compression ratio of 9.57—nearly eight times greater than that achievable using the lossless deflation algorithm described in Section 12.4.4. There is some loss of sharpness relative to the original image in (a) due to the size of the ranges, but the quality is reasonable. Figure 12.13(c) was produced using an error tolerance of 20. This almost halves the number of transformations required and doubles the compression ratio. However, image quality is significantly lower, with many of the 16×16 ranges visible as homogeneous blocks of pixels.

Decompression is much more straightforward and much faster than compression. It exploits one of the fundamental theorems of fractal image compression: the contractive mapping theorem. The details of this need not concern us here; instead, we simply note that the theorem allows us to reconstruct the original image from an arbitrary image—one that is completely black, for example—simply by the iterative application of the transformations that were computed by the compression algorithm. This procedure converges to a fixed

---

[1] In practice, it may be more expedient, computationally, to restrict or prevent overlap.

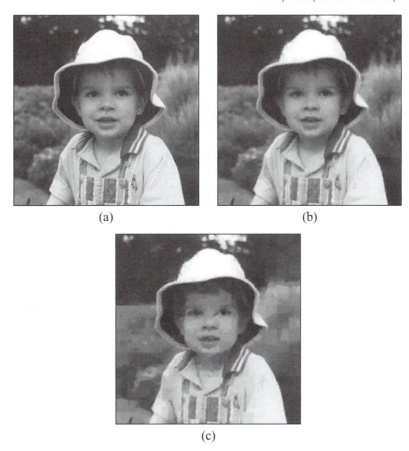

(a)   (b)

(c)

Figure 12.13 Examples of fractal image compression. (a) Original image. (b) Image compressed using 2194 transformations, giving a compression ratio of 9.57. (b) Image compressed using 1180 transformations, giving a compression ratio of 18.13.

point that is close to the original image, provided that a reasonable partitioning of the image was carried out during compression. It works because the transformations incorporate grey level information as well as geometric information. Figure 12.14 shows reconstructions of a fractally-compressed image after 1, 3 and 5 iterations. Beyond this point, the improvements to the reconstructed image are usually imperceptible.

An interesting and potentially useful feature of fractal decompression is that it is resolution-independent. The compressed image is merely a list of affine transformations, and these can be applied at any scale we desire. For example, we can compress a 100×100 image and decompress it into an image with dimensions of 300×300. We pay nothing, computationally, for scaling the image up in this manner. Also, the decompressed image will not have the blocky appearance characteristic of simple image magnification techniques such as pixel replication.

(a)   (b)

(c)

Figure 12.14 Iterative reconstruction of a fractally-compressed image. (a) After 1 iteration, starting from a random image. (b) After 3 iterations. (c) After 5 iterations. The visible effect of further iterations is negligible.

12.6   Compression of moving images

The need for high compression ratios is particularly acute in the case of video data. For this reason, digital video standards such as Apple's *QuickTime* or Microsoft's *Video for Windows* both support frame-by-frame JPEG compression and decompression. However, the JPEG algorithms were designed for the compression of still, rather than moving, images. The reductions in dataset size needed to fit an entire movie onto a CD, or to support video conferencing across networks with comparatively low bandwidths, cannot be achieved unless we additionally take into account interframe redundancy. In any video sequence, there will be areas that either do not change over a significant number of frames, or else change in a relatively smooth and continuous way. The human visual system gives much less emphasis to these regions, so they can be highly compressed in time without affecting video playback quality to any serious degree.

The Motion Picture Experts Group (MPEG) is responsible for developing worldwide standards for lossy video compression, similar to those developed by the JPEG organisation for still images. The current standards are known as MPEG-1 and MPEG-2. The former is suitable for low resolution sequences with data rates of up to 1.5 Mbit per second; the latter support higher resolutions (e.g., 640×480) with data rates of between 4 and 10 Mbit per second. Both support the simultaneous compression of video and audio data and the synchronisation of the two datastreams. A new standard, known as MPEG-4, is imminent.

The current MPEG standards use a DCT-based block coding scheme to compress a *reference frame*. These reference frames occur at regular intervals in the input sequence— e.g., once every fifteen frames. The next step is to carry out motion estimation for subsequent frames. This involves computing the correlation between blocks of pixels in the current frame and blocks in the reference frame. Blocks are moved around in sub-pixel increments to estimate their motion accurately. If it is determined that a block has no motion, a special 'no change' code can be output, signifying that the corresponding block of pixels from the reference frame can be used during decompression. If the block has motion, then it may be similar to a nearby block in the reference frame—in which case we can output the location of that block. If the correlation between a block and nearby blocks from the reference frame is not sufficiently high, the block must be coded as per JPEG compression. The cost of motion estimation is high, so the MPEG technique is highly asymmetric. In fact, compression is often hardware-assisted.

12.7 Further reading

For those interested in the general principles and practice of data compression, one of the definitive recent texts is the book by Nelson and Gailly [34]. This contains detailed descriptions of most of the techniques discussed in this chapter and presents implementations written in C. (Converting this code to Java should be relatively straightforward.)

LZ78 dictionary-based compression and its derivatives are not described here; for further details, see Nelson and Gailly [34]. The original paper by Ziv and Lempel [54] may be of historical interest. Implementations of LZ78-based algorithms written in C can be found in Nelson and Gailly's book and in the book by Pitas [37]. Documentation on the LZ77-based deflation algorithm is available online as the Internet Request For Comments document RFC1951. (See `http://sunsite.org.uk/pub/rfc` or do a web search for 'RFC1951' to locate a site near you.)

A useful information source for JPEG compression is the paper by Wallace [49]. Gonzalez and Woods [20] discuss a variety of techniques based on transform coding in some detail and present worked examples of JPEG compression and decompression. Practical algorithms for fractal image compression and decompression are dissected and implemented by Nelson and Gailly [34]. For those interested in the theoretical background to this technique, a number of books are now available [15, for example].

One new and promising technique not discussed here is wavelet-based image compression. This outperforms DCT-based compression to the extent that the forthcoming JPEG-2000 standard for lossy compression will abandon the DCT in favour of the wavelet transform. Like the DCT, a discrete wavelet transform (DWT) generates a frequency-based representation of an image. Unlike the DCT, the basis functions of a DWT have 'compact support'; that is, they are not infinite in extent. This makes them more suitable for the representation of highly localised structure such as edges. The enhanced information-packing capabilities of the DWT lead to greater redundancy when its coefficients are quantised and, hence, greater compression.

A brief introduction to wavelets in the context of image processing is given by Umbaugh [48]. Castleman [9] devotes an entire chapter to this subject. Press et al. [39] describe the theory and give some C code that demonstrates wavelet-based image compression. A Java prototype for a JPEG-2000 image decoder can be found at `http://ltswww.epfl.ch/~neximage/decoder/`.

The MPEG standards are described in a paper by Le Gall [16] and in various recent books [e.g., 32, 22]. Information can also be found online at `http://drogo.cselt.stet.it/mpeg/`, the official website of the MPEG committee, and at `http://www.mpeg.org`, an index of MPEG resources.

12.8   Exercises

1. The `DeltaEncoder` program compresses an image by delta compression. Implement a class `DeltaDecoder` that decompresses the datastream generated by `DeltaEncoder`. Test the two classes and verify that the compression is lossless.

2. Repeat Exercise 1 for `RunLengthEncoder`.

3. Suppose we have two images. One of these images has a broad, flat histogram and the other a narrow, highly-peaked histogram. Which image will compress better by means of Huffman coding?

4. Why does the JPEG technique employ 8×8 blocks of pixels? What would be the likely effect on an image of using a different block size, say 16×16 or 32×32?

5. Consult the references for further details of fractal image compression and implement this technique in Java.

Glossary of Image Processing Terms

Active imaging Mode of imaging in which an artificial source of energy is used.

Adaptive filter A filter whose behaviour changes in response to variations in local image properties.

Affine transformation First-order geometric transformation involving a combination of translation, scaling, rotation and skewing.

Aliasing Phenomenon occurring when an image is undersampled, i.e., when the sampling rate is less than twice the Nyquist frequency. Information with a high spatial frequency is incorrectly represented, manifesting itself as an artefact with a lower spatial frequency.

Alpha-trimmed mean filter A filter that sorts pixel values from a neighbourhood into ascending order, discards a certain number of values at either end of the list and then outputs the mean of the remaining values.

Amplitude spectrum Term given to the magnitudes of the complex numbers produced by the *Fourier transform* of an image. The amplitude spectrum is a measure of how much of each frequency component is present in the image.

Analogue-to-digital converter, ADC Hardware used to convert an analogue signal (e.g., serial video) into digital form.

Anti-aliasing Filtering operation designed to remove frequencies that exceed half the sampling rate achieved by an *analogue-to-digital converter*, thereby guaranteeing that the *Nyquist criterion* is met.

Aperture An opening that admits light into a camera; a hole of variable size, built into a lens, that controls the total amount of light falling on a sensor.

Backward mapping The process of determining values for pixels in a geometrically transformed image by applying the inverse transformation to pixel coordinates. This gives coordinates in the input image from which a pixel value can be interpolated.

Band pass filter Filter that passes a certain range of frequencies whilst suppressing others.

Band stop filter Filter that has the opposite effect to a *band pass filter*, suppressing a particular range of frequencies whilst passing others.

Barrel distortion Distortion caused by camera optics, in which straight lines appear to bend outwards, away from the image centre.

Basis function Term used to describe one of the two-dimensional sine or cosine functions that form the basis of a *Fourier series* representation of an image.

Bilinear transformation Geometric transformation characterised by eight coefficients, used in computing a piecewise warp of an image.

Binary image Two-level image; image in which pixels can take on one of two possible values (usually 0 and 1).

Block coding Term applied to a class of image compression techniques that operate on blocks of pixels.

Blocking artefacts Features visible in images that have been highly compressed by means of the *JPEG compression* algorithm, caused by discontinuity effects in the *discrete cosine transform* applied to 8 × 8 blocks of pixels.

Brightness adaption The means by which the eye adjusts its overall sensitivity to cope with a huge range of light intensities.

Butterworth low pass filter Popular form of low pass filter having a transfer function that varies smoothly with frequency.

Butterworth high pass filter Popular form of high pass filter having a transfer function that varies smoothly with frequency.

Canny edge detector A near-optimal edge detector combining a *Gaussian filter* for smoothing with *gradient vector* calculation, *non-maximal suppression* and *hysteresis thresholding*.

CCD Charge-coupled device; a solid-state sensor comprising a rectangular array of photosites formed from a semiconductor such as silicon.

Closing Morphological operation on a binary or greyscale image, defined as an iteration of *dilation* and *erosion*.

CMY model *Colour model* used in printing, in which colours are represented as a linear combination of cyan, magenta and yellow components.

CMYK model *Colour model* used in printing, in which the *CMY model* is extended by the addition of a true black component.

Coding redundancy A redundancy in the data used for image representation, arising when the *codewords* chosen to represent pixel values are not optimal.

Codewords Symbols used to represent pixel values in an image. The codewords used for images are normally the set of integer values that can be represented with a fixed number of bits (eight, typically).

Colour model Means of specifying colour in a standard, generally accepted way.

Coma Lens defect in which off-centre rays of obliquely-incident light come to a focus to one side of the central ray position, giving point objects a comet-like appearance.

Compression ratio Measure of the performance of a compression algorithm, defined as the ratio of input image size to compressed image size.

Cone Photoreceptor in the *retina* of the eye, responsible for colour vision.

Contextual segmentation *Segmentation* that takes into account the context of a pixel, i.e., the relationships that exist between a pixel and its neighbours.

Control point A landmark point in an image, used to define a geometric transformation of some kind (e.g., a warp that registers one image with another).

Convolution An operation that sums the products of pixel values from a neighbourhood and coefficients from a *convolution kernel*.

Convolution kernel Small array of coefficients that are multiplied by pixel values during *convolution*.

Convolution theorem Expression of the relationship between *convolution* and multiplication in the frequency domain.

Correlation Neighbourhood operation that closely resembles *convolution*.

Cumulative histogram Record of the cumulative frequency of occurrence of *grey levels* in an image. Used in *histogram equalisation*.

Dark current Signal produced by a *CCD* or some other sensor in the absence of illumination.

Deconvolution Reversal of convolution, typically implemented as an *inverse filter*.

Dilation Morphological operation on binary or greyscale images, characterised as hitting or intersection of a *structuring element* with an image.

Discrete cosine transform *Frequency domain* transformation used in *JPEG compression*.

Discrete Fourier transform A *Fourier transform* defined for sampled data.

Disparity Difference in the apparent position of a point from the scene in the left and right images of a 'stereo pair'.

Dither matrix Matrix of pseudorandom thresholds used for *dithering*.

Dithering Technique used to generate halftone versions of greyscale or colour images.

Electromagnetic (EM) spectrum The range of radiation produced by oscillations of electrically charged material, including such things as x-rays, microwaves and visible *light*.

Entropy Measure of disorder and information content in an image, which can be estimated from its *histogram*.

Erosion Morphological operation on binary or greyscale images, characterised as fitting of a *structuring element* into the image.

Error diffusion *Halftoning* technique in which the error that results from thresholding is propagated to neighbouring pixels.

Fast Fourier transform, FFT Efficient method for calculating the *Fourier transform* of an image.

Fidelity criteria Ways of measuring the effect of lossy compression techniques on images.

Field curvature Curvature of the surface of best focus for a lens.

Filter transfer function Two-dimensional function that is multiplied by the *Fourier transform* of an image in order to carry out *filtering*; Fourier transform of a *convolution kernel*.

First-order interpolation Method of computing output pixel grey level in a geometrically transformed image as a distance-weighted function of the grey levels of neighbouring pixels in the input image.

Focal length Distance from the lens plane to the point at which parallel incident rays converge; the standard measure of the magnifying power of a lens.

Forward mapping In geometric transformations, the process of mapping pixel values in the input image onto pixels in the transformed output image.

Fourier coefficients Weighting factors applied to the sine and cosine *basis functions* in a *Fourier series*.

Fourier series Representation of a periodic signal as a weighted sum of sine and cosine *basis functions*.

Fourier transform, FT Projection of a signal onto a set of sine and cosine *basis functions* of varying frequency.

Fovea Small region of the *retina* providing the most detailed information about a scene.

Fractal compression *Lossy compression* technique that exploits the similarity, under *affine transformation*, of different parts of an image.

Frequency domain Realm in which an image is represented as a set of *spatial frequencies*.

Gamma Parameter specifying the non-linearity in response of a monitor's cathode ray tube.

Gaussian filter Filter that blurs an image using a non-uniform *convolution kernel* whose coefficients are samples from a two-dimensional Gaussian function.

Gradient vector A way of representing the magnitude and direction of changes in *grey level* in the vicinity of a pixel.

Grey level *Quantisation* level used to represent intensity at a pixel, displayed as a shade of grey.

Greyscale A set of grey levels, ranging from black to white.

Halftoning Simulation of a greyscale or colour variation using binary patterns of black or coloured dots.

High pass filtering Filtering technique that attenuates low spatial frequencies whilst leaving high spatial frequencies unaffected.

Histogram Means of recording the frequency distribution of *grey levels* in an image.

Histogram equalisation Technique for contrast enhancement based on a flattening of an image *histogram*.

Histogram specification Technique for contrast modification in which a user can specify a desired shape for a *histogram*.

Hit and miss transform Morphological operation used for shape detection, in which a matched pair of *structuring elements* are used to probe the inside and outside of image features simultaneously.

HSI model *Colour model* in which colour is represented by hue, saturation and intensity components.

Huffman coding *Lossless compression* technique in which pixel values are represented by variable-length codes.

Hysteresis thresholding Technique used by the *Canny edge detector* to produce contours from edge pixels having high gradients.

Ideal low pass filter Filter that blocks all frequencies above a cutoff frequency.

Ideal high pass filter Filter that blocks all frequencies below a cutoff frequency.

Idempotence Property of *opening* and *closing* operators, whereby the effect of multiple iterations of the operator is no different from the effect of a single iteration.

Image registration Process by which two images of the same scene, obtained at different times or by different means, are matched geometrically.

Imaging Image acquisition; the process of sensing our surroundings and then representing the measurements that are made as an image.

Interframe redundancy Temporal redundancy in video data, arising from the fact that most pixels change very little or not at all between successive frames.

Interpixel redundancy Spatial redundancy in image data, arising because the values of neighbouring pixels are often strongly correlated.

Inverse filter *Deconvolution* technique in which degradation is removed by filtering an image with the inverse of the *point spread function*.

Inverse Fourier transform Reconstruction of a signal from its projections onto sine and cosine basis functions of varying frequency.

JPEG compression *Lossy compression* technique based on the *discrete cosine transform*.

Laplacian Second-order derivative of an image; a *convolution kernel* approximating the second-order derivative.

Light Visible electromagnetic energy with a wavelength between 400 and 700 nanometres.

Linear filtering Use of a linear operation (e.g., convolution) to modify the spatial information content of an image.

Look-up table, LUT Means of storing a precomputed grey level mapping, to speed up brightness/contrast enhancement.

Lossless compression Information-preserving compression; compression in which the reconstructed image is identical to the input image.

Lossy compression Compression with information loss; compression in which carefully chosen components of the information in an image are discarded deliberately in order to achieve high redundancy and hence high compression.

Low pass filtering Filtering technique that attenuates high spatial frequencies whilst allowing low frequencies to pass unattenuated.

Mach banding Phenomenon in which bands of uniform brightness appear to be brighter at their edges than at their centres.

Maximum filter Non-linear operation in which the central pixel of a neighbourhood is given the maximum value from that neighbourhood.

Mean filter Linear operation in which the central pixel of a neighbourhood is given the mean of the values in that neighbourhood.

Median filter Non-linear operation in which the central pixel of a neighbourhood is given the middle-ranked value from that neighbourhood.

Minimum filter Non-linear operation in which the central pixel of a neighbourhood is given the minimum value from that neighbourhood.

Minimum mean square error filter An *adaptive filter* whose smoothing effect depends on local *grey level* variance.

Modulation transfer function, MTF *Fourier transform* of the *point spread function* of an imaging system.

Morphing Technique for smoothly transforming one image into another, using geometric warping.

Morphological smoothing An *opening* and a *closing* applied in sequence to a greyscale image.

MPEG compression Video compression technique that attempts to eliminate interframe redundancy in image sequences.

Negation A mapping of *grey level* that gives the effect of a photographic negative, black become white and vice versa.

Neighbourhood operations The class of image processing operations in which a pixel's new value depends not only on its original value but also on the values of surrounding pixels.

Non-contextual segmentation *Segmentation* on the basis of some global attribute, without reference to the spatial relationships between pixels.

Non-maximal suppression A stage in the *Canny edge detector* whereby local maxima in grey level gradient are thinned down to ridges that are only one pixel wide.

Nyquist criterion Requirement that the sampling frequency for a digital signal should be at least double the highest frequency present in a signal.

Opening Morphological operation on binary or greyscale images, defined as an iteration of *erosion* and *dilation*.

Passive imaging Image acquisition using energy sources that are already present in the scene.

Patterning Simple *halftoning* technique in which a pixel of a greyscale image is replaced by a small pattern of black and white pixels taken from a fixed set of such patterns.

Period Duration of one cycle of a periodic signal.

Photopic vision 'Bright light' vision; vision involving *cones* in the *retina*.

Photoreceptor Generic term for *rods* and *cones*, the two types of light-sensitive cells in the *retina*.

Photosite A semiconductor junction acting as one of many discrete imaging elements in a *CCD*.

Pincushion distortion Distortion caused by camera optics, in which straight lines appear to bend inwards, towards the image centre.

Pixel Contraction of 'picture element'; a term for one of the array elements that constitute a digital image.

Point spread function, PSF Linear model of the blurring caused by the environment and the imaging system.

Power spectrum The square of the *amplitude spectrum*.

Prewitt kernels Well-known *convolution kernels* for computing grey level gradient in the x and y directions.

Psychovisual redundancy Redundancy in an image resulting from the insensitivity of the human visual system to particular image characteristics.

Quadratic warp Non-linear geometric transformation described by two transformation equations with terms up to x^2 and y^2.

Quantisation Digitisation of the values stored at each pixel of an image.

Quantisation level Value stored at a pixel after quantisation.

Rank filter Non-linear filter in which pixel values from a neighbourhood are sorted into order and the value with a particular rank in the sorted list is selected as the new value for a pixel.

Redundancy A term describing the presence of data that are not needed to convey the information in an image.

Region growing *Segmentation* technique that forms regions of similar, connected pixels.

Region of interest Area of an image, usually rectangular, that will be the subject of further processing or analysis.

Retina Light-sensitive layer of cells occupying the inner surface of the eye.

RGB model *Colour model* used by image acquisition and display devices, in which colour is represented as a linear combination of red, green and blue components.

Ringing Artefact of filtering or of reconstruction from a limited set of frequencies, in which edges create a pattern of ripples in the image.

Rod The more numerous of the two types of photoreceptor in the retina of the eye, sensitive to light intensity.

Run length encoding, RLE *Lossless compression* technique in which a run of pixels with the same value is replaced by the value and the length of the run.

Sampling Digitisation of the spatial coordinates of an image, so as to produce a discrete array of numerical data.

Sampling rate Rate at which a video signal is sampled during digitisation.

Segmentation Partitioning of an image into distinct regions that, ideally, correlate strongly with features of interest.

Scotopic vision 'Dim light' vision; vision involving only the *rods* in the *retina*.

Sliding window compression Dictionary-based compression technique in which the dictionary is a window of previously-seen data that slides along the datastream.

Sobel kernels Well-known *convolution kernels* for computing grey level gradient in the x and y directions.

Spatial domain The domain of the image, normally defined by pixels in a Cartesian coordinate system.

Spatial frequency Rate of change of intensity with distance moved in an image.

Spherical aberration Lens defect in which central and off-centre light rays are brought to a focus at different distances from the lens.

Split and merge algorithm *Segmentation* technique in which an image is divided into regions that are iteratively subdivided and merged until some measure of uniformity is achieved.

Structuring element, SE Shape or template used to probe an image in morphological operations.

Thresholding *Segmentation* technique in which pixels are assigned to one class or another, depending on whether an attribute (typically *grey level* or colour) exceeds a specified threshold.

Top-hat transform Morphological operation performed on greyscale images, obtained by subtracting an opened image from the original image.

Transform coding A technique in image compression, where we create a frequency-based representation of an image and discard some of the high frequencies to create redundancies.

Uniformity predicate Test used in *segmentation* to evaluate the similarity of a set of connected pixels.

Unsharp masking Process of subtracting from an image a blurred version of that image.

Volume Three-dimensional analogue of an image; 3D array of *voxels*.

Voxel Contraction of 'volume element'.

Wiener filter A noise-tolerant technique for the restoration of degraded images.

Zero crossing Point at which the second derivative of an image changes sign.

Zero-order interpolation Method of computing output pixel grey level in a geometrically transformed image by calculating coordinates for the corresponding point in the input image and rounding to the nearest integer.

Zero-phase-shift filter Term used in the *frequency domain* to describe filters that affect amplitude only, not phase.

24-bit colour Colour specified using three 8-bit integers, one for each component of the *colour model*.

4-neighbourhood Neighbourhood consisting of a pixel and the pixels that are adjacent vertically and horizontally.

8-neighbourhood Neighbourhood consisting of a pixel and the pixels that are adjacent vertically, horizontally or diagonally.

Bibliography

[1] Sinan Si Alhir. *UML in a Nutshell*. O'Reilly & Associates, 1998.

[2] H. C. Andrews and B. R. Hunt. *Digital Image Restoration*. Prentice Hall, 1977.

[3] J. T. Astola and T. G. Campbell. On computation of the running median. *IEEE Transactions on Acoustics, Speech and Signal Processing*, 37(4):572–574, 1989.

[4] G. J. Awcock and R. Thomas. *Applied Image Processing*. Macmillan Press, 1995.

[5] Gregory Baxes. *Digital Image Processing: Principles and Applications*. John Wiley & Sons, 1994.

[6] T. Beier and S. Neely. Feature-based image metamorphosis. *Computer Graphics*, 26(2):35–42, 1992.

[7] R. M. Bracewell. *The Fourier Transform And Its Applications*. McGraw-Hill, second edition, 1986.

[8] J. F. Canny. A computational approach to edge detection. *IEEE Transactions on Pattern Analysis and Machine Intelligence*, 8(6):679–698, November 1986.

[9] Kenneth R. Castleman. *Digital Image Processing*. Prentice Hall, 1996.

[10] J. W. Cooley and J. W. Tukey. An algorithm for the machine calculation of complex Fourier series. *Mathematical Computation*, 19:297–301, 1965.

[11] Randy Crane. *A Simplified Approach to Image Processing*. Prentice Hall, 1997.

[12] Edward R. Dougherty. *An Introduction to Morphological Image Processing*. SPIE Press, 1992.

[13] Bruce Eckel. *Thinking in Java*. Prentice Hall, 1998.

[14] Robert Eckstein, Marc Loy, and Dave Wood. *Java Swing*. O'Reilly & Associates, 1998.

[15] Yuval Fisher, editor. *Fractal Image Compression: Theory and Application*. Springer-Verlag, 1995.

[16] Didier Le Gall. MPEG: a video compression standard for multimedia applications. *Communications of the ACM*, 34(4):46–58, April 1991.

[17] Andrew S. Glassner. *Principles of Digital Image Synthesis*. Morgan Kaufmann Publishers, 1995.

[18] Jonas Gomes, Lucia Darsa, Bruno Costa, and Luiz Velho. *Warping and Morphing of Graphical Objects*. Morgan Kaufmann Publishers, 1998.

[19] Jonas Gomes and Luiz Velho. *Image Processing for Computer Graphics*. Springer-Verlag, 1997.

[20] Rafael Gonzalez and Richard Woods. *Digital Image Processing*. Addison-Wesley, third edition, 1993.

[21] Mark Grand and Jonathan Knudsen. *Java Fundamental Classes Reference*. O'Reilly & Associates, 1997.

[22] B. Haskell, A. Puri, and A Netravali. *Digital Video: An Introduction to MPEG-2*. Chapman & Hall, 1997.

[23] Cay S. Horstmann. *Practical Object-Oriented Development in C++ and Java*. John Wiley & Sons, 1997.

[24] T. S. Huang, G. T. Yang, and G. Y. Tang. A fast two-dimensional median filtering algorithm. *IEEE Transactions on Acoustics, Speech and Signal Processing*, 27(1):13–18, 1979.

[25] Ramesh Jain, Rangachar Kasturi, and Brian Schunk. *Machine Vision*. McGraw-Hill, 1995.

[26] J. R. Janesick, T. Elliot, S. Collins, M. M. Blouke, and J. Freeman. Scientific charge-coupled devices. *Optical Engineering*, pages 692–714, August 1987.

[27] Jonathan Knudsen. *Java 2D Graphics*. O'Reilly & Associates, 1999.

[28] Barthold Lichtenbelt, Randy Crane, and Shaz Naqvi. *Introduction to Volume Rendering*. Prentice Hall, 1998.

[29] Douglas A. Lyon. *Image Processing in Java*. Prentice Hall, 1999.

[30] D. Marr and E. C. Hildreth. Theory of edge detection. *Proceedings of the Royal Society of London B*, 207:187–217, 1980.

[31] Paul M. Mather. *Computer Processing of Remotely-Sensed Images: An Introduction*. John Wiley & Sons, second edition, 1999.

[32] Joan Mitchell, Didier Le Gall, and Chad Fogg. *The MPEG Video Compression Standard*. Chapman & Hall, 1996.

[33] James D. Murray and Willam van Ryper. *Encyclopedia of Graphics File Formats*. O'Reilly & Associates, second edition, 1996.

[34] Mark Nelson and Jean-Loup Gailly. *The Data Compression Book*. M&T Books, second edition, 1996.

[35] Patrick Niemeyer and Joshua Peck. *Exploring Java*. O'Reilly & Associates, 1996.

[36] J. R. Parker. *Algorithms for Image Processing and Computer Vision*. John Wiley & Sons, 1997.

[37] Ioannis Pitas. *Digital Image Processing Algorithms*. Prentice Hall, 1993.

[38] Rob Pooley and Perdita Stevens. *Using UML: Software Engineering with Objects and Components*. Addison-Wesley, 1999.

[39] William H. Press, Saul A. Teukolsky, William T. Vetterling, and Brian P. Flannery. *Numerical Recipes in C*. Cambridge University Press, second edition, 1992.

[40] J. M. S. Prewitt. Object enhancement and extraction. In B. S. Lipkin and A. Rosenfeld, editors, *Picture Processing and Psychopictorics*. Academic Press, 1970.

[41] S. J. Sangwine and R. E. N. Horne, editors. *The Colour Image Processing Handbook*. Chapman & Hall, 1998.

[42] Robert J. Schalkoff. *Digital Image Processing and Computer Vision*. John Wiley & Sons, 1989.

[43] Clifford A. Shaffer. *A Practical Introduction to Data Structures and Algorithm Analysis*. Prentice Hall, 1997.

[44] J. Shen and S. Castan. An optimal linear operator for step edge detection. *Computer Vision, Graphics and Image Processing: Graphical Models and Image Processing*, 54(2):112–133, 1992.

[45] Milan Sonka, Vaclav Hlavac, and Roger Boyle. *Image Processing, Analysis and Machine Vision*. International Thomson Computer Press, 1993.

[46] Emanuele Trucco and Alessandro Verri. *Introductory Techniques for 3-D Computer Vision*. Prentice Hall, 1998.

[47] R. Ulichney. *Digital Halftoning*. MIT Press, 1987.

[48] Scott E. Umbaugh. *Computer Vision and Image Processing*. Prentice Hall, 1998.

[49] Gregory Wallace. The JPEG still picture compression standard. *Communications of the ACM*, 34(4):30–44, 1991.

[50] Steven Webb, editor. *The Physics of Medical Imaging*. IOP Publishing, 1988.

[51] Russel Winder and Graham Roberts. *Developing Java Software*. John Wiley & Sons, 1998.

[52] G. W. Wolberg. *Digital Image Warping*. IEEE Computer Society Press, 1990.

[53] Jacob Ziv and Abraham Lempel. A universal algorithm for sequential data compression. *IEEE Transactions on Information Theory*, 23(3):337–343, May 1977.

[54] Jacob Ziv and Abraham Lempel. Compression of individual sequences via variable-rate coding. *IEEE Transactions on Information Theory*, 24(5):530–536, September 1978.

[55] John Zukowski. *Java AWT Reference*. O'Reilly & Associates, 1997.

Index

Note: Page references in *italics* refer to Figures; those in **bold** refer to Tables

IMPORTANT: READ CAREFULLY
WARNING: BY OPENING THE PACKAGE YOU AGREE TO BE BOUND BY THE TERMS OF THE LICENCE AGREEMENT BELOW.

This is a legally binding agreement between You (the user or purchaser) and Pearson Education Limited. By retaining this licence, any software media or accompanying written materials or carrying out any of the permitted activities You agree to be bound by the terms of the licence agreement below.

If You do not agree to these terms then promptly return the entire publication (this licence and all software, written materials, packaging and any other components received with it) with Your sales receipt to Your supplier for a full refund.

SINGLE USER LICENCE AGREEMENT

YOU ARE PERMITTED TO:

- Use (load into temporary memory or permanent storage) a single copy of the software on only one computer at a time. If this computer is linked to a network then the software may only be installed in a manner such that it is not accessible to other machines on the network.
- Make one copy of the software solely for backup purposes or copy it to a single hard disk, provided you keep the original solely for back up purposes.
- Transfer the software from one computer to another provided that you only use it on one computer at a time.

YOU MAY NOT:

- Rent or lease the software or any part of the publication.
- Copy any part of the documentation, except where specifically indicated otherwise.
- Make copies of the software, other than for backup purposes.
- Reverse engineer, decompile or disassemble the software.
- Use the software on more than one computer at a time.
- Install the software on any networked computer in a way that could allow access to it from more than one machine on the network.
- Use the software in any way not specified above without the prior written consent of Pearson Education Limited.

ONE COPY ONLY

This licence is for a single user copy of the software

PEARSON EDUCATION LIMITED RESERVES THE RIGHT TO TERMINATE THIS LICENCE BY WRITTEN NOTICE AND TO TAKE ACTION TO RECOVER ANY DAMAGES SUFFERED BY PEARSON EDUCATION LIMITED IF YOU BREACH ANY PROVISION OF THIS AGREEMENT.

Pearson Education Limited owns the software You only own the disk on which the software is supplied.

LIMITED WARRANTY

Pearson Education Limited warrants that the diskette or CD rom on which the software is supplied are free from defects in materials and workmanship under normal use for ninety (90) days from the date You receive them. This warranty is limited to You and is not transferable. Pearson Education Limited does not warrant that the functions of the software meet Your requirements or that the media is compatible with any computer system on which it is used or that the operation of the software will be unlimited or error free.

You assume responsibility for selecting the software to achieve Your intended results and for the installation of, the use of and the results obtained from the software. The entire liability of Pearson Education Limited and its suppliers and your only remedy shall be replacement of the components that do not meet this warranty free of charge. This limited warranty is void if any damage has resulted from accident, abuse, misapplication, service or modification by someone other than Pearson Education Limited. In no event shall Pearson Education Limited or its suppliers be liable for any damages whatsoever arising out of installation of the software , even if advised of the possibility of such damages. Pearson Education Limited will not be liable for any loss or damage of any nature suffered by any party as a result of reliance upon or reproduction of or any errors in the content of the publication.

Pearson Education Limited does not limit its liability for death or personal injury caused by its negligence.

This licence agreement shall be governed by and interpreted and construed in accordance with English law.